BURLESQUE WEST

Showgirls, Sex, and Sin in Postwar Vancouver

After the Second World War, Vancouver emerged as a hotbed of strip-tease talent. In *Burlesque West*, the first critical history of the city's notorious striptease scene, Becki Ross delves into the erotic entertainment industry at the northern end of the dancers' west coast tour – the North–South route from Los Angeles to Vancouver – which provided rotating work for dancers and variety for club clientele.

Drawing on extensive archival materials and interviews with fifty former dancers, strip-club owners, booking agents, choreographers, and musicians, Ross reveals stories that are deeply fascinating and evoke, in the words of ex-dancer Lindalee Tracey, an era before 'striptease fell from grace because the world stopped dreaming.' Ross demonstrates that Vancouver's glitzy nightclub scene, often condemned as a quasi-legal strain of urban blight, in fact greased the economic engine of the city. Though jobs in the industry are often perceived as having little in common with conventional types of labour, retired dancers' accounts resonate with those of contemporary service workers, particularly in regard to such matters as unionization and workplace benefits and hazards. Incorporating first-hand narrative with feminist, anti-racist, and queer analysis, Ross traces the evolution of the industry over several decades, examining its roots and efflorescence, as well as its subsequent devaluation and sanitization with the integration of striptease style and neo-burlesque trends into mass culture.

Lavishly illustrated and thoroughly documented, *Burlesque West* is an ambitious and engaging social history that looks at the convergence of the personal and the political in a phenomenon that combines sex, art and entertainment, and commerce. Like its subject, the book will stimulate, delight, and offend.

BECKI L. ROSS is an associate professor in the Department of Sociology and the Chair of the Women's and Gender Studies Program at the University of British Columbia.

BECKI L. ROSS

BURLESQUE WEST

Showgirls, Sex, and Sin in Postwar Vancouver

UNIVERSITY OF TORONTO PRESS
Toronto Buffalo London

© University of Toronto Press Incorporated 2009
Toronto Buffalo London
www.utppublishing.com
Printed in Canada

ISBN 978-0-8020-9698-2 (cloth)
ISBN 978-0-8020-9646-3 (paper)

Printed on acid-free paper

Library and Archives Canada Cataloguing in Publication

Ross, Becki, 1959–
Burlesque West : showgirls, sex and sin in postwar Vancouver / Becki L.
Ross.
Includes bibliographical references and index.
ISBN 978-0-8020-9698-2 (bound).   ISBN 978-0-8020-9646-3 (pbk.)

1. Burlesque (Theater) – British Columbia – Vancouver – History.
2. Stripteasers – British Columbia – Vancouver – History.   3. Showgirls. –
British Columbia – Vancouver – History.   4. Nightlife – British Columbia –
Vancouver – History.   5. Vancouver (B.C.) – History.   I. Title.

PN1949.S7R68 2009   792.7   C2009-901219-7

This book has been published with the help of a grant from the Canadian
Federation for the Humanities and Social Sciences, through the Aid to
Scholarly Publications Programme, using funds provided by the Social
Sciences and Humanities Research Council of Canada.

University of Toronto Press acknowledges the financial assistance to its
publishing program of the Canada Council for the Arts and the Ontario
Arts Council.

University of Toronto Press acknowledges the financial support for its
publishing activities of the Government of Canada through the Book
Publishing Industry Development Program (BPIDP).

For Tracy, my one, for always

Contents

Acknowledgments

As a contributor to feminist, anti-racist debates and activism for thirty years, in my journey to complete this book project I benefited, on many levels, from rich collaborations. I want to commend my stellar research assistants at the University of British Columbia: initially, Kim Greenwell and Michelle Swann; at later stages, Erin Bentley, Maureen Douglas, Christine Harris, Geneviève Lapointe, and Rachael Sullivan. Each woman's commitment to the project extended well beyond the scope of my hopes and expectations.

Eminent historians and friends Michael Fellman and Angus McClaren read an early draft of the manuscript. I am grateful to them, as well as to other comrades in the academy, including Santa Aloi, Eileen Boris, Deborah Brock, Elise Chenier, Gillian Creese, Dawn Currie, Wendy Frisby, Franca Iacovetta, Tom Kemple, Eva Mackey, Renisa Mawani, Steven Maynard, Patti Moore, Dianne Newell, Bryan Palmer, Joy Parr, Leila Rupp, Joy Sangster, Rima Wilkes, Cynthia Wright, and Patricia Vertinsky. Additional friends provided sustenance on myriad fronts: I thank Nancy Archbould, Stuart Blackley, Anita Braha, Jane Coombe, Bill Coombe, Aaron Devor, Jamie Lee Hamilton, Arlene McLaren, Mary Millen, Heather Mitton, Marina Morrow, Judy Parrack, Judy Sewell, Gill Thomas, Cynthia Wright, and the 'Sudbury girls' – Karen Beange, Liz Dow, Peg Evans, Marg Ghent, Penny Gingell, and Alison Strong. Each person, at various points, offered me uncommon insights, loving support, and much-appreciated humour.

I would like to honour my parents, Carol Ross, Sheila Ross, and Chucker Ross, and my siblings, Brenda, Larry, Karey, and Julie; every family member graciously indulged my passion for this work. My in-laws, Carol and Terry Porteous, wrapped me in prairie hospitality. I continue to mourn their deaths, in 2002 and 2007, respectively. My niece, Erin Porteous, championed my project; on my visits to Winnipeg she always made a point of asking me questions about sex. Her death from bone cancer at age twenty-seven on 19 June 2008 is a heartbreaking tragedy.

My friend Larry Wong assumed the role of informal publicist: he is a big-hearted booster and Chinese Canadian historian extraordinaire. Janet Leduc and Don Luxton at Heritage Vancouver, Bruce Watson at the Vancouver Historical Society, Beverly Sharp at the West Vancouver chapter of the Canadian Federation of University Women, curators Reid Shier and Helga Pakasaar at Presentation House Gallery, and Danny Filippone, proprietor of the Penthouse Cabaret, believed in the importance of sharing my work with non-academic audiences at local venues. I also commend the efficiency and expertise of graphics librarian Carolyn Soltau at the *Vancouver Sun/Province*.

I learned much from attentive students and faculty at locations away from home: Harvard University, Stanford University, University of California at Berkeley, Langara College, University of Toronto, University of Lethbridge, University College of the Cariboo (now Thompson Rivers University), Simon Fraser University, the University of Chicago, the University of Alberta, and Ewha University in Seoul, South Korea. With 1½ inch by 1½ inch slides (and later, PowerPoint) in hand, I relished taking my 'dog and pony show' to audiences on the road.

At the University of British Columbia (UBC), I have been challenged, generously, by graduate and undergraduate students in the Department of Sociology, Women's and Gender Studies, Canadian Studies, and our small but sturdy interdisciplinary program, Critical Studies in Sexuality (CSIS). While at UBC, I secured much-needed financial support from the Social Sciences and Humanities Research Council (1999–2003), the Hampton Fund (2003–5), and the Sociology Department's Burwell Book Fund. The chair of Women's and Gender Studies at UBC, Wendy Frisby, granted me a sizeable honorarium to assist with costs associated with the visual content of this book.

While many academics have a vexed relationship with the mainstream press, I am thankful for the careful coverage of my study by Ken MacQueen (*Vancouver Sun/Maclean's*), Dene Moore (Canadian Press), Ellen Schwartz (*Trek Magazine*), Tim Carlson (*Vancouver Sun*), Peter Birnie (*Vancouver Sun*), Alexandra Gill (*Globe and Mail*), Marilisa Racco (*Globe and Mail*), Fanny Kiefer (*Studio 4*, Shaw Cable), and Theresa Lalonde ('On the Coast,' CBC Radio). Each journalist approached me with genuine curiosity and a willingness to publicize my research without succumbing (as did many others) to the temptation of tawdry sensationalism. A twelve-month stint (2001–2) as a columnist at Vancouver's *Xtra! West* bi-weekly newspaper enabled me to share preliminary findings with savvy queer and feminist readers.

Sections of work that appear in this book were originally published, in altered form, in scholarly outlets: the journals *Labour / Le travail, Journal of Women's History,* and *Canadian Review of Sociology and Anthropology,* and the anthologies *Making Normal: Social Regulation in Canada* (2003), *Physical Culture, Power, and the Body* (2006), and *Creating Postwar Canada* (2008). Thank you to the editors/publishers for permission to reprint material.

Fifteen years ago, Virgil Duff, executive editor at the University of Toronto Press (UTP), oversaw the publication of my first book, *The House That Jill Built: A Lesbian Nation in Formation.* Wide-eyed back then, I deposited an unedited, unsolicited, and unrevised doctoral thesis on his desk! This time around, Virgil bestowed upon me the same steadfast grace, robust enthusiasm, and gentle patience. I applaud his capacity to assist scholars, both untried and tested, in a shared quest to convey discoveries about our vast, sometimes befuddling, and always-changing social world.

Also at UTP, ace copy-editor Margaret Allen worked her special magic, while managing editor Anne Laughlin firmly guided the production process. Publicists Doug Hildebrand, Andrea Wilson, and Jenna Germaine committed time and expertise to promoting my work. I especially appreciate Doug's help with the book's title and overall 'look.' Annette Lorek assiduously assembled the book's index.

I am deeply indebted to the fifty women and men who agreed to be interviewed. *Burlesque West: Showgirls, Sex, and Sin in Postwar Vancouver* would not exist without their bravery, rebellious spirit, and impassioned truth telling. While many wondered whether they would ever see this project completed, their funny, sad, amazing, intriguing, illuminating, sly, and lucid stories compelled me to keep going.

I stand in solidarity with sex worker activists – in Vancouver, Jamie Lee Hamilton, Ryann Rain, Trina Ricketts, Susan Davis, Stacey, Raven Bowen, Raigen D'Angelo, Idris Hudson, Andrew Sorfleet, and Matthew Taylor; in Toronto, Gwendolyn, Valerie Scott and Ryan Hotchkiss. I did not have the pleasure of meeting the late Lindalee Tracey, but her marvellous book, *Growing Up Naked: My Years in Bump and Grind* (1997), and her two-part documentary on the history of burlesque inspired me greatly. I continue to learn from business insiders in the sex industry about the intricacies of sexual commerce.

My lover, Tracy Porteous, has lived with me, and this project, from start to finish. Her tenderness, keen editorial eye, sharp intelligence, ethical clarity, and unwavering love have kept me 'real' and even-keeled. From her twenty-seven years in the trenches of feminist anti-violence research, policy analysis, and social justice activism, she reminds me of the confounding dynamics and dialectics of sexual danger and sexual pleasure. Our cozy retreat on Pender Island, British Columbia, granted me precious weeks each year to write in the company of hummingbirds, rufous-sided towhees, nuthatches, deer, mice, bald eagles, and carpenter ants.

Preface: Beginnings, Backlash, and Brazenness

My goal to explore the history of erotic entertainment – burlesque, go-go dancing, and striptease – has deep personal and political roots. I was born in 1959, at the end of the baby boom, in the northern mining town of Sudbury, Ontario. The eldest of five in a white, middle-class family, I grew up in a lakeside home built on the submerged cement pilings of an early-twentieth-century brothel and dance hall: a fitting foundation for my emergent passions. Since the late 1970s, I have lobbied for women's reproductive choice, lesbian/gay/bisexual liberation, and the rights of trans people (transgender, transsexual, and intersexed) to dignity and equality. I have agitated for access to state-confiscated queer pornography, funding for HIV/AIDS research and education, the decriminalization of prostitution, an end to systemic racism, and the joys of masturbation. While writing this book, I learned that my attraction to striptease is linked to my fierce, abiding love of athleticism, fashion, and music; my queer search for femme ancestors; and my escape from the poisonous, anti-sex venom of Catholicism. For me, compelled by all things erotic, excavating the complexities of 'bump and grind' became one strategy for combating the legacy of sexual shame, guilt, and silence imposed on all women who dare to push against the river of social conformity.

At seventeen, I attended the Folies-Bergère cabaret in Paris. At twenty-seven, I sat in awe of striptease artist Gwendolyn as she irreverently instructed male patrons in the mechanics of female orgasm at Le Strip on Yonge Street, Toronto's famed sin strip.[1] At thirty-seven, a resident of Vancouver in the late 1990s, I began frequenting strip shows at the No. 5 Orange, the Penthouse Cabaret, and the Cecil Hotel, with my lover Tracy at my side. And at forty-seven, I volunteered at the strip-a-thon organized by Exotic Dancers for Cancer to raise money for 'Rethink Breast Cancer' at Vancouver's Drake Show Lounge. After four decades, I am captivated, still, by female dancers' combination of glamour, sexiness, talent, skills, and ingenious use of costumes, props, and music. As a lesbian eager to witness other feminine women's sexy manipulations of femininity, I rarely feel aroused in strip clubs; rather, I identify with, and feel inspired by, stripteasers' public displays of sexual confidence.

Over years of research, I eagerly absorbed knowledge of retired dancers' efforts to achieve economic independence, to defend their craft as bold artistic expression, and to free their bawdy acts from the censorious, punishing gaze of politicians, journalists, clergy, police, criminologists, and feminist critics. The strip trade was (and is) a jumble of contradictions: it promised women more lucrative dividends than sales, service, or clerical work at the same time that it produced them as dangerous sexual 'Others'. Learning how dancers strove to reconcile these duelling poles of adulation *and* contempt became one of my principal preoccupations.

Plumbing the Irreverent

To chronicle the history of striptease after World War II, I needed research dollars. In June 1999, after two unsuccessful bids, I was awarded a grant totalling $50,900 by the Social Sciences and Humanities Research Council of Canada (SSHRCC). In June 2000, with the help of research assistants Kim Greenwell and Michelle Swann, I spent $400 on advertising in local community papers and faxing a press release to dozens of media outlets. Our aim was to profile the 'Striptease Project' in order to locate and recruit retired dancers, club owners, booking agents, musicians, choreographers, and photographers. We had encountered great difficulty in finding these folks, in part due to the stigma that still shrouds the business. Also, most of Vancouver's infamous striptease venues had disappeared, with many retired entertainers having left the city. Searching for clues at the provincial archives in Victoria, British Columbia, the City of Vancouver Archives, and the Special Collections archive at the University of British Columbia was like sifting for gold in the Fraser River. Many days we left weary, no wiser than when we entered. We learned that a cloaked, slippery topic like ours would require innovative strategies and some big-time luck.

In June 2000, two journalists, Ken MacQueen from *the Vancouver Sun* and Dene Moore from Canadian Press, responded to our ad in the *Cou-*

rier newspaper. After interviewing me, they played up my 'search for the naked truth.' In a photograph taken outside Vancouver's Penthouse Cabaret, I appear in front of the marquee: 'Pet of the Year' (a dubious distinction at best!) (see plate 1). MacQueen and Moore reported that I had received government funding to write this book.[2] Their articles were reprinted nationally and internationally, making the front page of the *Vancouver Sun, Globe and Mail, National Post, Winnipeg Free Press*, Victoria *Times Colonist*, and most other mainstream newspapers across Canada and the United States, as well as the *Bangkok News* and the *Iran Times*. I was subsequently contacted by journalists from across Canada, as well as from Switzerland, Australia, South Africa, California, New York, England, and Scotland. Eight prize-winning documentary filmmakers invited me to collaborate on a film, and I had yet to do the research! Between us, my research assistants and I did forty-five interviews for print, radio, TV, and film/video.[3]

Once I had been contacted by media pundits about my study, I expected a range of titillating angles, but I did not anticipate the relentless personal probing. I stick-handled my way around journalists' shared assumption that I moonlighted as a stripper. I joked that had I danced in strip clubs I would have paid off my student loan two decades earlier! Like a broken record, reporters asked: 'How do you justify spending taxpayers' dollars on studying strippers?' Numerous non-Canadian reporters said they were frankly astonished that (a) I took a 'frivolous' topic so seriously, and (b) I had funding from the public purse. On the media hot seat, I stressed the originality of my project and the need to redress the silences in the province's canonical history. I talked about how the money would fund skills training for my research assistants. Adapting the wisdom of feminist sociologist Dorothy E. Smith, I described my desire to treat former dancers, club owners, and other key players as the experts of their own lives. I outlined my plan to explore the dancers' contribution to local economies and performance traditions. From my preliminary findings, I discovered that ex-dancers had a stake in the allocation of tax dollars for research since they had paid personal income tax and sales tax, and some had invested in Canada Savings Bonds and registered retirement plans.

Righteous, Angry Canadians Sound Off

I was ill-prepared for the spiteful, even hateful e-mails, phone calls, and faxes. On talk-radio shows in Toronto, Calgary, and Vancouver, I was attacked by successive callers who were incensed that the government would 'waste *their* money' on such a 'useless, disgusting project.' Several male callers ventured that a history of male loggers and miners in British Columbia would be much more constructive. (Of course, they conveniently neglected to acknowledge the instrumental role played by female sex workers in the history of resource-based communities.)[4] On the Rafe Mair radio show in Vancouver, a male caller opined, 'I could have told you that men like to drink beer and look at naked women – fifty thousand dollars saved. I don't see what the point of this research is. It's a no-brainer, period.'[5] Mark Milke from the Canadian Taxpayers' Federation bellowed that the research 'was a joke.' He was quoted as saying, 'I'm almost speechless. What, strippers don't get "studied" enough every day as it is?' One cameraman at a local television station hissed, behind my back, that I was a stupid fool. In the federal House of Commons in Ottawa, the right-wing Reform party (newly merged with the Progressive Conservative party), castigated the Liberal majority for authorizing such a gross misuse of citizens' monies. Political cartoonists had their way with the scandal (see fig. P1). In the midst of the cacophony, thirty-five letters denouncing my project were sent to then Prime Minister Jean Chrétien and forwarded to my funder. Every letter received by SSHRCC made some reference to the project's funding as a farcical, absurd, worthless, and ridiculous squandering of taxpayers' dollars.

My survey of the sample of complaints reveals two main arguments: approximately half underscored the need to redirect government 'handouts' away from such offensive 'wastage' to more deserving projects: 'I resent hard earned tax dollars going to promote the stripper industry. How will people in need of affordable housing benefit directly from the study?'; 'There isn't an emergency hospital facility in the country that would not have welcomed a $51,000 donation'; 'If you can give frivolous grants for studying strippers surely to god you can return some tax money for a worthwhile project like the Toronto transit system'; 'It is unbelievable to us that our government can't cut taxes or lower the GST but can spend money on this nonsense. SHAME!!' And finally, 'This grant has no social value. Have you been down to the east side of Vancouver lately?'

The second, equally popular set of criticisms tackled the content of my study more directly: 'If I want to see someone strip naked, I will bring home a bottle of wine and ask my spouse to strip for me in the privacy of my house, not in some bar'; 'A person who is already struggling

Figure P1 Cartoonist Adrian Raeside lampoons the conservative backlash among Conservative (then Reform party) politicians. *Penticton Herald*, June 2000.

with moral/mental problems goes to a strip bar ... And we wonder why rape is rampant in Canada. Why not spend that money on seeing how we can stop these people with mental disorders from becoming violent offenders!'; 'Strippers usually don't do much besides perform banally repetitive "dances" in seedy strip joints. Not sure what viable research or "art" can be gleaned from that. What type of professor spends all her time in strip clubs, anyway?' And finally, from a conservative women's organization in Alberta: 'Our goal is to strengthen families, communities and our nation through educational and service programmes. We sincerely hope you will rescind this grant.' Though hardly representative of the views of an entire country's population, the hostile responses were nonetheless disquieting. Canadians, it seemed, were in an ornery mood, no doubt because of worries about the dismantling of social programs and national health care, a looming economic downturn, and the ongoing burden of the Goods and Services Tax (GST). And though

I share concerns about the erosion of the welfare state, the crisis of poverty, and the wrong-headedness of some government priorities (e.g., national defence funding and corporate tax shelters), my Striptease Project triggered animosity that seemed to far outstrip criticism of other federal spending initiatives.

I quickly realized that the backlash was partly linked to the ongoing scandal inside the ministry of Human Resources Development Canada (HRDC). In February 2000, news outlets across the country reported that an audit alleged that $30 million was unaccounted for, and the minister, Jane Stewart, was lambasted for mismanagement of taxpayers' money.[6] For a federal Liberal government with a reputation for financial competence and fiscal probity, charges of 'wasted money' dealt a serious blow. Though SSHRCC funded my project, not HRDC, it mattered little to exasperated citizens, who demanded that Prime Minister Chrétien veto my grant. I began to feel that academics, university administrators, and scholarly funding agencies need to work harder to make our procedures more transparent and our work more visible and relevant to communities beyond our campus gates. For instance, the council that bankrolls research in Social Sciences and Humanities oversees a highly competitive, peer-review process. The annually dispensed funds have enabled excellent, award-winning research and writing. But I suspect this is cold comfort to those who oppose all public subsidies to makers of history, art, and culture.

What distressed me most about the negative publicity was the popular belief that striptease was something to be ashamed of, stuffed under the carpet, and purged from public discourse. The overriding message: stripteasers were best dismissed as smelly trash, better off disqualified from national conversations about the allocation of tax dollars. Their citizenship status, including their democratic right to debate public policy, was under siege. Dancers were caricatured as anti-family and a threat to national sovereignty. And underlying the prevailing attack on dancers was veiled disgust towards 'sleazy strip joints' and the men who frequented them. My place as a scholar employed at the University of British Columbia – a reputable institute of higher learning – also came under fire as fellow Canadians publicly disapproved of my efforts to 'dignify' such an 'undignified,' even 'undignifiable' subject. Not only was the study deemed worthless, repellent, and unfundable; critics seemed to say that stripteasers were not worthy of anything but collective contempt. In fact, irate naysayers invoked the same impulse to differentiate the 'savage' from the 'civilized' as had misguided colonial explorers, scientists, politicians, physicians, women's groups, clergy, and journalists a century earlier.[7]

As much as the angry outburst upset us, my assistants and I scored over $1 million worth of publicity! Retired dancers and club owners contacted me from all over Canada, and from as far away as Italy, Virginia, Washington, Florida, and California. Emboldened by their desire to be heard above the chattering critics, they expressed a willingness to participate, and to put me in touch with others. In particular, the dancers' enthusiasm for the project assured me that the time was right. Both ex-dancers and other business insiders noted that many original movers and shakers in Vancouver's postwar burlesque and striptease scene had died. I also recognized that those still with us were aging, and that their passing would mean the loss of their memories and memorabilia.

Shaken by the reactionary mean-spiritedness, and disturbed by how strippers were being freakified, I quickly found that the scope and scale of the backlash strengthened my resolve. If ex-dancers were perverts, then I was too, proudly so. Theirs was a story worth telling, not one to be drowned out by barbed misogynist musings about how men's past experiences in timber, mining, and forestry were intrinsically more significant. Convinced of the importance of erotic entertainment as remembered by the women and men once pivotal to its staging, I strove to open up new, fresh terrain for historical inquiry. Pledging to listen to, learn from, and honour the brazen voices of business insiders heretofore disregarded, I plunged in with a thicker skin than when I had first imagined this research more than ten years ago.

BURLESQUE WEST:
SHOWGIRLS, SEX, AND SIN IN POSTWAR VANCOUVER

1 Uncloaking the Striptease Past

For more than a century in the West, commercial striptease has flagrantly exploited a demand for undressed female flesh.[1] Today, the tradition of a woman doffing her clothing for an audience still has legs, as it were. In the bare-it-all world of peeler pubs and upscale gentlemen's clubs, exotic dancers spread their wares fully nude on stage while marketing lap dances, massages, and table dances in Champagne and VIP rooms. Drive-through stripping is sold to customers in cars at the Climax Gentlemen's Club in Delmont, Pennsylvania. Based in Beverly Hills, Ecstasky Air staffs its jets with strippers who offer passengers a full bar, gourmet menu, massages, and 'exotic entertainment.'[2] Inside a downtown Toronto studio, women read the news on the Internet while gradually disrobing for four million viewers monthly.[3] Female environmentalists, water polo players, artists, and cross-country skiers pose naked in calendars to raise money for a host of causes. Russian tennis star Maria Sharapova and American golfer Natalie Gulbis attach their blond, youthful, and skimpily adorned personas to a dizzying array of consumer products. British supermodel Kate Moss performs a semi-naked pole dance in a music video by the *White Stripes*, while brass stripper poles are hawked by celebrities Pamela Anderson and Carmen Electra. Students of mine at the University of British Columbia enthusiastically register for on-campus pole-dancing lessons. Kerry Gold, a *Vancouver Sun* reporter, smartly summed up the scene: 'Since Oprah Winfrey giddily busted a few bump-and-grind moves on national television, ladies of every stripe are discovering their inner peeler.'[4]

The current appetite for 'tasteful' female nudity is matched by nostalgia for the spunk and mystery of nearly nudes in decades past. At Hollywood's Academy Awards ceremony in March 2002, host Whoopi

Goldberg, festooned in feathers, top hat, silver corset, fishnet stockings, and shiny stilettos, lampooned the film *Moulin Rouge* by descending from the ceiling on a trapeze. In *Mrs Henderson Presents* (2005), the one-and-only Dame Judi Dench takes a turn as the shrewd purveyor of a nude burlesque revue during World War II in London, England. The tantalizing culture of postwar striptease has also inspired two bracing Canadian novels – *Crazy about Lili* by William Weintraub (2005) and *Cease to Blush* by Billie Livingston (2005).[5] One of the enduring musical gems of Broadway, *Gypsy* – originally staged in 1959 – was remounted at the magnificent Stanley Industrial Stage in Vancouver in May 2007, to rave reviews. And the one-of-a-kind Exotic World Burlesque Museum was recently relocated from the California desert to Las Vegas and renamed the Burlesque Hall of Fame.[6]

Since the mid-to-late 1990s, neo-burlesque troupes across North America and in the United Kingdom have revived the magic of 'the tease,' 1950s-style.[7] Velvet Hammer (Los Angeles), Glamazons (New York), Scandelles (Toronto), Shim Shamettes (New Orleans), Ooh-La-La (Denver), and Smartie Pants and Sweet Soul Productions (Vancouver) have featured sassy, curvy vamps with pasties, feathers, g-strings, and live orchestras.[8] Not to be outdone by their straight sisters, the Vancouver-based Stilettos & Strap-Ons, and the Seattle-based BurlyQ troupes showcase queer sexuality with shows like 'The Good, the Bad, and the Femme.'[9] In California, women aged fifty to eighty – the Fabulous Palm Springs Follies – parade around in little more than sequins and stiletto heels, charming fans from around the globe.[10] Dita Von Teese, a glamorous, sequinned pin-up and neo-burlesque star, is rumoured to charge $2,500 for a ten-minute show.[11]

Without a doubt, the contemporary nudie craze signals the loosening of community standards, as well as evidence of our unrelenting curiosity, if not obsession, with all things sexual. As Michel Foucault smartly observed, debates about sex in the West have percolated robustly since the eighteenth century.[12] Religious leaders, politicians, medical professionals, and police have dedicated entire careers to defining, classifying, and surveying the minutiae of human sexual activity, inventing an emphatic vocabulary of sexual norms and abominations.[13] Marital, procreative, kink-free, heterosexual monogamy was named and propagandized as mature human sexual adjustment. Immature, abnormal sex deviance, it was argued, was embodied in the figures of the homosexual, hermaphrodite, adulterer/adulteress, nymphomaniac, showgirl, onanist (masturbator), prostitute, sadist, and sexually precocious child – all members of what Foucault called the 'numberless family of perverts.'[14]

In opposition to sex pessimism, twentieth-century pro-sex crusaders such as Oscar Wilde, Emma Goldman, Walt Whitman, Marie Stopes, Mae West, Alfred Kinsey, Marlon Riggs, Annie Sprinkle, Sue Johanson, Josey Vogels, and Kim Cattrall (of *Sex and the City* fame) fought to release non-conformist sexual acts and fantasies from the vice-grip of medico-moral, class-bound, and racialized categories of sexual pathology. What has remained constant is a turbulent sex war between those who aim to police sexual dangers and those who press for emancipation of sexual pleasures.[15] In December 2005, libertines saluted the landmark Canadian Supreme Court decision that decriminalized public consensual sex between adults in 'swingers' clubs' across the nation.[16] Writing for the majority in the seven-to-two decision, the judges ruled that sexual activity cannot be considered indecent unless it can be shown to cause harm to society. Outraged opponents, including editors at the *Globe and Mail*, wailed that the decision was a sign of degraded 'community standards' and a harbinger of ever more sordid debauchery to come.[17]

In spite of recent evidence of mainstreamed female nudity in popular culture, including inside swingers' clubs, professional striptease continues to be a lightning rod for contests about female sexuality. To ex-dancer Margaret Dragu, striptease performers have always played the role of conscientious objector by bravely testing and defying society's limits; they have experienced outsider status as 'sexual offenders.'[18] Members of the world's second-oldest profession, ecdysiasts in the West continue to thread their way through the dichotomy that perniciously divides women into Madonnas or whores. But where did the spectacle of striptease come from? Why has it endured? What competing factors structured its efflorescence and its repression? How has the business of 'bump and grind' changed over time? What, in fact, is especially unique, evocative, and illuminating about commercial striptease in the decades immediately after World War II?

Early-Twentieth-Century Burlesque and the Tease Factor

Contemporary fascination with the professional 'stripper' who dances for dollars has unique historical and geographical origins.[19] In the nineteenth century, knowledge of belly dancers from the north-African coast, Hindu erotic dancers in India, and snake dancers in Brazil influenced the emergence of commercial striptease in the West.[20] In the late 1860s, Lydia Thompson and her British Blondes, with their high-kicking legs and bawdy humour, scandalized and electrified North American audiences. A decade later, tableaux vivants cast women in full body stockings in poses of classical sculpture and paintings, backlit to emphasize their eroticism.[21] In 1893, six belly dancers, one of whom became known as the 'cooch' dancer Little Egypt, fed white consumers' fantasy of the exoticized 'Orient' at the Chicago World's Fair.[22] On the fairgrounds, crowds gawked at the dancers, whose movements were condemned by moral reformers as primitive and unladylike.[23]

Beginning in 1906, Toronto-born Maud Allen toured her 'Vision of Salomé' through Britain and Europe, and her erotic dance of thin veils and apparent nudity blurred the line between licit and illicit public performance.[24] In the 1910s through the 1940s across the United States and Canada, chorus girls danced with the Ziegfeld Follies and later Minsky's Follies – a New York-based musical variety show modelled after Paris's Folies-Bergère. In 1925, the owners of Minsky's burlesque theatre in New York were charged with presenting a performance likely to corrupt public morals: that night, Mademoiselle Fifi ended her show topless, hands stretched above her head.[25]

For the first half of the twentieth century across North America, bare-legged and often bare-breasted chorus girls in vaudeville and burlesque shows exhibited the ideals of white, (hetero)sexual beauty, glamour, and patriotism. They were admired by fans and paid relatively good wages. But they were also caricatured as 'gold diggers, vamps, unintelligent, and of weak moral fibre ... a different species of woman altogether.'[26] Popular dismissals of sex work *as work* licensed medical, legal, and moral experts to classify the stripper (and the prostitute) as nothing but a congenital type predisposed to sexual degeneracy, laziness, immorality, and criminality.[27] A bundle of contradictions, the showgirl was mythologized as 'a sexual predator as well as a corrupted innocent, an emblem of European wickedness as well as Broadway glitz.'[28] As historian Angela Latham contends, 'the chorus was a vehicle by which to "glorify the American girl," usually by emphasizing her sexual allure, and yet no profession except for prostitution so stigmatized women.'[29] By the 1910s when some actresses laid claim to legitimate and respectable theatrical careers, female burlesque dancers were scorned by critics as anti-actresses who indulged in indecent spectacle, ruinous to public morals. The wholesome, unthreatening, almost androgynous Ziegfeld girl was marketed to middle-class consumers and tolerated for her art and glamour; meanwhile, argues Robert Allen, the bourgeoisie were quick to label dancers in working-class burlesque as wild, potentially destructive amazons.[30] By the standards of upper-crust theatre patrons, a blatant strip act, even if justified by a narrative device (e.g., a woman changing before dinner), was definitely not the opera, the ballet, or Shakespearean drama.

Burlesque houses in working-class districts of Vancouver, Toronto, and Montreal became the routine target of police raids. Historian Charlene Kish has noted that in 1912, the owner/manager of Toronto's Star Burlesque house was charged with permitting the performance of an immoral show: the 'Darlings of Paris.'[31] In a debate about 'The Darlings,' the Rev. St Clair expressed outrage at the supposedly homosexual character in the performance, a 'sissified policeman, Archibald,' and a 'class of sissies and fairies whose acts exceed in grossness the actions of the inhabitants of Sodom and Gomorrah, as bad as anything ever attempted in the bathing place of ancient Rome.'[32] After a two-day trial, the owner/manager of the Star Burlesque House was acquitted by a jury of twelve men. Noteworthy for both its homosexual innuendo and its bawdy heterosexual double entendres, it was burlesque, Kish concluded, that had 'developed into a lively, amusing, and sexually exciting form of entertainment. For a single dime or quarter one could watch talented acrobats and comical sketches, hear heart-warming ballads, and best of all see dozens of beautiful young women in spectacular and revealing costumes.'[33] The direct address of female burlesque dancers and 'talking dolls' was designed to mock conventions of genteel femininity. Performers' risqué actions and provocative costumes meant that they were commonly associated with 'public women' or prostitutes. Similarly, in northern British Columbia, Yukon, and Alaska in the early 1900s, dance hall girls were routinely assumed to work as prostitutes. Both dancers and sex workers were regarded as fallen, wanton women.[34]

Censors Flex Their Muscle

By the 1920s, the popularity of burlesque in theatres across North America waned with the advent of motion pictures. In the 1930s, burlesque became synonymous with saucy striptease. A key to a stripper's success, argues historian Andrea Friedman, was not how much skin she revealed but how much people in the audience thought she revealed, and how much she promoted their desire that she reveal more.[35] Maintenance of the illusion of nudity afforded the striptease business some legal protection from obscenity laws. Italian American Ann Corio, a famous stripteaser throughout the 1930s, remembers incidences of state power over sexual representation, and the tricks employed to safeguard illicit shows:

> [At the Howard Theatre in Boston], once the ticket-taker saw the censor coming up the stairs he pressed his foot on a pedal. On stage, the show might be in full production. A stripper might be giving her all for mankind, shimmying and grinding. Clothes might be flying in all directions. The crowd would be yelling 'Take it off,' and the music might be crashing to a crescendo. Suddenly a red light would start blinking in the footlights. A censor had arrived ... Imagine Mickey Mantle trying to stop in the middle of his swing. That's what those stormy strippers would have to do ... Red light! Hold it! The hips would stop as if paralyzed. Those clothes would come flying back from the wings. The perspiring musicians would dissolve to a waltz. And by the time the censor reached the top of the stairs and looked down on the stage he would see – not a hip-swinging, hair-tossing, half-naked tigress – but a nun on a casual stroll through a most unlikely convent.[36]

The temperance-minded Vancouver Council of Women (VCW) and the city's chapter of the Women's Christian Temperance Union (WCTU) actively endorsed the censorship of vaudeville and burlesque shows that promoted 'looseness of thought' and 'undermined the sacredness of home and marriage.'[37] When Vancouver's Orpheum Theatre opened (for the fourth time) in 1927 on Granville Street as Canada's largest vaudeville house, the owner was determined to promote it as a reputable site for 'family entertainment.' An early communiqué warned managers that,

> There is a tendency on the part of certain artists to use in their act suggestive and objectionable material. This must not be tolerated by Managers. All unclean language, oaths, profanity, double-meaning jokes, suggestive songs, improper dances and offensive situations must be promptly eliminated ... Each individual Manager is charged with the responsibility of censoring the acts played at his theatre ... Managers and artists should cooperate so as to give our patrons only clean and wholesome entertainment.[38]

In New York, a decade-long campaign against burlesque waged by religious, anti-vice, and municipal activists, including Mayor Fiorello LaGuardia – resulted in a city-wide ban on burlesque entertainment in 1937.[39] Anxieties about the disorderliness and immorality of the male burlesque-goers – caricatured as 'sex-crazed perverts' – were at the heart of contests to eradicate sexual entertainment.[40] By 1942, every burlesque theatre licence in the Big Apple was revoked on the grounds that the shows promoted filth, vulgarity, queer innuendos, immorality, and male sexual violence. In effect, anti-burlesque initiatives were part of a larger set of strategies to regulate the sexual content of commercial culture – strategies that also targeted motion pictures, crime comics, and smutty magazines. Ironically, some mainstream magazines in Canada and the United States during World War II featured sizzling female dance hall and canteen entertainers in g-strings as morale builders for the troops. For a brief moment, soldiers and, by extension, 'the nation' depended on public displays of feminine sexiness. However, the entertainers' patriotism remained suspect because of their 'potential promiscuity' and 'descent into prostitution.'[41] And anti-obscenity activists insisted that burlesque shows corrupted normal masculine identity and depleted the virtue not only of soldiers, sailors, and marines but of all male citizens, imperilling the strength of the nation.

Clergy, public officials, women's groups, and the police alleged that low-class venues in urban centres spawned criminal elements and imperial decline. Reformers mobilized a range of municipal by-laws, provincial liquor laws, and federal Criminal Code provisions to protest the multifaceted scourge of 'lewd and obscene public performance' in disreputable nightspots.[42] In 1941, a special Police Delegation of religious and temperance leaders toured and inspected Vancouver's nightspots: they were known as the 'special constables' and were part of a long tradition of anthropological treatment of the city as, quoting historian Carolyn Strange, 'a laboratory full of troubling specimens of urban life.'[43] When they roamed city streets in search of flourishing vice, they became social geographers, mapping the locations of moral evils. Upon visiting what was likely the Mandarin Gardens Supper Club, Mrs McKay of the Vancouver Local Council of Women, representing seventy-eight women's groups, told reporters for the *Vancouver News Herald*, 'The floor show was objectionable, with girls naked except [for] brassieres and loin cloths.'[44] The Rev. Cook complained of 'immoral conduct highly suggestive of Sodom and Gomorrah.'[45] In 1945, members of the B.C. Temperance League, the Local Council of Women, and the United Church campaigned to prevent Hymie Singer from opening a new nightclub in Chinatown, citing the need to 'improve the moral life of the community.'[46]

In 1946, the State Burlesque Theatre on East Hastings Street was trans-

formed into Vancouver's first and only burlesque house. The original
Pantages theatre in 1908, and then the Royal Theatre, the State was *the*
spot to indulge one's passion for energetic, cabaret-style revues.[47] Well-
liked American entertainers Stinky Mason and Tom Farmer headlined
at the State, as did Cab Calloway, Peggy Lee, and Mel Tormé. Hollywood screen stars were the talk of the town, and the State's live shows
both preceded and followed screenings of the latest Hollywood films.
Owners Keith Lindforth, then Hymie Singer and Jack Aceman, and later, Isy Walters, guaranteed laughs by honouring the bawdy burlesque
tradition of treating 'low' subjects in a dignified, ceremonious manner
and 'high' subjects in a crude, undignified manner.[48] Favourite subjects
of burlesque – the 'poor man's musical comedy'[49] – were politics, domestic relations, and all facets of sex. Heterosexual lust was frequently
satirized; on occasion queer content was worked up through double-
entendres that spoofed limp-wristed homosexuals. Retired University
of British Columbia theatre professor and bon vivant Norman Young
recalls a typical burlesque sketch at the State by two comedians – Stinky
Mason and Tom Farmer: 'They're standing together on stage, and a
"walking doll" goes by – she parades around, has no lines, and looks
gorgeous – and Stinky makes panting noises. Tom says, "That's Liza.
Do you know that her left leg is insured for five hundred thousand
dollars?" Stinky replies: "Wow, wow, wow!" Liza comes back, and Tom
says, "There's Liza again. Do you know her right leg is insured for five
hundred thousand?" And Stinky retorts: "Hey, that's a million dollars
she's got between her legs!"'[50]

By middle-class standards of morality and respectability, burlesque
shows were considered indecent, risqué, and vulgar. The nudity, sexual
innuendo, and ribald jokes exploited by female dancers, comedians,
and clowns in burlesque and, later, striptease, catalysed moral panics
across North America as reformers, lawyers, judges, local pundits, and
police warned citizens to avoid the harmful consequences of sexually
suggestive entertainment.[51] Labelled 'factories of vice' and 'pest-breed-
ing theatres' that harboured coarse behaviour, 'bur-lee-cue' houses
were described in terms similar to those used by middle-class reformers in campaigns against prostitution, alcohol, and venereal disease:
they hastened the demise of an upstanding citizenry. At the same time,
burlesque shows in Vancouver and elsewhere were wildly popular. Big-
name American striptease dancers Gypsy Rose Lee, Yvette Dare and
her trained parrot, Faith Bacon and Sally Rand (both of whom claim to
have invented the fan dance), and Evelyn 'Hubba Hubba' West, with

Figure 1.1 Sally Rand, the feathered fan dancer, graced the stage of Vancouver's State Burlesque Theatre. She is pictured here in 1934.

breasts insured by Lloyds of London for $50,000, performed at the
600-seat State Burlesque Theatre (fig. 1.1). They were fronted by small
swing orchestras, backed by local showgirls such as Nena Marlene, and
co-billed with top-banana comedians, torch singers, magicians, accordion players, plate-twirlers, fire-eaters, tap dancers, and jugglers.

In the wake of the forced closure of burlesque halls in New York
City in the 1920s and 1930s, the State Burlesque Theatre was raided by
Vancouver's Morality Squad and its licence was revoked in September
1946.[52] In the courtroom, prosecutor Gordon Scott dangled before him
several flimsy garments, which he described as (1) a g-string, (2) 'what
purports to be a brassiere,' and (3) 'a pair of pink net panties.'[53] Later
that month, the licence was reissued by Vancouver City Council with
the proviso that 'none of the former comedians or striptease dancers, or
anything of a like nature be engaged.'[54] Defending his decision, License
Inspector Arthur Moore reminded the city council that members had
agreed to ban all strip and burlesque shows in 1946 – the same year
that fan-dancer Sally Rand was arrested for an 'indecent performance'
in San Francisco.[55] Again, in 1950 and 1951, the State had its licence
suspended for presenting 'an indecent strip act.'[56] Inspector Moore reported that 'A girl had taken off her clothing piece by piece until she
was wearing semi-transparent brassiere and panties, and from the back
rows, she appeared to be nude.'[57] Alderman Anna Sprott declared the
State's spicy show 'a bad influence on our young people.'[58] Though the
licence was quickly reissued by city councillors after owners assured
them they would offer 'clean entertainment with a little sex appeal,' the
club was raided again in January 1952.[59] Two exotic dancers and a male

comedian were arrested for 'bumps and grinds and suggestive jokes' in 'Holiday Spirits' – an 'indecent show,' and 'cheesecake pictures were seized from the State's marquee.'[60] Two weeks later, the three performers and two theatre owners were convicted in police court of 'presenting an indecent vaudeville performance'; all five were fined and the theatre's licence was revoked.[61] The State's manager, Charlie Nelson, was not amused: 'We had permission from city council to run a modified burlesque. If they call that indecent there's no use trying to show burlesque at all. It was like a Sunday school picnic compared to most shows in the U.S.'[62] The State's doors were firmly closed in 1952, marking the end of classic burlesque entertainment in Vancouver.

Postwar Contradictions

After World War II, the industry of striptease consolidated and expanded in the context of cold war politics and nuclear anxiety. It was a time of massive social, economic, political, and sexual upheaval across North America, when the imperatives of conformity and conservatism clashed with waves of youth rebellion, restlessness, and cultural radicalism.[63] At the end of the war, many hailed the burgeoning welfare state and accompanying notions of 'caring and sharing ... [as] ... central to our Canadian identity.'[64] Although personal disposable income more than doubled for Canadians between 1947 and 1960,[65] other realities also unfolded. First Nations peoples continued to suffer abuse in residential schools and the abduction or 'big scoop' of their children by non-Aboriginal adoption agencies.[66] African Canadian women faced displacement from hard-won factory positions occupied during the war.[67] Moral campaigns were engineered to make 'New Canadians' out of the vast influx of immigrants and refugees.[68] State surveillance targeted the Communist Party of Canada, the left, peace activism, women's groups, and the union movement with renewed vigour.[69]

American icons of domesticity June Cleaver, Donna Reed, and Betty Crocker propagandized the dividends of full-time wifedom, motherhood, and middle-class suburbia. Social scientists popularized their support for the nuclear family as *the* model for modern family life.[70] In the wake of war-related trauma, death, and turmoil, the marriage rate in Canada exploded. By 1956, the age of marriage had plummeted: on average, women married at 21.6 years and men at 24.5. 'Especially for women,' Doug Owram argues, 'the completion of [high] school, engagement, marriage, and the birth of the first child were more or less consecutive events.'[71] In contradictory fashion, the end of the war also spawned stories of sexual intrigue peddled in risqué comic books, *Playboy* magazine (launched in 1953), pin-up calendars, and lurid pulp novels. Hollywood's release of *Niagara* in 1953, starring the incomparable Marilyn Monroe, reinvigorated Niagara Falls (both in Ontario and New York) as a heterosexual theme park for honeymooners.[72] Zoologist Alfred Kinsey's *Sexual Behaviour in the Human Male* (1948) and *Sexual Behaviour in the Human Female* (1953) – both widely circulated in Canada – blew the cover off pre-marital sex, masturbation, female orgasm, and homosexual sex acts (37 per cent among men; 28 per cent among women).[73] The Kinsey Reports ignited moral panic *and* unleashed waves of excitement.[74] As historian Angus McLaren points out, Kinsey's name became a byword for scandalous sexual revelations.[75] In Hollywood films, 'bombshells' Marilyn Monroe, Jayne Mansfield, and Kim Novak ramped up the erotica quotient, expanding the inventory of titillation for sale.[76] Editors for the Canadian women's magazine *Chatelaine* communicated frank insights about birth control, masturbation, sexual abuse, lesbianism, and safe, legal abortions well before their American counterparts.[77]

By the 1960s, women were entering the Canadian labour force in unprecedented numbers. Whereas only fifty years earlier 42 per cent of employed women in British Columbia had worked in domestic service, new jobs – primarily in the sales, clerical, and service sectors – meant a variety of non-domestic options, though opinion about women's departure from the private sphere remained divided. Fears intensified about the corruption of impressionable teenagers who consumed dirty comic books, recreational drugs, and rock 'n' roll music.[78] Gary Kinsman shows that between 1958 and 1964, the Canadian federal government and the Royal Canadian Mounted Police (RCMP) purged hundreds of 'alleged' and 'confirmed' homosexuals from their jobs in the civil service (especially National Defence and External Affairs). Hundreds of gay men and women lost their livelihoods and their reputations as a result of the state's discriminatory belief that all homosexuals possessed an inherent 'character weakness' that made them vulnerable to blackmail, and hence a 'national security threat.'[79]

Vancouver Comes of Age

In British Columbia after World War II, the port city of Vancouver strengthened its place as a financial headquarters in western Canada, a central depot for the hinterland's resources and the world's largest grain-shipping centre. A boom in the export of oil, fish, natural gas, hydro-electric power, minerals, and forest products enriched the province's coffers.[80] On the political front, Social Credit premier W.A.C. Bennett took office in 1952 and ruled the provincial legislature for the next twenty years. Successive mayors of Vancouver sold the city as an attractive tourist destination, backboned by an expanding service sector, stepped-up hotel construction, the physical beauty of mountains, the Pacific Ocean, and the lushly wooded, 1,000-acre urban gem of Stanley Park.[81] By the 1950s, Vancouver was heralded as both a playground for outdoor recreation and a model of indoor cultural sophistication and night-time entertainment. Prohibitions against commercial entertainment on Sundays were revoked: Vancouver-born impresario Hugh Pickett helped to unlock the stranglehold of 'blue laws' by booking a world famous ballet troupe for a midnight Sunday show.[82]

Vancouver basked in growing economic affluence, optimism, and new opportunities for leisure.[83] After the long, penny-pinching years of the Depression, the tragedies of two world wars, and the disruption of familial and social networks, Vancouverites looked ahead to a rosier future. Beginning in the 1950s, the erection of sleek, modernist office towers, deluxe sports facilities, and diverse cultural venues announced the glitter and tinsel of a newly confident port city, deserving of civic pride.[84] By the 1960s, the entire city centre glowed from the electric energy of 18,000 neon signs. The eight-lane Granville Bridge (built in 1954) and the rezoned, densely developed West End enabled easier access to the city's core.[85] Inspired by the visionary urban planner Jane Jacobs, local citizens rejected the construction of an elevated freeway that would have splintered the centre of town: this decision not only distinguished Vancouver from most major North American cities; it showcased the city's downtown as a compact, intimate destination.[86] A de-industrializing trend saw manufacturing and light industry move out of False Creek and Granville Island, to be replaced with parks, an urban market, and water's-edge rental apartments and condominiums.

To the city's workers who toiled for long hours five days a week at dockyards, sawmills, factories, offices, shops, and department stores, a 'night out' on the weekend promised a much-welcome diversion from anxieties of the cold war, bomb shelters, and the fear of nuclear meltdown and communist invasion.[87] To suburban couples in New Westminster, Burnaby, Coquitlam, North Vancouver, Delta, Richmond, and Surrey, dressing up for night-time amusement meant temporarily escaping the comfort and familiarity of detached homes, small children, and shopping malls. To tourists on the lookout for adventure, the vibrant, pulsating beat of Vancouver's nightspots was as inviting as the city's dazzling natural beauty of mountains, forests, and ocean. Live big-band, swing, jazz, blues, soul, and rock 'n' roll music worked its magic on fun-seekers – young and old, urban and suburban, residents and visitors – who planned their evenings out in an era before television's monopoly on prime-time viewing kept people at home.[88] Vancouver's downtown exuded an aura of romance, and those attracted to its centre observed what Michael Johns calls 'sartorial decorum.' Having decided that going downtown was worth dressing up for, '[men and women] behaved with formality and dressed with restraint, even as a voluptuous sexuality lurked on all sides.'[89]

An economic upturn in Vancouver after World War II sparked renewed consumer spending that lasted until the mid-1970s, coinciding with the rapid growth of the city's independent nightclub scene. In the late 1940s and early 1950s, live stage acts prospered in Vancouver's core, and later in sprawling suburbs and small towns linked by improved transportation routes north to the province's northwest coast and the interior, and east to the Alberta border. By the early 1960s, the newly inaugurated Pacific Western Airlines, B.C. Airlines, and charter services of float planes transported loggers and miners from the interior and coastal regions to quick immersion in the city's simmering fleshpots.[90] Vancouver's reputation as 'home to the hottest nightclubs north of San Francisco' began to crystallize after the war, in large part because of the magnetic influence of *the* North American entertainment capital – Las Vegas.[91] No other city in Canada had the same geographical and symbolic linkage to 'Vegas.' But what, exactly, constituted the 'heat' that fired the furnaces of Vancouver's infamously 'hot' hotspots?

The Stain of Stigma, the Trouble with 'Deviance,' and the Dearth of Sleuths

My preliminary foray into researching Vancouver's erotic entertainment industry left me frustrated. Labour historians in Canada have uncovered the injustices of structural unemployment, ugly conflicts between workers and management, the exploitation of non-Anglo immigrants, the consolidation of a gender-segmented labour force, declining rates of unionization, and deepening class schisms as flagrant, wretched features of capitalist social formation.[92] Tales told of Vancouver's past by urban historians contain the odd, cursory mention of the sex trade but little about commercial striptease, past or present.[93] Contributors to the expanding field of feminist sexuality studies have explored histories of homosexuality, bisexuality, and heterosexuality, as well as past formations of sexual communities and the emergence of campaigns to police sexual danger and 'indecency.'[94] Again, however, I found almost no inquiry into the complexities and contours of postwar professional striptease. In all, an absence of sustained examination of exotic dance as work for performers and leisure for customers confirmed my suspicion that interlinked histories of labour, the city, recreation, and sexuality were significantly underdeveloped.[95]

Overshadowed by sagas of war, resource extraction and manufacturing, parliamentary politics, transportation systems, sporting heroes, and settlement patterns in the Lower Mainland, the particularities of Vancouver's striptease industry proved elusive. Even the impressive oeuvre of the late Pierre Berton – revered chronicler of railways, the Klondike gold rush, the mystique of Niagara Falls, and the tragedy of the Dionne quintuplets – was disappointingly mute on the question of bump and grind. The proverbial dilemma of locating sources germane to the story one wants to tell – whether case files, police records, personal scrapbooks, court transcripts, mayor's papers, diaries, or city directories – is especially acute for those of us who confront the legacy of (all varieties of) sex work as criminalized and largely unrecorded. For an employment sector so resiliently enduring, I unearthed little from conventional archival sources about the working conditions of Vancouver-based dancers who built careers, earned livelihoods, and steered their way around myths that revered *and* reviled them in the postwar era. Nor did I locate information on the men who produced and consumed erotic entertainment. A.W. Stencell's *Girl Show: Into the Canvas World of Bump and Grind* supplied a popular, richly visual account of twentieth-century striptease on fairgrounds. And two scholarly tomes were helpful – *Stripping in Time* by Lucinda Jarrett, and Rachel Shteir's *Striptease: The Untold History of the Girlie Show* – though neither focuses on the Canadian context, nor the pivotal decade of the 1970s.[96]

In the 1950s and 1960s, portraits of stripteasers in Hollywood films reinforced the dichotomy between proper, middle-class girls and wayward, working-class sex fiends.[97] Featuring morality tales of good versus evil, the 'stripper genre' peddles familiar tropes of the sordid business of burlesque, with few twists. Both *Gypsy* (1962) and *The Night They Raided Minsky's* (1967) depict a conventional portrait of burlesque/striptease as an entertainment culture both decadent and un-savory. Viewers are asked to empathize with an innocent, submissive, young woman manipulated and dominated by the stronger personalities around her. She enters into the world of burlesque either unwillingly or lacking understanding of how it is scorned as low-class, bawdy theatre. The heterosexual allure of her character only emerges when she is thrust in front of an audience and seems to stumble across her charms unwittingly. In the case of *Gypsy*, based on the memoir of strip-tease queen Gypsy Rose Lee, the suggestion is made that no respectable woman would enter the world of burlesque willingly, regardless of potential fortune. In effect, the character of Gypsy (Natalie Wood) invites sympathy solely because she is pushed into the business by her destructive, overbearing mother (Rosalind Russell), who repeatedly reminds Gypsy that 'she's still a lady.' The character Herbie (Karl Malden), representing the lone male voice of 'reason,' urges Rose to marry him and settle down in a normal family. But Rose rejects this proposal, forcing her daughter Louise/Gypsy into a risqué career, for which she is vilified on screen. Gypsy finally breaks away from her mother, telling her defiantly, 'I'm a star now – I have friends, I'm going places, up or down, wherever, I'm enjoying it.' The ending is more ambiguous than others in this genre – Gypsy exhibits a spunky resolve to overcome the odds. But the message is clear that the career of a stripteaser whom the press labelled a 'circus freak' and a 'novelty act' would never follow a straightforward path to stardom.

In the Oscar-winning blockbuster hit *The Graduate* (1967), striptease makes a cameo appearance. The newly minted, aimless university graduate Benjamin Braddock (Dustin Hoffman) is pressured to take Elaine Robinson (Katherine Ross) on a date. Elaine is the daughter of Benjamin's married, clandestine lover, Mrs Robinson (Anne Bancroft). By electing to take Elaine to a downtown strip club, Benjamin aims to publicly humiliate and punish the white, upper-class virgin by forcing her to witness the debauchery of stripteasers who twirl ornamental tassels from jewelled pasties double-dutch style and gyrate in g-strings for a living. Sickened and horrified by what she interprets as Benjamin's cruel assault on her modesty and respectability, Elaine breaks down crying. At the sight of Elaine's tears, Benjamin is jolted into white, class-conscious chivalry, does an about-turn, and lunges violently at the dancer on the stage. He then pursues a fleeing Elaine out of the club, and later comforts her with kisses and food in the safety of his stylish red convertible, the nasty underworld of the stripclub long for-gotten and Benjamin's transgression all but forgiven. When I watch this scene in *The Graduate*, I wish the camera had lingered on the nightclub's mesmerizing stage show, followed the voluptuous erotic dancers into dressing rooms, and made these much-maligned entertainers the protagonists, not the props. Alas, not a chance.[98]

In the late 1960s, American sociologists and criminologists 'discovered' striptease dancing. From observational fieldwork in nightclubs, they produced accounts of 'stripping as a deviant occupation' attractive to 'girls from unstable backgrounds' predisposed to 'exhibitionist behaviour' (having been denied affection from 'absent fathers') and in search of 'easy economic gain.'[99] Part of the broader trend within urban sociology to examine the 'subcultures' of gambling, prostitution, drug use, and prison systems, this literature on striptease is rife with generalizations and barely veiled judgments. Not only were these scholars unable to hide their own competing feelings of titillation and ambivalence (if not disgust) towards dancers; they were unable to accept striptease, or exotic dancing, as labour. Charles McCaghy and James Skipper adopt a condescending tone when they write that, 'Stripping is essentially an unskilled job'; and 'anyone who views ... strip acts will agree that "talent"... is notably lacking.'[100] Moreover, reminiscent of Alexander John Baptiste Parent-Duchatelet's nineteenth-century taxonomy of 'the prostitute' as plump, filthy, harsh-voiced, and lazy, McCaghy and Skipper isolate 'the stripper' as a physical type: 'taller, heavier, with larger hips, and much larger busts' when compared with the average American woman.[101] Notwithstanding the academics' efforts to interact with their 'informants,' dancers appear as specimens to be inspected, measured, and mocked rather than as workers whose rich biographies confound a facile 'deviance-begets-deviance' appraisal.

In the late 1970s and early 1980s, anti-pornography feminist activists emphasized the patriarchal degradation and oppression of strippers, porn models, prostitutes, and other sex workers.[102] To British ex-dancer Nickie Roberts, the no-win scenario prescribed by feminist critics was untenable: 'Either we were victims or we were repentant sinners to be hoisted up before the crowds like some confessing prisoner in a Stalinist plot.'[103] To those who rejected images of sexually contained, even asexual womanhood, feminist sex pessimism denied women their horny behaviour, their lust, and their longings to seduce. In the late 1970s, Gwendolyn faced the wrath of feminists on a 'Take Back the Night' march who screamed, 'Stripping is pornography' and 'Violence against women' outside a strip club in Toronto where she worked.[104] Writing about how she was misrepresented in the incendiary film *Not a Love Story: A Film about Pornography* (1981), retired dancer Lindalee

Tracey laid bare the scalding force of feminist Puritanism. Written six-teen years after appearing in the film, her searing condemnation of feminist filmmakers at the National Film Board (NFB) sounds a caution to all outsiders who dare to superimpose their moralizing assumptions on dancers' lives:

> I tell the women I want all my parts included, the poetry, the home, the performance art. I want to be whole so people know that strippers are complicated and not just bodies ... I wonder if the director is a middle-class tourist, just using me as her ticket into an exposé ... We film all the feminists [like Robin Morgan] in their own worlds, surrounded by their trinkets, not swallowed up in ugly places like the porn girls ... When the women from NFB finally show me the film, I'm stunned. How do you tell someone you like that you feel betrayed and sickened? I'm reduced to a porno queen; nothing of my studio or performance art, nothing but my function ... Then at the end, I'm a snappy, happy, born-again feminist penitent – a bad girl gone good. The film takes credit for my supposed conversion, as if I had no intellectual context before. The film is enormous ... I often feel like someone's pet being paraded at screenings and wom-en's talks, or that my opinions are being expropriated by more vigorous arguments. Now I am smothering under the weight of the film's lie: that I was re-created and liberated by the filmmakers ... The film cages my essence in a flat, single dimension. I'll have to learn to compete with that invented self on film.[105]

My book *Burlesque West* offers a departure from the misguided, sal-vationist rhetoric of some feminists, the sensationalist accounts of a corrupted, sex-deviant underworld by social scientists, stories of sorry strippers from the pens of Hollywood screenwriters, and the neglect of cultural historians. Here, I develop two central arguments. First, I challenge the popular assumption that postwar striptease constituted a marginal, inconsequential, and civicly embarrassing industry popu-lated by wayward degenerates and 'good girls gone bad.' Rather, I con-tend that commercial stripping oiled the economic engine of Vancouver (and other North American cities), much as prostitution did in the early twentieth century. More specifically, I show how the skin trade greased the levers of the seaside city's economy, all the while being treated by Puritan city fathers, police, and moral reformers as crude, quasi-legal titillation – a virulent strain of urban blight. Second, I trace how the stars of strip shows, the female dancers, participated in double-edged work: sexually empowering and financially rewarding, their career path was also burdened by patriarchal, racist expectations, occupational hazards, and myriad vulnerabilities. From 1945 to 1980, female dancers were benefactors of what historians term 'les trentes glorieuses' – the thirty glorious years of extended prosperity across postwar North America. Dancers benefited, but not without strife.[106]

Together, my two main claims deepen and extend Pierre Bourdieu's critique of 'the hierarchical, hierarchizing world of cultural works.'[107] Classified in collective consciousness as base, unrefined, dirty, and un-skilled – the diametrical opposite of ballet and opera – striptease was consigned to treacherous moral territory. At a time of intense confor-mity to norms of domesticity and nuclear family making, erotic dancers defied idealized hetero-feminine respectability to imagine belonging to a postwar nation bent on securing their exclusion. Yet as I note above, the resilience of stripping (in guises old and new) is legendary. As theatre historian Rachel Shteir argues, 'When reformers attacked strip-tease they did so in a way that always "nearly" eradicated it.'[108] Snared in a swirl of competing, contradictory forces, erotic dancers and their promoters spun a brand of super-natural bewitchery that trapped fans and foes alike under its alluring spell.

Economic Efflorescence: Thwarting the Abolitionists

From the late 1940s onward, Vancouver's independent nightclubs em-ployed thousands of workers – stripteasers, club owners, managers, booking agents, doormen, bouncers, ticket-sellers, hat-check girls, ciga-rette and cigar girls, go-go dancers, choreographers, photographers, costume designers, club secretaries, bookkeepers, MCs, DJs, cooks, kitchen staff, bus boys, prop, set, and lighting specialists, waiters and waitresses, cleaners, bartenders, musicians (who supplied dancers with live accompaniment until the mid-to-late 1970s), and lawyers (who de-fended clubs when busted by vice squads). Other workers whose earn-ings were derived from commercial striptease included specialty shoe, hosiery, make-up, and liquor suppliers, cab drivers, hair stylists, mani-curists, pedicurists, security guards, wig-makers, tanning salon opera-tors, clothing/fabric retailers, drug sellers, child care workers (who minded the kids of dancers), plastic surgeons (who did boob jobs), media pundits like gossip columnists Jack Wasserman and Denny Boyd, and the owners of the *Vancouver Sun, Vancouver Daily Province/ The Province,* and *Vancouver News Herald,* who raked in piles of dough by selling daily advertising spots to nightclub promoters. In all, commercial striptease became *as vital* to the city's postwar economic growth as its railway facilities, sawmills, and grain elevators.[109]

As its popularity grew, the striptease industry periodically attracted the scrutinizing, jaundiced eye of critics. Ironically, city officials benefited from the survival and surveillance of striptease: morality squads patrolled clubs (and sometimes extorted bribes); liquor and permit inspectors enforced rules; and prosecutors, judges, and court recorders managed courtroom adjudications of 'lewd and indecent public exhibition.' The city's coffers swelled with club owners' licensing fees, fines, property taxes, and utilities payments. Club owners and dancers encountered resistance from the same reformers who lobbied for restrictive gambling and liquor laws, as well as from stepped-up campaigns against venereal disease and for the censorship of 'obscenity.' In Montreal in 1951, the indomitable Lili St Cyr was arrested and subjected to a trial for giving an obscene and immoral performance; she was arrested again in 1967 before tourists arrived for Expo.[110] Perhaps because of St Cyr's tangle with the law, dancers in Montreal in the 1960s were known to wear 'merkins' – patches of artificial pubic hair glued to the pubic region – in order to avoid arrest for indecency.

After the war, across North American cities, tourists and conference-goers with expense accounts paid to stay in hotels, take cabs, dine out, and frequent night-time amusements. In 1948, tourist dollars spent in Vancouver topped $30 million.[111] And in 1975, the Greater Vancouver Visitors' and Convention Bureau estimated that the tourist and convention business pumped $200 million into the local economy. The economics of leisure dominated the speeches of ministers of recreation who promoted Vancouver as the spanking new 'Playground of North America.'[112] Civic boosters never included venues for striptease as legitimate grounds for play, or as choice bait to lure vacationers. However, the city's much-ballyhooed commercial striptease scene accounted for a healthy percentage of tourist-related revenues (though calculating exact figures is a dodgy enterprise).[113] That the economic and cultural heritage of Vancouver's striptease industry has been hidden, or at best treated as a source of collective shame – a punching bag for zealous moral conservatives – betokens the depth of unresolved cultural anxieties about flaunted, for-profit female sexuality.

In the late 1960s and 1970s, defenders of social purity across British Columbia combined nasty attacks against striptease (and sex work more broadly) with attacks against American draft resisters, Trotskyists, Maoists, drug users, marijuana growers, hippies, the Vancouver

Libertarian Front, and both the Women's Liberation and the Gay Liber-ation movements.[114] The *Georgia Straight*, Vancouver's 'free press,' was charged with three counts of obscenity, all of which were dismissed in 1969.[115] In Vancouver, in August 1970, twelve people were charged with indecency by the RCMP for appearing nude on Wreck Beach, and several weeks later the nudists stoked their campaign to protect the beach by staging a 'nude-in.'[116] In August 1971, the Vancouver Police turned a peaceful protest against federal marijuana laws – referred to as the 'Grasstown Smoke-In' – into the Gastown Riot.[117] Undaunted by reactionary forces, anti-authoritarian consciousness and action gained ground in the early 1970s to establish Vancouver as the centre of Can-ada's youth culture. Robert Hunter, the Vancouver-based co-founder of the environmentalist rebels of Greenpeace, made sense of the ripe political and cultural counter-culture into which his anti-nuclear jug-gernaut was born:

> In Vancouver ... we had the biggest concentration of tree-huggers, radi-calized students, garbage-dump stoppers, shit-disturbing unionists, free-way fighters, pot smokers and growers, aging Trotskyites, condo killers, farmland savers, fish preservationists, animal rights activists, back-to-the-landers, vegetarians, nudists, Buddhists, and anti-spraying, anti-pollution marchers and picketers in the country, per capita, in the world.[118]

Wilfully Plucky: Negotiating the Stripper Stigma

Amid this rich potpourri of cultural growth, political dissent, and sex-ual permissiveness, striptease dancers pursued careers in the world of show business. For this study, I asked how they got involved, what they loved and loathed about the business, how long they stayed, what re-tirement entailed, and why they insist that the pay, working conditions, and fans were superior in Vancouver to the scene in Las Vegas. From the outset, I mulled over niggling double standards: Why were scantily clad female figure skaters with the Canadian Ice Fantasy,[119] majorettes at sporting events, trapeze artists, and bathing suit contestants vying for the crown of Miss Pacific National Exhibition granted the status of 'family entertainer' while professional striptease dancers were not? Why was the work of stripteasers more likely to be ridiculed and yet more highly paid than the work of female cannery workers, fishers, bakers, stenographers, child-minders, and retail clerks? Indeed, why was the work of professional striptease performers so rarely granted the status of real work? Moreover, on what grounds were male night-club owners refused the legitimacy and respect extended to other successful entrepreneurs and business owners? Why did the vast majority of (male) jazz musicians who accompanied dancers on stage belong to a Vancouver union, Local 145, while dancers' efforts to unionize were repeatedly stymied?

The decades immediately following World War II marked a time of considerably more continuity than change in the striptease business. This period is often glorified as the glamorous 'golden era' of the tasteful tease before the rise of the explicit 'cunt show' in the late 1970s when, to quote ex-dancer Lindalee Tracey, 'striptease fell from grace because the world stopped dreaming.'[120] Conscious of Tracey's narrative of transition and eventual ruin, I sought to uncover the perspectives of business insiders who recalled striptease acts in an allegedly simpler, less raunchy, more entertaining time. Certainly, by the late 1960s, the sexual revolution that reverberated across North America had unleashed considerable sexual energy and experimentation prior to the HIV/AIDS crisis of the early-to-mid-1980s. From ex-dancers, I wanted to know what was 'golden' about the business, and what was not?

Unlocking the Memory Vault: Ethically Negotiating Oral Histories

While poring over primary documents, including dancers' autobiographies, photographic records, newspapers, and government files, I soon realized that the patchy archival and scholarly record necessitated in-depth interviewing. So, between 1998 and 2007 I conducted fifty interviews with business insiders: nineteen dancers who had worked before 1980, one transsexual entertainer (who was not a stripper per se), a retired modern/ballet dancer, six former nightclub staff, six musicians, four retired club owners/managers, two choreographers, three ex-booking agents, two former nightclub goers, two retired journalists, and four dancers who had worked after 1980.[121] I found interview participants, and they found me, through a combination of community ads, posters, snowball sampling, and intensive media publicity (outlined in the Preface). I feel deeply honoured by my narrators' trust in me, an industry outsider. During the process of interviewing, and afterwards, I never took this trust for granted. Initially, I suspected that my openly feminist identity might make ex-dancers suspicious of my motives. As I mentioned above, influential feminist critics have wrongly argued that all female sex workers were (and are) objectified, enslaved victims of lecherous, controlling men and their hydraulic, abusive lust.[122] And though I explained my significant disagreements with this abolitionist orthodoxy, I was never certain that interview participants were entirely reassured. That said, the vast majority of ex-dancers I interviewed self-defined as feminists *and* debunked the distorted rhetoric of their so-called feminist sisters.[123] These women were *insiders to feminism*. Unlike sex workers globally who have endured coercion, poverty, and sexual exchange for survival, the women who spoke to me chose to partici-pate in the sex industry from among other options. Many ex-dancers echoed the insights of contemporary American dancer/scholar Merri Lisa Johnson, who champions 'an economy of plenty' in contradistinc-tion to an economy of loss or shortage. Addressing feminist opponents, she dryly explains, 'We do not "use up" our sexuality by displaying it at the strip club. We do not render it cheap. We do not trade our self-respect for a sweaty dollar. There is always more where that came from.'[124]

Mindful of interviewing practice as multi-levelled negotiation, I strove for self-conscious clarity about my identity, what I endeavoured to do, and why. I was not a naive cultural tourist bent on extracting goods from 'native informants' in the nasty tradition of anthropologi-cal imperialism.[125] Instead, I sought awareness of the similarities and differences at play during interviews with my participants. I under-stand my lesbianism as non-normative sexuality akin, in some respects, to the sexuality of retired dancers in what Carol Queen calls a culture of erotophobia.[126] A femme fond of MAC lipstick, perfume, mascara, eye-liner, jewellery, bleached-blond hair, mini skirts, and high heels, I have weathered decades-long dismissal of me as a 'painted lady' with dubious feminist credentials.[127] As a sex educator, non-mother, and all-purpose violator of sex and gender norms, I relished opportunities to talk stripping with the pros. The ex-dancers were older than I was – and it was a pleasure to hold these elders, and their mixed feelings about striptease, in high esteem. Also older than I was, the men I interviewed were pleased – and surprised, I sensed – to be asked questions about their role in a business that intriguingly affirmed and undercut their entitlement to gendered power and control. While ex-dancers chose to be known in *Burlesque West* by their stage names, the men (e.g., club owners, staff, musicians, choreographers, agents) matter-of-factly con-sented to use of their given names – a subtle distinction that reveals the masculine privilege to be 'out' in the open.

Discovering connection with narrators was always gratifying, though it never erased the fact that, unlike me, the majority of retired producers and performers of striptease had once belonged to a gravely stigmatized profession. I anticipated that knowledge of my privileged job at the university would introduce an unbridgeable gap: as salaried instigator, analyst, and writer, I possessed the authority and resources to shape interviews, solicit personal reflections, and use narrators' stories as grist for my mill – a mill that Judith Stacey warns may have truly grinding power.[128] The class gap was felt most acutely in the company of the few ex-dancers who were struggling financially; it was least evident in interviews with those who were monetarily secure, including an Italian countess, a real-estate agent, a successful translator/ interpreter, and all four retired male club owners. As a white woman interviewing white and non-white participants, I made a conscious commitment to integrate queries about complex relations and performances of ethnicity and race/racism in the strip trade. In addition, my taken-for-granted ability to hear was challenged when interviewing a deaf ex-dancer who patiently conveyed her stories both verbally and non-verbally.

What seemed to matter most during interviews was my stated aim to unearth first-hand truths, re-evaluate urban myths, and ponder the past, present, and future of striptease culture from the standpoint of former business insiders. I explained to narrators that it was my job to communicate respect, ensure confidentiality, honour the gift of memory, and listen. Each person welcomed me (and my assistants), often with refreshments, into their homes – where their scrapbooks, photos, and old costumes were on display. The semi-structured interviews were two to four hours in length. In the spirit of reciprocity and respect, I endeavoured to send each narrator a copy of her/his transcript and, later, a book chapter I had written for publication. I solicited assistance with establishing correct dates, times, places, and acts, as well as feedback on my emerging analysis. Still, I am acutely aware that the women and men I interviewed constitute a small, unrepresentative group derived from word-of-mouth, snowball sampling, and a flurry of media stories. My narrators are the ones who survived; they felt strong enough and sure enough about the value of their experiences (and my role as a conduit) to contribute. Others, if alive and aware of my project, may have been either unwilling or unable to participate. I continue to wonder about all the insiders whom I did not locate.

Oral history is an excellent tool for recovering the otherwise unknown lives of marginalized, subaltern groups. However, an interview is never an unmediated oral source that provides a somehow 'purer' version of the past narrated by people who directly experienced it. According to Geoffrey Cubitt, 'Past experience is not a tape that memory can rewind, tracking backwards through a continuous series of remembered events until everything has been neatly recapitulated: remembering is always a somewhat speculative navigational labour.'[129] Writing about the construction of historical memory, Joan Sangster theorizes about how five women very differently remembered their collective participation in a textile strike in Peterborough, Ontario, in 1937. One woman emphasized her preoccupation with planning her wedding during the strike, while another portrayed the strike as a 'heyday,' a social diversion for the summer. To Sangster, a feminist labour historian, both tales were unexpected.[130] Some of my narrators may have embellished events, forgotten others, or become confused. Yet rather than invalidate memory as an unreliable resource, I follow Alessandro Portelli in holding that, 'The importance of oral testimony may often lie not in its adherence to facts but rather in its divergence from them, where imagination, symbolism, desire, break in.'[131] On occasion, I felt that I was privy to an oral tradition of storytelling among members of a community accustomed to sharing knowledge, secrets, and gossip to survive in a stigmatized industry. Where possible, I supplemented and corroborated the stories of all business insiders by referencing a range of primary documents – newspaper and magazine stories, booking diaries, maps, poetry, and film, among others.

I accept the fact that my narrators may have withheld information to protect themselves and their loved ones. While I refrained from asking dancers about past experiences of child sexual abuse, many volunteered stories of sexual violence they had suffered as adults. Acutely conscious of the stripper stigma, the ex-dancers I interviewed had largely positive stories to tell. It is possible that they emphasized the satisfactions of their craft to compensate for mistreatment endured in the past. I also interviewed them before the curious cultural phenomenon of stripper-chic appeared on the scene – an ironic fad that would have occasioned much spirited commentary. For some, memories of their striptease careers were thirty years old; for others, more than half a century. Just about every ex-dancer wistfully invoked mention of the 'piles of dough' she had made and spent back then. What is clear, borrowing from Sangster, is that their experiences were created not out of many possible discourses but out of a limited range of discourses expressive of structures of power and of individual and collective resistance to those structures.[132] My challenge became one of refusing to depict retired dancers and their promoters as either victims or romantic figures; such a polarization would have scuttled sensitivity to the messy, sometimes contradictory, deeply textured stuff of lives lived and recounted.

As an adult, I experimented with recreational ballet, jazz, modern, and Latin dance classes. While I still love to shake my booty at local nightclubs, I have never danced professionally. By the time I began this book, I was too old, too flat-chested, and (still) too inhibited to launch a striptease career. That said, I have always been curious about stripteasers' decisions to enter the business, the nature of their working conditions, and their longevity in a patriarchal, racist industry predicated on men's fantasies of naked women.[133] I am indebted to the retired dancers, primarily in the geopolitical north, who have found the resources to write their own autobiographies of exploitation *and* rebellion, resistance *and* accommodation.[134] Indeed, of late, the stripper memoir seems robust enough to merit designation as a new sub-genre. In *Burlesque West*, I build upon ex-dancers' individual stories by offering a window onto debates about gender relations, sexuality, racial stereotypes, morality, and labour in a uniquely western Canadian city. I patently disagree with ex-stripper Diablo Cody's portrayal of stripping as 'puddle-shallow and symbolically molecular.'[135] Indeed, the saucy tales that fill her 200-page 'tell-all' book, *Candy Girl*, contradict her flippant conclusion. Rather, in broad terms, my findings suggest fruitful insights into the sociology of work, feminist theories of the body, configurations of urban space, popular amusements, the quandary of citizenship, and (non)belonging to the postwar nation.

My book is informed by a pastiche of theoretical influences, including the poststructural, queer treasures of Michel Foucault and Judith Butler; the intricate facets of moral regulation by Pierre Bourdieu, Erving Goffman, Mariana Valverde, and Alan Hunt; the feminist materialism of Dorothy E. Smith, Gary Kinsman, Arlie Hochschild, and Beverly Skeggs; and the anti-racism of Edward Said, Anne McClintock, and Patricia Hill Collins. My concerted effort to integrate stories by white and non-white women and men fills a gap in scholarship that largely disregards diversities of race/ethnicity and gender. First and foremost, I understand former striptease dancers – working class and middle class, white and non-white, queer and straight – as women who worked for a living. I have attempted to borrow from the best of critical ethnography; my case study is indebted to and driven by first-person memories. And still, it marks a partial, incomplete account. Unlike researchers who observe the contemporary scene, including Bernadette Barton, Chris

Bruckert, Danielle Egan, Katherine Frank, Katherine Liepe-Levinson, and Mary Nell Trautner, I did not engage the technique of direct observation inside strip clubs: the dancers I interviewed had retired, and all save three of the strip clubs that appear in *Burlesque West* have disappeared. Nor did I make a priority of soliciting stories from spectators who paid for strip shows in the immediate postwar decades (though I was regaled with countless yummy anecdotes after every public talk). I invite others to pick up strands that I leave hanging, or to invent brand-new directions from the ones I have sketched here.

In chapter 2, I examine how men in postwar Vancouver were indispensable to the production of striptease as club owners, club staff, musicians, choreographers, booking agents, costume designers, and photographers. Behind the marquee, men called the shots, reaped the rewards of an often-lucrative business, and paid a price – emotionally, legally, and financially – for their transgressions. They also profited, as did other male employers of female service workers, from dancers' hard work, concessions, and accommodations. The female dancers who perfected gimmicks on Vancouver stages from 1945 to 1980 form the core of chapter 3. Here, I pay particular attention to the racialized expectations and queer dimensions of strip culture, as well as to the artistic, cosmetic, and athletic traditions that shaped – and were shaped by – dancers' repertoires. Accepting 'business insiders' as expert knowers, following the lead of Dorothy E. Smith, has meant discovering not only the identities of those who performed striptease but the meanings that these women attached to their craft.[136] In chapter 4, I explore dancers' working conditions, relationships with co-workers and patrons, efforts to supplement striptease income, and the pressure, by the early 1970s, to tour for a living. Chapter 5 is devoted to excavating the occupational hazards specific to the business: the stripper stigma, sexualized harassment, and vulnerability to violence. Here, dancers' campaigns to unionize, and obstacles that thwarted their organizing efforts, figure prominently. As well, I examine the blunt instrument of the law – how it was used to arrest, intimidate, and deny work to dancers and their promoters. Finally, in chapter 6, I explore ex-dancers' exits out of the trade, as well as the issues germane to stripping as a 'full contact sport' in the twenty-first century. The phenomenon of neo-burlesque and the curious marketing of pole-dancing lessons invite closer scrutiny. Increasingly billed as a 'world-class' city, Vancouver stands as an important case study of erotic entertainment with implications for urban sites across North America and beyond.

2 'I Ain't Rebecca, and This Ain't Sunny-brook Farm':[1] Men behind the Marquee

Fifteen to twenty police officers would come in on a raid and swoop down on you. But we had a system. Each club owner would phone: 'They just left my place. They're on the prowl.' And we had a man up on top of the roof of the Penthouse. If the lookout saw a cavalcade of cars coming down Seymour Street, he knew it was the police. So he would press the button to sound the alarm. That gave customers a chance to hide their bottles.

Ross Filippone, Interview, 2000[2]

Take a walk on the dark side, of Chinatown, where, like a sinister gargoyle, bird of carrion perched drooling on to the corner of Pender and Main, once stood, a perverse monument fully erected, to deviant, diabolical depravity, the notorious Kublai Khan ... where lying in wait for you ... femme fatale sirens, luring in the men ...

Sean Gunn, 'Kublai Khan Ten,' 2000[3]

As in Montreal, Las Vegas, Chicago, and New York, Vancouver's night-club business emerged as an occupational enclave for immigrant men – among them, Jewish, Italian, Irish, Ukrainian, Chinese, South Asian, and African Canadian. Constrained by barriers to meaningful, secure, well-paid employment in private and public sectors controlled by the port city's well-established Anglo elite, these non-Anglo men journeyed along a road less travelled. Intrepid impresarios in the fast-paced, edgy world of 'adult entertainment,' they endeavoured to pad their pockets, keep a tight grip on business, hire and fire strippers (and other per-formers), and dodge the intrusive surveillance of the law. Much like the Minsky brothers in New York, the Weinstein Brothers in Dallas, the O'Farrell brothers in San Francisco, Milt Schuster in Chicago, and Paul Raymond in London, England, nightclub operators in Vancouver sought self-employment – the satisfaction of being their own boss.[4] Whether it was the Gaiety, Apollo, or Republic in New York, the Rialto in Chicago, the Two O'Clock Club in Baltimore, the Burbank in Los Angeles, the Folly in Kansas City, or the Penthouse in Vancouver – running a club that featured 'exotics' meant engaging in a risky enterprise with the prospect of both high-stakes dividends and losses.

Until the mid-1970s, all of Vancouver's club owners and booking agents were men; they openly exploited other men's fascination with naked female bodies, they operated quasi-legal establishments, and they were widely stereotyped as sleazy, low-life mobsters and criminals.[5] In this chapter, male club owners' first-person memories of the 'stripper business,' supplemented by reflections of male musicians and 'night-beat' reporters, reveal the choices made, the deals done, and the bargains struck along the way. A sampling of some of the most popular nightclubs' architecture, location, clientele, and booking history underscores the reality that club owners, like the striptease artists they employed, experimented with gimmicks to attract patrons from week to week, month to month, and year to year. Their trade was sharply stratified along lines of socio-economic class, race/ethnicity, and geography, with implications for vulnerability to anti-vice policing and the wrath of moral reformers. Whatever a club owner's specific circumstance, competition for customers' entertainment dollars was intense – gauging consumer mood in a fickle sector that rode waves of economic up-turns and down-turns became a constant preoccupation. Not unlike the insecurities of free-lance photography, running a restaurant, or selling vacuums door-to-door, staging striptease for a living was a tricky proposition, one fraught with tensions, tangles, and tumult. At the same time, club owners – merchants of vice with outsized personalities – came to know the thrill of hobnobbing with celebrities, counting the money after a profitable night, and witnessing an unforgettable dancer's performance: all sure-fire compensations for the vagaries of show business.

Erotic Entertainment Heats Up after Dark

In the late 1940s, in the words of entertainment scribe Jack Wasserman, 'Vancouver erupted as the vaudeville capital of Canada, rivalling and finally outstripping Montreal in the east and San Francisco in the south as one of the few places where the brightest stars of the nightclub era could be glimpsed from behind a post, through a smoke-filled room, over the heads of $20 tippers at ringside. Only in Las Vegas and Miami Beach, in season, were more superstars available in nightclubs.'[6] *Vancouver Sun* journalist Patrick Nagle recalled a 'show business railway' that moved performers, including showgirls, up and down the Pacific coast on the 'west coast circuit' with stops in Los Angeles, San Francisco, Las Vegas, Reno, Portland, Seattle, and finally Vancouver, where rising American entertainers delivered their acts to loyal fans.[7] The geographical proximity of 'terminal city' to the western states meant that talent flowed steadily south-to-north across the U.S.-Canada border much more than it flowed east-to-west across the Rocky Mountains. In the context of a strong Canadian dollar, American nightclub acts were relatively affordable; moreover, entertainers often rehearsed brand-new material in Vancouver, sometimes at discounted rates, without the fear of influential negative press. In a city eager to show off its mid-century patina of sophistication, professional female striptease artists were advertised as juicy fare at a range of independent clubs (see table 2.1).

Fancy Nightclubs in the City's West End

As the lights went out in Vancouver's vaudeville and burlesque theatres – the Beacon and the State – in the early 1950s, nightclubs emerged in both the West End/uptown and East End/downtown districts. Indeed, the east-west spatial divide, with Main Street as the principal bisector, was an already well-established fact in the metropolis (see map, fig. 2.1). As summarized in the 1950s Gallery at the Vancouver Museum, 'In the 1950s, your neighbourhood, especially the side of Main Street you lived on, was likely to reflect your income, ethnic origin, religion, and political affiliation.' Asymmetries of wealth, income, status, and education date back to the late 1800s; moreover, racial and ethnic tensions have always been a central feature of life in the province's lower mainland.[8] In 1951, the city of 345,000 on the south-west coast of *British* Columbia comprised an Anglo-Canadian majority (93 per cent) and small communities of non-Anglo Canadians who were over-represented on the city's east side.[9] Like the colour line that divided Montreal's nightclub scene in the 1940s and 1950s, Vancouver's scene reflected and reinforced the city's longstanding class-based and racialized separation of east from west.[10]

Vancouver's largest and most enduring West End nightclubs – the

Table 2.1
Striptease staged in Vancouver's nightclubs, 1945–69

Nightclub name	Nightclub/hotel address
Palomar Supper Club	713 Burrard Street
Cave Supper Club	626 Hornby Street
Penthouse Cabaret	1019 Seymour Street
State Burlesque Theatre	142/144 East Hastings Street
Smilin' Buddha Cabaret	109 East Hastings Street
New Delhi Cabaret	544 Main Street
Harlem Nocturne Cabaret	343 East Hastings Street
Isy's Supper Club	1136 West Georgia Street
Isy's Strip City	1136 West Georgia Street
Gary Taylor's Show Lounge	661 Hornby Street
	750 Granville Street
Shanghi Junk (renamed Kublai Khan Supper Club)	442 Main Street
Oil Can Harry's	752 Thurlow Street
Zanzibar Cabaret (formerly The Torch Cabaret)	1129 Howe Street
Crazy Horse Cabaret	1024 Davie Street
Circus Circus	1082 Granville Street
Mandarin Gardens Supper Club	98 Pender Street
	64 East Hastings Street
Forbidden City Cabaret	90 East Pender Street
	3955 East Hastings, Burnaby
Pink Pussycat Cabaret	Corner of Water and West Cordova Streets
Shangri-La Cabaret	2550 Marine Drive, Burnaby
Narrows Supper Club	Main at St Denis, North Vancouver
Kit Kat Club	138 East Hastings Street

Cave Supper Club (1937–81), the Palomar Supper Club (1937–51), Isy's Supper Club (1958–72), and the Penthouse Cabaret (1947–present) – represented la crème of the city's nightspots. Swanky and upmarket, these clubs promised adventurous Vancouverites high-class acts, dancing to swing rhythms, and night-time razzle-dazzle. Much larger and more elegant than the East End cabarets (see below), they were renowned for showcasing tour stops by top-drawer entertainment, including the Everly Brothers, the Mills Brothers, Rosemary Clooney, Harry Belafonte, Lenny Bruce, Sophie Tucker, Liberace, the Platters, the Will Mastin Trio with Sammy Davis, Jr, Tony Bennett, Lena Horne, Mitzi Gaynor, Ella Fitzgerald, Milton Berle, and Juliet Prowse.[11] Until the

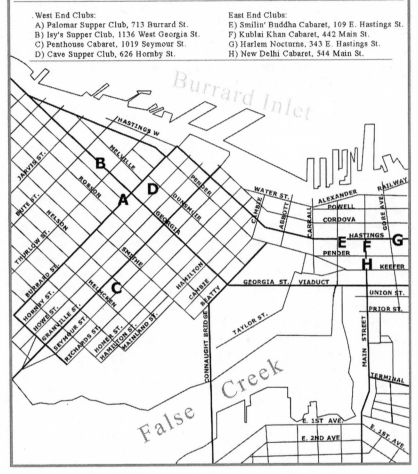

DOWNTOWN VANCOUVER NIGHT CLUBS (1955)

West End Clubs:
A) Palomar Supper Club, 713 Burrard St.
B) Isy's Supper Club, 1136 West Georgia St.
C) Penthouse Cabaret, 1019 Seymour St.
D) Cave Supper Club, 626 Hornby St.

East End Clubs:
E) Smilin' Buddha Cabaret, 109 E. Hastings St.
F) Kublai Khan Cabaret, 442 Main St.
G) Harlem Nocturne, 343 E. Hastings St.
H) New Delhi Cabaret, 544 Main St.

Figure 2.1 West versus East: Downtown Vancouver's geography, circa 1955.
Map designed by Rachael Sullivan, 2008

late 1950s, African American entertainers were refused accommodation at uptown hotels, including the Devonshire, the Hotel Vancouver, and the Georgia. African American tourists and mixed-race couples were also denied hotel rooms.[12] This racist policy, borrowed from Jim Crow segregationist practice in the southern United States, signalled to black performers their subhuman standing north of the forty-ninth parallel.

Initially, West End nightclubs had a dinner menu, with seating arranged around tables and booths. Patrons were no longer simply spectators; they sought out postwar nightclubs expecting to dance, eat, drink, and socialize. However, for decades in the province, strict liquor licensing laws meant it was illegal to purchase alcohol in free-standing nightclubs (with the exception of 'private,' members-only clubs like the Quadra Club, the Arctic Club, and the Pacific Athletic Club, or beer parlours that forbade entertainment, especially dancing and singing!).[13] So nightclubs like the Cave, Isy's, the Palomar, and the Penthouse were unlicensed bottle clubs.[14] Unhappy with restrictive liquor laws, nightclub patrons illegally smuggled bottled booze to the clubs in brown bags or large purses. Or, on occasion, patrons bought drinks from the bootlegged stash behind the bar. The possibility of being caught in a police raid during a fancy floor show only added to patrons' excitement.

The Palomar Supper Club was owned first by Hymie Singer, and then by Sandy DeSantis, who became the club's orchestra leader. Located at the corner of Georgia and Burrard Streets, the Palomar was a 1,200-seat wartime dance hall with opulent red decor and white Greek pillars. Sensing the shift away from big-name touring orchestras, DeSantis began booking big-name acts such as Louis Armstrong, a young Sammy Davis, Jr, and Carmen Miranda. Occasionally, in the 1940s and 1950s, the Palomar booked floor shows of scantily clad female dancers until the club closed because of bankruptcy in 1951 (see fig. 2.2).

Coinciding with the closure of the State Burlesque Theatre and the Palomar in the early 1950s, the owners of Vancouver's West End supper clubs gambled on making profits from risky acts. They were inspired by the topless yet tasteful production numbers that centre-staged female glamour and exotic allure in Las Vegas at the Stardust, the Tropicana, the Dunes, and the Desert Inn.[15] In fact, many of these shows were recycled and restaged from acts at the Folies-Bergère, the Moulin Rouge, the Crazy Horse, and the Lido in Paris, and from cabarets in Vienna, Berlin, and Zurich. Indeed, Europe was perceived as much more advanced than North America vis-à-vis cabaret-style nightlife and nudity. From their offices in Vancouver, Gordon King, Isy Walters,

Figure 2.2 Nena Marlene performs at the Palomar Supper Club, circa 1950.

Sandy DeSantis, Joe Philliponi, Ken Stauffer, and Bob Mitten stoked connections to booking agents in Vegas, Los Angeles, and San Francisco with an eye to fostering an appetite for bump and grind on the northwest coast of Canada. American striptease artists with mainstream, cross-over appeal began to grace Vancouver's stages, including Lili St Cyr, Ricki Covette, Gypsy Rose Lee, and Tempest Storm (still alive in her mid-eighties, writing books, and giving public talks). While large stadiums and arenas booked rock 'n' roll music (including Elvis Presley in 1957), and fancy theatres concentrated on 'respectable' acts after World War II, the 'horrible prettiness' of commercial striptease was cleverly marketed by club owners in other venues.[16]

Celebrities Work Their Magic amid Stalactites at the Cave Supper Club

First owned by Gordon King, a Winnipeg-born entrepreneur, the Cave

Figure 2.3 The Cave Supper Club, West Georgia Street, 1948

Supper Club was officially opened for business at 626 Hornby Street in 1937. It quickly became one of the city's favourite nightclubs (fig. 2.3).[17] Describing the club's interior for *Vancouver Life* magazine, Len Carlyle wrote that the King family ingeniously dipped burlap in wet plaster and moulded the material around two-by-four outcroppings from the ceiling and floor: dimly lit and painted khaki green, they imparted a cave-like atmosphere. The supper club changed hands many times: after King, it was owned by George Amato (from Portland, Oregon), then Isy Walters, and finally, in 1958, Ken Stauffer and his nephew-partner, Bob Mitten. Isy Walters ran the Cave from 1952 to 1958, and then left to open his own nightclub. To the late gossip columnist Denny Boyd, 'The Cave was semi-gothic. They had a sculptured ceiling with plastic stalactites hanging from it, dusty artificial palm trees. For years, it was so busy they didn't have time for renovations. There were line-ups to get in, people got dressed up – your best suit and tie, and the woman would wear a gown ... The crowd was not a stripper crowd, it was a Vegas entertainment crowd.'[18]

In 1954, the Cave, the Palomar, the Hotel Vancouver, the Hotel Devonshire, and the Montefiore Club were issued the first dining-lounge liquor licences, which legalized the sale of liquor, wine, and beer with meals from 6:00 p.m. until 1:00 a.m. daily. Cocktail-lounge licences were awarded to the Georgia, Vancouver, Devonshire, and Sylvia Hotels.[19] A provincial plebiscite held concurrently with the 1952 provincial election revealed that British Columbians were overwhelmingly in favour of liquor sold by the glass. In 1959, Isy's Supper Club followed suit. The sale of alcohol (at often highly inflated prices) together with ever-increasing cover charges made it possible to bankroll expensive professional entertainment, including female striptease acts. As historian Mariana Valverde notes, drinking moderate amounts of alcohol in public venues had, by the 1950s across Canada, assumed a degree of respectability as a method of enhancing social interaction, intimacy, and relaxation.[20] In spite of the temperance-leaning, Social Credit government of B.C. premier W.A.C. Bennett (in power from 1952 to 1972), Vancouverites sought the pleasure of each other's company in social spaces where alcohol consumption and nightly entertainment were jointly sold. For many, Freudian-inspired 'enlightened hedonism' supplanted the old-fashioned temperance ethos that had dominated the century's early decades.[21]

Once inside the Cave Supper Club, patrons were seated on two levels to have dinner and drinks, see a show, dance, and socialize. Though the club was licensed for 600, often 800 to 1,000 bodies were crammed in. For many years, the Cave had a sizeable dance floor and a crackerjack house band: saxophonist Fraser McPherson was the band leader who orchestrated dance music between shows. Each of the Cave's owners had a knack of booking successful celebrity acts. This was no easy feat, as it was the era 'when Uncle Miltie came on TV Tuesday nights and you could shoot a cannon down any main street on the continent and not hit anyone with the exception of the crowds standing around the free show in the TV shop window.'[22] From the mid-1950s through the 1960s, Cave operators drew folks away from their TV sets to view live American stars such as Dan Rowan and Dick Martin, Duke Ellington, Vic Damone, Jack Carter, Brenda Lee, the Righteous Brothers, Wayne Newton, the Barry Ashton Dancers, and Ginger Rogers, as well as Canadian Mimi Hines. Many performers, loving how they were treated by owners and patrons in Vancouver, worked for less than the puffed-up, slot machine-subsidized salary guaranteed in Las Vegas.[23] It was the indomitable Isy Walters, first at the Cave and then at the Pacific National Exhibition (PNE), who instigated the incorporation of sexy, bare-bosomed show girls into Las Vegas-style package shows. Walters was one of Vancouver's most intriguing, enduring, and compelling movers and shakers in the world of entertainment (fig. 2.4)

Born Isadore Waltuck in Odessa, Russia, in 1906, he arrived in Vancouver at age two with his working-class parents, Joseph and Marion Waltuck – Jewish immigrants in search of a new life where it was rumoured 'money was growing on the city's streets.'[24] As a young boy, 'bitten by the showbiz bug,' he sold candy and ice cream in every theatre in Vancouver. Walters left home at fourteen to travel across the United States and Canada with Browning Amusements and the Conklin and Garrett carnivals. Once settled in Vancouver, he was hired every summer at the Pacific National Exhibition to work the joints and games, and he spent winters making stuffed canvas dummies – Hitler and Mussolini – to throw balls at. He later bought a scrap metal business, Acme Machinery, which flourished in wartime until he sold it to try his luck with the nightclub business.[25] With seeming ease, Walters spread his thirst, skill, and sixth-sense for 'star attractions' around the lower mainland and Vancouver Island. In 1948, he owned both the State Burlesque Theatre on Hastings Street in Vancouver and the Scirocco nightclub in Victoria, British Columbia. He also had a part interest in the Mandarin Gardens Supper Club and the Narrows Supper Club. In 1952, having sold the State and the Scirocco, Walters bought the Cave Supper Club in downtown Vancouver and booked a wealth of acts over a seven-year period, including Mandrake the Magician (1953), comedian Sophie Tucker (1953), Paris-based dancer Josephine Baker (1955), male-to-female transsexual singer Christine Jorgensen (1955), the cast from the 'Amos 'n' Andy' television show (1956), and the Ink Spots (1957). A gifted, astute impresario, Walters summed up his career in an interview with Meyer Freedman in 1975: 'I have played practically every major star, when they were a star, and even before they became stars!' (fig. 2.5).

In an interview with me, Isy Walters's son, Richard Walters, noted that his father 'booked strippers' for Vancouver's PNE every August, beginning in the early 1950s: 'The married men would send the kids to the merry-go-round and they'd run to the girlie show. They weren't really called stripper shows, they were called girlie shows. Of course, it was stripping. They'd take it off to g-string and pasties, but it wasn't all the way down. These girls were coming from Los Angeles, they were coming from Vegas. They were strippers; they weren't amateurs.'[26]

Figure 2.4 Dancer and unicycle at the Cave Supper Club, circa 1945

Figure 2.5 Isy Walters outside his supper club on West Georgia Street, February 1976

While Vancouver's other renowned impresario, Hugh Pickett, was known to book striptease dancers for the Cave Supper Club through Famous Artists Limited, this fact is routinely erased. Instead, hailed as 'the nation's premier promoter' of celebrities in a recent CBC documentary film, Pickett was appointed to the Order of Canada in 1987, and later commemorated in stone on Granville Street's 'Star Walk' by the B.C. Entertainment Hall of Fame – an organization Pickett founded.[27] By contrast, while Pickett hobnobbed with the glitterati, Isy Walters was a carnie at heart. Unlike Pickett, Walters was not ashamed to acknowledge that he always liked to 'bring in the sex shows whenever things got quiet in the city.' In 1975, a year before his death, Isy Walters commented effusively, 'It just seems that the girls always got me out of [financial] trouble. At first, they got me into trouble [with the morality squad], and then in later years, they keep getting me out of trouble'[28] (fig. 2.6).

Isy Walters transferred his love of burlesque from the PNE to the

Figure 2.6 Isy Walters relaxes backstage at Isy's Supper Club, West Georgia Street, February 1976.

State, the Cave, and lastly Isy's Supper Club. Like circus czar P.T. Barnum decades earlier, Walters bridged the boundaries of high-class and low-class entertainment. At his PNE girlie shows he was the barker; his ashes reside on the PNE grounds. At the upscale Cave, Walters orchestrated Vancouver appearances of first-class 'exotics': Gyspy Rose Lee (1955), Lili St Cyr (1954), and Ricki Covette (1956). In addition to striptease acts, he appreciated that female dancers, regardless of their erotic explicitness, added dramatic action and sexy flare to any evening's program, so he booked lines of chorus girls and female dance troupes as warm-up acts for the feature performers.[29] After Walters left the Cave in 1958 to open his own nightclub, Isy's Supper Club (fig. 2.7), the Cave's new owners, Bob Mitten and Ken Stauffer, gradually turned away from chorus lines and showgirls to concentrate on rock bands until the club closed in 1981.

Richard Walters grew up inside his father's nightclubs, working alongside him to plan, book, and promote acts until his father's death

in 1976. 'We did six nights, never Sundays. Show time was ten to one
p.m. We were selling four hundred meals a night.' Now over eighty and
operating a talent agency in Palm Desert, California, Richard has lovingly conserved one of Isy Walters's booking diaries – it is a rich, precious chronicle of the names and dates of every act Walters booked at
the Cave Supper Club (1952–8), and Isy's Supper Club (1958–71).[30] At
the back of the booking diary is an eighteen-page address book chock
full of Walters's personal contacts with largely American entertainers,
including 'exotics,' comedians, singers, talkers, musicians, jugglers, as
well as costume designers, fishnet stocking suppliers (Albert's Hosiery
in Los Angeles), and talent agencies, such as Phil Downing and Associates in Portland, Washington; the Dave Sobel Agency in Spokane,
Washington; and the William Morris Agency in Beverly Hills, California. Lesser known 'exotics' listed in the back pages include Lulu Turner,
Sunny Day, Nona Andrews, Lili Marlene, and Tiny Bubbles. According
to Richard Walters, 'We had a lot of girls that were Australian or English. They were working in Vegas and then they'd be found by immigration and kicked out. So, they would come back to Canada and wait
for their papers. They would come directly to us and work for us for
awhile.'[31] Walters recalls that the showgirls were topless at the Cave,
but they always wore g-strings and fancy headgear: 'Mother would
come down and watch them the first time to make sure everything was
OK. We paid them $75 a week, which was not chicken feed – girls got
$25 a week in a grocery store. Plus working a production line at the
Cave was much more glamorous.' Most acts were booked for two-week
stints, with the most bankable offered extended engagements.

Isy Walters had high standards for dancers: he admired professional
stripteasers, not only from his standpoint as a risk-taking entrepreneur
but as a consumer and arbiter of female beauty, ever sensitive to the
vicissitudes of consumer tastes. Columnist Jack Wasserman commented in 1970, 'Isy meets the situation by staging "rawcous" shows with
a stage full of cuties in varying degrees of nakedness.'[32] Yet Isy was
known to have definite views about what he considered respectable,
proper female comportment. 'My father,' according to Della Walters,
'would never have let me become a dancer. Now there's a dichotomy
for you ... When I was a cocktail waitress, I was approached by a man
who wanted to take my picture for *Playboy* – twenty-five thousand dollars. I was eighteen or nineteen. Isy said, "No way my daughter's going
to be on every goddamned musician's wall all over North America.
No." I think his main objection was that I was separate from all that at

Figure 2.7 Showgirls with parasols at Isy's Supper Club, circa 1959

some level.' So on the one hand, Isy Walters refused to accept that stripping was cheap and tawdry, and on the other hand, he strove to protect his daughter from any involvement in the sex industry, hence reinforcing a moral hierarchy that divided good 'Marys' from evil 'Eves.'

Working alongside Walters for close to two decades was the irrepressible, gifted icon Jack Card. Born in Vancouver in 1934 to Irish Catholic immigrants, Card remembers the lure of show biz. At age ten, mesmerized by vaudeville, he snuck in to see Sally Rand perform her bubble dance at the Beacon Theatre while his grandparents shopped at Woodward's department store. Trained as a tap, jazz, and ballet dancer, as a young adult he worked as a professional choreographer first at the Cave Supper Club and later at Isy's Supper Club. A man who loved and respected women, he strove to combine female dance talent with sexiness on stage. 'We never had total nudity at the Cave. We had bare-breasted showgirls, parading with massive headdresses and feathers. They could dance but they weren't dancers. We were getting our show-girls out of Vegas. We'd bring them up for six weeks – no tattoos, no visible scars. We also started to hire local women. Two undercover policewomen thought our shows were pornographic so they placed an ad in a Vancouver newspaper to entrap showgirls. But we advertised openly, and we hired with decorum.'[33] In 1964, Card worked with Cave owners Mitten and Stauffer to book top-flight Las Vegas talent, 'Vive Les Girls,' imported directly from the Dunes Hotel in Las Vegas. Both this show and the extravaganza 'Viva La Roma' (1966) were staged at Isy's Supper Club (plate 2).

Very little of the city's night life escaped the eagle eye of Jack Wasserman, who became a front-row fixture at both the Cave and Isy's Supper Club. Born the only child of Jewish immigrant parents in Winnipeg in 1926, he moved with his family to Vancouver in 1935. Wasserman joined the staff of the *Vancouver Sun* in 1952 after dropping out of the law school at the University of British Columbia. Following in the tradition of Walter Winchell, an influential, syndicated American columnist, Wasserman wrote 'After Dark,' then 'About Town,' until his untimely death in 1976 at age fifty-one.[34] In 1966, he is quoted as saying, 'Going to the Cave for me is like going to the office for a stockbroker. It's what I do. I'm like a sportswriter at a football game … I'm a natural-born busybody.'[35] Famous for his cocksure, know-it-all persona, he was generous with his praise for talented acts, as well as quick to condemn unnecessary police surveillance. Aware that his passionately held attitudes were 'objectionable,' he felt he needed 'to work twice as hard as anybody.'[36] A master of tongue-in-cheek humour, Wasserman publicized and popularized night-time amusements, though his coverage was largely restricted to the West End/uptown entertainment scene. He brilliantly skewered hypocrisy when he smelled it; he delighted in double-entendres. In 1963, he fixed his gaze, as he frequently did, on striptease:

> The civic bluenoses who draw the line across the chests of mermaids appearing on coffee shop signs should trek down to Isy's this week for a peep at Betty Peters, known, professionally, as the Sea Goddess. She starts out dressed as a mermaid in a plastic tank containing 400 gallons of water and proceeds to remove her garments. She performs the feat under water, which is undoubtedly attributable to the fact that she has the largest lungs in show business.[37]

Married to Fran Gregory, an attractive blond entertainer from California, Wasserman was a cheerleader for live performance and a critic of unnecessarily tight liquor controls. He also had an uncanny knack for sniffing out trends in the world of show business, including the growing grip of commercial striptease on the minds and pocketbooks of night-club regulars.[38] That the city's major newspaper hired Wasserman as a full-time 'nightclub reporter' is a measure of his nose for a story and his supple grasp of his readers' taste for gossip. A fixture on Vancouver's night-time beat for more than a quarter-century, Wasserman influenced perceptions of female striptease as legitimate, albeit boundary-bending performance.

Deluxe Showgirls at Isy's Supper Club

Isy's Supper Club, which opened in December 1958, was granted a coveted dining-lounge liquor licence in 1959. Walters installed plush chairs, red velvet curtains, big tables, seating for 260, and air-conditioning, spending $100,000 to transform what was a former Chrysler garage.[39] One wall was mirrored, and another wall in the entryway was 'full of eight-by-ten black and white photographs of all the acts: signed, framed, and screwed onto the wall.'[40] Fresh from seven years at the Cave, Walters continued booking big American stars at Isy's, including Lenny Bruce, Duke Ellington and his band, and Richard Pryor. And between the late 1950s and the early 1960s, Walters booked lines of dancers, such as the Dancing Gibsons, to fill out his nightly bill – a strategy he first introduced at the State Burlesque Theatre. In mid-1963, Walters's diary plots a shift to more explicitly sexual numbers. The names of his sexy acts reflect his ongoing love affair with the flash, sparkle, and erotic mystery of Las Vegas and Paris: Burly Cue Revue, Vegas Girls, Les Girls Revue, and SKIN Exotics. Both Sally Rand and Tempest Storm graced Isy's stage in 1970. With the exception of the SKIN show in 1969, dancers shared the nightly limelight with comics, accordion players, singers, illusionists, and magicians. Isy's house band played behind an opaque curtain on the stage. In January 1971, Isy abandoned all pretence to a mixed, revue-style entertainment program. The soaring costs of Las Vegas-style acts had become prohibitive. To coincide with a 'Truck Loggers Convention,' he launched 'Strip City' – a weekly exclusive line-up of four or five local 'exotics.'

Jeannie Runnalls, who began her career at nineteen as a go-go dancer in Calgary, went to work at Isy's Supper Club, first as a cocktail waitress – 'black lace top, hot pink skirt, black nylons' – and later as Isy's personal secretary. 'Not only did Isy have a photographic memory,' recalled Runnalls, 'but he had the first liquor licence, the first Cadillac, the first penthouse.'[41] Upon meeting Isy Walters in his office, *Vancouver Sun* reporter Mike McRanor commented that the fast life had taken its toll: 'This man's face wasn't lined; it was a crater of steel wool, a lifetime of dreams and schemes worn like a balaclava. Raggedy Andy in the Flesh.'[42] Della Walters, Isy's step-daughter, described her father's hectic pace until his death of a heart attack while working in his nightclub in early March 1976:

He'd get up about ten in the morning and spend an hour getting ready. He'd be gone by noon. And he was home at six on the nose. Six-fifteen, he watched the news. Eat supper, watch the news, nap for a couple hours, then go and get changed and be gone again. He was a huge workaholic, didn't take vacations, except to California and Vegas – a mix of work and play. He was a big smoker, but he didn't drink. He was a master showman, huge charisma. He was larger than life. At his memorial strippers came up to me after and told me how much he had meant to them. You know, and my mother was upset because, 'Yeah, well they had him and I didn't.'[43]

The artistic force behind many of the large-scale production numbers that showcased showgirls was the aforementioned choreographer, Jack Card, who produced shows for both the Cave Supper Club and Isy's

Figure 2.8 Jack Card re-
hearses with showgirls at
Isy's Supper Club, March
1975.

Supper Club (fig. 2.8), and toured with dancers in the United States, including Gypsy Rose Lee. Card recalled: 'I had my sixteen dancers. We'd
do a big show opener, then there would be a comedian, or a comic or
an acrobatic act, or a magician or whatever. Then we'd do a production
number to bring the star on, and often we would follow the star with a
big closing.' Because Isy Walters wanted a 'Vegas look,' Card introduced
a topless, bare-breasted line of showgirls to the Cave and Isy's, typically
under the banner, 'Direct from 27 Triumphant Weeks in Las Vegas Revue.'[44] Jack Card is emphatic about the elegant character of his shows:
'The dancers had huge headpieces, cabbage roses, collars with feathers
sprouting, and rhinestone strapping everywhere – jewelled skirts, high-
cut. We took the bras off – it was all very tasteful – never bottomless. We
showed as much as we'd dare show, but with elegance and class. The
showgirls had to be gorgeous, perfect teeth, great bodies, very elegant,
and very, very classy. What they were doing out there was not Swan
Lake. They were doing a sexual tease. But any semi-nudity had to blend

Figure 2.9 Jack Card prepares dancers' headpieces, 1982.

in as a story production'[45] (fig. 2.9). The 'stories' were augmented with collapsible stairways, layers of curtains, expert lighting, waterfalls, and stage doors. A trademark of Card's designs was the dancers' transparent negligee, called a duster, in either chiffon or silk. Jazz saxophonist Dave Davies (née Harold Loretto) admired Jack Card: 'Jack was show biz, legit, old school, way up there. He didn't want long-haired, hippie guys with guitars on stage. He wanted them clean-cut.'

Victoria-born dancer and choreographer Patrick Kevin O'Hara started training as a dancer in England in 1949, at the age of nine. He continued training and studying in Canada, the United States, France, Denmark, and Russia 'with most of the great teachers and choreographers of the last century.'[46] In the late 1960s and early 1970s, O'Hara became involved in commercial striptease: 'In 1972, I had four shows that I had choreographed running concurrently in Paris. At the same time I was starring at Les Folies-Bergère doing very sexy cabaret acts as a dancer with my partners, as well as choreographing and dancing for TV.' Designing his own pas de deux and solos, O'Hara worked in Vancouver

Figure 2.10 'The Duvals' performing at Isy's Supper Club, 1975

with Jack Card during the 1970s, dancing with his first wife, Patricia, from 1974 to 1979 in a duo billed 'The Duvals' (fig. 2.10). One of the few straight men – 'an aberrant oddity in professional dance' – O'Hara infused the Vancouver night club scene with a distinctly Parisian sensuality and style, deliberately mixing his passion for classical ballet with a generous measure of purposeful eroticism.

Booking acts for his own club, Isy Walters confidently promoted dazzling 'exotics' as part of an evening's show, or a 'package deal,' to heterosexual couples, both locals and visitors. And yet both he and his son, Richard, were well aware of the need to ensure that what they viewed as tasteful did not slide into disgusting or offensive in the eyes of patrons, especially women. Richard Walters notes that women were quick to judge other women who doffed their clothing for a living: 'You've got to remember that in the fifties and sixties, the average woman looked down on strippers ... maybe they really wanted to do it. How many women went home from these shows and stripped for their husbands? I bet some did. But they were hypocrites – they all thought strippers

were prostitutes.' He also admitted that some prostitutes solicited customers at Isy's though 'only the classy gals. We never had the cheap
ones – we just wouldn't let them in. The Penthouse had more than anybody.' He continued: 'Isy knew the rounders, I knew the rounders. And
the pimps were there – they were the bottom line of bad guys. Nobody
wanted guys making money off girls.'[47]

The Penthouse Cabaret: The City's Oldest Stationary Funhouse

Like Isy Walters, Joe Philliponi[48] became an extraordinarily notorious,
colourful club owner and impresario. In 1929, as a small boy, he arrived
with his Italian immigrant parents in Extension, British Columbia, from
San Nicola, Italy. In 1933, the Filippone family relocated to Vancouver,
'the Manhattan of Canada.' After what Joe's younger brother Ross
Filippone remembered as a happy childhood, three sons – Joe, Ross,
and Mickey – served in the armed forces during World War II, and
brother Jimmy and sister Florence stayed home to operate the family's
messenger and delivery service, Eagle Time Delivery Company, out of
1019 Seymour Street, a building purchased in 1938.[49] After the war, the
family launched their Diamond Cab Company, which had the city's
first limousines, and they ran an amateur boxing gym. In 1947, Joe Philliponi began to entertain late-night guests at a private club in his loft
apartment, which he called the Eagle Time Athletic Club. According
to Ross Filippone, 'donations' to the Athletics Club underwrote the
family's sponsorship of amateur sports for youth, including lacrosse,
basketball, bowling, football, hockey, and boxing. A very popular after-
hours joint among celebrated invitees, Joe's loft was raided for liquor
infractions in 1949 and subsequently named the Penthouse. It was the
same year his father died of 'coal miner's lungs,' and the year that Joe
and his siblings joined Sandy DeSantis in running the Palomar Supper
Club, only to have the building sold out from under their noses. It was
turned into a skyscraper, an office building on Burrard Street, after they
had invested $100,000 in renovations.

The Penthouse Cabaret opened with a cabaret (non-liquor) licence
at 1019 Seymour Street officially in August 1950, and was owned and
run by the Filippone brothers – Joe, Ross, Mickey, and Jimmy, and their
sister Florence. Joe was the splashy playboy at the helm. Ross was the
'family man' and general manager of the club, Mickey ran the bar, Jimmy was the club's handyman, and Florence was the bookkeeper. Joe, a
life-long bachelor with a reputation as a shrewd businessman, booked

Figure 2.11 Joe Philliponi, relaxing in his office at the Penthouse Cabaret, 1982

all the acts, including the strippers. Ross told me stories about Joe with much fondness and admiration: 'He was always travelling south. It was like, if he's going to pay for it, he wants to see it. He doesn't want a picture, he doesn't want the word of the agent.'[50] Both Joe and Ross relished their role as dinner-jacketed hosts to the stars of stage, screen, and radio. Joe, in particular, cultivated a particular 'look.' *Vancouver Sun* scribe Denny Boyd noted that, 'Joe wasn't much more than five feet tall and he layered his dumpy body with a combination of checked suits, striped shirts and flowered ties that made him look like a ransacked closet'[51] (fig. 2.11). Like New Yorker Billy Minsky, who was also short in stature, Joe Philliponi had a nose for talent (fig. 2.12).

In the Penthouse's heyday in the 1950s and 1960s, six hundred patrons a night paid to enjoy the shows, which cost the Filippones upwards of $300,000 a year. The club sported a pink neon sign – in step with the neon craze that swept downtown Vancouver. Throughout the 1950s, the Penthouse had one of the few fine restaurants in town, the Steak Loft, and its brick-oven pizza and charcoal-broiled steaks – 'Grade "A"

Figure 2.12 Joe Philipponi at the Penthouse Cabaret, September 1978

Alberta Beef' – were legendary. Ross remembered the culinary land-scape: 'There were only two or three restaurants in the city that had edible food. There was Mammy's on Prior, and Vy and Bob Moore's on Union Street. And next door to us was the Dixie Chicken Inn, run by black people – Adele and Bob Smith. We had something different to offer.' Legendary too were the lavish spreads of food laid out annually by the Filippones for people who had nowhere else to go on Christmas and Boxing Day.[52] Couples frequented the Penthouse to dine, dance, and enjoy the acts of famous and up-and-coming performers from Las Vegas. In the club's vast Gold Room, show business celebrities Tony Bennett, Sophie Tucker, Sammy Davis, Jr, Liberace, Harry Belafonte, and Ella Fitzgerald entertained. Ross reminisced: 'We'd have the top people come to the club – lawyers, stockbrokers, doctors, professional athletes. Husbands came with the wives.' It was not the Orpheum. Nor was it the Palomar, the Cave, or Isy's, with their elaborate floor shows of skimpily clad dancing girls, intricate choreography, and sumptuous stage set. Yet it had heat. As heritage booster Maida Price wryly com-

Figure 2.13 The Penthouse Cabaret, 1019 Seymour Street, Vancouver, 1978

mented, 'It's the history of Vancouver, stuffed into that old building on Seymour Street like a stripper into a bustier'[53] (see fig. 2.13).

By the mid-1960s, in part to stay competitive with the Cave and Isy's Supper Club, Joe Philliponi began to explore the inclusion of showgirls in the nightly floor shows. In 1968, reporter Alex MacGillivray wrote that, 'The Penthouse ... is a watering spot for bookies and brokers, doctors and dentists, guys and dolls, ladies and gentlemen, and just about anybody who could smell a good time ... it was the city's oldest stationary funhouse.'[54] A decade later, in 1978, *Vancouver Sun* columnist Denny Boyd reflected on the club's first thirty years:

> It was the place to go after hours to get a steak, mixer for your bottle, see a show, run into a friend or find a hooker. Make no mistake about it, hookers came to the Penthouse. So did other club owners, musicians, lawyers, cabinet ministers, newspaper editors, off-duty policemen, civic politicians, safecrackers, corporation presidents, Hollywood starlets, cheating husbands, stockbrokers, school principals, gamblers, plainclothes RMCP

surveillance teams, PTA presidents, surgeons, drug-users, short-order cooks and – I suspect – the odd man of the cloth.[55]

The Penthouse was among the only West End clubs to introduce go-go dancing in the late 1960s, following the lead of East End cabarets such as the short-lived Pink Pussycat and the Kit Kat Club. On the heels of classical 1950s burlesque and in anticipation of bottomless exotic dancing in the 1970s, go-go dancing in go-go bars, such as the Whiskey A-Go-Go and Retinal Circus, sprang up in California in the early 1960s. Buoyed by the radicalism of the sixties counter-culture, women such as American Carol Doda doffed brassieres and pasties, donned bikini bottoms, and danced the twist, the mashed potato, and the swim inside North Beach nightspots, suspended in cages.[56] In 1966, recognizing that toplessness marked another advance towards total nudity, an agitated Vancouver mayor Bill Rathie told city council that San Francisco had tried to control the 'topless craze' and failed.[57] In Montreal in 1967, a topless dancer and a nightclub manager were fined for 'staging an indecent spectacle.'[58] In spite of spirited opposition to toplessness, the trend continued as Vancouver clubs began to advertise topless pool rooms, topless go-go girls, topless lunches, topless shoeshines, and, at the Flame Cabaret on Howe Street, a topless teeter-totter.[59] Bob Stork recalled that his flamboyant father, Lester, introduced topless waitresses at his unlicensed Bunkhouse café on Davie Street as a way to 'push the edge' by flogging the 'newest taboo.'[60] At Club Zanzibar, jazz pianist Gord Walkinshaw remembered that, 'Very often the waitresses would take a turn topless go-go dancing. At night you could rent a pair of roller skates – the go-go girls were on roller skates and the clients were allowed to wear roller skates and catch them.'

In 1967, Dee Dee Special, a much-loved striptease dancer from the East Coast, inaugurated the Gold Room at the Penthouse, bumping in time with a nine-piece jazz orchestra (fig. 2.14). Two years later, in 1969, an advertisement for the Penthouse in the *Vancouver Sun* announced: '"Girls!" Dee Dee, a spectacular dancer, Miss Lovie, Afro Cuban artist of rhythm, Big Miller, big in size, bigger in talent, Miss 007, Risqué Exotic!, Daring 2 shows, 11 and 1:30 am.'[61] As much as 'exotics' attracted loyal locals and intrepid visitors, Penthouse owners began to feel the pinch of lost revenues as a new, revolutionary advance in media technology kept people at home. While only 29 per cent of households in British Columbia owned televisions in 1955, by 1975 this figure had increased to 95 per cent.[62] Ross astutely observed, 'Television hurt the

Figure 2.14 Joe Philipponi and Dee Dee Special at the Penthouse, 1982

nightclubs. People sat in their living room and turned on the tube. They saw Ed Sullivan with all the name acts you could possibly mention, all in one hour! Four or five top-name acts in the business. And it didn't cost. So people stayed home – they didn't want to pay $1.75 for a drink.' Of course, professional striptease was never staged on the *Ed Sullivan Show,* which contributed, in part, to its enduring mystique: for those who ventured out to a nightclub there was always the promise of something new, something special, and something daring alongside acts popularized on TV.

Part of what made the Vancouver strip club scene so successful was the antiquated system of liquor licensing. Until the late 1960s, the Penthouse Cabaret was a bottle club. While the Cave, Palomar, and Isy's were all awarded liquor licences in the 1950s, the Penthouse and all of the East End cabarets were shut out. In 1964, Police Chief Ralph Booth publicized his disdain for 'foolish, unenforceable' liquor laws.[63] He noted that of twenty-seven night clubs in Vancouver, only five had liquor licences, and the unlicensed spots were 'crowded with hundreds of juveniles who are allowed to drink liquor, and turn the premises into cesspools of violence, sex, and crime.'[64] In 1965, Booth harshly criticized city councillors for issuing operating licences to cabarets without first ensuring that the clubs would be granted liquor licences by the Liquor Control Board.[65] By September of that year, police raided downtown cabarets for twelve consecutive weekends; the charges laid increased in number to 325, an increase over the total of 280 in 1964.[66]

To pay their entertainers, the Penthouse sold patrons ice and mix and sometimes illegal booze; they turned a blind eye to customers who arrived with liquor bottles in brown bags. Unfamiliar with the politics of liquor control in the mid-1960s, tourists were intrigued by the 'quaint-ness' of the city's unlicensed 'dry' cabarets.[67] Looking back, Ross Filip-pone was frank about the situation: 'You couldn't survive strictly as a bottle club when you're bringing in big-name acts. You had to have extra revenue. And the only way you could get revenue was by selling drinks.' He maintains that the hotels had a monopoly on liquor sales – they could legally sell draft beer and 'it was all political.' Rumoured to be at the helm of the 'Vancouver Mafia,' the Filippones vigorously de-nied any association; Joe liked to point his finger at the Petroni brothers, who allegedly controlled the nightclub scene in Montreal.[68] Ross told me that the Penthouse was raided and harassed weekly in the 1950s and 1960s by fifteen to twenty Vancouver police officers at a time.[69] On the one hand, the pernicious police pressure incensed bottle club own-ers; on the other hand, the owners realized that the availability of illegal alcohol, especially after 2:00 a.m., plus the heat of ever more risqué ex-otic dancing, afforded their clubs a distinctly 'forbidden' allure.

To prepare for imminent police busts, Ross's brother Joe arranged a lookout on the nightclub's roof to watch for the detective crew. Much like the ticket-taker who set red lights flashing when a Vice Squad member entered Minsky's theatre on New York's Lower East Side in the 1930s,[70] when Joe spotted police he sounded an alarm that alerted the bar staff downstairs. Waiters then warned patrons to hide their jugs on built-in ledges, like utensil drawers, under the tables, and to deny any wrong-doing to the gun-and-holstered boys in blue. Ross Filippone expressed indignation about the routine harassment: 'It was a big farce. It was like the Keystone Kops coming in looking under tables for bot-tles with little flashlights. They'd never go to Hotel Vancouver. They'd never go to the Commodore. They'd never go to the Palomar. They would never go to the Cave, because those places were high class'[71] (fig. 2.15).

Effectively, the double standard reflected the city's class-stratified hierarchy of nightclubs, with the 'high-status' clubs exempt from anti-vice raids – though the Penthouse was higher on the ladder than its East End rivals. At long last, in December 1968 after years of lobby-ing by Joe Philliponi and the West Coast Cabaret Owners' Association (with Joe as president), and after ten failed applications, the most strin-gent liquor laws in North America were relaxed enough to award the Penthouse a dining-lounge liquor licence. The licence formally ended the hypocrisy of police harassment for 'harbouring criminals' who had legally purchased booze at twenty-four-hour, government-run liquor

Figure 2.15 Ross Filippone peruses dancers' promotional photographs at the Penthouse Cabaret, 1978.

stores. It also meant an end to the lucrative revenue the city collected from liquor fines.

Touted as a minor-league equivalent to the Eiffel Tower and the Empire State Building, the Penthouse earned a reputation as the best place in the city to meet elite sex workers who frequented the club, bought food and drinks, and charmed a loyal clientele of locals and tourists.[72] Penthouse patron Larry Wong remembers being 'kicked out by a hooker' who claimed that his table was in her territory.[73] Indeed, sex workers operated a lively sex trade inside the city's independent nightclubs, in part because, until the early 1970s, unattached men and unattached women were physically segregated in hotel beer parlours – a strategy implemented during World War II to curtail illicit sexual commerce by 'undesirable' prostitutes, and to enhance the pubs' claim to decency.[74] Unfettered by the same restrictions that governed hotel pubs, nightclubs offered sex workers prime heterosocial milieux in which to search for clients while they enjoyed the floor shows.

Jazz musician Doug Cuthbert who worked at the Penthouse in the early 1970s later observed that, 'It was not a place for a woman to go if she wasn't looking to make some money.'[75] As Dave Davies, a saxophone player who worked at the Penthouse, remarked, 'There were resident hookers. And my recollection is that some of those hookers at the Penthouse were just goddesses. They were just stunning women. Beautiful women. Real style, class, dressed to the nines, cultured women.' On any given night, between 100 and 150 prostitutes used the club as their workplace; many later escorted their clients to nearby hotels or their West End apartments. To singer Ron Small, the dynamic between working women in nightclubs was unique: 'The hookers were not dancers, but they respected dancers. They would bring people in to see the dancers because they want to get you turned on!'[76] To their credit, the Filippone brothers did not discriminate against working girls. In fact, Ross Filippone appreciated their self-sufficient, entrepreneurial spirit: 'You had to admire the fact that they were doing what they were doing and there was nothing shameful about it. What I didn't like was that some of them had pimps. And to me, a pimp was the lowest creature on the scale 'cause he would take her money and beat her up.'

East End Nightclubs: Smilin' Buddha, New Delhi, Kublai Khan

Throughout the 1950s, 1960s, and 1970s, Vancouver's West End night clubs – the Cave, Isy's, and the Penthouse – were owned by white (albeit non-Anglo) men, they regularly featured white striptease headliners, and they catered to a predominantly white, well-heeled clientele (initially gender mixed, then primarily male professionals). In the East End, by contrast, a tightly knit circuit of nightclubs emerged that were deemed 'minor league' or 'B-List' in comparison to the West End's 'A-List' nightclubs (see map, fig. 2.1). Smaller and more run-down than West End venues, leased by men of colour, the East End venues began to regularly feature 'B- and C-grade' striptease acts in the early to mid-1950s. Refused liquor licences since the 1940s, these bottle clubs – like 'blind pigs' during the Prohibition era – were subject to police scrutiny, patrol, and attack until the late 1960s.[77]

In and around the working-class neighbourhood of Chinatown – a city in miniature – Lachman Das Jir's Smilin' Buddha (1953–89), Leo Bagry's New Delhi (1956–73), Jimmy Yuen's Kublai Khan (1970–80), formerly the Shanghai Junk), and Ernie King's Harlem Nocturne (1957–68) were more racially diverse than their West End competition in terms

Figure 2.16 Advertisment for the Kublai Khan's floor show, 1960

Figure 2.17 Advertisement for the New Delhi Cabaret, 1959

of staff, clientele, and audience. Part of the postwar transformation of Chinatown into a tourist site – the city's premiere 'exotic' destination – these East End nightclubs marketed consumer taste in the extraordinary and the unusual, as dictated by the discursive tradition of what the late Edward Said termed orientalism[78] (figs 2.16, 2.17. 2.18, plate 3). In her book *Vancouver's Chinatown*, Kay Anderson argues that hegemonic notions of a quintessential racial 'Other' produced and managed Chinatown as a segregated enclave of adventure, intrigue, vice, and immorality – a destination for 'entertainment spice, colour and romance.'[79] At the same time, the names of the East End cabarets – Kublai Khan, Smilin' Buddha, New Delhi, and Harlem Nocturne – belie the myth of Chinatown's homogeneity and suggest that in the area's nightclub scene a range of communities of colour converged, carving a space

Figure 2.18 Advertisement for the Harlem Nocturne, 17 May 1965, and advertisement for the Smilin' Buddha, 3 May 1963

for themselves that was unavailable in other parts of the city.[80] Representing a mix of residential and commercial interests, Chinatown business owners capitalized on the locale's renewed energy and optimism after the war, though Chinese Canadians were well aware of stubborn racist stereotypes and practices. The area's nightclubs were renowned for informal drug dealing, recreational pot use, an active sex trade, and a visible police presence far removed from the upper-crust, West Side enclaves of Shaughnessy, Kerrisdale, and Point Grey. They were also the first to introduce topless dancers minus pasties, though initially the City Licensing Department required that the women appear motionless.

Former Vancouver-based dancers, booking agents, and musicians acknowledge that there was a definite hierarchy dividing the city's high-end and low-end nightclubs. For many people of colour in Vancouver, the cheaper, more accessible, and less formal Chinatown clubs were 'the place to be.' Alex Louie, who operated the Marco Polo nightclub in the 1950s, recalled that Chinatown was a booming place peppered with restaurants, shops, and nightclubs – a 'vibrant, very colourful area' where 'people partied every night' and where his 'all-you-can-eat Chinese smorgasbord' boosted club revenues.[81] Chinatown clubs were a popular destination for thrill-seeking white Vancouverites and tourists, who crossed the city after seeing the 'big stars' at the Cave Supper Club and Isy's Supper Club, much as white New Yorkers traversed neighbourhood borders to Harlem nightspots like the Hot Feet, the Clambake, and the Cotton Club, and white San Franciscans sought out their city's Chinatown clubs.[82] To adapt the insight of Kevin Mumford, the interzone of Vancouver's interracial, East End district promised non-residents entrée to somewhere exotic, foreign, and supposedly inferior.[83] Here in the 'contact zone,' disparate cultures met, clashed, and grappled with each other.[84] For some white Vancouverites, voyaging from the West End to the East End clubs was considered slumming it, in part because the East End lay adjacent to the historic Skid Road – Vancouver's first so-called slum district, which overlapped with the city's original red light district.[85] Inhabited by waves of immigrants, unemployed poor, drifters, and mobile labourers for close to a century, the East End/Chinatown area was dotted with single-room occupancy hotels and lodging houses. Choreographer Kevin Patrick O'Hara conveyed a keen memory of the East End clubs: 'The vicarious thrill of sitting next to gangsters, dope fiends, pimps and whores was the drawing card … The reputation of [these clubs] was uniformly and universally damned from every sanctimonious pulpit in the city and therefore the clubs were very popular and always full.' He added, dryly, that 'White Vancouverites have always been a pretentious lot of culture vultures who like to frequent low-life venues to reassure themselves of their intrinsic superiority …'[86]

In the 1950s and 1960s, the East End's reputation jostled between Chinatown's brave tourism and elected officials' view that the neighbourhood was a disorderly home to male addicts, criminals, alcoholics, and sex deviates. In 1970, journalist Eric Nichol described the area as 'alcoholism's ghetto – to which gravitated the walking wounded from the hinterland: the chokerman crippled by a log, the failed fisherman, the prospector finding his last glint of gold in a bottle of bay rum.'[87] Coincidentally, the city's police station was located on the edge of Chinatown, affording the overwhelmingly white police force easy access to what they deemed the 'trouble zone.'[88] Men had always outnumbered women among non-Aboriginals in Vancouver (until 1971), though the numerical discrepancy between the sexes was especially pronounced in the East End, in part because of the historical concentration of male labourers compounded by racist immigration barriers that created Chinese bachelor communities.[89] Geographer Jeff Sommers contends that the East End was a location where damaged masculinity, symbolized by the skid-row derelict, was linked to the deterioration of the central-city landscape.[90] At the same time, the neighbourhood's long-time majority population of male transients and resource workers meant a steady supply of patrons for relatively inexpensive floor shows.

In the late 1950s, Master of Ceremonies (MC) and yo-yo specialist Harvey Lo recalls that the Marco Polo nightclub featured a chorus line of 'four, pretty Chinese girls' in strapless bras, short skirts, and fishnet stockings – a spin-off from San Francisco's Forbidden City nightclub, owned and operated by Chinese American impresario Charlie Low.[91] Electric bass player Sean Gunn, a Chinese Canadian and a self-described 'people's proletariat musician,' cut his teeth at the Marco Polo club, later forming the house band with 'Lito, the Filipino keyboardist,' and 'Owen, the Hong Kong percussionist,' at the Kublai Khan, where they accompanied strippers in the 1970s.[92] A club that attracted a mix of white and Chinese men, and a regular complement of twenty to thirty prostitutes, the Kublai Khan was upstairs at 442 Main Street. Gunn memorializes the 'sleazy pleasure dome' in his brilliant epic poem, 'Kublai Khan Ten':

> Formerly known, as the Shanghai Junk, it was Vancouver's one and only,
> and probably, ever, to be [thank heaven] totally debauched, vilely despica-
> ble, fiendishly nefarious, scum-sucking beyond redemption
> Chinatown strip joint, where, the official door policy, was, that everybody
> (everybody being defined, as non-Asians) had to pay the cover charge,
> with the notable
> exception, of us
> the indigenous, lost yellow sheep, of the epicanthic fold who were
> unofficially, exempt
> and thus, being racially excluded, from paying, we, of course [now don't
> tell anybody]
> got in for free
> a sort of, reverse racist head tax, and as well, a small measure, of poetic
> justice
> historically speaking, a tiny, but somehow satisfying, drop in the bucket,
> of long over due,
> pay back time precipitated, through, an ironic act, of Asian exclusion.
> Inside, once you got around, the one armed bandit, or a doorman
> a self-professed, one hand style, Kung Fu expert [if there ever was,
> such an animal]
> you were seduced, penetrating deeply, into a sensuous-bawdy, raucous,
> lewd, lascivious,
> slimy, grimy, carcinogenic smoke-filled, purgatory, where, lying for you,
> in the shadows,
> laid, the women.[93]

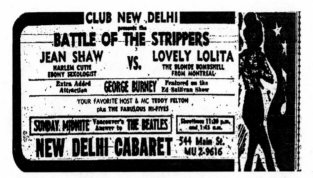

Figure 2.19 Club New Delhi's floor show pits the 'Ebony Sexologist' from Harlem against the 'Blonde Bombshell from Montreal,' 21 February 1965.

Reminiscing about the notorious Kublai Khan nightclub, Gunn not only takes wry pleasure in the free cover charge for Asian patrons; he subsequently documents the commercial, physical, and emotional mystique of the 'ubiquitous peelers' in the 'deviant, diabolical, and depraved' Chinatown strip clubs. The Kublai Khan was not alone: an advertisement in the *Vancouver Sun* for the New Delhi Cabaret in February 1964 reads, '"Battle of the Strippers," Jean Shaw, Harlem Cutie, Ebony Sexologist vs. Lovely Lolita, the blonde bombshell from Montreal, MC Teddy Felton, and George Burney, featured on Ed Sullivan'[94] (fig. 2.19). In fact, neither 'stripper' nor 'exotic' was used in promotional material for Isy's Supper Club or the Penthouse until the early 1970s. In July 1969, another advertisement for the New Delhi was published: 'Stripperama, Vancouver's sin-sational, sex-sational girlie show, featuring direct from Hollywood, Susie Starr, Miss Ruthie, Frisky Miss Marcie, Stunning Miss Lena, 2 topless go-go girls, plus new chorus line.'[95] Similarly this ad for the Smilin' Buddha Cabaret appeared in 1969: 'The Big Sexciting Girlie Show, Laverne, the body beautiful, Miss Lulu she's a lulu, Miss Karen, a go-go, Miss 69, lovely eyeful, Pat Petite M.M. Good, Lauren Paul, Sweetheart of song, held over Pat Morgan, Teddy F. MC.'[96]

Jazz saxophonist Dave Davies recalls that Teddy Felton worked both the Smilin' Buddha and the New Delhi: 'He was wonderful. A black fellow. Skinny. A prototype announcer, a jack of all trades, a front man for what was a pretty lame floor show. He would try to make it look good. B-Grade strippers, dancers, comedians.' Ron Small was also an African American entertainer who moved to Vancouver in the early 1960s after leaving military service and the army big band. He first sang with the 'Fabulous Pearls' at Isy's Supper Club in 1959, and chose to relocate to Vancouver when he fell in love. In the mid- to late 1960s, Small worked as a singer and MC alongside striptease artists and other variety-show performers at the Smilin' Buddha and the New Delhi 'when the city was zooming.'[97] He later opened his own club, the Riverboat Queen, in 1967 on Davie Street. Small recalls his musical accompaniment: 'I sang for Lawanda, and Kay Nelson – she was a Hawaiian girl. And their acts were very sexy.' Dave Davies also recalled that the New Delhi was renowned for booking African American dancers who, he claims, 'brought the intensity and the excitement with them. It's like meeting somebody from New York. You almost instantly know that they're from some place that is really happening. It radiates out of them.'

By the late 1960s, bare-breasted exotics were *the* prized performers in the East End clubs; typically supplemented by an MC and a singer, they practically owned the marquee at the Smilin' Buddha and the New Delhi. Jazz musician Mike Kalanj remembers the New Delhi: 'It had a warm atmosphere – tables and chairs – the dancers had closets for dressing rooms. The dance floor was a hardwood floor in the middle of the room with a rope around it. They served East Indian and Canadian food. It was at Keefer and Main. You'd go up this long staircase and at the top was a ticket booth. Through the hole in the glass, you'd buy your ticket, they'd ring the buzzer and open the door. You couldn't just walk in.'[98] The two-dollar admission charge covered the cost of one entrée – curried chicken, fried rice, veal cutlet, or pork chop.[99] Another local musician, Doug Cuthbert, remembers that to qualify for a cabaret licence, 'club owners had to have a three-piece band and at least a vocalist.' An unintended consequence of this state-mandated facet of cabaret life was the orchestrated, mutually beneficial bond between professional, live music making and professional striptease that survived until the late 1970s.

Choreographer Jack Card, whose own production numbers were influenced by the legendary musical director Florenz Ziegfeld, Jr, and choreographer Busby Berkeley, stated that most of the city's black striptease performers danced at the 'Main Street clubs' in and around Chinatown, often featured as 'B-dancers,' 'novelty acts' or 'Afro-Cuban' dancers. And some of these dancers found extra work at carnival girlie shows like 'Harlem and Havana' at the Pacific National Exhibition. Card notes that the East End clubs and the PNE simply lacked the same status and prestige, dancers were not paid as well, and they had to make do without the elaborate stage lights, collapsible stairways, trap doors, velvet curtains, big orchestras, and professional choreography enjoyed by the almost exclusively white dancers in the West End clubs. As I show in chapter 3, a colour line separated the downscale East End from the upscale West End nightclubs, though the stratification of commercial striptease was somewhat flattened out by the early 1970s as hotel beer parlours proliferated and independent nightclubs spiralled into oblivion.

Shrewdly trading in the allure of the racial and sexual 'Other' to tantalize prospective customers was likely the wisest and most profitable strategy for East End clubs to compete with prestigious West End clubs, though drawing dollars away from well-heeled patrons was never easy. In January 1964, the New Delhi Cabaret advertised its 'All Star Imported Show Direct from America's Leading Nightclubs and Burlesque Shows,' including 'Leah Dawson, songstress from Hollywood, Ca, Miss K.K. Exotic Dancer from Portland, Oregon, Virginia Dare, Exotic Stripper from L.A., Dave Yuen, singer, and from Montreal, Harry Walker and the Hi-Fives for your Dancing Pleasure.'[100] However, also in January 1964, Isy's Supper Club in the city's West End boldly proclaimed the unveiling of 'Show Girls USA, The Only Big Imported Floor Show in Town.' Both line-ups reflect the preference for imported (non-local) talent shared by club owners at the New Delhi and Isy's. However, it seems that Isy's publicity move was designed to trump the competition and to reassert Isy's as *the* one and only nightclub equipped to reward its discerning patrons with the biggest, the best, and the 'most Vegas' of evening delights. And Isy's, the Penthouse, and the Palomar advertised the city's best orchestras, which again reflected the geographical distribution of entertainers – musicians and dancers – along an East-West divide. As pianist Gerry Palken, a former band leader at Isy's, recalled, 'I never played the East End. We all looked down our noses at those clubs – you didn't get paid very much. It was pretty low life down there – all the down-and-outers. There was a little café down there that drilled holes in the spoons so the junkies wouldn't steal them to cook up. I just didn't want to work down there.'[101] Isy's Supper Club strove to distinguish itself by emphasizing tasteful production numbers as opposed to second-tier exotics who strutted their stuff in 'Stripperamas' to B-grade music for drunks and riff-raff in Chinatown. By contrast, East End clubs openly promoted dancers of colour, especially black women, as 'Harlem cuties, ebony sexologists, and Afro-Cuban specialists.' And musician Gord Walkinshaw claims that the New Delhi was the home of the first transvestites and 'sex changes,' some of whom worked as professional striptease dancers. There is little doubt that the East End cabarets pushed hardest against the limits of 'community standards.' What remains uncertain is the extent to which East End and West End nightclubs actually competed in the 1950s and 1960s. Former Harlem Nocturne boss Ernie King recalls that there was seldom an intersection between 'the two different worlds.'[102]

Shakin' It Up at the Harlem Nocturne

Ernie King was born in Edmonton, Alberta, in 1919, the son of African Americans who left Oklahoma and the racism of the American south to make better lives in Canada.[103] His family moved to Vancouver in 1930 when King was a young boy; he later quit school to work at Hammonds Furniture Company for four years. After serving in the army during World War II and playing in the army band, King became a professional trombonist and started his own all-black band, the Harlem Kings. While touring with his band in Edmonton, King met his future bride. Married in 1948 and settled in Vancouver, King joined the musicians' union, Local 145, and began working in East End cabarets. He is very clear about barriers to better paying and more esteemed gigs in the West End supper clubs:

> I was qualified enough to play in the Cave, but they didn't want a guy like me. The owners wanted an all-white band, not a coloured band with me sitting in there. I would have never got a job as a houseman, in the house band at the Cave – there were never any black musicians, unless it was a black band from the States. They knew our black musicians had as much talent or more than anybody else ... So I said I'd prefer to be with a couple of coloured guys, and maybe a couple of white guys, in the East End clubs.[104]

Anti-black racism percolated throughout Vancouver in the 1950s and 1960s. Though its expression was less virulent than in the southern United States, performers and mixed-race couples were denied hotel rooms in both the West End and the East End, and black men and women encountered a segregated labour force.[105] A former 'cigarette girl' at the Cave Supper Club, Megan Carvell Davis married Mel, a Harlem Globetrotter, in the early 1960s. Not only was she labelled a 'nigger lover,' but she recalled that Mel was refused a room at the Hotel

Vancouver.[106] Ernie King noted that black men in Vancouver tended to work with the railways either as porters or observation-car stewards. Unwilling to follow in their footsteps, King rented the main floor of 343 East Hastings Street, one and a half blocks from Main Street. He opened the Harlem Nocturne in 1957. Following the lead of all-black clubs in the United States, including the Club DeLisa in Chicago, the Riviera in St Louis, and the Flame Show Bar in Detroit, King ran the only black nightclub in Vancouver.

Ernie King described the process of establishing his business: 'I rented from the Chinese man upstairs who owned the building. Me and the guys in the band pitched in, we painted it, cleaned it up, put a hardwood dance floor in. I built all the tables – little square tables, twenty-eight inches square, to seat four people. I bought a hundred chairs. I had booths coming along the east side, with a couple on the west side. The kitchen was in the back. The dance floor was about ten feet by twenty feet. I raised the bandstand, so guys played up. I had a small band, and the guys could cook it up – R and B Louis Jordan-style, and some Latin music.' One of King's artistic touches was the club's mural, which he designed and painted himself, inspired by a local mural painter whose style he 'borrowed' and adapted (fig. 2.20).

American sailors in port for three to four days and regulars from Seattle frequented the Harlem, as did locals from the East End neighbourhood. Performers and tourists who travelled by train and bus to Vancouver found both stations within several blocks of the Main Street nightclubs. In addition to his wife, Choo Choo Williams, King booked other striptease acts, including Lottie the Body, Miss Lovie, and Tequila Lopez (see chapters 3 and 4). Ernie King chuckled, 'Our cook Doris weighed three hundred pounds. We put her on the floor show one time and she did good! Very light on her feet. Later that week, a guy came in and said, "I heard you had a big fat woman in here dancing. That's what I came to see."' Other black entertainers enlivened the scene, nurtured by Ernie and Choo Choo: 'We had the Mills Brothers, Ike Turner, Montgomery Brothers, Pearl Brown, Thelma Gibson, Ruth Brown – a jazz singer, Billy Daniels, Ernestine Anderson, T-Bone Walker did a solo act, he'd work the Delhi and then come over to the Harlem' (fig. 2.21).

The Harlem Nocturne drew loyal patrons from nearby Hogan's Alley, Vancouver's working-class black community, and the larger white working-class East End community. Like the owners of the Penthouse Cabaret, who believed in redirecting time and profits to community-based activities, King and Williams sponsored a men's Senior

Figure 2.20 Ernie King, trombonist, bandleader, and club boss,
Harlem Nocturne, circa 1960

A basketball team, the Harlem Nocturnes, in the early 1960s. Then, in 1968, King sold his share in the Harlem Nocturne just before Hogan's Alley was designated a 'slum in need of clearance' by a City Council enamoured of the same urban renewal ideology deployed to justify the destruction of the black Nova Scotian community of Africville.[107] Hogan's Alley was subsequently bulldozed to the ground to make room for the Georgia Street viaduct.[108] Though King and Williams had never depended wholly on Hogan's Alley residents for patronage (and by the 1960s the community had dispersed), they were unhappy about the lack of consultation with residents and small business operators.

Denied liquor licences until the late 1960s, East End nightclub owners like Ernie King, Leo Bagry, Lachman Das Jir, and Jimmy Yuen milked the 'forbidden' aura of their unlicensed bottle clubs, but suffered much more intense police scrutiny than their West End rivals.[109] In 1959, the *Vancouver Sun*'s night-beat reporter Jack Wasserman forewarned readers: 'An east end club is in for more trouble as the result of the dry

Figure 2.21 The Harlem Nocturne's Ernie King, with singer Pearl Brown, 1955

squad.'[110] Later that year, Wasserman urged the provincial government to grant 'rough' East End clubs 'cabaret-type' liquor licences to 'give East Enders a chance to drink like human beings.'[111] In 1965, the Harlem Nocturne was raided by liquor squad detectives; the Smilin' Buddha and the Penthouse were included in the sweep.[112] And in 1967, the Harlem Nocturne was one of thirteen bottle clubs raided 107 times in January and February of 1967.[113] Ernie King harbours bitter memories of police surveillance and heavy-handed incursions. One night stands out:

> I had a doorman, Roy Brooks, and he was bootlegging mickeys and whisky. People would order bottles from him, so one night he sold some liquor to an undercover cop. I hadn't sold any liquor but they put me in handcuffs. My cousin, Walter Towns, a big powerful guy, didn't know they were cops, and hit one guy. Boom! Twenty cops came, and took us down – me, Streeter, Towns, Mike Taylor – my piano player, and kept us overnight. The next day in court, two stool pigeons confessed they'd gotten the

wrong guy, so my case was completely thrown out. My lawyer was Ann Sutherland – she was close to two hundred pounds and she could argue … she just bamboozled the cops.[114]

King was not alone in devising strategies to subvert police action and the threat of arrest. Laughing, he recalls a creative tactic: 'I trained my customers. I had them put their booze in an empty Coke bottle, or Seven-Up bottle, and they'd pour rum in there, or vodka or gin. And the cops never bothered them! It took the cops a year to wise up!' Other Chinatown clubs put liquor in teapots. At the Penthouse Cabaret, a bottle club until 1968, Joe Philliponi also suffered years of police intimidation (see below), which suggests that the Penthouse occupied a liminal third space somewhere between Vancouver's East and West sides. However, the Harlem Nocturne was subject to unique pressures that Ernie King insists must never be minimized or forgotten: 'No one was harassed more than me. No one. It got to the point they would harass me two or three times a night. Because I was the only man that owned a black nightclub! I couldn't get a liquor licence. I could only sell food and soft drinks. After ten years of owning that place and fighting with the cops and letting them get away with all kinds of stuff, I finally said "To hell with it, I'm closing up." I sold the place and I got on out of there. I went into the trucking business and I didn't have to be harassed by the police.'[115] King's recollection of the regulatory times was confirmed by gossip columnist Denny Boyd: 'Vancouver Vice Squad was insane in those days! It was probably the perceptions of a couple of high-ranking cops that, "We must stamp out evil. We must shape the morals of our citizens. We can't let them condemn themselves to hell."' Italian Canadian Dave Davies, who had numerous black friends and lovers, observed that, 'Black people in the city like Ernie King were racially profiled to death, only that word wasn't known in those days.'

In 1966, fourteen years after the State Burlesque Theatre was raided for the third time, the city's chief licence inspector, Mitch Harrell, cautioned the Harlem Nocturne and another club: 'Two cabarets were warned: the attire on their girls was too skimpy. One involved dancers with transparent, black chiffon blouses. The by-law forbids any person to produce in any building or place in the city any immoral or lewd theatrical performance of any kind.'[116] To quell fears of unchecked permissiveness, and to justify their own regulatory practices (and budgets), law enforcers and social reformers sought, through a variety of techniques, to administer striptease as a social problem that called for normalizing interventions, particularly in the East End clubs.[117] In a two-year period, from April 1967 to March 1969, the B.C. Liquor Control Board Annual Reports of 'Unlawful Sale of Liquor' registered 168 cases and a total of $8,060 fines collected – the vast majority paid by offending club owners.[118]

By necessity, club owners, staff, and entertainers balanced what was at times a lucrative (though often fickle) business with tense relations with police and moral reformers. Even after full nudity was decriminalized in 1972 (see below), strip joints remained easy prey for moral conservatives and their clean-up campaigns. How much policing of the Harlem Nocturne and other East End nightclubs was fired by vestiges of the early-twentieth-century temperance ideology? What about institutionalized police and societal racism, including the congealed, intractable myth of exotic Chinatown as a vice town, and myths of black people as criminally predisposed? [119] What role was played by the century-old conflation of the East End with female prostitution and 'sex deviance' in general? Certainly, multiple factors were involved; calculating the strength of each at any given time is a vexing task, largely because they continually reinforced one another. What is clear is that Vancouver's East End nightclubs were relentlessly scapegoated in the 1950s, 1960s, and 1970s.

Hotel Explosion in the City and Beyond

As the early 1970s ushered in a new era of liberalism, dancers and club owners across Canada and the United States played with the edges of 'full disclosure.' In Toronto, when the nude scene in the musical *Hair* evaded police censorship, dancers at a number of downtown strip clubs and hotel bars shed the g-string, though morality squad officers insisted on its reinstatement in November 1971.[120] In Vancouver, the Club Zanzibar (formerly the Torch Cabaret), the Factory, and Café Kobenhavn began introducing bottomless dancing in the fall of 1971. Following a visit to the Penthouse in October 1971, the inveterate night-beat columnist Jack Wasserman pronounced that, 'Nudity is now the staple of night time "entertainment" in our town ... There doesn't seem to be any point in bemoaning what has passed. As the fisherman said loudly to Emcee Tony Pisani, "Bring on the girls." That's what's going these days.'[121] Using his *Vancouver Sun* column 'Saloon Crawler's Notebook' to develop a more detailed meditation on the transition, Wasserman opined that

The viability of flesh as a commodity is amply demonstrated by the success of Isy's Strip City which rescued the club from financial disaster induced by massive public indifference to such name performers as Sarah Vaughn. In its own quiet way Vancouver has become the San Francisco of the north, with more toplessness, bottomlessness, and assorted variations of full disclosure than most other cities in the country. The trend is disquieting because of what it represents in terms of pure exploitation, mostly of the males in the audience.[122]

In December 1971, B.C. Attorney General Leslie Peterson issued a warning to nightclubs that nude dancing must stop, identifying the Criminal Code and the Liquor Act as appropriate instruments to end topless and bottomless performances.[123] On 17 February 1972, the Café Kobenhavn, an East End after-hours club at 968 Main Street run by a biker gang, the Satan's Angels, was raided by the Morality Squad, authorized by Peterson. In April 1972, five dancers and three club workers were charged with unlawfully presenting an obscene performance – as cited in Section 163, subsection 1, of the Criminal Code.[124] At the hearing in early September, 1972, a witness called by the defence, entertainment reporter Michael Walsh, argued that the public tolerates a great variety of sex acts in movies on Granville Street's theatre row, and that upon a recent visit to Wreck Beach, he had counted 29 females and 111 males sunbathing in the nude.[125] On 12 September 1972, provincial Judge David Moffett dismissed all obscenity charges, saying that he was 'satisfied the performance which has been described to me is not obscene in the light of the modern day approach of Canadian society, in a closed club type of atmosphere.'[126] Moffett made reference to a sign outside the Kobenhavn warning of nude dancing; as well, he acknowledged the trend to greater explicitness in mass-circulated magazines and films. Jazz musician Doug Cuthbert recalled the details: 'When the law was changed and the NDP [New Democratic Party] was voted into power in 1972, the g-strings came off. It was like, "We want to free people from the Social Credit party. We're going to change the world."' Two years later, after hearing an appeal by the crown in 1974, Judge D.B. MacKinnon ruled that the show at Café Kobenhavn *was* offensive to modesty and decency, and suggestive of lewd thoughts. Without having attended the show himself, he relied on testimony from Constable William Baker, who objected to 'undulating contortions' and 'simulated sex acts' on stage.[127] Judge MacKinnon elaborated: 'It tends to corrupt and, in my view, the dominant characteristic of the performance was the undue exploitation of sex.'[128]

In spite of contradictory legal rulings, and the decidedly muddy legal picture, 'peeler pubs' in hotels mushroomed in Vancouver: the horse, as it were, was out of the barn. Hurt by economic recession, hotel owners and managers across the province turned to nude floor shows to boost sagging alcohol sales. Ironically, whereas women's presence in these hotel pubs had been prohibited as 'indecent and disorderly' in the 1920s,[129] and women had been consigned to the partitioned 'ladies and escorts' section, women who 'peeled' in the 1970s became every downtown hotel's ticket out of financial ruin. The clout once wielded by prohibitionist forces had been considerably blunted. By 1975, there were close to thirty locales specializing in striptease in Vancouver, and scores of others in the surrounding suburbs of New Westminster, Surrey, Richmond, Delta, Coquitlam, and Burnaby (see table 2.2). Strip bars competed for the coveted entertainment dollar with an additional thirty major nightclubs specializing in mainstream entertainment that drew 40,000 patrons a week and banked revenues of $20 million a year.[130] Revenue rolled in from tourists from the state of Washington, south of the British Columbia border, where strip clubs prohibited full nudity with the sale of alcohol.

A veteran manager of Vancouver nightclubs in the 1960s and 1970s, Gary Taylor began his career in the late 1950s as a teenaged drummer backing up striptease dancers at the Smilin' Buddha, New Delhi, Harlem Nocturne, and 'girlie shows' at the Pacific National Exhibition (where he worked for Isy Walters). After short gigs at the Penthouse Cabaret, the Zanzibar, and the King of Clubs in the early 1970s, Taylor opened Gary Taylor's Show Lounge on Granville Street, where 'beautiful, innocent-looking women' were hired to strip, accompanied by jazz and blues musicians.[131] It was rumoured that Taylor was a smooth, fast-talking operator who bet strangers on the street that he could get a woman to take her clothes off on his stage.[132] A long-time friend joked that Taylor could talk a nun into going on stage.[133] When I interviewed him in 2007, Taylor emphatically dismissed those who judged him as 'some kind of whore monger'; rather he claimed to have been at the forefront of a 'pure and innovative' trend to enable women who were 'amateurs' to 'discover themselves' on stage and 'have a lot of fun doing it'[134] (fig. 2.22).

While pub owners like Taylor scrambled to install small stages for

Figure 2.22 Club owner Gary Taylor inside his downtown Vancouver Show Lounge, 1977

exotic dancers, bookings for Las Vegas-style acts at the Cave, Isy's, and the Penthouse dried up. The acts became too expensive, and competition from hotels meant the need to trim costs dramatically. To quote Richard Walters, 'All of a sudden acts like the Everly Brothers, which we used to buy for seventy-five hundred a week, wanted seventy thousand a week and no nightclub could do it. It killed it. Isy had the girlie shows at the PNE. He'd make thirty or forty thousand in three weeks, and that helped the club for a while, but even that disappeared by the mid-seventies.'[135] To compete with the hotels, according to Jack Card, 'Isy and his sidekick Foxy [Harold Fox] bought six rubber blow-up sex dolls, dressed them up in fringe panties, and bras, glued on cheap wigs from Army and Navy, put high-heeled shoes on them, filled them with helium, put wires around their ankles, and set them in the air about twenty feet on top of his club, flying all over Georgia Street!'[136]

After Isy Walters abandoned his allegiance to big-name acts, his son Richard noted that, 'Isy made a lot of money from "Strip City," but also from booking acts outside the city through WaltCard – the booking agency co-owned by Isy Walters and Jack Card. The Kelowna hotel bars, the Kamloops hotel bars, they were all coming through WaltCard.' By contrast, Joe Philliponi continued to mix striptease dancers with singers, MCs, and comics in a variety-style revue at the Penthouse Cabaret; meanwhile, his brother Ross watched the hotels steal their business: 'The hotels started to bring in top-line girls, a better class of girls. They were giving the public what they wanted. No cover charge. We charged cover. Cabarets could only stay open from seven o'clock at night to two o'clock in the morning. A hotel with the same type of entertainment could open from noon to two o'clock in the morning – that's fourteen hours against our seven hours. The hotels had the best deal from day one.' In conversation with *The Province* columnist Roy Shields in 1975, Larry Thiesson, manager of the St Regis Hotel, remarked that skin was good for business, and that 'hotels aren't churches.'[137] Not only did hotels begin to exploit the novelty of female nudity by scheduling exclusive slates of exotic dancers, including lunch-hour specials; their liquor licences allowed for twice as many hours a day as the very cabarets that had pioneered professional striptease decades earlier.

After Isy Walters's death in 1976, Jack Card renamed WaltCard booking agency 'International Artists' and ran it with Isy's former secretary, Jeannie Runnalls. Card remembers that hotels were quick to book strippers: 'The Niagara Hotel and the St Regis Hotel were among the first – girls did five shows a day, ten dollars a show. Then it was the Richmond Inn, the Surrey Inn. Every hotel wanted strippers. We were booking two hundred and eighty girls a week.' Runnalls remarked on the rapid shifts in the business and the exodus of striptease artists who were unwilling to adjust: 'Nobody had really tested the obscenity law, and overnight the law changed. The rush was unbelievable. I had to find a ton of dancers and very quick. At least half of the originals that did the Vegas show stuff left the business because there was zero market left. Jackie, Danielle, Belva, Shirley, Lovie – they said "No" to the first transition, which was nudity. Then the second major transition was to the spread show, and the queen of the spread was Leanne.'[138] Runnalls described recruiting women in public bathrooms, classifying dancers as 'A, B, or C,' and 'matching the right dancer with the right room.' In Runnalls's estimation the A-grade hotels included the Drake, the Cecil, No. 5 Orange, and the Marr; the Yale hotel was B-grade, and the Cobalt, American, and Marble Arch hotels were C-grade.

Almost overnight, booking agencies – International Artists, Choice

Table 2.2
Striptease staged in Vancouver hotels and pubs, 1970–1980+

Hotel name	Hotel address
No. 5 Orange Hotel	205 Main Street
Austin Hotel	221 Granville Street
American Hotel	928 Main Street
St Helen's Hotel	159/61/63 Granville Street
Royal Hotel	1025/29 Granville Street
Niagara Hotel	435 West Pender Street
St Regis Hotel	602 Dunsmuir Street
Drake Hotel	606 Powell Street
Marr Hotel	403 Powell Street
Nelson Place Hotel	1006 Granville Street
Balmoral Hotel	159 East Hastings Street
Castle Hotel	750 Granville Street
New Fountain Hotel	41 Cordova Street
Fraser Arms Hotel	1450 SouthWest Marine Drive
Marble Arch Hotel	514 Richards Street
Piccadilly	612 West Pender Street
	620 and 622 West Pender Street
Yale Hotel	1302/1304/1306 Granville Street
Cobalt Hotel	917 Main Street
Dufferin Hotel	900 Seymour Street
Vanport Hotel	645 Main Street
The Barn/Barn Cabaret	1138 Granville Street
Cecil Hotel	1336 Granville Street
The Factory	1042 Davie Street

Source: Vancouver City Archives, Vancouver: City Directories[139]

Entertainment, and Deluxe – emerged to handle the vast demand for topless and, later, bottomless dancers. In the early to mid-1970s, agents worked closely with a new generation of hotel staff. Leon and Harry Brandolini ran the No. 5 Orange Hotel, Gary Taylor ran Gary Taylor's Show Lounge, Danny Baceda owned Oil Can Harry's and Baceda's, Sam Sorich ran the Cecil Hotel, and Darcy Taylor and Jack Cooney managed the Marr and the Drake Hotels on Powell Street in the East End, two blocks from the No. 5 Orange. The Brandolinis, Cooney, and Taylor were among the first to expand and upgrade their small stages with fancy lights, poles, showers, and decent dressing rooms off stage (fig. 2.23). Club owners and managers were eager to attract not only a new generation of locals but also the lucrative tourist trade. A bartender named Buddy worked at the No. 5 Orange Hotel in the late 1970s:

Figure 2.23 Jack Cooney (left) and Darcy Taylor transformed the Marr and the Drake Hotels into show lounges featuring non-stop exotic dancers, 1982.

We'd get visitors from the States, because [stripping] was nowhere as explicit in the States. In fact, there were no strip clubs with full nudity in Edmonton in the seventies. So, we got all kinds of guys from Seattle, Bellingham … not to mention guys from Portland, at a convention, or the Shriners or the Lions from St Louis, Missouri, or Desmoines, Iowa. They'd take off the little fancy hat, put on a t-shirt and jeans, get right into the fire … You'd also see maybe a dozen Filipino guys, the deck hands on some boat moored in the harbour. They'd come to town like every couple of months or three or four months. They'd get a room and we'd see them every day, sometimes a couple of times a day, and then you wouldn't see them for three or four more months.

Once a bar for longshoremen and mill workers, the Drake Hotel was renovated in the mid-1970s, and the Marr Hotel in 1979. Into the Marr went $35,000 worth of sound equipment, a stage with a hydraulically rising centre platform, and a $12,000 package of lights. The combined capital outlay of $375,000 transformed the two hotels from 'snake pits' to glittering 'show lounges' – which together constituted a dual-shafted gold mine featuring continuous exotic dancers.[140] In 1980, rival Sam Sorich dedicated $160,000 to remaking the Cecil Hotel on Granville Street into a high-volume strip showroom packed with 'cleaner shows' than the 'raunchy acts' at the Drake and the Marr.[141]

Legal Conundrums: Hounded by the Law Post-Decriminalization

Despite the legalization of nude dancing in British Columbia in September 1972, strip clubs never escaped the heavy-handed rule of law. Nor were book sellers spared: law enforcers lashed out against the sale of 'obscene' novels, magazines, and 'super-hardcore pornography' throughout the 1970s in Vancouver and other Canadian cities, registering successive attacks against the growing mood of sexual permissiveness.[142] In 1973, the B.C. Liquor Control Board launched a crackdown on 'nudie clubs' by ruling that all nightclub entertainers must be accompanied by a three-piece orchestra. Insulted by the directive from a 'back door Gestapo,' Bob Reeds of the Barn Cabaret explained that 'This demand simply prices nude dancing out of existence for the working man.'[143] In Vancouver in November 1973, Gary Taylor was charged with 'presenting an obscene performance' at his Show Lounge.[144] A month later, municipal councillors in the suburbs of Delta and Surrey debated the 'suitability' of nude dancers at the Scottsdale Inn and the Newton Inn. Delta alderman Bill Reid protested that, 'We're not grown up enough in Delta.'[145] Surrey Mayor Bill Vander Zalm led the charge to ban nude entertainment in neighbourhood pubs so that his municipality could remain a 'square community.'[146]

In 1974, following a year of legal deliberations, Gary Taylor won his obscenity case. In a fifteen-page decision, Judge Jack McGivern dismissed charges against Taylor and five female performers.[147] Taylor recalled the case as a triumphant victory for the adult entertainment industry, and for himself as a self-named pioneer. In the spirit of the purely carnivalesque, Taylor and his lawyer, Tony Pantages, defended the strip club by re-enacting the 'obscene' performance at the Show Lounge with police, the crown prosecutor, and Judge McGivern in attendance. Taylor recounted the improbable story with glee: 'After we were charged, we did the whole thing in the club … Peaches and another girl danced, the lighting was the same, and boom, boom, the band started – it was a great drama … one hell of a defence. When they busted us, the cops said that you could see the girls' anus and clitoris at twenty feet. Whatever you saw in the dark, [we said] it's the human body, and is the human body obscene? We won hands down, and we celebrated.'[148]

While all Vancouver strip clubs were vulnerable to obscenity-related charges in the 1970s, it was the Penthouse Cabaret that was raided after a twelve-month undercover operation. In spite of the live-and-let-live nonchalance of Penthouse staff, and the lack of citizens' complaints, prostitution-related charges were laid against club personnel on 22 December 1975. That night, following the defeat of Dave Barrett's NDP by Bill Bennett's Social Credit party in the provincial election, the Filippone brothers – Joe, Mickey, and Ross – cashiers Minerva Kelly and Rose Filippone (Mickey's daughter), and doorman Jan Sedlack, under the umbrella of Celebrity Enterprises, were arraigned on charges of 'living on the avails of prostitution' and 'creating public mischief with intent to corrupt public morals.' In his guidebook *The Fortnightly Restaurant Magazine*, Dick MacLean summarized the police plot: 'The full operation, which involved twelve officers, included surveillance by means of electronic eavesdropping devices, hidden cameras, motor vehicle surveillance, and male officers entering the club to pose as prostitutes' clients.'[149] Female officers also posed as prostitutes. For months prior to the arrest, Morality Squad members, led by Inspector Vic Lake, had staked out the club and taken photographs of every man leaving the club with a woman on his arm. According to historian Brian Salmi, 200 photos (of 700 taken) were entered as evidence in the courtroom, and one officer described the stack that never made it into court as a 'blackmailer's wet dream,' containing photos of doctors, lawyers, politicians, celebrities, and numerous members of Vancouver's establishment.[150]

In the now infamous case known as *Regina v. Celebrity Enterprises*, a six-week preliminary hearing was followed by a trial in September 1976 (lasting until May 1977) before Judge William Trainor. To Ross Filippone, the lengthy battle resulted in painful consequences for his family: 'My kids got ribbed. It was embarrassing. Didn't help my marriage, either. I sat the kids down and told them, "I want you to know one thing – we're not ashamed of anything. You can keep your heads up high, and you can know that your Dad did nothing wrong." But inside they were hurt.' According to the *Vancouver Sun*'s 'Around Town' columnist Denny Boyd, 'When people accused Joe of harbouring hookers and strippers, and living off the avails, he replied, "I ain't Rebecca, and this ain't Sunnybrook Farm."'[151] During the trial, in a move to rehabilitate the club's shaken reputation, Joe Philliponi (the booking agent) assured Judge Trainor that full nudity was never allowed on stage even though, he noted, dancers had been performing bottomless in San Francisco since the mid-1960s.[152] However, the disciplinary gaze of the police was squarely on prostitution-related activity in the club rather than on the g-strings of featured exotics.

In both the media and the courtroom, the Filippones were likened to pimps who profited from the tips and cover charges paid by prostitutes who solicited customers inside.[153] In court, Detective Kenneth Johnstone, a Vice Squad officer, argued that the Penthouse management granted customers cash advances on their MasterCharge credit cards at a surcharge of 20 per cent to enable payment for sex with women who treated the club as a 'union shop' for prostitutes.[154] Struck by the hypocrisy of law-enforcement agencies, columnist Denny Boyd supported the Filippones' crusade for justice: 'Is the Safeway where [the prostitute] buys her groceries living off the avails? Is her hairdresser, her landlord, the Hydro Company, B.C. Telephone? And if she pays taxes on her illicit income, is the Solicitor General living off the avails?'[155] In an interview decades later, Ross Filippone angrily echoed Boyd's critique of the glaring double standard: 'We argued in our defence that the Hudson's Bay [department store] sells working girls clothes, so why aren't they charged with living off the avails?' In his closing argument, defence lawyer Russell Chamberlain insisted that the Penthouse had spent $180,000 in 1975 to hire professional entertainers, which was not a cost incurred by operators of a bordello.[156] Crown prosecutor Roy Jaques contended that the Penthouse's 'marketplace for prostitution' constituted 'a scandal in the community.'[157]

Finally, in September 1978, after sixty-one trial days over six months, testimony from forty-five witnesses, a padlocked closure lasting almost three years, conviction at county court, acquittal by three judges at the B.C. Appeal Court, $1.5 million in litigation fees, a Supreme Court appearance where nine judges dismissed the case, and hundreds of thousands in lost revenues, the accused were fully acquitted. The Penthouse Cabaret reopened for business, bruised but not broken[158] (fig. 2.24). Joe Philliponi estimated lost revenues at $400,000, with an additional $100,000 spent in legal fees.[159] At the end of it all, columnist Denny Boyd claimed that one of the club's defence lawyers, Angelo Branca, 'seared the buttons off Inspector Vic Lake's uniform, charging the Vancouver Police Department officer with creating a Penthouse dossier that was "a bundle of half-truths, quarter-truths, and un-truths."'[160] Boyd was

Figure 2.24 Joe Philliponi (left) and Ross Filippone celebrate the reopening of the Penthouse Cabaret, September 1978.

not alone in his condemnation of the expensive, farcical morality play. Erotic dancers and club staff lost earnings, and sex workers were forced to relocate outside to far more dangerous street strolls. In 1977, journalist Allan Fotheringham queried the logic and timing of the assault on the Penthouse in an era of 'sex on the open market.'[161] Fotheringham speculated that the city's chief of police, Don Winterton, and Inspector Lake – the Filippones' long-time adversary – abhorred the casual kickback system of the old days. Indeed, Winterton's beefed-up 'law and order' mandate worked to deflect much-needed attention away from the city's more pressing social and economic problems. And the club's forced closure did nothing to dampen the collective appetite for erotic entertainment.

Changing Times

With the Penthouse padlocked in the mid-1970s, the bottomless trend

gripped hotel bars. The sudden bloom, like cherry blossoms explod-
ing on a warm February day in Vancouver, meant that dancers were
in demand not only in the lower mainland, but across the province.
Those who travelled were paid a higher rate to compensate for the in-
convenience. The Columbus and the Drifter in Prince George, the Le-
land in Kamloops, Rock Creek near the Kootenays, a converted barn in
Nelson, the Hope Hotel, and the Grasslands in Merritt were among the
pit-stops. And until the mid- to late 1970s, dancers worked with jazz
musicians, both on and off the road. Supplying live musical accompaniment to dancers (and all other cabaret entertainers) was *the* bread-
and-butter gig for the city's best jazz musicians in the 1950s, 1960s,
and into the 1970s. When hotel owners and managers took over the
booking of 'peelers,' they squeezed out live music, replacing musicians
with tape-recorded top-forty hits. Independent nightclub owners had
trouble paying the musicians union scale. After the reopening in 1978,
Penthouse operator Ross Filippone explained, 'We went into records
and DJs, and we still had to pay royalties, which cost us thousands a
year.' As musician Mike Kalanj put it, 'the money started getting too
skinny.'

As Della Walters, Isy Walters's step-daughter recalled, 'There was a
huge economic downturn at the beginning of the seventies and people
didn't have the money anymore. And many of us in my generation
didn't want to go to a place like that.'[162] A new feminist involved in the
women's liberation movement, Walters began questioning what she
saw as the objectification of women's bodies for (men's) profit. In addition, other entertainment genres, including disco, rock 'n' roll, and folk
music, gathered steam. By the early 1970s, straight couples rarely went
to a nightclub together. To musician Doug Cuthbert, 'It was a different
time and place. Today, to get exercise people spend a hundred bucks a
month in an aerobics club. But they used to go dancing all the time. And
the clubs lost the female audiences. It ended up being a boys' club do-
main. It used to be a show. Then there was no show.' Jazz pianist Gord
Walkinshaw witnessed the shift away from mixed-gender crowds: 'It
got to the point that only ten per cent of the audience was women, and
some of those were strippers on their night off visiting their friends. Or
if they were working, they'd finish a set, and go off in the audience, get
free drinks and socialize.' Vancouver's hotel strip bars emerged as a
bastion for men of all kinds, on their own or in the company of friends
and acquaintances.

Tarred by the Brush of Immorality

Male nightclub owners who routinely booked striptease dancers never took for granted the respect extended to so-called legitimate small business operators, even within their own ethnic communities, whether Italian, Jewish, Chinese, South Asian, Irish, Ukrainian, or African Canadian. Like the Jewish American brothers of burlesque, the Minskys, Vancouver's nightclub owners and pub managers 'made it' – they were gainfully employed, paid taxes, set down roots in the city, married, raised children, and supported community activities such as sports teams, boxing, and the Variety Club.[163] These businessmen contributed significantly to Vancouver's postwar embrace of capitalist expansionism, in part through 'selling British Columbia.'[164] By most conventional measures, they were model Canadian citizens. In fact, Joe Philliponi, Isy Walters, and Ernie King served as soldiers during World War II. Yet in the eyes of critics, the combination of *who* they were (non-Anglo immigrants), *what* they did (promote striptease), *where* (in nightclubs and pubs), and *when* (well past midnight), disqualified them from the roster of 'businessmen of distinction.' Though each made his mark as an innovative impresario, not one has his name in the British Columbia Entertainment Hall of Fame, or stamped into concrete for posterity on 'Starwalk' outside the Orpheum on Granville Street's historic Theatre Row.

Though never hobbled – as dancers were – by the unflinching stripper stigma, nightclub owners habitually faced pressure from anti-vice factions to clean up the acts. Raids, fines, arrests, and closures engineered to stamp out immorality, revitalize law and order discourse, and justify a bigger policing budget were commonplace; they took a toll on all business insiders, particularly East Enders. Both Isy Walters and Joe Philliponi died in their clubs – Isy of a heart attack in 1976, and Joe of a bullet to the head in 1983.[165] Vancouver hotspots were never shut down en masse à la New York City in the late 1930s.[166] However, clubs such as the Penthouse Cabaret, Harlem Nocturne, Café Kobenhavn, New Delhi, Smilin' Buddha, and Kublai Khan were forever at risk of incursion. Nightclubs were routinely pilloried as raunchy breeding grounds for rapists, sex perverts, and murderers.[167] Even in 1980, the Penthouse was the subject of a police report by undercover officers who objected to 'a vulgar and improper act' on stage.[168] Vancouver police exercised significant discretionary power to lay charges of obscenity, illegal liquor sales and consumption, gambling, minors on the premises, and myriad prostitution-related offences.[169] Striptease in particular was perceived by many as evidence of the city's sinful, overly tolerant nature.[170] As nightclub-goer and former waitress Lynn Ross put it, the port city's 'Victorian mentality had not worn off,' even by the 1970s.[171] Ironically, as I posit in chapter 1, Vancouver's economy needed erotic spectacle, yet moral reformers screeched that it ruined communities and family values.

Nightclub and hotel bar owners who invested in striptease made a comfortable living as hard-working entrepreneurs, yet they never escaped insidious moral opprobrium. Even Joe Philliponi's long-standing membership in the province's conservative Social Credit party and his support for the city's conservative Non-Partisan Association (NPA) did not shield him from the scalding heat of police action.[172] In 1982, Joe told journalist Les Wiseman that he went after, and got, many things, notably money, women, success, the celebrity life, and friendships with stars. Wiseman championed Joe's reputation as one of the city's most reliable and generous philanthropists. And yet Wiseman could not resist the jab that Joe Philliponi was 'a hustler, in the best sense of the word and perhaps in the worst.'[173]

The tricks employed by clubmen like Philliponi, the risks they took, the profits they made, and the lines they both crossed and buttressed solidified their larger-than-life personas. On the one hand, they were grudgingly admired for not only surviving but thriving. Like seasoned boxers, once down, they fought to get back in the fight. On the other hand, commonplace lore alleged that they aided and abetted men's sexual perversions, degraded and victimized women, and took part in a range of illicit activity. Male strip club owners had money, yet they possessed insufficient symbolic capital or pedigree of the kind necessary to belong to the city's posh private clubs, including the Vancouver Club, the Royal Vancouver Yacht Club, the Shaughnessy Golf Club, and the Georgian Club.[174] No amount of Vegas-style glamour, profit-making, or humanitarian goodwill could erase the perception of male club owners as shady, seamy hoodlums who stimulated and capitalized on other men's desire for 'exotics.' Club owners did not make money from women's bodies any more than male employers made money from the bodies of female domestics, factory workers, waitresses, shop clerks, or fashion models. Rather, they made money from women's labour. Regardless, clubmen were caricatured as low-down pimps. Unentitled to membership in the city's wealthy, Anglo business and professional class, they were perpetual outsiders.

Throughout the 1950s, 1960s, and 1970s, men supplied the infrastructure of Vancouver's flourishing striptease scene; professional female dancers constituted the backbone, the *raison d'être* of the industry. Dancers were worshipped by some; they were judged harshly by most others for abandoning and/or mocking the venerated matrix of stay-at-home, full-time marriage, wifedom, and motherhood. Even in the late 1960s, as the sexual revolution unleashed its pro-sex sensibility across North America, Britain, and Europe, erotic dancers were subjected to popular disapproval. Because striptease was staged behind closed doors in nightclubs associated with forbidden, quasi-criminal actors and activity, dancers – even famous, internationally renowned ones – were stained by their presumed involvement in dodgy, underworld goings-on. At the same time, dancers were applauded for their acts, moxie, style, glamour, and practised sexiness. Their stories of triumph and toil are next.

3 'We Were Like Snowflakes – No Two Were Alike:'[1] Dancers and Their Gimmicks

I had to dance at the Harlem [Nocturne] because we couldn't afford to hire a lot of entertainment. Our dancers were mostly local. Thelma Gibson was a singer; Pearl Brown sang. I wasn't in a chorus line, I was a single. Ernie's cousin said, 'I read about this dancer called Choo Choo Williams,' and I thought, 'Geez, that's a good name for me' ... So I made my own costumes, I loved to dance, and I loved music. I was worried that word was going to get back to Edmonton that I'm dancing, with no clothes on! But I didn't feel that I was a stripper because I didn't get down. Stripping wasn't allowed: they would have freaked out if I got down to pasties.

Choo Choo Williams, Interview, 2002[2]

The Fox usually opens with a rock 'n' roll set in a glamorous brocade out-fit with a 12-foot feather boa to Paul McCartney's 'Monkberry Moon De-light'. Her clothes seem to melt off. You seldom notice her fumbling with a zipper because every gesture is part of the overall effect. Everything she does is suggestive; nothing is lewd. It seems to take her five minutes to take off her bra. She dances with the straps undone, cradling her breasts with obvious pleasure in both arms, offering them to some fellow fresh in from Surrey, wearing his new leather car coat. She stretches straps out, looks lovingly inside, fondles, strokes, twirls the bra over her head (they duck at stageside tables) and finally gets down to her floor routine in time with 'Easy Evil,' by, of all people, Toni Tenille.

Sean Rossiter, 1979[3]

After World War II, striptease dancers performed what were ostensibly private acts in public, making the art of undressing spectacular, often funny, and almost always mesmerizing in Houdini-esque fashion. From curvy, coy, and deluxe-costumed 'teasers' in the 1950s to caged go-go dancers in bikinis in the 1960s to bottomless 'hippie chicks,' 'gymnasts,' 'aerobics-specialists,' and 'spreaders' in the 1970s, strippers met and exceeded what historian Rachel Shteir calls a cultural 'craving for the fabulous.'[4] Charismatic, improvisational, and self-reliant, they were assigned the status of gender and sexual 'outlaw' for defiance of societal conventions. In the 1950s, Michael Johns argues, women's breasts in 'middle America' had to be alluring and controlled, but 'holstered' in stiff, pointy-cupped bras at all times. In a moment of unprecedented conformity to a dress code, women were permitted snug-fitting tops and even some cleavage, but short dresses or pants were rare.[5] By contrast, the decidedly unholstered breasts, bare (lengthy!) legs, rhinestone-encrusted stilettos, peekaboo devices, transparent wraps, and smouldering erotic aura of striptease professionals shook the foundations of culturally monitored female respectability and reserve.

While ordinary women wrestled with opposing messages that mixed together little-girl innocence with sensual but restrained sophistication leveraged to both attract and keep a man, extraordinary bump-and-grinders openly communicated non-conformist sexual suggestiveness via multiple, innovative techniques. Dancers and their acts were measured against the idealized contours of slim, buxom, white, able-bodied, young, glamorous, and heterosexy bodies sought by male club owners and booking agents. In spite of this tightly circumscribed fantasy creation, *stripteaser* was never a homogeneous category of identity, occupation, and performance. In this chapter, I explore how dancers' diverse aesthetic repertoires – the gimmicks they chose to express their artistry – were contoured by differences of race/ethnicity, social class, age, sexuality, and gender. I also examine how all dancers manipulated props, costumes, style, and g-strings in the context of ever-intensifying pressure, by the early 1970s, to bare *all* secrets of the flesh, from top to bottom. Vancouver's richly faceted nightclub scene invited dancers to brandish their wares.

Undressing for Success: White American Queens of Striptease Set the Glamour Bar

In contrast to earlier decades, striptease queens in the 1950s and 1960s began to deliver saucier, bolder eroticism that scandalized many onlookers (though their acts would seem downright modest by today's

XXX-rated standards). The vast majority of headliners mined the rich reservoir of symbols of white glamour, pageantry, and feminine magnetism embodied in the 'goddesses' of Hollywood's silver screen: Mae West, Marilyn Monroe, Brigitte Bardot, and Kim Novak. At the same time, stripteasers were trend-setters in their own right; they borrowed from numerous artistic, cultural, aesthetic, athletic, and musical traditions, and invented more. They daringly tweaked the conventions of female propriety, and their cutting-edge styles and brazen sexiness were widely copied and adapted, albeit in sanitized fashion, by mainstream female entertainers across North America.[6] For instance, female big-band, jazz, and swing instrumentalists in the 1940s and 1950s were made to 'look like strippers' with 'gowns revealing plenty of bosoms.'[7] And baseball players for the All American Girls' Professional Baseball League (1943–54) were mandated to wear short-skirted uniforms, attend Charm School, and appear 'sexy' to fans.[8]

Top-drawer erotic dancers who performed in Vancouver were white, American-born women who milked Canadians' fascination with talent imported from south of the forty-ninth parallel. Lili St Cyr, Ricki Covette, Evelyn West, Blaze Starr, Gypsy Rose Lee, and Tempest Storm were featured at high-end Vancouver nightclubs in the affluent and predominantly white West End. These awe-invoking entertainers with their Vegas-style costumes, props, and sets were familiar to Canadian consumers of girlie magazines – *Cabaret Quarterly, Modern Man, Bare, Vue, Foto-Rama, Gala, Bachelor, Frolic, Night & Day,* and *Eyeful,* as well as Hollywood films such as 'Strip-o-Rama' (1953) starring Lili St Cyr, Georgia Sothern, Rosita Royce, and Bettie Page. Bringing their world-class sex appeal to fans in the flesh, the flashy headliners were professionally managed, commanded celebrity status, and invested a sizeable chunk of their earnings in expensive gowns, dance training, choreography, props, music, and make-up. According to Rachel Shteir, Georgia-born Tempest Storm honed her act by stripping to three standards: Harold Arlen's classic 'Stormy Weather,' Arthur Freed and Nacio Herb Brown's 'Temptation,' and the Ira Gershwin/Harold Arlen torch song 'The Man That Got Away.'[9] In the mid-1960s at the Cave Supper Club, Storm's wild red mane and legendary proportions (40–21–34), made a lasting impression on choreographer Jack Card:

> She'd come out in her negligée – all feathers and jewels, making small talk with the audience. She'd get a phone call on the couch, and pretend to make love to her lover's picture. After she put the phone down, she'd

Figure 3.1 Lili St Cyr performs at the Cave Supper Club. Advertisement in *Vancouver Sun*, 28 June 1954

pretend she was taking a shower behind a screen, bubbles would come up and she'd pat herself all down. Back in front she'd slowly powder and perfume herself everywhere; she'd wink at all the guys ringside. It looked like her g-string was still on – a little patch with a very fine, flesh-coloured elastic attached. She'd get up – keeping her powder puff in front of her, and put on a frilly corselet, boom. Then she'd lie back on the couch putting on her stockings. In the first part of her act, when she undressed, she'd spring her stockings to the audience with her toe. Then she'd get up, strut around the stage a little bit, give herself a little more perfume. Then she'd go behind and get into a dress, come out front, sit down and make a BIG production of putting her shoes on. She'd throw a fur stole on that trailed ten feet behind her. As she left the stage, the lights dimmed down, and as she got to the end she'd turn on a little red light near her shower room, behind the couch and table, wink at the audience and strut off stage. That was a twenty-five-minute act. She'd work with the house band, but she had her own orchestrations, musical director, and her own dresser. She never, ever in Vancouver took it all off. She went bare-breasted. But she never took her g-string off and she never spread her legs.[10]

Lili St Cyr (born Willis Marie Van Shaak in Minneapolis in 1918 of Swedish-Dutch heritage), spent many years in Montreal, beginning in 1944 at the Gayety Theatre. Crowned 'queen of the strippers,' she was well-known for her on-stage bubble-baths, her acts as a jungle goddess and a biblical temptress, and her fondness for eccentric story telling.[11] A Vancouver favourite (fig. 3.1), St Cyr performed her trademark bubble baths in a transparent glass tub, dried off with a tiny towel, and then slowly proceeded to get dressed, a striptease in reverse.[12] It was widely reported that the highlight of her act came when an invisible fishing line tugged off her g-string over the heads of the audience while the house lights faded to darkness.[13] By the mid-1950s, St Cyr had become 'as much a fixture in Las Vegas as the roulette wheels.'[14] She was known to work 365 days a year; her tastes were expensive, her shows unique. As she noted, women attended her shows to see the dazzling array of dresses and jewellery; men came to see her remove them.[15]

At Vancouver's Cave Supper Club in 1952, Lady Godiva hit the boards and made a fortune. She danced and sang on stage, and after a huge explosion, the lights changed and she was on a horse totally nude, but with her hair covering everything up. In local news media Lois De Fee was advertised as 'Superwoman, a world famous stripteuse, 6'4" tall and 200 pounds of seductive, tantalizing curves.'[16] Adorned in false eyelashes, leopard prints, and fishnet stockings, all of the strippers who danced at the State Burlesque Theatre, according to Nena Marlene, were 'real ladies' who stripped with talent, but never down too far: 'They would do the tease – take a sequined glove off, put it back on, take it off again. Some would just take off an earring and dangle it. The show builds up until they take their top off to a net bra – no pasties back then.' Jack Card recalls: 'The girls would bounce across the stage so their big gazongas would go ba-doom, ba-doom, ba-doom, ba-doom. But they'd be dressed, back then. They would bump and grind a lot and the drummer would go, rrrrrrrrrrr-BOOM!'[17] One popular striptease act at the State Burlesque Theatre was New York-based 'Tons of Fun': '900 pounds, 3 girls, 300 pounds each, and they danced like fairies.'[18]

In the 1962 Hollywood film *Gypsy*, starring Natalie Wood and Rosalind Russell, an entire production number, with music by Stephen Sondheim, reinforces the art of plying a gimmick. Three striptease dancers serenade Gypsy: 'You can pull all the stops out, till they call the cops out, grind till you're fined or you're banned. But you've got to have a gimmick, if you want to get a hand. You can sacrifice your sacro, working in the back row, bump in a dump till you're dead. But you've got to have a gimmick, if you want to get ahead.' The inspiration for *Gypsy* was the Seattle-born show-stopper Gypsy Rose Lee who worked and travelled with Jack Card for a short time. Gypsy, known for her high-class manners and literary tastes, performed for rapturous fans in Vancouver shows and, more regularly, in extravagant Las Vegas revues where each of her costumes carried a $5,000 price tag.

Headliners became quickly familiar with the art of costuming: sumptuous fabrics of silk, velvet, organza, tulle, satin, and chiffon were spun into magnificent gowns, overcoats, hats, shawls, jackets, capes, dusters, and negligées, all with specialized snaps, clasps, and zippers for easy removal. Before bottomless acts were legalized in Vancouver in the early 1970s, striptease dancers cunningly peeled off their sequined gowns, furs, and peekaboo devices to reveal pasties and g-strings, often worn layered over one another up to three at a time. The g-string, Italian American Ann Corio slyly observed, 'was a tiny jewel-like bauble on a string around the waist covering up its specific subject.'[19] As well, notes Jack Card, under g-strings, some dancers experimented with rhinestone clips in the 1950s and 1960s: v-shaped and glittery, made of sprung steel, they fitted over the pubic area and inserted into the vagina.

Eschewing the script for full-time motherhood and wifedom, erotic dancers were bombshells, and a bombshell, to quote historian Kristina Zarlengo, was a 'deeply desirable, unattainable woman with an inflated body and intense sexuality – a steadfast atomic age feminine ideal ... who represented raw power of a kind frequently associated with the atom bomb.'[20] Retired Vancouver journalist Denny Boyd appreciated the image a professional teaser could evoke: 'She's tall, long legs, big boobs. She had personal and physical grace. There's no fantasy with the short, squat girl ... you wouldn't even date that girl in high school for heaven's sake!'

Impersonating the Exotic 'Other'

The striptease industry at mid-twentieth century depended on the appropriation of the allegedly inherent sensuality and 'exoticism' of non-Anglo cultures. Circus and carnival histories illustrate how white burlesque and striptease performers commonly disguised themselves as Algerian, Egyptian, South Asian, Arabian, or Hawaiian in order to fill the demand for Salomés, belly dancers, and harem girls. The Dutch-born Mata Hari (née Margaretha Geertruida Zelle) performed her 'Oriental dance' snugly fitted into a nude body stocking under diaphanous gowns in Paris in the early 1900s prior to her rather unsuccessful and brief espionage career.[21] Egyptian acts for showgirls typically showcased mummy cases with creaky doors, snakes, pipes, swords, turbans, and Eurocentric versions of Arabian dancing. In her book *Rank Ladies*, M. Alison Kibler remarks that white female vaudevillians in the United States donned corked-up racial masquerades while black performers

Figure 3.2 Lili St Cyr performs orientalism, circa 1955.

were discouraged from trying to look or act white.[22] At the same time,
historian Linda Mizejewski notes that in the 1910s and 1920s, café au
lait make-up – light-skin or mulatto-effect blackface – became a 'standard sexual mask for the more daring Ziegfeld girls' performances, a
way to appropriate but also to distance a racially structured, forbidden
sensuality.'[23]

From the turn of the twentieth century onwards, dancing girls at Canadian and American carnivals were regularly described as 'Oriental
dancers,' and shows had names like 'Persian Palace,' 'Turkish Village,'
'Little Egypt,' 'A Trip to Babylon,' 'Mecca,' and 'A Street in Cairo.' Here,
the tourist discourse of escape used to lure white travellers to destinations out of the ordinary, especially robust after World War II, was
materialized in Vancouver. 'Naked girls' from 'far-away villages' and
'palaces' were marketed by nightclub owners and carnival program-
mers as cheap alternatives to vacation sites outside provincial borders.
In particular, the treatment of colonized India in girl shows worked implicitly to sanction British imperial rule, and to promote the superiority
of *British* Columbian spectators.[24] Decades later, white stripteasers still
played with eroticized images of 'other' ethnicities and peddled (however unwittingly) the racist discourse of orientalism (fig. 3.2).[25]

At the Beacon Theatre in Vancouver in 1945, white headliner Yvette
Dare, whose trained parrot helped her to disrobe on stage, was billed
as presenting a 'Balinese dance to the bird god.' In an interview with
Vancouver Sun reporter Ray Gardner, Dare admitted using brown
make-up all over her body and revealed that Jeta, her parrot, was not
actually from the 'exotic isle of Bali' as advertised, but rather was 'a
New York department store bargain' who had 'never been nearer to

Figure 3.3 Nena Marlene, circa 1950, at the State Burlesque Theatre

Bali than Macy's basement.'[26] Indeed, publicly calling one's own bluff suggests a uniquely situated form of 'passing' intended to deceive no one. Clearly, some white women could don and commodify trappings of racial otherness while avoiding the indelible stain of racial difference in a city governed and numerically dominated by Anglo-Canadians until the 1970s. Vancouver-based showgirl Nena Marlene recalled the 'exotic' repertoire at the State Burlesque Theatre in the late 1940s, and the industry's broad demands for otherness at the same time that she self-reflexively gestured to her own duplicity: 'Our line of showgirls filled in between the comedians, the accordion player, and the magician, and before the headlining strippers. We'd do Hawaiian dances, and Indian tom-tom dances because we had to keep changing themes, but we weren't authentic one bit'[27] (fig. 3.3).White dancers like Nena Marlene, and on rare occasions biracial First Nations dancers, donned standardized symbols of Indianness to cash in on the trappings of the mythic 'noble princess' à la Pocahontas. In 1956, 'Princess Do May – the Cherokee Half Breed' was photographed in full feather headdress,

Figure 3.4 Yvette Monjour, star performer at the 'Viva la Roma' revue, Isy's Supper Club, 1966

beaded headband, and drum. However, in reality, I suspect that she possessed neither Cherokee heritage, nor Cherokee traditional dress – the costume in the photo is a hodge-podge of disparate, unrelated ephemera meant to signal to white viewers the exotic *and* the familiar – the ultimate in non-threatening otherness.

While postwar Vancouver's East End/Chinatown cabarets promoted interracial socializing and performance by dancers of colour (see below), West End Vancouver nightclubs attempted to maximize their shows' appeal by presenting an incongruous blend of white women impersonating eroticized 'Others.' At Isy's Supper Club in 1963, audiences saw 'A Night in a Turkish Harem' featuring 'Norwegian Beauty, Ann Inga.'[28] In 1966 at Isy's, Jack Card choreographed 'Viva La Roma,' a 'Luxurious Italian Revue,' featuring 'The Girls of Napoli' and the Hungarian-born dancer Yvette Monjour as 'La Belle de Rome' (fig. 3.4). Kitty Kelly, a Seattle-based striptease entertainer was well-known to Vancouver audiences as the 'Irish Venus' in the 1960s.[29]

While dancers of colour adopted racializing signifiers in their acts (see below), white dancers borrowed from race-based repertoires as a way of flirting with the danger of otherness. Scandinavian American superstar Lili St Cyr danced at the Cave, Isy's, and the Penthouse in the mid-1950s through the 1960s. Among St Cyr's favourite routines were 'In a Persian Harem,' 'The Chinese Virgin,' and 'The Love Bird,' which, according to Steve Sullivan, 'was set in the jungle amidst a tribe of beautiful savage women.'[30] Giant Spanish and Aboriginal headdresses were standard pieces of St Cyr's repertoire, as was a Japanese bath-house that she had assembled on stage. As a result of St Cyr's lineage as unquestionably white and 'naturally' blond, she was free to dabble in non-white, non-Anglo exotica because it left no trace. She was not Japanese or First Nations, nor was she Latina, Chinese, or Arabic, and that was the point: St Cyr belonged to a long list of celebrities all of whom traded in non-white racial markers because they could and it was profitable, not because, like entertainers of colour, they had to and it was a struggle.

Diversities Abounded among Locals in the Port City

As Vancouver residents demonstrated a hearty appetite for bump and grind after the war, and the independent nightclub sector boomed, a local industry of dancers, choreographers, make-up artists, costume designers, and musicians sprang up to supplement imported acts. Following my publicity campaign, I interviewed nineteen former strip-tease dancers who had lived and worked in Vancouver between 1945 and 1980. Several retired dancers declined an interview, others had left the province and were unreachable, and others still may have chosen not to participate. So, nineteen is a non-representative sample: indeed, it is likely composed of dancers who viewed their careers as successful, hence deserving of recollection. Dancers who lasted a few months or less, dancers whose drug or alcohol addictions forced their early exit, and dancers who moved sporadically in and out of the business are not included here. In addition, a number of dancers were murdered during the period under study, and their voices have been forever silenced. Still, there is some diversity within the group, as outlined in table 3.1.[31] At least one dancer worked in each of the four decades under study; thirteen women are white and six women are non-white (three African Canadians, one Latina Canadian, two biracial First Nations); fifteen identify as heterosexual and three as lesbian or bisexual; one of

Table 3.1
Dancer profiles: Race, sexuality, dance training, starting age, children, time span of career

Name	Racial / ethnic identity	Sexual identity	Formal dance classes	Age when started dancing	Raised children while dancing	Time span of dancing career
Nena Marlene	white	heterosexual	tap, ballet	20	yes	1946–52
Choo Choo Williams	African Canadian	heterosexual	none	23	yes	1954–67
Miss Lovie	African Canadian	heterosexual	none	24	no	1964–73
Roxanne	French, Russian, and Cree	lesbian	some Celtic, tap, and ballet	21	yes	1965–75
Princess Lillian	white	heterosexual	none	19	yes	1968–86
Coco Fontaine	African Canadian	heterosexual	some jazz dance	18	yes	1968–83
Bonnie Scott	white and First Nations	heterosexual	none	14	no	1969–86
Foxy Lady/ The Fox	white	heterosexual	none	24	no	1971–83
Tarren Rae	white	heterosexual	none	16	no	1973–83
Virginia	white	heterosexual	movement classes at SFU	24	yes	1973–5
Shelinda	white	heterosexual	some ballet and jazz	17	no	1974–88
Cascade	white	heterosexual	no dance; some gymnastics	19	no	1974–9

Table 3.1 (*Continued*)

Name	Racial / ethnic identity	Sexual identity	Formal dance classes	Age when started dancing	Raised children while dancing	Time span of dancing career
Scarlett Lake	white	bisexual?	dance, theatre	21	no	1974–6, 1979–81
April Paris	white	heterosexual	none	26	no	1975–86
Sarita Melita	Latina Canadian	heterosexual	ballet, modern, tap, theatre	19	yes	1976–84
Jasmine Tea	white	heterosexual	some ballet and modern	18	yes	1978–86
Klute	white	lesbian	none	24	no	1979–86
Bambi	white	bisexual	none	17	no	1979–2002
Shalimar	white	heterosexual	ballet	17	yes	1983–9

Source: Interviews with former dancers, 1999–2004

the dancers is deaf; the youngest of the group entered the business at fourteen and the oldest at twenty-six, with twenty as the average age of entry. Twelve of nineteen dancers (63 per cent) began dancing when they were under the age of twenty-one, which made them vulnerable to arrest as minors in licensed nightclubs and pubs. The dancers' careers averaged ten years. Ten of the nineteen women (53 per cent) had dance or gymnastics training. Eleven women (58 per cent) worked past the age of thirty, which would be considered rare in today's youth-driven market. Nine (47 per cent) raised children while working in striptease, while more than half elected either to postpone or to forgo mother-hood altogether. As table 3.2 shows, nine women (47 per cent) identify as working class, three (16 per cent) as lower middle class, and seven (37 per cent) as middle or upper class; six women (31.5 per cent) grew up in single-parent families and thirteen (68.5 per cent) in two-parent families; twelve (63 per cent) are high school graduates (with three later returning to graduate). These portraits, textured by the dancers' own first-person accounts, capture realities that put into question enduring negative stereotypes of strippers as uneducated, untrained, from broken families, raised by poor single mothers, and flighty, undependable, and otherwise unemployable.

White Vancouver Dancers Perfect a Gimmick

In Vancouver, as elsewhere, imported American headliners or feature dancers in the 1940s, 1950s, and 1960s secured bookings at posh West End nightclubs. Local talent was relatively rare in the 1940s and 1950s, though a handful of Vancouver-based showgirls such as Nena Marlene and Norma Norelle broke into the local burlesque scene. Born in Vancouver in 1924, Nena Marlene, the daughter of a B.C. Electric labourer and a homemaker, was the youngest of eight children.[32] After years of dance lessons (partly paid for by her sister), and years of retail employment, she worked 'in the line full-time' from 1946 to 1952 at the State Burlesque Theatre on East Hastings Street alongside dancers such as Norelle and Mimi Hines. Their chorus line, known as the State-ettes, performed before and after the 'big acts' – American singers, comedians, and stripteasers – and they were accompanied by live orchestras in the pit. In her twenties, alongside other showgirls – who were also called exotic dancers – Nena Marlene, also known as "Little Bits,' performed three to four dances a show, two to three shows a day, six days a week. She reminisced: 'My ambition was not to be a stripper, I didn't

Table 3.2
Dancer profiles: Social class, schooling, family of origin

Name	Social class background	Level of formal schooling while dancing	Family of origin
Nena Marlene	lower middle class	high school graduate	two-parent family, siblings
Choo Choo Williams	working class	high school graduate	two-parent family, siblings
Miss Lovie	working class	high school graduate, two years art college; nursing training	single mother (until age 14), 3 siblings
Roxanne	working class	high school graduate	single mother (after age 5), 1 sibling
Princess Lillian	working class	high school graduate	parents separated, only child
Coco Fontaine	working class	dropped out of high school	two-parent family, siblings
Bonnie Scott	working class	dropped out of high school	single mother, siblings
Foxy Lady/The Fox	middle class	high school graduate, one year university	two-parent family, siblings
Tarren Rae	middle class	dropped out of high school	two-parent family, 1 sibling
Virginia	middle class	high school graduate, nursing training	two-parent family, only child
Shelinda	middle class	dropped out of high school; got diploma while dancing	two-parent family, siblings
Cascade	upper middle class	high school graduate, some college	two-parent family, siblings
Scarlett Lake	upper middle class	high school graduate	two-parent family, 2 siblings
April Paris	lower middle class	dropped out of high school	two-parent family, 10 siblings
Sarita Melita	working class	dropped out of high school	single mother, 8 siblings
Jasmine Tea	upper class	high school graduate	two-parent family, siblings
Klute	lower middle class	high school graduate, degree in horse training	two-parent family, 1 sibling
Bambi	working class	dropped out of high school	single mother, siblings
Shalimar	middle class	high school graduate	two-parent family, adopted, only child

Source: Interviews with former dancers, 1999–2004

Figure 3.5 Nena Marlene (right) in a burlesque sketch at the Mandarin Gardens, circa 1950

have the beauty. After knowing you're a pony in a chorus line, you're a pony. You can't grow up and be a gorgeous, glamorous girl. You don't take a little dump like me and try and make her a beauty, because it's not going to work. I could talk to her belly button!' In Nena Marlene's words, 'To be a headliner stripper you had to have class – we worked with Sally Rand, Evelyn West, Rosita Royce, Zorita, Zandra, and Lois De Fee – they were majestic.' Nena Marlene combined dancing at the State Burlesque Theatre with late night shows at the Narrows Supper Club in North Vancouver and midnight shows at the Mandarin Gardens Supper Club in Chinatown – both clubs regularly integrated striptease into choreographed floor shows (fig. 3.5). Nena Marlene also had more prestigious club dates at the Commodore and the Hotel Vancouver, but as a tap dancer or one-half of a balancing duo, not as a burlesque dancer. She later used her experience to springboard her into a successful, international touring career with the Maylo Trio.[33]

In the mid- to late 1960s, Canadian striptease dancers were 'discovered' and promoted for the 'star quality' once monopolized by their American sisters. A hippie generation of zesty dancers across Canada belonged to a youth movement committed to flouting social taboos of all kinds. Dancers were caught up in the zeitgeist of anti-authoritarian movements world wide, including student protests and mounting criticism of the American war in Vietnam, grassroots women's liberation, the Quebec sovereignty movement, the Red Power and Black Power movements, and gay rights activism. The gregarious, raunchy act of Janis Joplin, the rock and blues singer 'with the bordello voice,' was an inspiration for dancers who admired and identified with Joplin's dynamism and sexual abandon.[34] Lindalee Tracey, a professional stripper in Montreal in the 1970s, writes in her memoir that striptease not only snubbed authority but afforded her a 'gigantic' outlet for artistry, comedy, poetry, and sassiness.[35] In Vancouver specifically, women's entrée into professional striptease in the 1960s coincided with the founding of the Greenpeace environmental juggernaut, agitation to decriminalize marijuana, the launching of Vancouver's alternative, shit-kicking weekly *The Georgia Straight: Vancouver's Free Press* (1967), and the Abortion Caravan (1970).[36]

The retired dancers I interviewed varied in their allegiance to anti-establishment politics, including feminism and Marxist critiques of the military-industrial complex. What they shared (among other things) was a time and place of idealism and change: they played a role as architects and engineers of a new geography of labour and leisure, all the while experimenting with rebellion on and off the stage. They joined the business of erotic entertainment as most of the 'old-time' strippers of the 1940s and 1950s were 'greying,' retiring, or scaling back their public appearances. The 'queens' – Sally Rand, Blaze Starr, Gypsy Rose Lee, Lili St Cyr, and Tempest Storm, who had never performed entirely naked, were highly critical of the trend to toplessness and later bottomlessness adopted by young dancers caught up in the sexual revolution that swept across North America in the 1960s.[37] Expressions of public nudity in *Hair* and *Oh! Calcutta!* redefined undressing as political activity. In this context of openness, erotic dancers transformed the conventions of burlesque into something new (plate 4).

Some of the most popular local headliners who performed in Vancouver from the mid-1960s to the early 1980s included Miss Lovie, Dee Dee Special, April Paris, Princess Lillian, Suzanne Vegas, Marilyn Marquis, Lili Marlene, Tia Maria, Tequila, Jasmine Tea, Foxy Lady, Bonnie Scott, Michelle, Danielle, CoCo Fontaine, and Tarren Rae. A small number began their stripping careers at the Pink Pussycat and Oil Can Harry's as go-go dancers, performing in cages or on small boxes. Influenced by new trends in California and England in the mid-1960s, they had little in the way of costumes, routines, or elaborate props. However, because go-go dancing paid so poorly, many dancers like Roxanne quickly abandoned their iron cages and bikinis to pursue full-time exotic dancing careers.

The city's aspiring erotic dancers learned that a career, especially as a headliner within the city and beyond, demanded significant financial investment in costumes, shoes, props, wigs, hairpieces, expensive make-up, stockings, sheet music, and, by the late 1970s, tape-recorded music. Indeed, all dancers spent money to ramp up their marquee status, and their ranking on the 'pay and prestige' scale. Dancers were keenly aware of what sociologist Pierre Bourdieu identified as a correspondence between cosmetic investments and the chances of profit for those whose physical appearance is valorized on the job. 'Beauty care' to cultivate the 'market value' of their bodies, observed Bourdieu, commanded dancers' time and effort, sacrifices, and money.[38] Springolater shoes sold near Pike Place Market in Seattle, Washington, were coveted by many erotic dancers: high spike heels with a steel shaft 'they were like Barbie doll shoes' says April Paris, 'made for strippers.' The top-drawer West End nightclubs expected dancers to assemble a professional wardrobe, and while some sewed their own outfits, others purchased top-of-the-line creations from local designers who specialized in striptease fashions, many of which sported upside-down 'stripper zippers.' Eager to maintain a 'certain look and style,' West End club owners such as Joe Philipponi and Isy Walters subcontracted costume-making to talented and experienced local seamstresses – some of whom were retired dancers. Dazzled by the outfits, dancers at the Cave, Isy's, and the Penthouse were invited to 'work off' the price tag in instalments over several weeks or months. In figure 3.6, the late Vancouver-based artist Theodore Wan caught a moment of exuberantly feathered and bejewelled choreography on film.[39]

Originally from California, gay costume expert Jerry Satan became known as 'the man who sewed for the stars.' He moved to Vancouver with dancer Daquiri St John in the 1960s, and in addition to St John's wardrobe, supplied unique ensembles to many striptease performers, as well as Liberace and Elvis Presley. Following in the tradition of American costume designers Rex Huntington on the east coast and Gussie Cross on the west coast,[40] Clyde Dubois, a gay Francophone

Figure 3.6 Three exotic dancers 'hit it hard' in a burlesque revue on a Vancouver stage, circa 1977.

designer from Quebec, settled in Vancouver in the late 1960s. Dubois became famous for his extravagant, signature gowns, his panache, and his fancy sewing machine. According to Bonnie Scott, 'Clyde Dubois used to live on Grant Street and his basement was a costume factory. He was THE costume guy in Vancouver. He did the costumes for Jack Card's shows – hand-beaded with glass beads and sequins.' Foxy Lady noted that Dubois outfitted Michelle and Danielle, both of whom became 'A-dancers' with elaborate, popular shows. Foxy Lady herself purchased several items from a 'very generous' Dubois: 'He made costumes for girls on a mere deposit, because they needed the costume to get the job. He would front them. He and his sister, Rose, worked on the machines in his house.' Back and forth for gigs between Vancouver and Europe in the 1970s, choreographer Patrick Kevin O'Hara gave Dubois the patterns for costumes from the big Paris shows such as the Lido, Moulin Rouge, and Folies-Bergère. As O'Hara explained, 'This may also have played a part in the quality of the look that was part of the hot Vancouver scene.'[41]

In addition to clothing, Vancouver dancers further customized their acts by experimenting with elements of magic, puppetry, theatre, gymnastics, pantomime, comedy, and dance training. Some incorporated props such as electric trapezes, parrots, live doves, Siberian tigers, cockatiels, roller skates, boa constrictors, fireballs on stage, and glow-in-the-dark body paints, while others made creative use of bird cages, oversized fish bowls, and bubble machines, not to mention strategically utilized ping pong balls and cigarettes! Suzanne took to blowing bubbles in a bubble bath on stage (plate 5). Most adopted false and/or dyed eyelashes, wigs, dyed or bleached hair, regular manicures, pedicures, and hair removal. Several musicians recall that a handful of strippers started singing tunes like 'Stormy Monday,' 'Sunny,' and early Beatles' songs like 'Maggie May' and 'Something.'[42] At Isy's Strip City in 1971, Rickey Brazil arrived on stage in a pink and silver pantsuit under a maxi-length coat she had designed herself, sang a ballad, and then undressed.[43]

Born in Edmonton, Alberta, Bonnie Scott grew up in a low-income household with a working-class mother and siblings. She ran away to Vancouver at thirteen and began to dance at fourteen at the Satan's Angels' biker bar on Main Street, the Café Kobenhavn. She remembers the Kobenhavn as dark, with cement walls and a cement floor on which bikers rode their 'hogs' after hours. Bonnie Scott and another dancer were arrested in 1972 for bottomless dancing but acquitted when nude performance was decriminalized in September 1972. After the arrest, Scott turned her career around. Following a short stint go-go dancing at the Shanghai Junk in the East End, she moved permanently west to Isy's Supper Club and the Penthouse under the paternal tutelage of Isy Walters and Jack Card. Scott recalls that, 'Isy was like my Dad – the Dad I never had. He kind of took me under his wing. He taught me how to be a professional dancer. I learned from Isy: you had to be professional, you had to have shows, you had to have class, you had to be a lady, you had to show up on time.' Part First Nations but light enough to pass as white, Bonnie Scott perfected her show-stopping extravaganza in Vancouver's 'A-clubs'– Isy's and the Penthouse, and later, the Cecil, the Marr, and the Drake Hotels – and across the country. After Isy's death in 1976, Scott was booked by Katie Lynch at Choice Entertainment. A dancer who achieved true headliner status in Vancouver, on stage under pink lights she stripped off her super-deluxe, beaded gown (designed by Clyde Dubois), climbed a ladder, and, once inside her six-foot-tall, transparent champagne glass, struck sexy poses amid the bubbles. She explains:

> To be a feature, you had the wardrobe, costuming, the music, the choreography. It mattered how well you were known, how long you'd been in the business, what kind of costumes you had, what kind of act you had, what kind of portfolio you had. I did that champagne show for eight years. The show was, at that time, worth about twelve thousand dollars. The gown was twelve hundred dollars, the glass was worth about three thousand dollars. I had a wrought-iron staircase that went up into the glass. I had a little wrought-iron powder table, I had a wrought-iron clothes hanger that I hung my costume on. I had a bubble machine, a fog machine. When I went out of town, I had my own black lights. I had a negligée for when I finished my show and I had a matching pink plush bathmat and pink towel. I used to buy my bubble bath from Avon because its bubbles lasted the longest. The whole show was twenty to twenty-five minutes – Jack [Card] helped me choreograph it. I got a four thousand dollar fox stole from my boyfriend, and an ivory cigarette holder and I'd do Eartha Kitt: 'My champagne case and your beer bottle bucket ...' (fig. 3.7)

Scott designed myriad routines over her fifteen-year career: 'I had "Dance of the Seven Veils," a Southern Belle show, a Fan Dance, and a Pink Panther routine, and Mae West shows. I had a show with a giant clam shell, and I did a dominatrix-style act with a whip – my "bitch act."'When she retired in 1984, she had invented a magic act where she booked herself and kept her clothes on. But she was also angry about the direction in which the striptease business was going, she had a chronic back injury, and she had a drug problem that prompted her journey to sobriety, her pursuit of university education, and yet another career.

Princess Lillian was born in Vancouver in 1948 and, like Bonnie Scott, raised by a working-class single mother. Anglo-Canadian, she began go-go dancing at Oil Can Harry's in the late 1960s, and, bucking the trend of American dancers working in Vancouver, she danced in Waikiki, Hawaii, in 1969–70, after which an uncle booked her into a club in Los Angeles for six months. Deaf from birth, a survivor of physical abuse at Jericho School for the Deaf, skilled in sign language, and a lip-reader for my benefit, Princess Lillian danced at Isy's, the Factory, the Penthouse, and by the mid-1970s, a host of downtown beer parlours.

Figure 3.7 Bonnie Scott, a spectacular feature dancer in Vancouver, 1975

To her, the Smilin' Buddha and the Kublai Khan were 'too low class.' One of the few professional dancers with a disability, Princess Lillian had movie star aspirations.[44] Resurrecting the comic tassel twirling of Cleveland's Carrie Finnell in the 1920s, Lillian learned moves and gimmicks from choreographer Jack Card at Isy's: 'I had tassels, and I'd make them twirl like an airplane propeller. I used to have a snake in my show – a hundred and ten pounds. I played the drums and accordion on stage; I worked with a baton, I had a belly dancer costume, I did some Scottish dancing, I did a cowboy/Indian theme. I had a biker theme: leather and a whip. People LOVED my show. I was very Las Vegas, and my show was very classy. I was an entertainer.' Princess Lillian maintains that nobody knew that she was deaf: 'I had the music turned up loud, I danced to the beat. I was the first deaf dancer in Vancouver – the first and only. Some of my friends in the deaf community said I was awful and dirty, but they were just jealous of me.'[45] She began in 1968 and ended her career in 1987 at the age of thirty-nine.

In 1961, at age fourteen, Foxy Lady moved to Vancouver with her white, middle-class family from Copper Mountain, British Columbia. She remembers that as a child she would dance where people would see her: 'As a little kid I thought I was just the greatest little star. I just really loved dancing. Later I became a show-off dancer.' A graduate from Magee High School where she was a schoolmate of actor Margot Kidder, the rebellious Foxy Lady travelled for several years with a carnival before returning to clerical jobs at Office Overload. Launching her dancing career in 1971 at the age of twenty-four, and quitting the business twelve years later, in 1983, she was first promoted by Isy Walters as 'Salem from Damascus' then 'Yolanda Torrez from Spain.' Preferring Foxy Lady, or Fox , after a short stint as a go-go dancer she began performing 'nude, without pasties, but not bottomless' at the Zanzibar in her high school graduation dress 'cut down' by her Mom, a Home Economics teacher. A six-month gig as a house dancer at the Zanzibar followed: 'I had a show, "Black Magic Woman," which was a Santana song. I dyed my hair black, the girlfriend of a guy in the band made me costumes. She made me a thick gold belt with fringes hanging down between my legs. It was a fringe panel. Long gold gloves, a choker, gold lace-up boots, a black bra with little gold fringes. And then she made me panties and the g-string. Of course everyone had to have a g-string! Everything unhooked from the front. You could get all kinds of things up at the East Indian shops on Main, or at DressSew on Hastings – fringe, feathers, boas, ostrich plumes.' Foxy Lady became a feature performer at Isy's, the Cecil, the Marr, and the No. 5 Orange. In 1979, journalist Sean Rossiter voted Foxy Lady/the Fox 'one of the best' who 'stands out from the rest' in his long, admiring essay, 'They Call Her Fox,' for *Vancouver Magazine*:

> [Her] second act is pure glamour. Plus a touch of kink ... She comes out in a glittery outfit covered entirely in rhinestones. The underwear alone is worth $200 ... She seems to be doing an awful lot of sashaying back and forth in this blinding getup, swishing her chiffon wrap around ... Just then, she walks away from us, slides the wrap out of the way and you see what she has been hiding all along: the seat has been cut out of her dress! She is mooning the Room! It is too outrageous: this Mae West design original gown with the ass cut out of it![46]

Virginia grew up in London, England, the only child of white, middle-class parents – her father was a church minister. Once in Vancouver, she became a registered nurse but left the 'flipping long hours' and poor pay to explore hippie-dom and try something new. She was a twenty-four-year-old wife and mother when she entered striptease culture at the Barn on Granville Street in 1973. At the Barn, she recalls, 'I was a topless barmaid. You'd serve the steaks topless for the lunch crowd and then your music would come on and you'd drop everything, including your underwear, and you'd do a little number for an hour, then you'd slip back into your clothes and you'd either continue serving or work the bar.' Six months later, Isy Walters became her agent; cognizant of her preference for lunch-time slots, he booked her into Isy's Supper Club, the Factory, and the St Regis, Dufferin, No. Five Orange, Yale, and Cecil Hotels. Though her first audition was at the Kublai Khan, she did not feel safe in the East End clubs or hotels. In beads and long, wrap-around skirts, she was inspired by rock sensation Janis Joplin's 'Better Move Over' and 'Get Down.' For the three years she stayed in the business, she successfully juggled striptease and child care and found ample work in the flourishing hotel scene. Opting for style on a budget, she sewed sequins on T-bars and g-strings: 'The top one was red velvet with glass beads on it hanging down your leg. When I took it off, it had a triangle underneath – an extra layer to tantalize the audience before you took it off.' In 1973, an advertisement for the Factory in *Dick MacLean's Leisure Magazine* read: 'A continuous stream of strippers, and topless and bottomless dancers offer their parts for your viewing pleasure ... to assist the slower members of the audience, the lighting arrangement highlights critical areas of each girl's anatomy.'[47] Well aware of club owners' official expectations that strippers disrobe fully, Virginia shared her coworkers' discomfort with the trend to bottomless acts. At the same time, she strove to be approachable on stage, 'not a sex goddess or an ice queen,' and she found that this stance disarmed men because it was 'too familiar, like coming on to a daughter or a sister.' One downtown beer parlour left a lasting impression: 'The St Regis Hotel had a great big plate-glass mirror all along one wall and I remember seeing myself there. It was quite interesting because I had never thought of myself as sexy.'

At age ten, in 1967, Tarren Rae moved to Vancouver with her white, middle-class family – parents and older brother – from Lachine, Quebec. At sixteen in 1973, a high school dropout and survivor of unhappy foster care, she was serving pancakes at a downtown restaurant when club owner Gary Taylor spotted her on the street and promised her a job as a cocktail waitress at his show lounge on Hornby Street.

He invited me into the club, sat me down, and plied me with incredible amounts of liquor – 'Between the Sheets' [laughs]. After I was totally hosed, he says, 'Why don't you get up and dance?' 'Oh, all right, sure!' So I got up there and I danced, sort of. Then I got really pissed off. I felt totally manipulated. So I went back to Gary's as a cocktail waitress. Later, I realized I didn't need to waitress when I could have fun, hang out with the girls, dance, make better money, and not have to work my butt off. Within six months I was dancing.[48]

When she started exotic dancing in 1973, Tarren Rae stated that while some dancers glued fake pubic hair onto their g-strings, "No one was ever caught dead totally naked on stage. You might be naked as a go-go girl. But a stripper was a performer, an entertainer. You had lights, you had real music, costumes, and live bands to back you up.' Growing up with parents who were nudists, vacationing as a child at a nudist camp in Aldergrove, and sun-tanning at Wreck Beach as an adult, Tarren Rae was comfortable undressed. She described what made her act unique and popular: 'I was really good at gymnastics. I started really young, I was very flexible. I learned how to balance. Everybody did headstands at Gary Taylor's, everybody did splits, everybody did walk-overs. Strippers weren't doing that – they were strutting, barely touching the floor. So I took the two cultures and meshed them together. I had a lot of dance, theme shows like Star Wars, a Cabaret show, a Glen Miller show, and a girl hippie thing.'

Similarly to Tarren Rae, Shelinda left the white, middle-class comfort of her West Vancouver home at seventeen and moved to play guitar on the 'happening streets' of Kitsilano. She began waiting on tables at White Spot for a dollar an hour, and in 1974, at seventeen, she began her fourteen-year career with a seven-year stint at Gary Taylor's Show Lounge. Also like Tarren Rae, Shelinda was recruited by Taylor himself: free drinks, free cocaine, and a tripled salary were incentives he offered to seduce young prospects. 'All of his girls were under nineteen,' says Shelinda. As a house dancer paid by the hour, she worked fourteen hours a day, from noon to 2:00 a.m. To wind down after a long day, she hung out with friends from the business at the Music Room, an after-hours gay bar on Seymour Street. Like several other dancers in the mid-1970s, Shelinda aimed for a more 'natural, organic look' on stage, with no make-up, bare feet, leotards, nightgowns, and Danskin body suits. Later, she got bookings at the No. 5 Orange, the Marr, the Drake, and the Cecil Hotels, where she began to wear make-up and 'get some costumes together':

Costume makers went around with their wares. They'd come trucking in on payday, Saturday. I always made my own. I did buy one thing from Clyde [Dubois]. I've always been thrifty ... I couldn't see paying three hundred dollars for a bodysuit that I could make myself. Nobody but Bonnie Scott wore the big beaded gowns – no big headpieces, no beads. The most you would do was a gauntlet –a glove without a hand – up to the elbow, with matching choker, then costume pieces, and g-string: a whole accessorized outfit. We free-winged it. No props, no choreography. Each girl developed her own style. One thing I was admired for: I did not do repeated moves.

Shelinda studied ballet for a year as a girl, and while starting her professional striptease career she also took jazz dance classes at a dance school on Hamilton Street. There, she recalls, she learned special moves, including spins and stretches. 'I could do a high kick, and I'd have to make sure my shoe didn't hit me in the nose. I was very athletic ... a "healthy looking brunette." I'd wear my hair up, and it would come down on the last song.' Shelinda told me that she appealed to a white-collar crowd – the Cecil Hotel at lunch-time was full of polite, silver-haired businessmen. She says that she loved to make them stop and pay attention: 'What I did was sensual, never any blatant sexuality to it, like touching myself on stage, or making a move that looked like intercourse.' She maintains that she did not remove her g-string until the last song.

Born in Edmonton in 1949, April Paris was the eldest of eleven in a lower-middle-class, Irish-Canadian Catholic family. Seeking adventure, she moved to Vancouver in 1969 at nineteen to become a hippie, a vegetarian, a Buddhist, and a feminist. Buoyed by the 'love-ins' and 'be-ins' in Stanley Park, 'smoke-ins' in Gastown, revolutionary music, and the women's movement, she remarked on the exciting, heady times: 'You just assumed that people you met had left some non-happening place to come to where it was happening!' April Paris worked at Lifestream health food store at Burrard and West Fourth, hung out at Banyan Books, did yoga classes, rode her bicycle everywhere, forfeited television, and devoured jazz music. Like other 'hippie chicks' who embodied West Coast mellowness, she embraced a relaxed approach to dress that emphasized loose-flowing cotton and hemp, patchouli oil, and minimal adornment or artifice. In 1975, at the age of twenty-six, April Paris launched her twelve-year career as a professional exotic dancer first at the Crazy Horse pub – 'a very nice pub on Davie, very

Playboy-mansion style, soft furniture, low key, not tacky' – and then at Gary Taylor's, and the No. 5 Orange, Drake, and Marr Hotels. Like most other dancers, she was resourceful: 'I had blond hair down to my waist and nice tits … I worked my hair! The men would always yell "let it down." I'd get saris from the little Indian stores, I'd cover the bra cup, make my own g-strings. I had a sewing machine. I'd make satin pants or get a hat from the Sally Ann [Salvation Army] and improvise.'

Though she 'ran off to Italy to get married in 1977,' April Paris returned to Vancouver every year to dance for two months until retirement in 1986. Like other white striptease dancers who entered the business in the early to mid-1970s during the hippie era – including Virginia, Tarren Rae, and Shelinda – she eschewed the 'old-fashioned bump and grind' and in its place opted for 'artsy and innovative' routines that incorporated yoga, aerobics, gymnastics, jazz, and a 'free-flowing philosophy' of 'nakedness is beautiful.'

Reporting for the *Vancouver Sun*, Christopher Dafoe attended the 'businessman's lunch' at the Crazy Horse in 1976; his assessment of changes internal to the trade echoed comments by April Paris and others. Dafoe struck a philosophical note: 'Missing … are the tiresome bumps and grinds that used to be mandatory when clothing was shed on stage. The frantic and often hilarious gyrations of the old-time strippers have given way to the supple grace of gymnastics and the expressive movements of modern dance.'[49] Two years later, in 1979, freelance writer John Masters paid tribute to the fresh-faced 'New Strippers,' whose graceful moves to the music of Joan Armatrading and Chuck Mangione reflected their ballet, jazz, and gym training.[50] Masters added that their reputation stretched 'across Canada, south to Los Angeles, and, via sailors, to Moscow and Peking.' Even the welder-turned-erotic dancer played by Jennifer Beals in the 1983 film *Flashdance* embraced the trend to leg warmers, body suits, and aerobic fitness led by Vancouver's dancers.

April Paris was a house dancer rather than an 'agency girl,' in part because she had no interest in touring. She explained the concept of 'house' employment: 'It was like working at the post office, year after year.' She also distanced herself from her glittery, elaborately head-dressed predecessors:

The burlesque dancers – most of them were from the States – strutted. They always wore their heels, and lots of make-up, which was very strange. They had costumes they brought in steamer trunks. Bras with rhinestones and big t-bars that go up the hip and then you just flip them off and underneath you've got a g-string, which is just the little triangle with elastic up the butt encrusted with rhinestones. We felt that we had to get down there on our hands and knees on the hardwood floor. We couldn't do three or four songs standing up – we would get down on the floor in bare feet and stretchy Capezios – our Danskin bodysuits, and we would do our gymnastic splits, stand on our head. I was yogic, I could stand on my head – I was like a corkscrew. My head was there and my legs were swirling around. That was my move. You can't steal a move – that was your livelihood.

Cascade grew up in a white, upper-middle class, two-parent family in the tony Vancouver neighbourhood of Kerrisdale, the youngest of three. She attended a girls' private grade school, and in the context of trouble at home, she got pregnant at sixteen, 'had a baby when she was a baby,' and put the child up for adoption. Several years later, Cascade graduated from Point Grey High School, took courses at Langara College, and then dropped out and found work in the retail and service sectors – Fairweather's clothing, a telephone company, and Internal Revenue. In 1974 she applied to waitress at Gary Taylor's Show Lounge in the Castle Hotel when she met Taylor himself – 'a great talker who could sell a refrigerator to an Inuit!' Cascade never did waitress: the next night, coached by Taylor from the side of the stage, she began her five-year career as a dancer. In spite of the lack of formal dance training, she had some gymnastics, and she loved dancing with a live band to the tunes of Gino Vanelli and Dionne Warwick. As she recalls, 'The original Gary Taylor's had two stages, both were very small: If you did the splits, your feet were off the end. It was hilarious. You did your dance on the first stage, got dressed, walked over to the next stage, and there you went again, two songs on each stage.' Cascade stressed that what she did for an audience was 'erotic, not graphic,' hence distinguishing her approach from the trend to 'spreading' and table-dancing that had gripped the business by the late 1970s. She continued, 'I'd whip the g-string off during the last two or three notes of the last song. And that was it – ta-dah!' Gary Taylor's was so casual, Cascade noted, that she and other house dancers shopped at Ruby's consignment store for slips and vintage wear. Though she made less money than A-list dancers such as Bonnie Scott, Foxy Lady, and Princess Lillian (explored further in chapter 4), Cascade appreciated the job security, the lack of competition amongst dancers, the funky, low-cost wardrobe, and the latitude that allowed for the kind of wacky improvisation and artsy acts intrinsic to *The Gong Show* on television:

> The audiences at Gary Taylor's put up with anything. We had Little Mary, and she was tiny, tiny, about four foot ten. She had a ripped, second-hand robe from Ruby's. She had a broken cigarette hanging out of her mouth, she put her hair in curlers, she put cold cream on her cheeks ... Another time, she went up and lay down in a bathing suit and pretended she was sun-tanning. At the Number Five she came out as the unknown stripper with a paper bag over her head and got dressed – like the 'unknown comic.' Men in the audience didn't know if they were supposed to clap or not!

Cascade remembers the raid and closure of the Penthouse Cabaret in 1975, and the influx of dancers who scrambled for work at Gary Taylor's while avoiding the cops. Dancers were quickly absorbed into the pub scene – there was plenty of work in the downtown beer parlours, though Cascade and other dancers criticized the heavy-handed, 'big bust' on the Penthouse and its closure for almost three years. When she injured her back and could no longer dance, Cascade waited on tables in restaurants, never forgetting the standing ovations she had earned, the money she had made, or her sense of having belonged to one big, supportive family.

Born in Nelson, British Columbia, and raised in a white, upper-middle-class family in North Vancouver, Scarlett Lake rebelled against the stifling artificiality of suburbia where she saw her mother's unfulfilled life. She remembered her attraction to the promise of 'gritty stuff downtown where people were really interacting.'[51] Employed in garment factories and later at Eaton's department store, she began stripping at Isy's in 1976 after accompanying a boyfriend to the club. Stating that the nine-to-five grind felt like a prison to her, she danced on and off for six years, channelling her desire to be an actress into the strip trade in Vancouver, and later in Victoria, where she specialized in 'strip-o-grams.' Five feet tall, blond, and 'very curvy,' she adopted Rose Rogers as her stage name. Her signature costume was a 'drop-dead long velvet red gown with a rose choker.' Scarlett has a vivid memory of assembling her wardrobe:

> Isy had an office that was ten square feet. There was a little ladder attached to the wall that went up into a hole in the ceiling and you could climb

up to the attic where there was a whole bunch of costumes that different women had for sale. Isy was selling their costumes on consignment to new girls coming in to the business, saying 'If you find anything up there, bring it down and I'll give you a price.'

A seamstress who parlayed her skills into costume design, Scarlett mixed items she purchased from Isy Walters with pieces rummaged from antique stores that she dyed, trimmed or altered with an eye to 'making sure zippers were in places they weren't in ordinary clothes: sometimes they operated backward from where you would normally go. I had a pant-suit thing and it zipped down the side so the pants could just fall off in one motion.' Relishing the physical workout and being in good shape, Scarlett enjoyed being appreciated by customers who told her she was beautiful, had a fabulous body, and was a good dancer.

Also raised in a white, upper-class family, Jasmine Tea grew up in Montreal taking dance classes and clashing with her parents about her hopes for a professional dance career. Upon graduating from high school, she fled to Vancouver in 1978 at eighteen, where she began selling roses in downtown clubs and cafés. At the No. Five Orange Hotel, she sold a rose to a man who asked her to give it to a dancer on stage. Invited backstage by the dancer, whose hands were full of costumes, Jasmine Tea remembers thinking, '"Oh god, there's going to be needles sticking out their arms, there's going to be some pimp in there trying to hook me." Instead, I saw needles, but they were knitting needles!' Within the year, she began exotic dancing, first on the road in Squamish, then in Dawson Creek and Prince George. She danced in Vancouver hotels only sporadically, as she feared her parents would find out and disapprove. In Vancouver, she enrolled in modern dance and ballet classes, and yoga at Synergy studio. Caught up in the hippie zeitgeist, she hung out at Wreck Beach and lived in hippie houses. Her dream of the National Ballet dashed – 'my bones were too big and my turn-out wasn't good enough' – she choreographed her own original routines for small, cramped hotel stages like the one at Gary Taylor's Rock Room: 'I used to do the splits against the wall, backwards, and then go up into a handstand on the wall, and then go into a one-arm handstand in the splits. I took off an outer g-string with my one hand, while I was up on the other hand ... I danced hard, I liked to sweat, and I enjoyed the applause: it was my creative outlet.' Believing in dance as 'the most beautiful art form there is,' Jasmine Tea showed her audience 'another side of dance.' She developed a secretary set with a three-piece suit, eye glasses, and her hair in a bun. A regular customer at vintage and thrift stores, she made a raven costume from a black unitard. And, she reminisces, 'I had a tuxedo suit for doing the theme to *Peter Gunn* ... I danced a lot in ballet shoes and jazz shoes. I found that got me a lot of respect.'

Like Jasmine Tea, Bambi was born in Montreal, the youngest of three from a working-class, Anglo-Canadian family. At fifteen, she moved out, dropped out of school, and two years later in 1979 landed in Vancouver where she began a twenty-three-year dance career at the age of seventeen. A regular performer upstairs at the Penthouse for more than twenty years, Bambi remembered her start: 'I was getting into bars – I had the big boobs at fifteen – and I thought, "They're going to treat me like a slut, I might as well go out and make some money." So I started out as a topless bartender in a nightclub in Richmond.' Later, at Circus Circus, Bambi go-go danced in a cage with g-strings, pasties, and feather boas, and remembers thinking that it was like being on the TV set of *Hee Haw*. Her musical tastes depended on her mood – her favourites included AC/DC and tunes from the soundtrack of the film *Saturday Night Fever* (1977). As a house dancer at Circus Circus, she was accustomed to work shifts from 9:00 p.m. to 2:00 a.m., and 'party shifts' from 2:00 a.m. to 5:00 a.m. Though Bambi has always seen herself as shy and insecure, she noted that a primary motivation to enter the industry was her love of dance and her feeling that exotic dancing permitted her to 'explore the exhibitionist inside.' A bisexual who insists that dancing is work and 'not nearly as easy as it looks,' Bambi noted the substantial effort necessary to convince each man in the audience that 'he's the special one.' She compared today's 'A-girls' – 'they're under twenty-one,' have 'double-D tits,' and are 'pimped out by their agents' – to dancers in the late 1970s, who had significant licence to be themselves: 'There were a lot of heavier dancers back then, all real boobs, their own personalities ... and guys loved them. My girlfriend, Portia, she was big-boned on the bottom, but she had a class act.' A witness to myriad changes in the business since the late 1970s, and a survivor who 'drank her pay cheque away,' Bambi says she made attempts to leave the business and yet uncertainty about her future kept her dancing – part of the big Penthouse family – until 2002.

Born Anglo-Canadian in the Salvation Army Hospital for unwed mothers in Toronto, Shalimar was adopted at an early age by an older, middle-class couple and raised north of the city. She graduated from Catholic high school with honours and was a member of the school council, debating team, and cheerleading squad; but she also sold acid in the school's smoking corner. In 1982, after winning 'amateur night' at a strip club in Toronto, she moved to Vancouver and danced full-time for six years. At the Penthouse and local hotels – the Cecil, Drake, Marble Arch, Drake, Austin, and Zanzibar – she specialized in theme shows, using her gymnastics and jazz dance training to maximum effect: 'I could just stand there, look at you, drop and land in the splits.' Like Tarren Rae, Shelinda, April Paris, and Jasmine Tea, Shalimar combined her athleticism and dance background with her love of theatrics: she adored being on stage. 'I'd come out as Raggedy Ann in crinolines, bloomers, and little boots; I had a little pony and a teddy bear for one song, "Candy Girl," and I'd pull lollipops out of my pigtails and hand them to the audience.' I had another show where I'd dress up like a little girl and do a puppet show at the end with "Clyde the muff-diving monkey" – I got him from the Sears catalogue for fourteen ninety-nine.' She also used 'lick 'em and stick 'em' cardboard matches to light her nipples on fire. At the Wild Duck in the suburb of Burnaby, she enjoyed the stage with its brass railing and the businessmen in gynaecology row: 'I'd walk up to them and I'd grab their ties and, "Oooh, I love a man on a leash," and tie him to the bar and crawl away.'

Shalimar explained that she needed a minimum of six costumes and six shows because 'you're like a comedian, you can't tell the same jokes every day.' A believer in the old adage 'to make money you had to spend money,' she purchased some items from costume sellers in the early 1980s, including Nancy Campbell, Cleo Creations, Alexis of California, and Cashmere Gold, who had a shop at the booking agency Choice Entertainment. Many other items – black, stretchy dresses, silver lamé bodysuits, and catsuits with holes strategically cut out – Shalimar made herself. One of her floor shows was inspired by the *Rocky Horror Picture Show*, and she danced to hits from the rock band Kiss – 'Take Me to Your Captain,' 'Spaceship Superstar,' 'Night Flight to Venus' – as well as Aerosmith, Joe Cocker, and popular Canadian rockers Bachman Turner Overdrive (BTO). While she said it was incumbent upon all dancers to keep male customers entertained, happy, and booze-consuming – 'like women who worked saloons in the Old West' – she defined a headliner as someone 'serving at Hy's Steakhouse' and a 'B-dancer' as someone 'slinging fries at Martha's diner.' A headliner, she continued, 'had good music, good costumes, and a professional attitude. She was always on time, had a good body, kept it in shape, and didn't eat three Twinkies after her show.'

Racy Acts: Black Stripteasers and the White Imagination

In chapter 2, I argue that Vancouver's nightclub culture was stratified by socio-economic class and geography (West vs East), and by race (white vs non-white). Club owners and musicians encountered a balkanized city rooted in hierarchies; some benefited more than others from the spoils of erotic spectacle. In her book *From Mae to Madonna*, June Sochen argues that black female vaudevillians not only faced the whorish image associated with show business; the additional barrier of the colour line meant that dark-skinned women were rarely booked into shows.[52] In a similar vein, Linda Mizejewski notes that musical director Florenz Ziegfeld's 'Glorified American Girls [1920s–40s] were not supposed to be recent immigrants from southern and eastern Europe, hence not ethnic, dark-skinned, or Jewish'; Ziegfeld rewarded his (white) girls for not getting summer suntans.[53] In one way or another, Andrea Stuart argues, the showgirl has always been linked to racial difference, exoticism, the power of darkness, and corruptions of the blood.[54] In her book *Black Sexual Politics*, Patricia Hill Collins shows how Western science, medicine, law, and popular culture reduced an African-derived aesthetic of sensuality, expressiveness, and spirituality to an ideology about black promiscuity.[55]

Though not officially a striptease performer, African American Josephine Baker found success in Paris in the 1920s, 1930s, and 1940s as a burlesque entertainer. She was cast in the shows 'La Revue Nègre' (1925) and 'La Folie du Jour' (1926) at the Folies-Bergère as a 'tribal, uncivilized savage' from a prehistoric era. Consigned to anachronistic space, Baker was rendered intelligible and digestible to white voyeurs as an oversexed Jezebel.[56] Narrating the fantasy of the jungle bunny, while her show represented slavery, discrimination, and liberation,' she danced in banana skirt and feathers.[57] In other shows straight out of the racist minstrel tradition, Baker 'was a ragamuffin in black face wearing bright cotton smocks and clown shoes'[58] (fig. 3.8).

White dancers in Vancouver tended to regard the city's East End clubs as shady destinations that they generally sought to avoid. April Paris recalled that the East End clubs failed to shake-off 'that opium-tinged' connotation and seemed like 'dark and strange places' to her and other white performers.[59] Many black dancers, both locals and imports, were promoted as 'novelty dancers' who tended to work a tightly knit rotation of lower-end clubs – New Delhi, Smilin' Buddha, Harlem Nocturne, and Kublai Khan in the East End. In addition, some

Figure 3.8 Josephine Baker from the Folies-Bergère production of 'Un Vent de Folie,' 1928

worked in 'girlie shows' on the grounds of the Pacific National Exhibition (PNE). Alongside the merry-go-round, arcade, shooting gallery, and sideshows spotlighting the 'bearded lady,' 'half-man half-woman,' 'alligator skin boy,' and 'mule-faced woman,' stripteasers were main features.[60] In fact, the girl show had become a staple of the touring carnival and circus across North America, beginning in the late 1800s, and was showcased at the Chicago World's Fair in 1893.[61] A.W. Stencell notes that the hoochie-coochie dancers of the Far East (some from as far east as New York City) and 'the fairs' half-naked "savages" from strange distant lands (many of them local Black people) provided white Americans and Canadians with a grand opportunity for a subliminal journey into the recesses of their own repressed desires and fantasies.'[62]

Though girl shows at the Pacific National Exhibition were wildly popular on the East Vancouver fairgrounds from 1910 until the early 1970s, knowledge of who performed, who attended, and how shows changed in style and emphasis, is conspicuously excluded from the fair's official history.[63] At the same time, the exhibition was famous for nation-affirming spectacles such as the celebration of white, middle-class femininity in the Miss Vancouver and Miss PNE pageants (as well as for the use of the fairgrounds to process more than 8,000 Japanese Canadians who were evacuated from the coast of British Columbia in 1942).[64] For decades during Vancouver's PNE, impresario Isy Walters booked striptease acts and milked connotations of excitement and immorality, the risky and the risqué. Most of the striptease performers were older, brought up from the United States, near their career's end, or as Jack Card puts it, 'Hard-boiled, over-thirty-five women who had been in the business for years.'[65] In the 1950s and 1960s, when Walters sent local dancers to work at the PNE, Card recalls that they were most often black women for whom the carnival girlie shows presented a rare opportunity to 'get off Main Street.'

In the eyes of the vast majority of white Canadians (and Americans) in the postwar era, including Vancouverites such as Isy Walters, black stripteasers epitomized the lascivious sensuality and wild rhythms presumed natural to their race; at the same time, outnumbered by white dancers, they were construed as ethnic novelties.[66] Walters's dancers were often segregated in separate tents for the 'White Show' and the 'Harlem and Havana' show – white and black dancers did not share the exhibition stage until the late 1960s. As Jack Card recalls, patrons entered the 'Black Show' between the legs of a fifty-foot-high plywood cut-out of a black dancer, all the while tantalized by the lurid bleating of the carnival barker: '"The African Queen, DIRECT from the jungles of Africa! You won't believe your eyes. We can't bring her out here yet, but we'll bring her slave girls out," and behind there'd be the Nubian slave girls in chains, a thumping and a bumping.'[67] Della Walters, Isy Walters's stepdaughter, remembers that her father, 'a product of his times,' could be 'crass, quite coarse, and had racist ways. He believed that it was even nastier to go look at the black strippers than to look at white strippers ... there was more titillation.'[68]

Far from being an isolated episode, Walters's staging of the 'Black Show' was mired in a century-old tradition of showcasing the 'Other' in carnival performance.[69] And yet, the story of black bodies in carnivals is more complicated. Born in 1929, Choo Choo Williams grew up in the black community of Amber Valley, Alberta. Her father was from Texas, her mother was from Oklahoma, and they were part of the migration

Figure 3.9 Choo Choo Williams, featured at the New Delhi Cabaret. Advertisement in the *Vancouver Sun*, 19 May 1965

from the southern states by African Americans who had been promised free land for homesteading in Canada in the 1910s and 1920s.[70] After moving to Vancouver in 1948 to marry band leader and trombonist Ernie King, Choo Choo began a twelve-year dancing career (1954–66) as a professional showgirl, first at the New Delhi and the Smilin' Buddha nightclubs and later at the Harlem Nocturne, which she co-owned with her husband, from 1957 to 1968. Williams was initially inspired to launch her striptease career after witnessing other black dancers 'shimmy and shake' at Vancouver's PNE in the early 1950s. After the birth of her son, she looked for a job and unexpectedly found her metier: 'I went to the "Harlem and Havana" show and I seen these girls up there wearing these costumes and dancing and shaking. I thought to myself, "Gee, do they make money doing that?" I thought, "Well, jeez, I can do that!" I seen this girl named August May Walker and she was cute. So I went and got myself some work'[71] (fig. 3.9).

With little money to spend on training or lavish Vegas-style costumes and accoutrements, Choo Choo Williams sewed her own Carmen Miranda outfit and did the limbo to a Latin beat: 'I had a sewing machine, so I made a turban, sewed a bunch of fruit on top. I had a chiffon skirt with hooks on the front, I'd take it off and dance. I had a leopard costume, I had bras and panties with sequins and fringes in different colours – a red one and a flesh-coloured one. Fishnet stockings ... I was pretty good for a country girl who had no training. As I got older, I got bolder [laughs] ... I always liked music, and I liked dancing' (fig. 3.10).

Feeling that she needed a bit more confidence, she took dance lessons

Figure 3.10 Choo Choo Williams at
the Harlem Nocturne, circa 1964

with Leonard Gibson, Thelma Gibson's brother.[72] Running the Harlem
Nocturne – Vancouver's only black nightclub – was truly a family affair,
and husband Ernie King was her biggest fan: 'I used to like to watch
the show. I got a kick out of looking at her. She could shake it up! She
had some shake-up costumes! I wasn't jealous. She was being paid to
dance, and I was being paid to play the trombone, and I'm playing the
trombone on the stage above her and I'm keeping her in line!'[73] When
she finished her floor show, Choo Choo changed her clothes and either
worked on the cash or waited on tables at the club.[74] She also shared
the stage at the Harlem with other black showgirls, including Joanne
Howard, Carol Curtis, and Rosalind Keene.

At the same time that both Choo Choo Williams and Ernie King enjoyed a measure of fame in East End entertainment circles, each noted
that the doors to the West End's Cave Supper Club and Palomar Supper
Club 'were pretty much closed to them.'[75] Choo Choo ventured to the
Cave Supper Club only once: in 1955 she attended the performance of

her idol, Josephine Baker. At forty-nine, Baker performed in Vancouver at the Cave more overdressed than underdressed. Baker's status as an international legend assured her top billing on the nightclub's marquee, though it is likely that her performance stirred anti-black sentiment as her appearance in Vancouver came only a few years after singer Lena Horne was denied a room by racist proprietors at the Hotel Vancouver, the Georgia Hotel, and the Devonshire Hotel.[76] Importantly, Baker is credited with desegregating Las Vegas nightclubs in the 1950s by being the first black dancer to refuse to perform for a white-only audience.

Miss Lovie, who worked for ten years, from 1965 to 1975, was Vancouver's most successful black dancer. Born in Texas and raised in Chicago by a working-class single mother, Miss Lovie was a paediatric nurse in Seattle when she realized there was more money to be made as a professional striptease dancer.[77] She recalls her start in the business: 'I met another dancer, Tequila. She was the one that told me, "Girl, you don't need to be at that. Get out of there, you dance too good!" So, I started dancing in a little black and tan (mixed-race) club in Seattle, with Big Mama Thornton on the bill.' After seeing Miss Lovie's show in Seattle, Leo Bagry, owner of the New Delhi nightclub in the city's East End, recruited her to perform for him in Vancouver. By the time she moved permanently to Vancouver in 1964, she had developed an act for the New Delhi in which, bikini-clad, she sat on the floor facing away from her audience, rhythmically twitching the muscles in her legs and buttocks to the beat of numerous Conga drums. She explained her signature act:

> I made things happen with my body. I'd sit on the floor, I'd stick my legs up high, up above my head, and I'd make my butt pop. I made my buttocks work like drums through muscle control. I could move around the floor like a clock, in a circle. I did the splits. I used to do a lot of black light dancing, and I used to wear a lot of glitter all over my body. That used to be my thing: I glittered.[78]

Miss Lovie quickly became a regular feature at East End nightclubs, where she was advertised as 'the world's foremost exponent of Afro-Cuban dancing' and an 'Artist of Rhythm' inspired by the showgirls at the spectacular Tropicana nightclub in Havana.[79] An advertisement for the New Delhi Cabaret appeared in the *Vancouver Sun* newspaper throughout the late 1960s[80] (fig. 3.11). Here, Miss Lovie poses on the ground wearing a zebra-striped bikini top, fur anklets, bracelets, and

Figure 3.11 Miss Lovie in zebra-skin attire. Advertisment for the New Delhi, *Vancouver Sun*, 14 March 1969

ears. As with white racist projections on the black athletic bodies of American bodybuilder Carla Dunlap in the 1980s, figure skater Surya Bonaly of France in the 1990s, and American tennis stars Venus and Serena Williams, it was expected that Miss Lovie would exhibit a raw, animalistic physicality.[81] And like Choo Choo Williams and other black dancers, Miss Lovie found steady work in the East End night-clubs.[82] The Penthouse Cabaret was the only West End nightclub Miss Lovie worked; she remained one of the few black dancers to cross over from the East End venues, though by the early 1970s the Penthouse had lost some of its lustre. Resistant to bottomless dancing in the early 1970s, and insistent that she 'never took it all off,' Miss Lovie donned a belly dancer outfit one night at the Penthouse and started to sing: 'I was shaking like a leaf. I think I sang "Girl from Ipanema" or "Shadow of Your Smile." So I did twenty minutes of singing, and twenty minutes of dancing for a while.' Miss Lovie later returned to work at the Zanzibar strip bar, where she hired and coordinated 'the ladies' and the musi-cians until the club burned down in 1973.

Other black women who danced in Vancouver were packaged within the racialized category of novelty act. Miss Wiggles stripped to pasties and g-string upside down with her head on a chair. Lottie the Body was an American dancer who, like Miss Lovie, invented a repertoire based on Afro-Cuban music and movement. She was also known to have balanced a chair in her teeth, near-naked. A 'fierce performer' with a 'truck driver's mouth on her,' Lottie danced at a range of East End nightclubs.[83] In the documentary film *Standing in the Shadows of Motown* (2002), she described herself as 'one of the greatest exotic dancers in the world.' Uriel Jones, a Motown jazz musician and member of the legendary Funk Brothers, reminisced about Lottie: 'If she moved one cheek, there was a certain drum she wanted you to hit; if she moved her left foot you had to catch all of that stuff, plus keep in rhythm with the band.'[84] In a similar vein, Vancouver-based jazz drummer Dave Davies developed a special relationship with African American dancer Lawanda Page in the 1960s:

> She was a big black woman. She and I were tight, tight friends for years. She used to be a stripper in the New Delhi Cabaret amongst other places. She had an incredible figure in those days and she called herself Lawanda the Bronze Goddess and she did a fire act. She'd light her finger and go around lighting guys' cigarettes in the club. Then the lights would go off and she'd light up the tassels on her pasties and spin them like propellers, in opposite directions. It was wonderful. After the gig, Lawanda and I would go back to the Regent Hotel, which was a sleazy place on Hastings Street. We'd sit up all night and talk while she sewed beads in sequences. She was a real free spirit.[85]

Perhaps most notoriously, Mitzi Duprée, originally from Los Angeles, was a crowd favourite in Vancouver, across the province of British Columbia, and throughout Alberta. Beginning in the late 1970s, Mitzi dextrously sprayed ping pong balls and played 'Mary Had a Little Lamb' and 'Frère Jacques' on the flute with her vagina. Wildly popular and 'playing the police like a fiddle,' she disclosed that she went through 600 ping-pong balls a week doing five daily shows.[86] Klute recalls Mitzi and her act with fondness: 'She was not an amazingly gorgeous black woman, but she had this amazing talent. She was really good at PR: she'd get on radio stations after she was banned, and then the clubs would be full to the rafters. She'd have people laughing, in stitches, and having great baseball games with these ping pong balls.'[87]

Coco Fontaine was born in Calgary to working-class African Canadian parents, the eldest of four children. She began dancing in Calgary in 1968, moving to work full-time in Vancouver in 1973. Following the lead of other club owners who renamed their dancers, Isy Walters fabricated her stage name – Coco Fontaine – and a fictitious birthplace – Chicago – in order to manufacture a more exotic mystique.[88] Painfully aware that 'there were only certain jobs black women were allowed to get into,' Coco relates a pivotal conversation with her mother, who had also worked as a burlesque dancer with the Royal American carnival shows: '"Mom, I can be a chambermaid all my life. Or I can dance." And my Mom just laughed and said, "Okay, if you're going to be one, be a damn good one!"' Coco made some of her costumes with her mother's assistance. She added dusters – 'the see-through housecoat' that was a Jack Card trademark. She recalls with delight how she was coached by Miss Lovie for two months: 'Lovie was at the Zanzibar – she was the MC and singer, and she stuck up for me. She's a powerhouse! She was my idol. I saw her perform with her legs straight up in the air, she'd do the splits, she'd have her muscles twitching, first that part, then that part ... "Oh, I said, now *that's* an entertainer!"'

When asked whether she felt pressure to perform a primal, jungle-bunny routine, Coco laughed and said she didn't need to be told. She 'danced primitive' on advice from her father to 'do what they expect you to do, but beat them at their own game.' As a born-in-Alberta girl dancing to the beat of the supposed jungle, she remembers laughing to herself and thinking, 'Oh, god, you stupid fools.' With satirical parody disguised within their performances, black dancers clearly resisted racialized, sexualized expectations internally, at the same time that they staged them outwardly.[89] Some experimented with skin lighteners and hair straighteners to carve out real and psychic spaces within bump and grind, and in opposition to racist stereotypes of grinning, fat mammies and Aunt Jemimas.

Former Vancouver-based booking agent Jeannie Runnalls admits that 'a lot of nightclubs didn't want black girls,' and that it was 'harder for black dancers to get booked in the "A"-rooms.'[90] White dancer Tarren Rae adds that black dancers 'weren't as marketable.' She continues: 'Club owners were like, "drop one in there amongst the mix, but don't give me a whole line up. Don't give me two black girls, or two Chinese girls. Don't give me small tits." There was a lot of prejudice. There was a feeling about Lovie, "Okay, well, we'll have her once, but we're not going to have her back for at least a month or two or three."'Jazz pianist Gerry Palken adds that 'Black dancers were expected to be more erotic, more loose, do more things that supposedly would turn men on.'[91] Even in the 1970s when there were more stages than dancers to fill them, jazz drummer Dave Davies recalls that 'Most of the girls at

Isy's, the Penthouse, and Zanzibar that I played for were white, but down at the Hastings and Main Street strip, it was more a concentration of black girls.' Pressured by club owners, booking agents, promoters, and patrons, sometimes subtly, sometimes blatantly, black dancers tended to incorporate props, costumes, music, and make-up that fitted racialized and sexualized colonial tropes of African primitivism and hypersexuality.[92] The racist imagery and expectations routinely cast black women as tragic mulattas, comic maids, or jungle bunnies, and these narrowly defined roles constricted black stripteasers' power to perform unencumbered by white racist fantasies.[93] And yet Miss Lovie argues that being an African Canadian in Vancouver in the 1960s accorded her, and other black entertainers such as singer Ron Small and MC Teddy Felton, special status as a novelty. She reminisces: 'We were spoiled. Everybody wanted to be around you.' Far from making her feel tokenized, Miss Lovie says the attention made her feel 'wonderful.' Through her dancing she may well have mined an otherwise rare opportunity to celebrate Afro-Cuban traditions of dance and music.[94]

None of the striptease dancers of colour who worked Vancouver venues achieved the stardom enjoyed by some of their white peers, though as Choo Choo Williams commented, light-skinned or 'high yellow' dancers were more likely to reach higher heights than darker-skinned women. Working-class black dancers had difficulty purchasing super-expensive costumes, dance lessons, props, and promotional photographs. Even if they possessed the resources necessary to attain a career as a headliner, the colour line persisted, sutured into place by stubborn, racist beliefs about the 'nature' of black dancers and where they did or did not belong. Shalimar, a white dancer, was surprisingly frank about her racist view: "Black dancers were mouthy, they were arrogant, they had that very aggressive female attitude and it did not go over well. A lot of men like black pussy as a novelty and that's it.' Unlike Lili St Cyr and her white competitors, black dancers could never fully escape the imperative to act black, be black, and stay black in a white-dominated city.

Gawking at dancers of colour and white women who impersonated the 'Other,' white Vancouverites were reassured of their own normality and cultural dominance. Social boundaries between spectators and performers, the 'civilized' and the 'uncivilized,' were conserved; until major demographic shifts in the 1970s, the near homogeneity of postwar Anglo Vancouver was affirmed. Pre-existing racial and gender stereotypes were animated in the interests of showmen and booking

Figure 3.12 China Girl Revue at the Cave on Hornby Street. Advertisement in *Vancouver Sun*, 19 October 1953

agents who were smartly fluent in the common-sense, naturalized precepts of mass entertainment. Similarly, for decades, African American actor Hattie McDaniel, African American ballet dancer Raven Wilkinson, and African Canadian tap dancer Jenni LeGon were black women subjected to racist discrimination.[95] Before her death in 1952, at the age of fifty-nine, McDaniel had played more than a hundred maids, slaves, and cooks. And yet like McDaniel, Wilkinson, and LeGon, striptease dancers of colour refused the label of exploited victim. The first-person accounts of Choo Choo, Miss Lovie, and Coco, among others, reveal resilient subjectivities that both accommodated and exceeded the terms of white voyeurism.

Chinese, Latina, South Asian, and First Nations Dancers: More Absent Than Present

Despite the fact that so many nightclubs were located in and around Chinatown, no one I interviewed was able to recall more than a handful of Asian dancers.[96] In fact, when Asian dancers were seen in Vancouver, they appeared as part of a 'song-and-dance' show during the 1950s at the Marco Polo club in Chinatown, then later, 'direct from New York,' at the Cave and Isy's, as the China Dolls or China Girls Revue (fig. 3.12).[97] Many Chinese American women began their careers as nightclub entertainers in the chorus line at Forbidden City nightclub on the outskirts of San Francisco's Chinatown.[98] In 1969, Miss Sumi travelled with the China Doll Revue to Isy's Supper Club. Her act incorporated a gradual disrobing behind a Japanese shoji screen, her silhouette in plain view.

In spite of Vancouver's growing Asian Canadian population, few Asian women became professional stripteasers. Choreographer Jack Card claims that, 'There were a lot of oriental girls in the city studying ballet, in the dance schools, but their families didn't want them working nightclubs.' Like dancers Sen Lee Fu, memorialized as 'The Most Exotic Dancer of Them All,' and Noel Toy, billed as the 'Chinese Sally Rand' and 'Chinese Fan-Tasy,' the handful of local Asian Canadian women who found work in the business highlighted their exotic ethnicity in order to capitalize on their 'novel,' albeit limited, marketability.

Interview narrators tell of local Asian dancer Suzie Wong, who wore traditional Chinese dresses and used make-up to emphasize the shape of her eyes; Damien incorporated fans and jade ornaments into her act. Chinese Canadian Sean Gunn, who worked in the house band at the Kublai Khan, observed that the 'so called exotica' were Asian hostesses, the 'so called erotica,' the 'ubiquitous peelers and working girls,' were primarily white women, and the men in the audience were invariably Asian 'Caucasian-philes.'[99] Gunn also remembers that third-generation Japanese stripper Miss Sumi was the Kublai Khan's 'only token, bona fide, embodied culmination of the great mythological, Asian Canadian, exotic-erotic mystique, and thus, of course, naturally, the featured, marquee attraction'[100] on the city's East Side. Similarly, in the airline industry, carriers servicing Hawaii and the Caribbean began to selectively employ Latina and Hawaiian stewardesses to lend 'exoticized authenticity' to appeal to the increasing number of postwar tourists bound for these romanticized destinations.[101]

Sarita Melita was one of the few Latina striptease dancers to live and work in Vancouver. Originally from 'the war zone of east Los Angeles' and the eldest of nine children raised by a single, working-class Puerto Rican mother, in 1973 Sarita fled to Vancouver with her draft-dodging boyfriend and was granted landed immigrant status. She began dancing in local nightclubs and on the road in 1975 at age nineteen after years of poorly paid secretarial, service, and clerical jobs. She recalled that, 'In those days, you had to be blond, and you had to be white, tall, long legs, big boobs. I was exotic. I had long black hair, I had darker skin, I had a darker look – a Middle-Eastern look, and my look was not in.'[102] Like Coco Fontaine's mother, Sarita's mother – 'a mango in a white man's land' – had also been an exotic dancer. She had worked in Los Angeles; from her trials and tribulations Sarita learned that 'Hell would have frozen over before a black, Puerto Rican, or Mexican Hispanic woman was granted marquee status.'[103] In spite of similar economic and racial barriers to achieving her own headliner status, Sarita, like her mother before her, appropriated racialized signifiers for her own purposes, emphasizing her passion for dance and costuming, her Latin roots, and her physicality and grace of movement. She laughed when she recalled poking fun at customers who insisted she remove her g-string: 'They'd say "show us pink" and I'd say, "I can't because mine's not pink. Mine's all chocolate." And they were like, "Oh, well, show us the chocolate," and I'd say, "No, no, no honey. That I save for my husband."' Like Miss Lovie, Sarita experimented with body paints on stage:

> I put gold greasepaint all over my entire body, and with the Queen Nefer-titi costume I looked like an animated statue. I used authentic Egyptian music, it was haunting, and had very sexual rhythms. Then, I did a salsa, because I'm Puerto Rican – it was a tribute, and I did a *West Side Story* thing. I had a tight red ballroom-dancing gown, and I did a lot of mambo, rumba – it was music right from Puerto Rico – hot Latin music.

At the Penthouse in the 1970s, Sarita expanded her repertoire beyond her Puerto-Rican roots, yet was careful to play within the borders of racialized, sexual otherness. From the Hollywood tradition of images representing Latinos as inherently musical, she had learned to wear her 'sexualized identity for a white audience at the drop of a hat ... doing exactly what [she was] expected to do: singing and dancing the night away.'[104] Playing with the poetics of female impersonation, Sarita mixed her typically Latin acts with interpretations of black and South Pacific culture:

> Clyde [Dubois] made me a blue top hat and a blue outfit that was a Tina Turner funk thing – I wore gloves, and it was a tribute to black music and funk. I did a Polynesian dance – came out with full Polynesian regalia that they loved – no one else could do that. I did a Motown act: I came out with my hair teased up in a flute, with a gardenia in my hair, a black gown with rhinestone spaghetti straps, long rhinestone earrings, white gloves, white mules: it was all black and white, and on stage I did Diana Ross.

Other women of colour were neither exoticized nor misrepresented on Vancouver's stages: they were simply absent, unrepresented as spectacles of even the most graphically racialized sexuality. Interviews suggest that several Aboriginal women who danced in Vancouver had successful careers because they were, like Princess Do May, 'part-Native' and light-skinned enough to pass as white, and in the case of Tia Maria, to pass as Asian. Virginia remembered 'a handful of Native dancers in the 1970s, but they were always booked into the low-end hotels like the Balmoral.' The absence of Aboriginal women in strip-tease performance suggests that while colonial discourse cast them as thoroughly sexualized 'squaws,' as historian Jean Barman has shown, it rarely cast them as 'sexy' in the idealized, ultra-feminine sense of the term.[105] The fact that a biracial dancer's best chance of success lay in passing herself off as anything other than Aboriginal reveals the uniquely denigrated status of Aboriginal women's sexuality in a nation long-steeped in anti-Aboriginal discourse and practice. Decades later, reflecting on her short stripping career, Marissa Crazytrain noted that as a Cree woman from Saskatchewan she fit the stereotype of the 'Indian Princess' but chose, instead, to create a nationality for her dancer persona – half Malaysian and half Italian. She made it clear that she could not see herself 'coming out on stage dressed in a long feather war bonnet and buckskin bikini accessorized with black-light war paint.'[106] The racist disqualification of Aboriginal women from the (white) beauty regime, the widespread assumption that Aboriginal women were hookers not dancers, and the decades-long prohibition against First Nations men and women in bars (as either dancers or patrons), severely restricted the chances Aboriginal women had to earn the title of burlesque queen.[107]

Because only six women of colour were interviewed for this book, I asked white participants in the business of striptease to speculate about the relatively small numbers of non-white dancers. In the case of black women, for example, white narrators normalized the sparse representation by referring to the absence of blacks in Vancouver in general. In this case, ignorance of the black neighbourhood, Hogan's Alley,[108] and the larger African Canadian community in Vancouver props up assumptions that there were few black women in the business because black people simply did not live in Vancouver. For white narrators, it was likely easier to reference a 'non-existent' black community in the 1950s, 1960s, and 1970s than to reflect critically on how the idealization of white, sexy bodies (even those that staged 'exotic' otherness only to discard it at night's end) operated both to shape the appetites and desires of Vancouver audiences and to shrink opportunities for non-white dancers in the city.[109]

Researching women's work as showgirls in San Francisco, Lorraine

Dong found that the conservative Chinese community considered such work immoral.[110] Of course, Anglo-Canadian dancers also came from families that similarly stigmatized their profession. Whether or not Asian and South Asian women faced harsher prohibitions against careers in professional striptease than white women, the well-documented anti-Asian history of Vancouver suggests that Asian dancers may have had limited purchase before an audience beset with warnings of unassimilable 'yellow hordes' from the East.[111] White dancer Shalimar was vocal about her opinion: 'The typical Asian woman is a little, submissive woman with little boobs – a cute little girl, and men didn't want to watch that. The Asian men that came into the clubs didn't want to watch Asian women.' Again, for Shalimar and like-minded others, it was likely easier to accept racist caricatures of 'Asian pussy' (or 'black pussy') than to probe the social, historical, and economic factors that enabled white dancers' monopoly, with few exceptions, on beauty, glamour, and sexiness across the North American nightclub circuit. Klute recalled her unease concerning a double standard: 'I never saw Asian women strip. But the bathrobe of choice was the cheap kimono from Chinatown. It was weird – here are these white girls doing their little stripping and they're all in these tacky, cheap versions of geisha outfits. So we were all these little white geishas.'[112]

Hoochie Coochie Queers Work Terminal City

Postwar striptease in Vancouver (and other urban centres) was replete with expressions of sexual and gender non-conformity, as well as being a microcosm of racial and ethnic differences. For instance, the industry promoted the sale of (predominantly white) heterosexual lust, and yet queers were definitely afoot. Jack Card recollected that some of the most beautiful showgirls he knew were gay, as were many dancing boys with their bare chests and false eyelashes.[113] Former erotic dancers Maud Allan, Josephine Baker, Lili St Cyr, and Gypsy Rose Lee are rumoured to have had female lovers. Openly bisexual stripper Anita Berber danced in fashionable lesbian clubs in Berlin and Vienna in the 1920s.[114] In 1958, lesbian historian Lillian Faderman began stripping in California clubs to defray the costs of attending college.[115] In their 1965 study of women's prisons in the United States, David Ward and Gene Kassebaum quote a maxim of prison life: 'strippers and models are likely to be homosexual.'[116] In 1969, American sociologists James Skipper and Charles McCaghy interviewed thirty-five 'exotic dancers' who informed them that approximately 50 per cent of their colleagues engaged in either prostitution or lesbian activities.[117] And in 1971, Canadian researcher Marilyn Salutin stated that, according to her informants, 75 per cent of female strippers were lesbians – a figure she argued reflects 'an occupational contingency' born of an 'understandable contempt for men.'[118] Though the social scientific accuracy of Salutin's statistic is dubious, and only two of the former dancers I interviewed (Roxanne and Klute) were self-identified lesbians, most narrators witnessed substantial same-sex sexual experimentation in the 1960s and 1970s – a time of free love, 'swinging,' and non-monogamy for youth of all sexualities in the West.[119]

On stage, whether striptease dancers were lesbians or not did not seem to matter; they accepted the contract to appeal overtly and unapologetically to men's desire for enactment of sexual fantasies on men's terms. At the same time, all of the ex-dancers I interviewed spoke at length of the sexual control and empowerment they experienced on stage as they manipulated their own *and* their clients' sexuality for profit.[120] Bass guitar player Sean Gunn recalled a lesbian exotic dancer 'with attitude' at the Kublai Khan who was 'attended by her royal consort, a definitive study in pompadoured, butch-cake, grease lunch bucket incognito, enough to pass for just another good old home boy hooting it up with the best of the peeping-Tongs.'[121] Vancouver-based lesbian dancer Kitty Wells is fondly remembered for her elegant gowns, beehive hairdo, 'personality plus,' and ladylike behaviour on stage, until she baited her queer audience at the New Fountain Hotel: 'You wanna know why I call myself Kitty, Kitty?' She'd grab her crotch and say, 'Puss, puss, puss.'[122] Indeed, as they had at nightclubs in Harlem, Greenwich Village, and Coney Island during the Jazz Age, gay, bisexual, and lesbian dancers, choreographers, make-up artists, prop-makers, costume designers, wig-makers, and customers found a home in the business of striptease.[123] Some like Wells – channelling the comic brilliance of Fanny Brice in the 1930s – used her act to send up or spoof striptease, to decidedly queer effect.

Born in Vancouver of Russian, French, and Cree heritage, though she passed as white, Roxanne was raised in Edmonton and escaped her working-class, abusive home at sixteen. After several years of living on the street, she finished high school, dropped out of business school, and, after a series of poorly paid menial jobs, began her dancing career at age twenty-two in 1965. Roxanne entered the strip business as a topless waitress at the Barn, and then as a go-go dancer at the Vanport, a rough bar on the edge of Chinatown with a mixed clientele of working-class gay women and longshoremen: 'We were very territorial – this was our space. Once this little straight guy wandered over to hassle us and we ganged up on him and I beat him over the head with my purse. The club also had this great big guy sitting outside the women's washroom handing out the toilet paper and checking to see if the dykes were fooling around in the can.' Labelled a femme because she wore high heels, flounces, skimpy outfits, beads, wigs, and long fingernails, Roxanne felt ostracized by the politicized women's community because she entertained men. During her ten years of dancing in Vancouver, Montreal, Toronto, and San Francisco, Roxanne met few other lesbians in the business. She commented wryly, however, on the unspoken homoeroticism among women in a career so focused on female bodies, beauty, glamour, and sexiness: 'We'd watch each other's shows all the time. We liked looking at each other, and there were lots of elements of bisexuality or lesbianism in there [laughs].' While several of the women I interviewed had boyfriends who depended on them financially, Roxanne helped to support her girlfriend: 'My salary subsidized my lover's, and our household. It was harder for the butch women to get jobs because of the way they looked.' She felt lucky that her early lessons in Highland fling, tap, and ballet had helped her develop dance themes and routines.

Almost twenty years before the invention of 'Xena: Warrior Princess' on prime-time TV, Klute, a white lesbian dancer, successfully reworked themes from 'Conan the Barbarian' as an s/m dominatrix, and played with the fantasies of men who longed to be topped. She counted herself lucky as a lesbian because, 'What men thought of me didn't really bother me too much, because I did not have to have a personal relationship with any of these guys.' Born in Toronto, she began a striptease career in earnest in the late 1970s at the age of twenty-four; after five years of travelling and working across the country, including in the west, she packed it in to pursue her love of horses and wrought iron-sculpture. Klute recalls that she never fit the 'high femme, mega-feature look.' Instead, she played with gender ambiguity on stage and interrupted 'the chemistry that is supposed to exist between boys and girls in a strip club.' She remembers being ostracized by club owners for being too dykey at the same time that she was shunned, as was Roxanne, by the women's community for not being dykey enough. 'The assumption [among feminists] was that strippers were sex trade workers buying into the whole male system, the pornography system. And how could a righteous dyke do something like that? When I would go into the clubs, women would be very suspicious – they thought for sure I was a straight woman, spying.' To stay in the striptease business, and to thrive, Klute needed to invent her own crafty strategies:

> I had some classy, elegant Bob Mackie gowns, but I felt like a female impersonator in them. So, I did a Michael Jackson show, I did a Grace Jones show. I did fire shows – risky things you did not want to be high or drunk for. I had two large fans and I did a show under black lights so it looked neat. I had three sets of conga drums. I did a cowboy show – chaps and a g-string – that's a good look, but I perverted it by using Frank Zappa music, like 'Moving to Montana.' I did a military show in which I did really rude things to guns. And I'd come out in mechanics' coveralls and do rude things to ratchet sets.[124]

Scarlett Lake, a straight dancer, enjoyed watching other women dance: a favourite memory is of a woman known colloquially as the 'Bermuda Triangle,' dancing in the late 1970s at the Yale pub: 'She was a truck driver type, the butch type, and I remember seeing her doing her thing. She used to take this Eatmore candy bar, and she would stuff it in her while she was doing her act, and then take it out, throw it out to the audience. She was sticking it in their faces. She had this giant cavern and everything near it would disappear. She would hold her parts wide open and move all the way around the stage, so that everybody could have a good look up inside. She was definitely a lesbian, probably a bit of a raging one, but one with a great sense of humour and personality. She was a white trash type, and her girlfriend was usually there in the bar with her. She was hilarious.'[125] Indeed, this lesbian's anti-assimilationist tactics foreshadowed the guerilla-style, direct action mandate of Queer Nation members across North America in the early 1990s.[126]

A small group of ultra-feminine female impersonators, most of whom were gay men, found a home in the business. Some were male-to-female transsexuals who successfully passed as bona fide stripteasers on stage in the 1950s and 1960s as sexy girls in full view of adoring (straight?) male fans. In *Girl Show*, A.W. Stencell claims that, 'Gays were often found in 10-in-1 side shows doing the half-man/half-woman act and working in drag on carnival girl shows. Many of the dancers who worked gay cabarets during the winter went with carnival shows in the summer ... it was a safe world where you were judged only on the job you did.'[127] After her highly publicized gender reassignment surgery in Denmark in 1952, American ex-soldier Christine Jorgensen became a popular singer and sexy nightclub star – she performed at Vancouver's Cave Supper Club in 1956. Hedy Jo Star was a male-to-female transsexual who enjoyed a successful striptease career and later owned a touring carnival in the United States.[128]

American Jaydee Easton, a female impersonator in the 1950s, flashed in drag by looping her penis with an elastic band, attaching it to a small rubber ball, and inserting it into her anus.[129] Other female impersonators such as Jackie Starr performed as female erotic dancers in straight nightclubs and gay cabarets until the 1970s, when full nudity in strip clubs made male-to-female drag virtually impossible.[130] Starr, who replaced an ill Gypsy Rose Lee several times on music hall stages in New York in the 1940s, was the top headliner at the Garden of Allah in Seattle for ten years. In Montreal, transvestites Lana St Cyr and Lili St Clair polished their striptease routines in the city's nightclubs throughout the 1950s and 1960s.[131]

Butch lesbians in postwar cities were unlikely candidates for professional striptease, given their penchant for breast-binding and men's clothing, hairstyles, cologne, and shoes. However, some became singers and masters of ceremonies in the 1950s, 1960s, and 1970s. Talented 'drag artistes' like Blackie – a popular figure in New York's Greenwich Village – impersonated men on nightclub stages and dazzled female fans, both straight and queer. [132] Others were fans who accompanied their femme lovers to nightclubs, or attended floor shows in the company of queer friends. In 1965, Tom Hazlitt of Vancouver's *Province* newspaper commented, 'The city's cabarets are crowded with bottle-packing juveniles. Drunkenness and fights are commonplace. So is drug addiction, prostitution, and erotic dancing of a bizarre nature. Some places are frequented by men who dress up as women and women who dress up as men.'[133] Reminiscent of Berlin's pre-fascist, above-ground queer cabarets in the 1920s and 1930s, nightspots in the city's working-class East End became home to gender and sexual outlaws.[134] Not only did sexually marginalized communities, including sex workers, share a sinful pathology in the expert and popular imagination, but they also shared an urban geography – an area in many cities designated as the locus of the sexual underworld.[135]

Just as dancers of colour were more likely to work the East End stages in the 1950s and 1960s, female impersonators and male-to-female transsexuals, or 'sex changes' as they were called, worked as striptease dancers in the same cabarets. Immersed in the world of live performance, many pursued a transition to female gender identity through breast implants, hormones, electrolysis, penile tucking, and, on occasion, vaginoplasty. In Vancouver, Princess Lillian remembers a male friend in the business who had a sex change in Japan for $9,000: 'She looked perfect. She looked like a real woman. She was a dancer. She danced in bathing suits and g-strings, and then she got married and adopted kids.'[136] Daquiri St John was a female impersonator and, according to MC Ron Small, a well-known stripper. Musician Doug Cuthbert played in the New Delhi house band: 'There were a lot of loggers in the East End area. They'd see shows, pick up drag queens turning tricks and doing floor shows. The New Delhi seemed to be controlled by the drag queens, and some of them were strippers, some had sex changes. Linda Crystal and Sandra Taylor were two female impersonators that come to mind. Nobody really knew. The only thing you could tell was the curves weren't quite real.' Musician Mike Kalanj chimed in: 'We learned pretty quick down there at the Delhi. We'd look at the arms, the hands, the Adam's apple, if they had implants, if they were going through electrolysis. But I don't think a lot were changed down below.'

Booking agent Jeannie Runnalls represented several transsexual dancers: 'At Isy's, one of my dancers was a sex-change called Goldfinger. He had it lopped off, he was all painted gold and he was six foot three with silicone implants.' Before full nudity was decriminalized and mainstreamed in hotel beer parlours, female impersonators (whether or not they invested in surgery and hormone treatments) perfected striptease routines that traded in the standard tricks of mystery and illusion.[137] Jazz musician Dave Davies remembers a transvestite exotic dancer, Zsa Zsa, at the Smilin' Buddha: 'There were a lot of sailors because it was that part of the city. Zsa Zsa would come out. He'd be really decked out and he'd do a real thing. And then he'd get a chair and place it in the centre of the dance floor and he would start sitting in the chair and flipping his legs up. Then he'd go over and grab one of the sailors and sit the sailor on his lap and start necking with him. And then at the end of the routine, Zsa Zsa would rip off his bra, and of course he was a guy. He'd take the guy back to his chair and sit him down, give him a peck on the forehead and that was the end of that routine.' Perpetrating the hoax of the century, to quote musician Sean Gunn, was the female transvestite performer at the Kublai Khan nightclub who dazzled a 'totally unsuspecting, homophobic male audience ... through the surreptitious application of a generous dab of glue liberally spread onto the underside of a furry, cod-piece, pastie.'[138]

As former dancer Foxy Lady recalled, 'Liz Lyons was an emcee. She was in her sixties, she had a sex change way back. She called herself the "Phyllis Diller of Burlesque." She'd come up from the States for a booking at Isy's and stay six months. She'd get to know all the dancers and introduce us. She was really popular – I don't think people knew she was a sex change. She wore her hair up, had lots of costumes, she'd wear a big boa, she was fat, a big sort of funny body.' Roxanne also recalls meeting gay men, drag queens, and sex changes – some of whom were professional strippers – at the New Fountain, another rough-and-tumble pub frequented by longshoremen and queers in the 1960s: 'The [male-to-female] sex changes were different then,' she remembered, 'because they were the experiments. They would be so proud of their sex change that they would take us into the cubicles in the women's washroom and show us.' In the process of gender transition, male-to-female transsexuals had supreme difficulty finding paid work anywhere, and were vulnerable to violence on and off the street.[139]

For many trans women, erotic entertainment offered one of the few relatively safe, supportive enclaves to make a living.[140] Male-to-female transsexual Tricia Foxx performed as a gender illusionist at BJ's cabaret, a gay after-hours speakeasy on West Pender Street (near Main Street) in the 1970s: 'I did impersonations of Liza Minelli, Bette Midler, and Cher. We also did Las Vegas-style revues with costumes, lots of lamé. I would strip down, though not completely naked. I had little pasties, little breasts, and a g-string ... You didn't want to show all the goodies. I had a very good tuck'[141] (see fig. 3.13). In nightclub dressing rooms, Goldfinger, Daquiri, and Sandra learned from biological women the intricacies of 'doing' sexy femininity and making themselves appear hetero-desirable. Poet and novelist Peter Trower observed the colourful patrons inside the New Fountain in the 1960s through the eyes of his fictional straight man Terry Belshaw: 'The customers were mostly women, some of them in black leather jackets and ultra-short haircuts and making no secret of their sexual preference. I recognized Mitch the Witch with a smashing brunette. He acknowledged me with his decadent choir boy smirk. On tighter scrutiny, I saw that his seemingly-female companion was a man in drag.'[142]

The presence of lesbians, gay men, bisexuals, and trans folks inside the striptease business in Vancouver and elsewhere unsettled the naturalized presumption that nightclubs were incontrovertibly heterosexual milieux. To retired performer Tricia Foxx, 'the entertainment culture, historically, has always been close to what we call gay culture ... We

Figure 3.13 Gender illusionist and performer Tricia Foxx, at BJ's cabaret, 1981

were like-minded communities that shared.'[143] Acting out moments of what philosopher Judith Butler calls 'insurrectionary queerness' inside nightclubs and at outdoor carnivals, queer performers, staff, and fans subverted the hetero-normative imperative; trans performers transgressed the rigid gender binary of masculine men versus feminine women.[144] On-stage duos – two women who danced together – served to 'double the pleasure' of male customers in the late 1970s and early 1980s at the same time that 'lezzie spreads' became popular in *Hustler* and *Penthouse*. However, faking lesbian desire on stage to lubricate men's arousal was one thing; announcing one's authentic lesbian identity and signalling one's unavailability to male customers was another thing altogether.

In spite of the emergence of feminist and gay/lesbian social movements that championed an 'out and proud' visibility in the mid-1970s, it was safer and more lucrative for lesbian and bisexual dancers to stay in the closet at work.[145] Gay and lesbian culture in Vancouver was under siege in the 1970s: the *Vancouver Sun* refused to print an advertisement from the Gay Alliance towards Equality (GATE), gay nightclubs were routinely denied liquor licences, and club-goers faced hard-nosed police surveillance and harassment.[146] Most queers in the striptease industry sought the same subterfuge that had sheltered Hollywood he-men Rock Hudson and Raymond Burr for so long.

Playing the Striptease Game

In 1957, French theorist Roland Barthes published 'Striptease,' summarizing what he saw: 'We see the professionals ... wrap themselves in the miraculous ease which constantly clothes them, makes them remote, gives them the icy indifference of skillful practitioners, haughtily taking refuge in the sureness of their technique: their science clothes them like a garment.'[147] Though Barthes grudgingly acknowledged the science, skill, and professionalism of striptease dancers, he also articulated a jaundiced, one-dimensional view of dancers that confined them (all) to caricature. And yet, rather than seeing themselves as remote, haughty, or coldly indifferent to their careers or their customers, both the white and the non-white dancers I interviewed emphasized a passionate commitment to their craft, an irrepressible love of dancing and music, and complex relationships with fans, lovers, and co-workers. Notwithstanding the significant differences among dancers sketched above, or the hazardous character of their work (examined in chapter 5), each woman spoke of the power of performing, the ways that dancing elevated her self-esteem, and her sense of pride in putting on a good show. For dancers, satisfying themselves, bosses, and patrons was never easy; it was contingent on physically, creatively, and emotionally demanding *work*. To augment their marketability, light-skinned dancers of colour made efforts to pass as white; male-to-female transsexuals passed as female; queer women passed as straight; small-breasted women passed as buxom. Manipulations of illusion, disguise, closetry, and surgery permitted some dancers a provisional approximation of iconic, white, hetero-feminine sexiness, thus the promise of bigger paycheques and greater notoriety.

The late 1970s heralded a raft of changes that forced dancers to adapt or depart. By 1980, Isy's Supper Club, the Cave, the Palomar, the Penthouse, the Smilin' Buddha, the New Delhi, the Kublai Khan, and the Harlem Nocturne had closed, stopped booking dancers, or, in the case of the Penthouse, fallen on hard times. The emerging coterie of male club owners at the city's beer parlours-turned-stripclubs introduced poles and showers on stage; dancers faced intense pressure to do 'split beavers' or 'show the pink.' In chapter 4, dancers reflect on their salaries, working conditions, touring schedules, relationships with co-workers, and the unstoppable McDonaldization of their trade.

Plate 1 Becki Ross outside the Penthouse Cabaret, Vancouver, June 2000

Plate 2 Showgirls in the revue 'Viva La Roma,' Isy's Supper Club, 1966. Program cover

Plate 3 Neon signage for the Smilin' Buddha Cabaret, 109 East Hastings Street, Vancouver

Plate 4 The Penthouse Cabaret promoted its 'Topless Exotic Dancers,' 1975.

Plate 5 Suzanne enjoys a bubble bath onstage, 1982.

Plate 6 Jane Jones perfecting her fire act in Vancouver, 1994

Plate 7 Barbara Ann Scott, Canadian Olympic and World Figure Skating
Champion, Maclean's magazine, February 1948

Plate 8 Dan Murphy expresses his displeasure at the insulting decision made by the Breast Cancer Society of Canada to refuse the exotic dancers' donation, 11 February 2007.

Diamond Minx

Plate 9 Diamond Minx, Vancouver-based neo-burlesque dancer, channels fan dancer Sally Rand, 2008.

4 'Peelers Sell Beer, and the Money Was Huge': The Shifting Conditions of Selling Fantasy

Men are the ones who paid our salaries. Men are the ones who told us when to jump and how high. But we were the ones who controlled that twenty minutes on stage. We did five shows a day – that kept me in shape. You might have an hour and a half between shows. We'd hang out, read, knit, watch soap operas, talk, go out, visit with a boyfriend or girlfriend. Six days a week, Monday to Saturday. You'd want to get your last show at 11 p.m. so you could go out and party at an after-hours club.

Tarren Rae, Interview, 2000[1]

In the early eighties, the clubs got into this mega-quick buck, shaky-shaky, wet t-shirt shit. All these bimbos and rocker girls came in: big hair, spandex dresses, silicon boobs, high heels and leg warmers – the Flashdance thing. All of a sudden it's six girls, twenty bucks a show, not two girls for fifty. A lot of girls went down to a couple of costumes and a couple of tapes thrown together. They cheapened the industry by taking away the pride and the showmanship. It all deteriorated. The big shows were too costly. So girls wandered around the stage in high heels saying, 'Look, I have a pussy. Oh, it's winking at you.'

Shalimar, Interview, 2000[2]

Commercial striptease venues in postwar Vancouver were diverse in location, clientele, and style. In this chapter, ex-dancers' recollections are textured by lively memories of working conditions, including club interiors, pay scales, travel, and the transition to brass poles, showers, and full nudity on stage. Though wages rose steadily, dancers' income varied, as did the quality of dressing-room and performance space, lighting, music, food services, promotion, and treatment by management and staff. By the early 1970s, dancers found themselves negotiating with agents who scheduled their bookings on 'the circuit' around the province. Like all service workers, dancers developed relationships with co-workers and patrons, some good, some bad. The promise of a financial windfall motivated dancers to choose striptease over other pink-collar jobs that entailed their own messy mixture of hardship and reward. Dreaming of stratospheric earnings, cross-over Hollywood status, and the notoriety garnered by a handful of white American 'queens,' stripteasers came to appreciate the lucrative nature of the work, as well as the freedom they exerted as independent contractors. This job, they insisted, was like no other.

'Ladies and Genitals, Let's Tickle Your Pickle, Heat Your Meat, and Pop Your Cork'[3]

A showgirl at the State Burlesque Theatre from 1946 to 1952, Nena Marlene remembered that Vancouver was the only place that had a true burlesque venue: 'Calgary was a cow-town, Edmonton was nothing, Victoria was dead. But Vancouver's State was the hub.' She also recollected that 'the State was beneath many entertainers,' but she loved to entertain there because she was well paid and her working hours allowed her to care for her sick mother.[4] Relegated to dressing in the State's basement while the big stars had private dressing rooms upstairs, Nena Marlene and other chorus-line dancers worked with American-born Karen Due Varney (the wife of the MC, Jack Gordon), who put the dances together and sewed the costumes for the theatre's shows (fig. 4.1)

Across the city on Georgia Street in the West End, Isy's Supper Club was renowned for interior walls covered with black-and-white photographs of famous stars, a live orchestra, a big stage, plush velvet curtains, an in-house light man, and a choreographer, Jack Card. Foxy Lady has strong recollections of Isy's, initially as a teenager and later as a dancer: 'I first went to Isy's with my parents to see Mitzi Gaynor. Years later when I worked there, we all had dressing rooms up there like the old times: lights, mirrors, and we'd sit up there at the big dressing table. You'd get your place for the week and that's where you put your make-up on. You always got paid on time. Isy would bug you if he thought you weren't looking good. He'd say, "Oh, you're getting too chubby," or "I don't like you with that hair." He'd call you into his little

Figure 4.1 Nena Marlene was a 'State-ette' at the State Burlesque Theatre, circa 1950.

office right behind the bar.'[5] Isy's was Bonnie Scott's home base, and Isy was her mentor. The club was 'old school' – a large pit with tables and chairs, a runway, and carpeting on the floor. As Scott reminisced, 'I'd work at Isy's for six weeks or eight weeks and then I'd go out of town for a little stint and then I'd come back, work for another six or eight weeks, and I'd go out of town for awhile, then I'd come back. Maybe I'd go over to the Penthouse for a month.'[6]

Throughout the 1950s and 1960s, the Penthouse on Seymour Street was an after-hours bar that specialized in Las Vegas-style entertainment packages. Bonnie Scott appeared regularly at the Penthouse: 'It was a really nice club in the old days because they used to have the burlesque theatre downstairs, and upstairs they had a restaurant. They had working girls there and they had a lot of rounders.' In the late 1960s, Miss Lovie was hired by Joe Philliponi at the Penthouse: 'He was a sweetheart. A little cheap, but you had a good band, good lighting, they always fed you – that's where they made up the difference.'[7] By the

mid-1970s, before the Penthouse was raided and shut down by Vancouver's morality squad in 1975 (detailed in chapter 2), the consensus
among dancers was that the club had commenced its downward slide.
Critical of the place and the staff, Tarren Rae did not pull any punches:
'They didn't pay very well. Joe would pull out his old mothy cigar box
and pay you out in dollar bills. It was just gross ... I didn't like working
there. It was all kind of moth-ridden, sort of seedy, with hookers in the
audience.' In the 1970s, Shelinda remembered that the Penthouse 'was
a little slice of history that stood still in time. The business was evolv-
ing, but the Penthouse had "Miss So-and-So" from the States who had
done the same act for who knows how long, with the big props and
costumes.'[8] In October 1974, columnist Jack Wasserman crowned Joe
Philliponi the 'last centurion guarding against complete nudity ... an
anachronism in these permissive days.'[9]

While many white dancers steered clear of dates at nightclubs in
the working-class district of Chinatown/Main Street, African Canadian Miss Lovie performed regularly at the New Delhi Cabaret and
the Smilin' Buddha. She remembered that the Buddha's owners displayed a large photograph of her clad in a zebra-skin bikini in the club's
window, and kept it there long after she retired from dancing. In the
late 1950s and early 1960s, Choo Choo Williams 'shook it up' at the
New Delhi, the Smilin' Buddha, and at the club she operated with her
husband, the Harlem Nocturne: 'We got a lot of American sailors. Any
time a battleship came in, all the sailors would come to the Harlem.
They'd be in port for three or four days.'[10] Though they suffered police
harassment and liquor-related fines at 'the Harlem,' Choo Choo said
that business was good on weekends: 'It was crammed like sardines.
The little dance floor would hold about fifty people, and it was crowded. The joint was jumping! Friday and Saturday it was leaping! We
were licensed [for food and entertainment] for a hundred, but we sometimes had two hundred in there.' She added that both black and white
customers came for the food, the limbo dance, the floor shows, and the
'rhythm and blues' (see fig. 4.2).

Former headliner Tarren Rae recalled performing for boisterous
crowds of stomping, whistling women at working-class pubs in the
Vanport Hotel and the New Fountain Hotel, two of Vancouver's renowned gay nightspots in the city's East End.[11] She left the stage one
night, 'dancing to "Rock the boat, don't rock the boat, baby," and after,
this woman came up to me – a big biker and a total dyke. She grabbed
me by the arm and pulled me over. She said, "You're going to have a

Figure 4.2 Choo Choo Williams, inspired by Carmen Miranda, at the Harlem Nocturne, circa 1965

beer with me, aren't you?" I said, "Oh, oh, oh … yes!" I went backstage, grabbed my costumes, and left. But I actually liked working there. I felt if I could impress that audience, it was more of an achievement. I thought the women were more appreciative of dancers … Women are harder to please – you have to entertain them.'

Musician Gord Walkinshaw has vivid memories of accompanying striptease dancers at the Vanport Hotel in the 1970s: 'The lesbian joint was the Vanport Hotel – a real serious dyke, prison guard, truck driver bar. I used to play there with a duo. I had a drum machine. All the girls had duck tails, pretty tough looking, cigarette packs. Once in a while some goofy guy would wander in and ask somebody to dance, but he'd be pushed away.'[12] Like Tarren Rae, Coco Fontaine worked as a dancer at the Vanport: 'Isy put me in the Vanport, in Chinatown. And I said, "Okay, cool, I'll dance there." The longshoremen were in there. It was a rough bar. I watched two fights when I was there, and they were drag 'em out, knock 'em down types. One butch woman against a longshoreman, and she won! If you went in the afternoon, it was kind of the feminine side. After five, it was very, very rough.'[13] Barred from entry to 'Eveless' (men-only) beer parlours in the 1920s, and confined for decades to the partitioned 'ladies and escorts' section, erotic dancers became hot commodities for hotel beer parlours in the early 1970s.[14] Inside the often dank, dark, and smelly caverns, dancers were forced to scale down their acts to fit stages that were small, sometimes dirty, roughly assembled, and poorly lit. The gymnastically endowed Tarren Rae remembered that the stages at Gary Taylor's Lounge were not much bigger than the tables. She laughed as she conjured up one memorable routine: 'I'd start at the top stage and do a walk-over to the second stage. One time I landed on my heels wonky and I shot backwards. I've only got my g-string on and I ended up right in this guy's lap!' Before hotel pubs were pressed to undertake major renovations in the late 1970s, few had adequate dressing rooms. At Gary Taylor's, recalled Shelinda, dancers used the women's washroom: 'Imagine fourteen girls in a two-stall bathroom!' By the mid- to late 1970s, live musicians and MCs had been expelled from the clubs, and dancers were initially expected to supply their own tape-recorded music, though DJs later took over. Cascade was not the only frustrated performer:

I worked at Gary Taylor's, and at the Number Five Orange. I also worked at the Drake but there were fleas in the dressing room, and the Cecil before it was fixed up was nasty – you had to flip on your own lights, there was indoor/outdoor carpet on the stage, the tape deck was right on the stage and every time your bent over you'd hit your butt on the tape deck.[15]

Foxy Lady referred to her debut at the Cecil Hotel (fig. 4.3) as horrible: 'They didn't have a proper stage. And they had an old eight-track tape-player and the thing got stuck.' When the No. 5 Orange Hotel opened near Main and Powell Streets in the mid-1970s (fig. 4.4), dancers were drawn to its 'Mom and Pop-shop' character. April Paris offered a commonly held observation: 'The Brandolinis ran it like you were their children. They renovated and had a good stage with a staircase, plexigass, lights, a real good dressing room with showers and towels provided. It wasn't the best money, but it was a family operation. You could suntan on the roof, bike to work, go for crab at the Only's during your break.' By contrast, on the lowest register of the 'C-scale' was the Cobalt Hotel, also on Main Street. Shelinda had a miserable time there; it gave her the creeps long after she refused to return. As she explained, 'The stage was

Figure 4.3 Cecil Hotel, Showroom Pub, Seymour Street, Vancouver

small, in middle of the room. The dressing room was big, but dirty and grungy. I remember I was at the counter, and I felt something on my leg. I was going to swipe it off and I realized it was a cockroach running up my leg.' Similarly, Shalimar was struck by the Cobalt's poor pay, compounded by the vermin factor. She spat out her critique: 'Seventeen dollars a show was garbage. It was the scummiest, most horrible and most disgusting, cockroach-infested place. We'd sit there and throw our high heels at the walls to see who could hit the most cockroaches.'[16] April Paris recalled the working conditions in many small hotel pubs, including dangerous nails in the stage, unclean poles, and dirty carpets from which dancers routinely acquired rug burn and infections.[17] In spite of the serious limitations of 'C-grade' hotels, there were other benefits that the expanding hotel scene supplied. As Foxy Lady explained, 'One good thing: when the pubs opened up, you could work days if you didn't want to work nights, or you could work doubles – the pubs during the day, Isy's at night. The work wasn't seasonal, it was all the time. And you always had bigger crowds on the weekends.'

Figure 4.4 No. 5 Orange Hotel, Showroom Pub, Main Street, Vancouver

Money: Making It and Spending It

Whatever the working conditions, the promise of a big-figure pay-cheque was an attractive incentive to all women who undressed for a living. When American headliners Sally Rand, Gypsy Rose Lee, Ricki Covette, Lili St Cyr, and Tempest Storm performed in Vancouver during the 1950s and 1960s, they netted top price – upwards of $5,000 per week even after they turned forty.[18] Blaze Starr earned $60,000 one year. While most female service workers were paid low wages, earning 57 per cent of what men earned doing similar work, only a small number of women in corporations and in the professions of law and medicine matched the incomes of white features following World War II. Like prostitution, striptease was so removed from the dominant culture of respectability and gender-appropriate roles that dancers' wages were not as depressed as those of mainstream working women.[19] By rejecting the requirements of respectability and propriety, they commanded better-than-average salaries as compensation for their transgression. In addition, their elevated economic agency attests to the significant value of their industry to the local economy, the lack of competition from women (and men) prepared to take similar risks, and the time-limited character of their careers.[20] To quote ex-dancer Bonnie Scott, 'What was ironic was being looked upon as lesser than life and getting the best salary you could get out there. Not too many people made more money than we did. We got paid very highly to be the object of men's desire.'

Like most employed women in the 1950s, 1960s, and 1970s, Vancouver-based dancers began their working lives in the 'straight' or 'square' job sectors of sales, service, manufacturing, and clerical work prior to entering the striptease industry. For example, Nena Marlene worked at a shoe factory, an aircraft factory, and later Woodward's department store; April Paris was a retail clerk at the Bay and then a secretary at Shell Oil; Miss Lovie and Virginia were nurses; Choo Choo Williams, Shelinda, Shalimar, Sarita, and Tarren Rae were waitresses; Scarlett Lake sewed clothes in garment factories; Foxy Lady was a clerk for Office Overload and a carnival worker; Cascade sold roses and taught piano; and Jasmine Tea trained as a telephone operator and sold clothing. Through a variety of avenues – newspaper ads, encouragement by boyfriends, conversations with club owners or recommendations by other 'business insiders,' attendance at striptease shows, or chance meetings with working dancers – they learned that a striptease career promised more money than low-paying, dead-end, pink-collar employment, as well as opportunities to travel, and greater control over when, where, and how they worked. As historian Rachel Shteir discovered, strippers in the United States in mid-century defended their decision to shed clothes in public by insisting that stripping was easier than standing behind a cosmetics counter, wielding a broom, or sweating over a conveyor belt for skimpy wages.[21]

As I noted in chapter 3, half of the women I interviewed were high school graduates; but no one had a college or university degree when she began dancing. All were clear that the money to be made as a 'professional exotic' was their 'number one' rationale for entering the industry. Other than two women who married during their careers, the dancers I interviewed were self-supporting; they relied on their own income to survive. In this way, without the economic support of a husband or long-term boyfriend, they followed the path cleared by other working women who, in earlier decades, were self-employed dressmakers, milliners, lodging-house keepers, hairdressers, private arts teachers, madams, and prostitutes.[22]

From 1945 to 1980, erotic dancers across British Columbia customarily signed an employment contract; they were typically paid in cash. Because it was illegal to touch a dancer on stage in British Columbia, tipping was not widely practised. Instead, once hired, dancers were guaranteed the security of a weekly salary. In the late 1940s and early 1950s, Nena Marlene worked as a showgirl at the State Burlesque Theatre on East Hastings Street. Having lost her husband in an airplane crash, she was left to raise her baby girl with her mother's help. She needed to take care of herself and her child as well as contribute to her parents' household economy. Nena Marlene recalls making less money than the out-of-town marquee performers but considerably more than friends in the retail trade: 'We locals were cheap opening acts for the big names. We didn't have agents back then. We were lucky to get anything they offered! But Hymie [Singer] was giving me $25 a week, which was a lot of money. And he paid better than Woodward's [department store].'

Dancing at East End nightclubs in the 1950s, Choo Choo Williams remembers that she was paid about fifty dollars a week, sometimes a hundred dollars if it was a special gig. She stated that, 'The white women probably made more money, but I didn't work with any. The only white women I worked with were singers, like Judy Hope and Eleanor Powell.'[23] In the mid- to late 1960s, Miss Lovie was paid approximately $150 to $200 per week; this figure increased with more bookings at the Penthouse and hotel pubs in the 1970s. She reckoned that she earned the equivalent of her week's salary as a nurse in three days as a striptease dancer. Though Miss Lovie knew that she earned less than white features who were booked at Isy's and the Cave, she felt fortunate to be able to work steadily, forty-eight weeks per year.

Beginning in the late 1960s, as the number of local dancers and nightclub stages rose steeply in the city, club owners, promoters, and booking agents arrived at a loose agreement to implement hiring and performance standards: a professional striptease dancer was contracted to perform a set of twenty to twenty-two minutes (five to six songs) every hour over the course of a designated shift, six days a week. Each dancer was required to pay her booking agent 10 per cent of her weekly wage. Dancers were assigned an 'A', 'B,' or 'C' ranking by agents that corresponded to bookings in 'A,' 'B,' or 'C' nightclubs, with pay according to a salary scale – 'A' at the top and 'C' at the bottom. The classification system had deep roots in earlier distinctions made between dancers, and between venues. In the popular film *Gypsy* (1962), the headliner, Gypsy Rose Lee, is constructed as superior to her 'back-ups' – the walking/talking dolls and regular house strippers. From her privileged spot in an elegant, soft-seat theatre, Gypsy educates viewers about the difference: 'I'm not a cheap stripper, I'm the highest paid in the business.' Vancouver's nightclub scene was stratified by entrenched divisions of class and race, as described in chapter 2. 'A-grade' nightclubs were the white, West End, upscale clubs such as the Cave Supper Club, Isy's Supper Club, and the Penthouse Cabaret, and they attracted 'A-grade,' predominantly white dancers. 'B' and 'C' nightclubs were clustered in the Chinatown/Main Street district in the city's working-class East End, and they had a long history of hiring 'B' and 'C-grade' entertainers, many of whom were non-white. Club owners across the East-West divide – Joe Philliponi, Hymie Singer, Isy Walters, Ken Stauffer, Leo Bagry, Ernie King, and others – operated in the dual capacity of club owner and booking agent in the 1940s, 1950s, and 1960s. By the early 1970s, commercial booking agencies had sprung up to serve the needs of exotic dancers and club owners in the context of a rapidly growing industry.

The proliferation of hotel beer parlours in and outside of Vancouver's lower mainland (which coincided with the demise of independent nightclubs) meant a massive increase in the demand for striptease dancers and a smudging, to some degree, of the city's colour line. Hotel owners and pub managers scrambled to locate entertainment for day-time and night-time shifts, and, convinced that 'peelers sold beer,' they turned to the new stable of agents, who began to play a pivotal, intermediary role between dancers seeking work and club/pub owners seeking talent. Unlike Nena Marlene, Choo Choo Williams, and Miss Lovie, who did not need agents in the 1950s and early 1960s, striptease dancers in the 1970s actively sought representation by WaltCard, International Artists, Amalgamated Artists, or Choice Entertainment. By the mid-1970s, the best-known agents, those with the most influence, included Jack Card, Jeannie Runnalls, Katy Lynch, Jack Cooney, Darcy Taylor, Tom Longstaff, and Gary Taylor. Both Runnalls and Lynch were former dancers themselves, and Card was a popular choreographer who joined Isy Walters to form WaltCard. In the late 1970s, Jeannie Runnalls' International was the largest and highest-profile agency, supplying 200 female and 30 male dancers at a time to 105 hotels throughout British Columbia.[24]

It became the agent's job to secure dancers the best possible gigs and wages, which by the early 1970s included the option of touring hotel stages throughout British Columbia and Alberta. Agents were also expected to troubleshoot, put out fires for dancers when problems arose, lobby on dancers' behalf, and keep club/pub owners happy by disciplining dancers who bent or broke the rules. On occasion, dancers paid fines to club owners for minor infractions such as showing up late or skipping a gig without adequate notice. Several dancers recalled that the Drake and the Marr Hotels had a fining system whereby dancers were penalized if they were late, if they performed routines under regulation length, or if they wore leg warmers, smoked pot in the dressing room, sported tattoos, or danced to the same song twice in a row.

In headliner Tarren Rae's experience, the (sometimes lengthy) tenure of a B-grade house dancer at one club meant she did not rely on a booking agent in the same way that A-grade features did: 'When you worked at like Gary Taylor's or Major Bagshot's or the Number Five [Hotel], it was more kind of a family thing. You stayed there, it was a regular job. You worked there every day, you knew the bartenders – you'd probably dated half of them. Working with an agent was more professional. It meant more money because you got booked into places. You had to have costumes, you had to be there for certain times, and a twenty- to twenty-five-minute show was required.' Shelinda echoed Tarren Rae's observations: 'At Gary Taylor's as a house girl, I made maybe seven dollars an hour. We were in a cocoon as house dancers ... We didn't know other dancers, booking agents, or salaries. Once you got on the circuit, with an agency, being booked out every week, you always got paid better.'

Without minimizing their complaints (explored in chapter 5), Vancouver-based dancers argued that they experienced better working conditions than the bulk of their American counterparts who worked primarily in the United States. Several Canadian dancers had firsthand experience of the poor pay and working conditions in Las Vegas, Nevada – an ironic twist given the city's reputation as *the* place for showgirls and lavish stage productions. Dancers – both locals and imports – preferred the Vancouver scene as it evolved and expanded in the 1960s and 1970s. Foxy Lady knew American striptease dancers who travelled to live and work in Vancouver on a short-term, six-month work permit; they were not permitted permanent entry to Canada. In order to cross the border, they needed to obtain sponsorship from a club owner, or risk deportation. When their permit ran out, they crossed the border back into Blaine, Washington. Foxy Lady elaborated: 'There was more money to be made up here. The girls from the States didn't have a lot of places to work. Strippers weren't even

Figure 4.5 Big Fannie Annie crossed the Canada-U.S. border regularly to perform in Vancouver strip clubs.

allowed in the main part of the city of Las Vegas – they were in the outlying areas. They had to hustle more to sell drinks to customers. The girls here had guaranteed wages.' American dancer Big Fannie Annie performed for enthusiastic fans in Vancouver strip clubs, beginning in the late 1970s (fig. 4.5).

By the early 1970s, the demand also began to exceed the supply, affording dancers greater choice and control over working hours. Licensed beer parlours already open for 'adult entertainment' until 2:00 a.m. added topless (and then bottomless) floor shows at lunch-time that became especially popular with stockbrokers, lawyers, bankers, accountants, and other businessmen who toiled in the city's financial hub. Dancers who 'did luncheons' earned less money on the day shift, but Foxy Lady noted that the work was plentiful: 'All the clubs started having a lunch crowd, and they were always trying to steal each other's customers.' Choosing the night shift, April Paris had the days free; in the summer months she and other dancers loved to sunbathe at Wreck Beach – the city's only nude beach.

Retired choreographer/booking agent Jack Card emphasized the pots of money to be made in the industry throughout the 1970s: 'The money for dancers went from ten dollars a show to twenty-five dollars a show, five shows a day, eight girls in each club. The money was huge in the early to mid-1970s when hotels entered the game. If you were an 'A-dancer,' you got twenty-five dollars a show, five shows in the afternoon, six days a week. Some doubled it because they were working a night shift too. And they might do a quick club date if close by for a hundred and twenty-five a couple of nights a week. That adds up to two thousand to three thousand dollars a week, minus ten per cent for the agent.'[25] What was more realistic, according to the women I interviewed, was an average of $900 to $1,500 per week for 'A' dancers in the 1970s, and $400 to $900 a week for 'B' and 'C' dancers. Ex-dancer Virginia, like Miss Lovie, vacated the profession of nursing because, as she recollects, 'Nurses were not well paid. It was something like three hundred to five hundred dollars a month. And [as a house dancer at the Factory] I made that in two weeks.' She earned enough to pay for her husband's university education, making more money dancing than her husband did after he landed his first high school teaching job. According to Jasmine Tea, some women employed by local jazz, modern, and ballet companies moonlighted at downtown striptease venues such as the No. 5 Orange Hotel to supplement their poor, irregular income.

Even B-grade and C-grade dancers at the low end of the wage scale earned more than chambermaids, restaurant workers, office staff, daycare and bank workers, drycleaners, and stewardesses in the female-dominated service industry. For instance, in 1971 in Vancouver, female senior clerks were paid an average weekly salary of $125, while senior female bookkeepers averaged $123, less than one-third of what stripteasers earned.[26] In 1980, female telephone operators averaged $184 per week, chambermaids averaged $170, and saleswomen averaged $245. Most dancers who worked full time made more money per week than nurses, social workers, and teachers.[27] In an interview with New York-born Elyssa Danton at a Vancouver strip club, *Vancouver Sun* reporter Diana Ricardo learned that Danton's earnings 'as a classic ballerina could never match her present income as a dancer.' Making reference to all 'exotic dancers,' Ricardo concluded that, 'The salaries these girls earn beat the steno pool by a country mile.'[28]

Tarren Rae encapsulated her understanding of the ranking system that slotted dancers from top-to-bottom: 'I was an A-dancer, and A-dancers could pick and choose where to work. You worked the best clubs, had the best conditions. A B-dancer filled in when they didn't have enough A-dancers. She was usually not as attractive, not in as good shape, not as great a dancer. B-dancers could work A-clubs every once in a while. C-dancers never worked A-clubs. They worked the sleazy, scummy places like the Balmoral on Hastings Street. These were "people who were drinking their welfare cheque" kind of places. C-dancers usually had problems: they were hooked on drugs, they had lots of tattoos. They were at the bottom of the food chain.' Princess Lillian, also an A-dancer, earned $1,000 per week in the mid- to late 1970s. In Montreal, dancers' salaries were comparable, which prompted Lindalee Tracey (aka Fonda Peters) to correct judgmental naysayers in her autobiography *Growing Up Naked*: 'Exploitation is about poor people with lunch buckets working in factories, workers who get stiffed for their pay or their hours. I'm making close to a thousand dollars a week … I'm not exploited.'[29] Similarly, April Paris noted that

> I didn't feel like I was a victim. I wasn't degraded and I wasn't an object. We live in a superficial society, and I wouldn't have been given that job if I didn't look good. I thought I looked damn good. It was a choice I made; I considered myself a feminist, and dancing was very liberating. I liked being able to dress like I wanted to ... and especially with this money. I was wearing [Charles Jourdan] boots after a while; and I thought, 'No one I know at Shell Oil can afford this.' It was the best job, I liked the hours, I liked the people, I liked the creative freedom I had – giving my creativity a place to blossom ... I was empowered by this.

When she started dancing in 1969, Bonnie Scott paid the monthly rent on her apartment from the money she earned in five nights. In the mid-1970s, she claimed that the women who had the headlining acts – herself, Danielle, and Michelle – made the most money in the days before 'the women who showed the most pussy became the highest-paid dancers.' In 1983, upon leaving the business, Scott owned $40,000 worth of equipment, including a van, stage lights, fancy costumes, a huge champagne glass, and machines that produced bubbles and fog. She left behind a lucrative striptease career: 'When I quit I was making six thousand dollars a month, fifteen hundred a week, and even now that is a lot of money.'

African Canadian Coco Fontaine remembers going to Isy's nightclub to audition in 1973 and meeting Isy's son, Richard: 'He thought I was a working girl, which was very rude. I was choked. I was tired of people thinking this.' As one of the very few black dancers to ever work at Isy's, Coco had mixed feelings about Isy and his peculiar tactics inside his office: 'He said, "Close the door," then he said: "Okay, lift your top. Take your bra off. I want to take a look." I'm like, "Oh no! Dirty old guy!" He said, "No, no, it's nothing like that. Just lift up, I want to see." So I lift up, and he says, "You're good material. Can you dance?"' Until his death in 1976, Isy Walters's trademark, in Coco's words, was his intimate, occasionally 'over the top' involvement with dancers:

> Isy had meetings with dancers on Sundays … what girls were goofing up – he'd let us know, and it would be so humiliating. He didn't like us coming in in blue jeans, with hair sloppy. He'd say, 'You will not get drunk. You are *not* the girl next door. Anybody could be the girl next door. You are *me*. When you're representing me, you will represent this club in yourselves.' He gave us lectures: how we were supposed to shave when we had our g-strings, how we should be looking, how to cover yourself, how to present yourself – 'Do not show too much because you won't be coming back'… Isy would say, 'You're not in a woman's world, you're in a man's world.' So, he said, 'Your prime priority is *that man*. Give him that fantasy.'

To 'prove [Coco Fontaine] could handle the crowds' before she got the okay to work in Vancouver, Isy first booked her in Kamloops, where she was making $350 a week in 1974. By the late 1970s, she was performing four shows a night, six nights a week, still largely on the road, where she made a maximum of $800 per week before retiring from the industry in 1983. In general, she noted, white feature dancers tended to work less, were paid more than dancers of colour, and had first choice of music and colour of costumes. Klute, a white dancer, confirmed Coco's view of the racist barriers she and others faced: 'Women of colour had it very hard in this business. It was very hard for them to get booked. And they didn't get as much money as I did. It was totally unfair. When I'd see black women dancing, they often had the imitation lion-skin stuff on and they were playing on the expected fantasy.'

Tarren Rae, a talented, feisty, white headliner, watched her earning power increase exponentially over the course of her fifteen-year career: 'At Gary Taylor's I was making about eighty dollars a week to start, then one seventy-five to three hundred, then it went to between five hundred and seven hundred, then between nine hundred and twelve hundred, and then fifteen hundred.' In 1983, at the 'Strip-Tease Artists' Roundup' – the first Strippers' Convention, at the Sahara Hotel in

Figure 4.6 Golden G-String winner Tarren Rae perfects her routine, 1984.

Las Vegas, Rae competed against forty-five dancers from across North America and was crowned the best exotic dancer on the continent.[30] Thrilled with her 'Golden G-String' title, she went 'zooming up to as much as five thousand dollars per week' (fig. 4.6).

Several dancers mentioned Isy Walters's insistence that dancers pay taxes, keep receipts to show legitimate deductions, and seek investment advice. Not all dancers heeded his advice, however, and few matched the take-home pay of Tarren Rae. Throughout the 1970s, dancers like Virginia, Jasmine Tea, April Paris, Shelinda, Coco Fontaine, Cascade, and Bambi made an average of $400 to $800 per week, while a handful accepted payment as low as $250 per week at 'skuzzy' East End hotels like the Vanport and the Cobalt. Still, their incomes were two-to-three times higher than those of female workers in sales, service, and clerical jobs.

British-born Virginia claimed that she made more money, had more freedom, worked fewer hours, and had more control over work than the waitresses, nurses, teachers, chambermaids, and secretaries she knew. Going home to her family every day and not running up a bar tab meant that it was easier to sock money away. Other former dancers like Klute had a tougher time: 'I was raised Catholic, so it was like, you gotta have savings, but I had no money management skills whatsoever. When I retired, I pissed it all away on living for a year and a half, and on love. A dollar was like a penny to me. I could piss away money faster than anything ... that career did not set me up for being good with money.' Every ex-dancer I interviewed said that saving and investing the money they earned was very difficult, if not next to impossible. All expressed some measure of regret that they had not had the inclination, the foresight, the support, or the willpower to handle their finances better while employed in the business. Several women mused about the ethos of 'living for the moment.' As Roxanne put it, 'The kind of person who went into stripping was very free-spirited, had a sense of adventure, you wanted to travel. No one saved for their old age.'[31] To April Paris, spending was easy: 'You spent money – a car, restaurants, clothes, drugs, living in a fancy place in the West End rather than sharing a communal flat in Kitsilano.'

Few dancers were accustomed to pocketing so much money so fast – many told me stories of giving it away, spending it on luxury items, sharing it with friends and family, and redirecting it back into their career. Foxy Lady commented, 'The first part of my career in dancing, I spent it. I spent it on costumes, I spent it on make-up. You bought a car to get from job to job, and especially if you were working at night or out of town. Or you'd take a cab and haul your costumes in and out of cabs.' By the mid- to late 1970s, the hotel pubs began to refuse to pay dancers in cash; hence dancers were advised strenuously by Isy Walters, Jack Card, and other agents to file income tax returns. As Foxy Lady recalled, 'We started paying taxes when the hotels started issuing cheques. I started paying taxes in 1975, I bought RRSPs, we bought new cars – I had a black Trans Am, a friend had a big white Monte Carlo – very flashy ... I paid an accountant to help me with deductions, and later I became an accountant!' Similarly, Shalimar knew that she had to spend money to make money on the stage, though this was an expensive undertaking. She reminisced, 'You make a lot of money as a dancer, but you spend a lot – hairdressing, sexy nails, you have to look perfect. You can't just go buy a Sally Hansen nail kit and throw it on. I probably spent more money dancing than I'll ever make from my education.' Shalimar, who began her career in the early 1980s, was one of the few dancers who adopted a shrewd approach to the business: 'I was making twelve hundred dollars a week, fifteen hundred on the road, fifty dollars a show, doing five, six shows a day for six days straight. Cha-ching, cha-ching, cha-ching! I saved to pay for my university education, and no student loans. At tax time, I wrote it all off: every pair of high heels, every lipstick, every tampon I bought.'

For the nine women I interviewed who raised children while dancing (47 per cent), a striptease career was attractive because it enabled a healthy income and flexible scheduling in the absence of reliable, high-quality daycare options. Mothers who danced rarely left the city to tour; instead, they elected to string together club dates in Vancouver and its surrounding suburbs. In the early 1960s, Choo Choo Williams coordinated her dance timetable to accommodate her responsibility for child-rearing: 'I could be home with my kid in the daytime and then go out and dance at night.' After the birth of her son, Jasmine Tea was a single mother and lived on welfare for a brief stint before returning to dancing: 'I only worked three weeks a month, and took one week off to spend time with my son.' Roxanne also juggled her mothering duties with her need to earn a decent wage as a single parent:

> Because I had kids, I could like take time off. The main thing, even more than the money, was that I was my own boss. You could work two weeks and then you could take a week off, then you could work a month and then you could take two weeks off. You didn't have to wait till the end of the year for your two bloody weeks off. I hired a babysitter when they were young. When they were in school, you could run home real fast between shows, be with them, take them shopping.

Dancers and Their Co-Workers

Wherever striptease performers worked, in whatever conditions, they did not work alone. Until the late 1970s, all dancers were accompanied by all-male in-house jazz and swing bands.[32] Though backing up striptease artists was not for everyone, the nightclubs paid union scale and supplied bread-and-butter gigs for working musicians. To American musician Art Hess, playing for strippers in a burlesque orchestra during the 1930s was a 'dog-catcher's job' – steady, nightly work.[33] Many of Vancouver's hottest jazz musicians worked with dancers at West End and East End venues, including Fraser McPherson, Cuddles Johnson, Chris Gage, Stu Barnett, Dave Davies, Doug Cuthbert, Gerry

Palken, Sean Gunn, Mike Kalanj, Gord Walkinshaw, Ernie King, Harry Harvey, Peter Batt, and David Lee.[34] A typical combo consisted of a trio of saxophone or bass, organ or piano, and drums, though the orchestras at the State Burlesque Theatre, Cave Supper Club, Isy's Supper Club, and Palomar Supper Club were considerably larger. Members of the musicians' union Local 145, players worked the clubs six nights a week, and when hotel bars opened up, many did two shifts a night – noon to 8:00 p.m. at one club, and 8:00 p.m. to 2:00 a.m. at another.

In spite of the benefits, musicians like Mike Kalanj acknowledged the stigma: 'My parents frowned on it. But I was working six nights a week, I belonged to the musicians' union, getting paid, it was legit. It was where I was working that was the problem. I was from a classical background.' Vancouver-born jazz musician Doug Cuthbert worked for many years in the house band at the New Delhi cabaret, though he recalls, laughing, that his parents didn't know he was 'playing at a stripclub on weekends.' He joined the Delhi band in 1963: 'It was mostly singers and dancers at the Delhi. Teddy Felton was the MC – he was a hold-over from the 1940s – a lot like Sammy Davis Junior. He'd sing a few songs, then introduce the dancers, who couldn't go bottomless at that time. They all had costumes. Better ones had really elaborate costumes. And the ones that had the better costumes and the really good acts would get really good money. They'd do their little number with three or four changes, and we'd back them up.' Sean Gunn, who was born in Vernon, British Columbia, played electric bass in a small band at the Kublai Khan in the 1970s, though his Chinese Canadian parents did not approve. He said he could not imagine inviting his mother to a gig. At the club, Gunn's band played four sets, one alone, and three for the dancers. He laughed: 'We faked our way through. No one was really listening anyway.' He remembered sharing the dressing room with dancers and playing Santana's 'Black Magic Woman' a lot.

There was abundant work for musicians in the 1970s after the hotel pubs opened up and before the transition to tape-recorded music made live music obsolete. Pianist and bass player Gord Walkinshaw commented on the lunch-time specials at the Zanzibar: 'You'd work noon until two p.m. non-stop. There would be one of the older strippers, some go-go girls. We'd play a couple of songs, two strippers each did three songs. And the go-go girls would close at two. It was pretty easy money for us – a hundred and twenty-five a week. These weren't classy jobs. The other musicians looked down on us. They probably made one-sixty a week at the Hotel Vancouver.' Saxophonist Dave

Davies reflected on the pay scale: 'The go-go girls made less than we did, but the strippers made more than we did. I didn't mind because they were working harder. Dancers were making three to five hundred a week.' Added Mike Kalanj, 'Dancers made way more than we did. I bet you some of them were pulling down a thousand bucks a week.'

Dancers and musicians agreed that the full-time striptease dancers made more money than their musician brothers, though many dancers lamented the fact that the musicians were unionized and they were not. As Foxy Lady put it, everyone knew that dancers were the drawing card, not the musicians. Dancers selected sheet music for the musicians to play: 'There was a music store on Georgia Street named Kelly's. You'd love a song and have to find the sheet music. The guys, especially at Isy's, could all read music: they were jazz guys, really good musicians, studio musicians. That was the best. We used to fight for the songs we wanted.' Dave Davies concurred: 'A lot of the girls had their own charts. They'd have all kinds of tunes and they'd have all the right moves: "Caravan," "Night Train," "Watermelon Man," and "Hey, Big Spender," all the songs that sound bumpy and grindy.' Gord Walkinshaw chimed in, 'The strippers were pretty fussy. They were especially hard on drummers, there's always a drum solo. We backed them up and learned what they wanted.' Dancers spent hours finding sheet music and rehearsing with musicians; from the mid-1970s on, they spent hours selecting music and paying for it to be recorded on eight-track tapes.

In spite of the stigma, both Gord Walkinshaw and Dave Davies insisted that they enjoyed backing up dancers. Davies snorted, 'Hell, I was proud of it. I'd tell my friends, "You should have seen the beautiful girls I saw today." I bragged about it.' Walkinshaw did not hesitate to express his bliss: 'Here we are looking at naked women, twenty or thirty of them all day, and that's our job. How many people get paid for that? I felt like I'd died and gone to heaven.' Pianist Gerry Palken noted the esteem attached to dating a dancer: 'A new dancer came in and she was always a challenge for the band, to see who'd be the first one … Well, we weren't scared of AIDS. Those days, if you got a dose you went to the hospital, got a shot, didn't drink for three days, and you're back in action … I had a couple six-month sort-of affairs with dancers.' Bass player Sean Gunn also talked about fantasies of strippers, and the sure-fire fate of becoming 'just another lovelorn road kill.'[35]

Ex-dancers typically referred to other ex-dancers as former co-workers, though they rarely shared the same stage. Like other groups of wage-earning women, dancers in the striptease business found female friendship and intimacy, as well as competition, jealousy, and distrust. Tarren Rae drew a parallel between the striptease world and an all-girls' school: 'You had your cliques, and you knew who hung out with who, and who you had to watch your p's and q's around. The core of my friends today are people I've had from my dancing years.' For Jasmine Tea, striptease supplied a unique setting for the development of close bonds with other dancers. Her career, she recalled, offered her the chance to be 'really real' in the company of other outlaws: 'We'd smoke a joint, laugh, do each other's nails and hair. There was lots of camaraderie; it was very, very nice. I never got that with any other job. It was tight-knit because you exposed yourself to each other, skin-wise, and internally. I think as you peel off layers of your clothes, you peel off layers of your persona, down to who you really are.' For women who had left behind unhappy, tension-filled histories with family members, relationships forged within the industry provided a meaningful alternative. 'Striptease,' said Cascade, 'was a family for many of us, it was a support system that we didn't have.' Retired British stripper Nickie Roberts mused about working in Soho, the 'sex heart' of London in the early 1970s: 'Strip club dressing rooms were my first experience of "women-only" spaces and we had some of the best times there ... There was a real solidarity among the working girls. There had to be, really, we were all sitting there naked together, measuring and comparing our clitorises. That's solidarity!'[36] For some dancers, membership in 'the life' entailed a reformulation of kinship relations similar to those carved out by the working-class black and Latin American trans/queer drag performers, who collectively manufactured fashion 'houses,' voguing, 'mothers,' and drag balls in New York in the late 1980s.[37]

In the down-time between shifts, women traded tales about life and love – pay and working conditions, ups and downs with lovers, plots and characters of daily soap operas, recipes, abortions, kids, landlords, and emerging women's liberation. Miss Lovie, Coco Fontaine, and Klute acknowledged the mentorship of older dancers, who taught them the ropes, passed on tips, made them costumes, and warned them against harm of all sorts. Coco Fontaine mentioned that an older dancer occasionally gave her a costume and 'that was considered good luck.' Klute chuckled when she recalled how several older strutters from the burlesque days took her under their wing: 'I was kidnapped by a couple of them one time. They said, "You're so pretty but you don't wear enough make-up." So they'd teach me how to put it on.' Klute also got to know a broad range of women in the business, and her description skewers the notion of a homogeneous lot: 'I remember a really interesting mixture of women, everything from the women totally driven by drugs to really super strong, famous women like Chesty Morgan and Annie Ample – they were mega-business women.'

Princess Lillian explained that she was not hampered on stage by her deafness, but relations off stage with hearing dancers were sometimes a strain. She said, 'It was lonely for me and frustrating because I had a hard time communicating. I'd always ask, "What are you saying, what are you talking about?" They didn't have much patience.' So, relations between dancers were never entirely rosy or chummy-chummy. Some dancers blamed or were blamed by other dancers for stealing costumes, jewellery, props, moves, music, and lovers. And yet for many dancers, in spite of the dramas, tensions, and disagreements that erupted in the workplace, friendships made in 'the life' were forged, nurtured, and remain strong decades later. Moreover, periodic drives for unionization (described in chapter 5) enhanced solidarity across differences of personal temperament, race/ethnicity, age, ability, and class background.

Dancers' Relationships with Patrons

While striptease dancers worked for male nightclub owners, alongside other dancers, and with male musicians, they depended on customers whose expenditures paid their salaries. In the 1950s and 1960s, some women accompanied men to see Vegas-style showgirls at the upscale West End supper clubs and the East End nightclubs. However, during the postwar decades, men were consistently the dancers' most ardent, loyal, and dependable fans. Some men went to strip clubs with business associates; some attended sporadically for a special event or bachelor party; some went alone.[38] Many male patrons bragged about their patronage, some lied about it, others hid it; some did all three. Men who regularly attended strip shows were (and still are) stereotyped variously as maladjusted sex perverts; lonely, single geezers in greasy trenchcoats; lecherous business-types who cheat on their wives; and fraternity boys with hormones run amok. Based on her own participant observation at two strip clubs in New England, sociologist Danielle Egan argues that regulars were both economically privileged and 'played' by the dancers.[39] Similarly, in Vancouver, men's longing, projected onto dancers as desired objects, was premised on a hierarchical, non-reciprocal exchange and, ultimately, an unobtainable fantasy.

Yet rather than occupy the static stance of object – the 'whorish wife' – dancers employed tactics to exploit patrons' fantasies to their own (lucrative) ends.

Virginia captured some of the complexities of male spectatorship that she witnessed: 'A lot of men were embarrassed that they were there, that they were peeping. Businessmen would come – they were just having their businessman's lunch and hoping that nobody they knew saw them there. They were always very quiet. But then you'd always get the loudmouth … I liked talking to them. They treated me with respect. They told me their problems, how their wives had died, how unhappy they were, various stories of their lives.' The ex-dancers I spoke with engaged in what sociologist Arlie Hochschild terms emotional labour – managing feeling to create a publicly observable facial and bodily display, disguising fatigue and irritation, and offering care to customers as part of the service itself, in exchange for a wage.[40] Emotion work by dancers constituted an invisible, taken-for-granted element of their relationships with patrons as well as club staff and booking agents. For instance, not only were dancers obliged to smile (much like flight attendants and waitresses), they were expected to conjure up some warmth behind it.[41] In general, with access to less power, authority, and status than their male clients and bosses, dancers consciously honed their allegedly innate 'feminine wiles' to enhance their earning capacity.

Retired dancers acknowledged the multiple needs and desires of patrons: most men harboured fantasies of female beauty, glamour, and sexiness. 'Groupies' or 'stage-door johnnies' wanted to date and 'bag' a dancer; other men sought an emotional connection. Decades before the invention of lap dancing and tableside massages, Tarren Rae emphasized the limited physical interaction with male customers in nightclubs, and the fact that men who were 'out of hand' were routinely thrown out of the club. In an interview for the *Vancouver Sun*, dancer Shelley More defended erotic performance as a social safety valve to control men's innate sexual urges: 'We're doing the public a service. We've saved a lot of marriages and [prevented] a lot of sex offences against children.'[42] Debbie, a feature dancer at the Drake Hotel in the late 1970s, perfected a Florence Nightingale routine in white high heels, cap, and spangled smock. Like Shelley, she had no illusions about herself as a 'fantasy figure' for her male customers: 'The men who come to see us come to see the entertainment value. They don't think about us when we go home to our children, to our husbands or girlfriends. They don't think about us washing dishes, cooking supper, washing floors, and doing the laundry. They see the entertainment value; they see an image up there.'[43]

Few dancers spoke to customers while they performed on stage, though April Paris remembered a funny incident: 'In one of the bars, the first video game, *Pac-Man* – with its horrible sound – was right in front of the stage. This guy's playing, and I'm taking my clothes off. I said, "You know, it's either me or *Pac-Man!*" And he laughed.' Much of the time, Shalimar, like Virginia, felt that she was expected to play the role of companion and counsellor offstage: 'The men want something they can't have. It's the same reason they buy a magazine or they watch a video. They always want to feel that that beautiful woman is paying attention to them. The men go for companionship – not with their wife, but with someone else that's going to listen to them bitch about how she does this and that and how she doesn't understand me, and the kids, and the job, and the boss, and the guy down the street ... Women have Harlequin Romance novels ... Strip clubs have been the den of the man going to escape.'

Buddy, a bartender at the No. 5 Orange Hotel in the late 1970s, witnessed many interactions between patrons and dancers, some of which infringed the club's rules. To protect dancers, a tight bunch of security-minded enforcers formed among bouncers, waiters, and bartenders:

> You'd have some young construction worker who had a few drinks too many, sitting in gynaecology row. The girl has, in the course of her danc-ing, kicked off a shoe, and he reaches out and grabs it, only to be instantly set upon by a couple of extremely brutal guys, who would just pound the living crap out of this guy. Throw him out into the back alley and pound the crap out of him some more. The policy was well known: you never touched the stage, you never touched anything on the stage, and you cer-tainly never even thought about touching a dancer.

Pleasing customers (from a safe physical and psychic distance) was each dancer's primary objective on stage, and ex-dancers agreed that this goal was relatively easy to achieve. As April Paris commented, 'You could do the tiniest little gesture and they'd have their mouths open. You didn't have to be naked either. They knew that you would eventu-ally be naked, so whatever you did in the meantime, they were waiting for it. I knew that that was a lot of power to have. Bosses would tell me, "Smile, smile. Make it look as if you're enjoying it." I was enjoying my-self, but I was doing it for me, I wasn't doing it for them. I saw them like little dogs with their tails between their legs and their tongue hanging out ... I learned where my power comes from.' Similarly, Jasmine Tea refuted the harmful stereotype that strippers were manipulated and oppressed by men in the audience. She explained: 'The adrenaline rush that you get when you're dancing is very addicting. It's like a drug. It's very powerful to have that much control over that many people.' For Klute, a butch lesbian, enacting a powerful presence on stage afforded her a measure of control:

> The way to survive, for me at least, was to take total power and that's why I became a feature and had shows that lasted half an hour and had a whole plot to them ... I liked doing really scary, really powerful women. It was my security blanket in the business. It got me through without doing drugs. I liked going on stage and grabbing the audience by the balls and holding them there until I was finished.

As dancers developed their act, profile, and reputation, they attracted loyal followers, much like other professional entertainers who drew fans to their gigs. Foxy Lady grinned when she remembered her popularity: 'I had about four, five little old guys that would always ask me, "Where are you dancing next?" They followed me around. One guy went all the way out to Maple Ridge!' Roxanne, who appreciated her male admirers, criticized the hypocrisy of women who at once condemned and imitated her: 'You'd get your regular customers who'd be there and would know you, and had a big smile on their faces. It kind of made you feel good because they were lonely men ... Sometimes the wives would come with their husbands and for the most part they would sneer and then they'd go home and practice in front of the mirror.'

In spite of their feelings of power and control on stage, dancers approached interactions with male customers with caution. The vast majority refused to date customers, and yet they strove to appear friendly, attentive, and sexy while on the job. At times, this meant submerging their misgivings about men in the club, especially those who occupied 'wanker row.' As Topaz, a dancer at the Drake Hotel and a self-named 'untouchable,' explained in an interview with Les Wiseman, 'Men are there for the pink, but that doesn't mean you have to show them any. I try to block out all the slosh (weirdos) out there. Luckily, I don't have very good eyesight.'[44] Several dancers wore wedding rings or made mention of husbands in conversation with male customers to communicate their lack of interest in more than friendly banter. At all times, dancers were wary of the threat of sexual harassment and assault (addressed in chapter 5). Years later, in the early 1990s, Diana Atkinson wrote about stripping gigs throughout British Columbia in her book *Highways and Dancehalls*. Using the unnerving metaphor of combustion, she captured her competing feelings of self-assurance and vulnerability: 'It exhilarates me to walk through the crowded bar after midnight, the only female in the room, wearing one square foot of fabric and a chiffon scarf. A piece of oil-soaked paper strolling through a forest of matches.'[45]

Bonnie Scott recalls a surprising and heart-warming encounter in the Fraser Arms Hotel: 'A local bridge-building engineer used to come in. We'd sit in the lounge between my shows – he'd buy me a drink. I was telling him how tired I was, and he says, "You need a holiday." And he went out the next day, bought me a return ticket to Hawaii, all paid – hotel and everything. He's like, "Here. You need that holiday, take a holiday."' While working at the Vanport Hotel, Tarren Rae inspired the beneficence of one generous regular: 'I had this one guy who was a fisherman. At the end of my show, he'd come up and he'd drop this big, huge salmon on the stage. And I'd go, "Oh, thank-you." And I'd pick the salmon up, naked. I'd put my cover-up on, and carry the salmon over to the bar, put it down, and say, "I'll be right back." I'd get changed then go down to the fish joint on Powell Street, get them to chop it up into steaks, and then I'd hand it out to the other dancers. What a sweetheart!'

Upon retiring from the scene in Vancouver in 1975, Virginia received a 'solid silver tea service from the gentlemen, the skid row types' – her regular customers. *Vancouver Sun* columnist Denny Boyd made it clear to me that he respected 'the ladies' on his nights out to local strip clubs. He once compared stripper Tempest Storm's obsession with zippers to safety commercials featuring B.C. Lions linebacker Paul Giroday and Canucks goalie Glen Hanlon suiting up, carefully pulling on each layer and giving each pad a slap test (fig. 4.7). In addition, he compared the smooth moves of Miss Storm in shimmering black sequins to 'Guy Lafleur going one on one with Moose Dupont.'[46] Acknowledging his own chequered marital history, he mused about the double standard: 'If more wives knew a little bit about undressing, like stripping, then more marriages would last. You didn't marry the bad girl, you married the Madonna. Five years into the marriage, you're thinking, "Jesus Christ, I could have married Hot Dot!"'[47]

Figure 4.7 Burlesque queen Tempest Storm, backstage at the Penthouse Cabaret, 1982

Travelling the Circuit

In the postwar era, North American entertainers sought paying engagements at home and beyond. In the Pacific Northwest, a 'west coast wheel' linked cities from San Diego, California, to Vancouver, British Columbia, to Anchorage, Alaska. Circus and carnival performers; sports stars such as the Harlem Globetrotters, the B.C. Lions football team, and the Vancouver Canucks hockey franchise; and countless musicians, magicians (such as Mandrake, and Velvet, his assistant), comedians, figure skaters with the Canadian Ice Fantasy, and showgirls packed suitcases and travelled for weeks, sometimes months on end.[48] Vancouver was a popular destination for professional entertainers of all sorts, as well as a springboard to points north, south, and east. Headlining striptease dancers were part of this migrant, mobile labour force, on the move from town to town in search of paying gigs and appreciative audiences.

Beginning in the late 1960s, Vancouver-based erotic dancers toured the province by bus, car, and air to perform at hotels in small cities and towns such as Victoria, Nanaimo, Vernon, Terrace, Prince George, Powell River, Cranbrook, and Kamloops. [49] Until the late 1970s, they often travelled with musicians, who accompanied them on the stages of out-of-town hotels. Work on the road paid better than work in Vancouver – dancers were compensated for leaving the familiarity and comfort of home, though their memories of touring were mixed. Shelinda and Klute told stories of long, twelve-hour days, split shifts 'on an invisible leash,' and six-day weeks cooped up in 'ratty hotels with broken-down beds and cockroaches … in small towns with people who had more keys to your room than you did.' But as Klute added, 'You got addicted to travelling. It was like joining the navy and seeing the world.' For dancers who had limited travel experience, a succession of bookings opened up new vistas and possibilities for adventure, though gigs out of town typically combined positive and negative elements. Few of the hotels were equipped with luxuries, and some lacked basic essentials. In lieu of dressing rooms, dancers were often told to change in the one women's public bathroom or the bar coolers where beer and draught were stored. Bonnie Scott made do in circumstances that left much to be desired:

> I danced in Nanaimo, the Playgirl in Prince George, the Campbell River Lodge. A club in Langley owned by the guy who owned Circus Circus. Wells Grey, Clearwater, Dawson Creek – I hated working in those places because they had no class. They just gave you some box in the corner, or you'd be dancing on the dance floor. It was ridiculous. That's why I had my own lights eventually. I didn't necessarily like the fact that they had a crappy stage and no lights, but if they treated you half decent then it wasn't so bad.

According to Foxy Lady, the Wild Duck Hotel in Port Moody was one of the first beer parlours in the Lower Mainland to introduce striptease dancers in the mid-1970s: 'They went to Isy [Walters] and asked him to book dancers for them. But they had carpeted little platforms. There was no room for big costumes. That's when costumes became downsized.' To April Paris, the shift signalled the end of 'strutting': 'The hotel pubs did not have real stages. The strutters floated down the stage at Isy's with these dusters on – long capes with one button that sort of covered the breasts, and chiffon over their legs – the effect was stunning. They needed a huge stage.' Not only did the small stages restrict a dancer's wardrobe choices; they narrowed her repertoire of moves and mobility. Adapting to the changing environment of hotel bars in the 1970s was non-negotiable, noted Klute: 'Hotel stages were eight feet by ten feet, so you got really good at expressively dancing in short, small spaces.

The ceiling wasn't usually too far from your head, the sound systems had blown speakers, the lighting was sad, the DJs were sometimes non-existent or a bartender put a tape in.' From Klute's standpoint, it was a rare treat to work with a 'real DJ' and a superior lighting system. In her experience, the customers in small, resource-based towns were a colourful, raucous bunch: 'You'd look out into the audience and there'd be all these guys in baseball caps and lumberjack shirts, hooting and hollering and commenting on every facet of your body from your toe-nails to your hair, and particularly your private parts.' On the B.C. coast in the mid-1970s, Sarita Mileta's experience of fan participation was a positive one:

> In Kitimat, there were Greek sailors on shore at the local nightclub. I did a Middle Eastern gypsy type of act. I balanced the beer on my head and I wore a coin belt and coin robe with a little vest and a long gypsy skirt; I brought out a tambourine and they went insane. They loved me so much, they treated me like a princess. Men would tell me, 'Don't take this the wrong way, but taking your clothes off ruins it. You have a beautiful body and we're coming here to watch you dance.'[50]

In the late 1970s, Bambi was booked into a hotel in Grand Forks, Alberta; she ruefully remembered her twelve-hour bus-ride:

> They stuck me on a bus – I get to the hotel and it says 'Condemned Hotel, Except for Dancer.' My first out-of-town gig, and they paid me eight hundred for the week. All they got there was Doukhobors and bikers and you couldn't tell them apart because they all had the long beards. You paid your transportation and food – they supplied the hotel room, which had no lock on the door, and no running water. We had to swim in the lake to wash … Another time, they flew me in to the middle of the bush on a private plane – you're the only girl and they fly you in to this bush camp and all these guys come out three times a day to see your show. Other places, you had to put quarters into the jukebox to make sure your three songs came to twenty minutes.

Jasmine Tea recalled her experiences of audiences on the road as diverse and unpredictable: 'I was in Prince George, making six hundred and fifty for the week. The stage was the size of a kitchen table. One night all the guys were in chairs pulled right up to the edge – they wouldn't watch until I had everything off. And then they're, "Come on, spread 'em!"' I was mortified. Another night, they paid me not to dance because a big hockey game was on a brand-new TV. They pooled their money together so that I wouldn't do my show. That was devastating.' In Sooke, on the southern tip of Vancouver Island, Jasmine Tea had a very different experience. During her week-long engagement, male patrons who frequented the strip club took her out for dinner or invited her to their house where they cooked her dinner, and then returned her to the hotel: 'They treated me like a queen,' she recalls. 'They never laid a hand on me, there was no sexual tension. Maybe for them it was the novelty of telling their buddies that they took the stripper home.' Similarly, Cascade said that she was given the 'kid glove treatment' by the men in small towns, but snubbed by the women: 'At Funky John's in Trail, B.C. – you'd be the celebrity! The women didn't like you very much! [laughs] All of sudden, there's a new dancer in town and the guys are going night after night ... The guys just wanted to hang out with you. And they were respectful, they were pretty good to talk to. They were very protective. You'd be taken out for breakfast, lunch, and dinner ... a different fellow would just want to hang around with you.'

To Princess Lillian, touring stirred up unpleasant memories: 'A lot of guys in the small towns – Port Hardy, Kamloops, think that the dancer is a hooker. Guys would come to my room, and I had to phone the manager. I got upset. And you were expected to pretend you didn't have a boyfriend, when I had one.' Another hazard of touring mentioned by several dancers was the separation from family, friends, and loved ones. To Shelinda, travelling was not cost-effective: 'I spent so much money on phone calls to my boyfriend, it didn't make it worth the extra money to go.' For vegetarians like Foxy Lady, finding a decent meal in a 'meat and potatoes town' was a challenge. As she laughingly recalled, 'I lived on cheese and tomato sandwiches.' At the mercy of older hotels' faulty boiler systems in the winter, dancers remembered suffering through gigs with no heat or hot water, compounded by the isolation of being 'stuck' in a strange locale without a car, scrutinized by women who, as Foxy Lady said, 'hated you because you were the dancer.' Val Scott, a retired dancer from Toronto, captured her experience this way: 'In small towns, everyone knew you were the stripper ... The men ogled you in restaurants, and the women all looked at you with stiletto eyes like they wanted to kill you.'[51] It was commonplace for a dancer to feel conspicuous as 'the dancer' in town – a target for both fans and foes.

Dancers of colour were apprehensive about performing for overwhelmingly white, small-town crowds. Black dancer Coco Fontaine spent many years on the road: 'I travelled all over the province. To Granisle, B.C., which is very north, only five hundred people, a gold town. In Fort St John I thought I was going to be lynched.' By contrast, Miss Lovie, another black dancer, recounted a heart-warming experience: 'There was a gay Indian guy in Prince George. He was my bodyguard. He just loved me! He'd come and get me early in the morning, "Lovie, it's time to come have some breakfast now. Come on, you know I don't want you walking around here by yourself!" He was so sweet.'

Supplementing Striptease Work

On occasion, erotic dancers supplemented their nightclub earnings by modelling, movie-related work, magazine work, all-male stag events (which date back to the late 1800s), and non-striptease dancing in chorus lines and with jazz troupes. In the 1960s, Choo Choo Williams posed nude for Vancouver-based painter Jack Shadbolt and other artists at the Vancouver Art School, but under her married name, not her stage name, so 'nobody would know.' Beginning in the mid-1960s, some dancers augmented their striptease wages by performing a fifteen-minute act between pornography reels on the stage of the Chinese-owned Venus movie house on Main Street near the Cobalt Hotel on the edge of Chinatown. Coco Fontaine has a vivid memory of the 'Venus': 'It was a sleazy little theatre where you could see porn. It was punishment for me, because I do not like having a guy come, and all the coats and the flashing. But you only danced for ten minutes. You'd go onstage, finish, and head on back to Isy's, or the Smilin' Buddha or Kublai Khan – you'd have a cab waiting.' Like other dancers featured in TV and print commercials, Jasmine Tea modelled for a body lotion company, and found modelling to be 'way more sleazy than dancing. The number of people that think they can touch you ... It was dog-eat-dog.' Other dancers used the time between sets to learn lines for (poorly) paid parts in theatre productions.

Making extra money also motivated some dancers to promote and publicize their assets off stage. In her memoir, the late Montreal-based dancer Lindalee Tracey writes that by the late 1970s dancers had started to 'hype themselves' by doing anything to get on television, including holding up round-cards at boxing matches, modelling bikinis at car shows, and posing for corner-store calendars.[52] In Vancouver, several dancers were 'ring girls' at professional wrestling events at the Pacific

Coliseum and the Agridome. Appearing in *Playboy* magazine also afforded significant cachet to those dancers in search of greater exposure and a competitive edge. In the late 1970s, Shelinda was dancing in local clubs when approached by Vancouver wedding photographer and *Playboy* scout Ken Honey: 'He went around to stripclubs and took photos of girls and tried to get them in *Playboy*. He tried to get me in the magazine.' On the prowl for 'Girls of Canada' since the early 1960s, in the summer of 1978 Honey scored big: he photographed eighteen-year-old Dorothy Stratten (born Dorothy Ruth Hoogstraten in suburban Coquitlam), who became *Playboy's* centrefold in August 1978, and then the magazine's Playmate of the Year for 1979 – two Canadian firsts. Stratten soared to unexpected heights; her success, though tragically cut short by her brutal murder at the hands of ex-boyfriend Bob Snider in 1980, generated international buzz about Vancouver as a seed-bed for sexy blonds.[53]

Private stags and parties offered dancers a lucrative supplement to their stage acts in clubs. Some dancers, however, refused to put themselves at risk in a situation that was less monitored and potentially more volatile than a nightclub or hotel pub. In Bonnie Scott's words, 'Stags were always bad. The worst stag I probably ever worked was at the Royal Roads College in Victoria. That was the absolute worst. They got him naked, chained him in the chair, and got you to paint his balls blue, with blue paint. Some girls agreed to be raffled off as a door prize, some didn't.' Most dancers preferred the safety and security of a nightclub or hotel stage. Foxy Lady exposed the underhanded tactics of one club owner: 'Stags were scary, but they paid well. People tipped and threw money at you. Marty, the owner of Zanzibar, was really sleazy. He subcontracted us out to work at a hall, a stag, when we're supposed to be at the Zanzibar, and we'd get paid the same. He'd be paid more for the stag, but he skimmed off the money. We didn't get it.' Shalimar did a lot of stags, but she told me that she always made it clear that she wasn't the door prize, nor was she there to do the 'sex thing.' She charged $250 a show in the early 1980s, out of which she paid a bouncer to escort her to the gigs and pick up her costumes. Also in the early 1980s, some dancers worked part-time for Strip-A-Gram – introduced to Vancouver by entrepreneur Bill Keeton from Olympia, Washington, as a business to 'rent out' strippers for special occasions – anniversaries, birthdays, and business parties.[54]

While it is likely that a small percentage of Vancouver dancers combined striptease with prostitution (agent Jeannie Runnalls estimates it was 5 per cent), only one of the retired dancers I interviewed disclosed involvement in the exchange of sex for money. In 1976, Scarlett Lake was recruited on stage by a black MC at Isy's: 'He put me on to a client the first night I danced there, so to me dancing and escort went kind of hand in hand ... And out of town I thought, "Hey, there's nobody here I know. I'm going to be hanging out here for a whole week, I mean I might as well make some extra money."' Noting that she possessed a 'strong sexuality' and a desire 'to meet all kinds of potential partners,' Scarlett explained: 'Soon as I started dancing, I started meeting men left, right, and centre. I remember a two-week period where I looked back and I went, "Oh my God, I'm exhausted." I had two or three dates a day for two weeks.' Keeping her escort work quiet and private, she managed the stigma at the same time that she acknowledged its potency: 'I'm sure there were other women who turned tricks, as they called it in those days. Maybe some looked for a guy who would be a sugar daddy so they could feel a little bit better about it.' Unashamed, unapologetic, and still working in the escort trade thirty years later, Scarlett was refreshingly frank about the strictures that bind women sexually: 'I don't buy into the Madonna-whore thing – it's absurd. It's a male construct, it's a Catholic church construct, and it doesn't help us get ahead. We're so busy sitting around trying to prove how sweet or pure or innocent we are, and in the meantime we just lose touch with the women we really are. We've got huge ranges of being bitches and whores, from the ugly to the beautiful.'

The majority of retired dancers I interviewed, by contrast, emphasized their careers as artists and either implicitly or explicitly set themselves apart from prostitutes (especially street-involved, outdoor workers), who laboured under more severe criminal sanctions, stigma, and the acute threat of violence. Black singer and MC Ron Small recalled a largely unacknowledged symbiotic relationship between prostitutes and dancers. He noted that the top call girls 'had diamonds, were classy, and dressed to the nines,' and rather than 'standing out on Victoria and Kingsway [in the East End],' they worked the up-scale nightclubs, and 'brought people in to see the dancers because they want to get you turned on!' However, rather than mutual respect, striptease dancers were much more likely to imagine solidarity with early-twentieth-century can-can dancers, mid-century Vegas show queens, and Hollywood starlets than with prostitutes, who in the eyes of many dancers gave stripteasers a 'bad name.' Brave women like Scarlett Lake who both danced and sold sexual services were, as she put it, a 'breed apart.'

Augmenting Marketability

In the 1950s and 1960s, according to April Paris, there was some acceptance by club owners and booking agents of a range of body types, from 'voluptuous, really Rubenesque, to flat as a pancake.' However, throughout the 1970s, expectations narrowed dramatically, and oversized breasts became de rigueur in the skin trade – a trend capitalized on more recently by west coast Canadian blond Pamela Anderson and the late Anna Nicole Smith.[55] As historian Lucinda Jarrett observed, 'Reviews [of strip shows] praised the statistics of a girl in the same way a prize horse or new model of car might be evaluated.'[56] Fantastically top-loaded women graced the pages of *Playboy* magazine – the first 'boob job' mentioned is Miss April 1965 – and Hugh Hefner both reflected and created the axiom that *breasts count* in the fantasy marketplace.[57] In the striptease industry, the legendary breast size of white Americans Annie Ample, Morganna – The Kissing Bandit, and Chesty Morgan guaranteed their billing as feature acts.[58] Morganna made no secret of her measurements: 60-24-39.[59] Val Scott, a Toronto-based dancer 'bought tits as part of buying a costume' and claimed them as a 'professional development' deduction on her income tax return.[60] According to the women I interviewed, breast implants became increasingly common among Vancouver-based dancers in the mid- to late 1970s – an embodiment of what sociologist Pierre Bourdieu might call 'the art of self-embellishment' for believers in the virtue of 'cosmetic voluntarism.'[61] In fact, the silicone implant was an improvement on the strategies of the 1950s. Choreographer Jack Card told me a story about Las Vegas showgirls who ran out at rehearsal breaks to get silicone injected directly into their breasts: 'They didn't do implants in those days. They had injections right into the fatty tissue. And then the bubbles would start three years later and the tearing apart of their boobs – it was terrible.'

Former booking agent Jeannie Runnalls recalled that in the 1970s, 'Nightmare boob jobs happened. Some poor girls had operation after operation after operation for corrections. It looked like you were wearing two softballs. There was no blending.' Roxanne has regrets about her surgery: 'I had a boob job in the seventies and it was a disaster. I had them removed. We were programmed to think, "Well, if we had this operation and had bigger boobs, then we would make more money." And of course, you fell for it, right? But it wasn't worth it.' Shelinda refused to get implants, though her mother, a former dancer, recommended them to her. Tarren Rae was happy she was 'a 34-B with good legs.' And Princess Lillian was an 'all-natural 36-C.' However, by the early 1980s, like the male professional body builders and football, basketball, and baseball players who 'juiced up' on steroids, dancers confronted acute pressure to approximate the ever-inflating ideal in order to boost and lengthen their careers. And yet Shelinda observed that, 'Men hooted and hollered because they thought they were supposed to like large breasts.' Tiana, who danced in Vancouver in the 1980s, told a male booking agent that she would get breast implants if he underwent penis elongation. Whether or not all men genuinely fetishized large 'hooters,' many dancers kept the cash flowing by enhancing their shape; and local cosmetic surgeons were eager to oblige.

Commensurate with sociologist Dorothy E. Smith's analysis of femininity as a social accomplishment, dancers produced their bodily appearance through thought, planning, exercise of judgment, use of resources, and expenditure of time and money on skilled shopping and materials.[62] Smith asserts that women become expert, knowledgeable practitioners of the norm to 'look good.' Lauding women's technical competence in deciphering a world of gendered texts and capitalist markets, she explains that, 'Behind [feminine] appearance and its interpretation is secreted a subject who is fully an agent.'[63] Striptease dancers sought myriad avenues for exhibiting their own agency in a business that was as rife with opportunities as with minefields.

Transition to Poles and Showers on Hotel Stages

In the late-1970s, the No. 5 Orange and the Wild Duck Hotels were among the first to install brass poles on stage. Debuting 'under the canvas big top' on fairgrounds decades earlier,[64] the pole reappeared in California as an offshoot of club owners' desire to market something novel. With the explosion of striptease stages in hotel beer parlours across Vancouver and the Lower Mainland, club owners scrambled to spruce up and spice up their menu of goods and services. A retired bartender, Buddy, was an enthusiastic fan of pole-dancing at the No. 5 Orange: 'I was quite impressed with the musculature of some of these ladies, in the legs, the arms, and the upper body, to do those pole moves, spinning around the poles, upside-down, right side up, every sort of position in-between ... Those girls made it look easy. And when you're that good, you make it look easy, like Wayne Gretzky made hockey look easy.'

Though opinions about poles varied, the dancers I interviewed uniformly denounced the simultaneous introduction of showers on stage as a crass ploy invented by men to stoke straight men's fantasies of wet female bodies in the service of profits. No longer guaranteed the freedom to design their own acts, dancers resisted the overt intervention and control of club owners. Shelinda resented the pressure to conform to the expectations of club owners and staff, and the ways in which showering constricted her performance choices: 'The DJ got this interactive conversation going with the audience, which I'd never experienced before. "Do you want her to do her shower guys?" And the guys in the front row were just chanting, chanting, chanting. I felt angry. I refused to do a shower for a long time.' So when she finally complied, the feisty, gutsy Shelinda publicly showered on her own terms: 'I got myself completely soaked and I came out and I just shook my hair all over the guys in the front row. I stomped around like a proud horse.'

In the late 1970s, some feature dancers like Tarren Rae hated showering on stage; she simply refused to do it. Indeed, Tarren Rae's marquee status offered her a rare instance of protection that was denied to non-headlining dancers, though by the early 1980s similar acts of defiance had largely disappeared. Shalimar fought the shift to what she disdainfully termed 'shower power' on the grounds that it compromised hygiene and aesthetics: 'It pissed me off. You spent how much time doing your hair? You spent how much time putting on your make-up? For what? So I can go in here and wreck it? Plus, I don't see anybody up there with the Ajax scrubbing that shower down every night. You know, they clean the bar but not the stage or the shower. And when was the last time that carpet was shampooed?' In the same vein, Bambi abhorred the public spectacle of what was otherwise a private pleasure. She recalls that, 'It was totally degrading to get into a shower in front of everybody at the Number Five and the Marble Arch. The Wild Duck had the drain in the middle of the dance floor, and it was just hilarious. They had to have some old guy come and mop it up after every show.' In the early 1980s, Tiana danced with a woman at a club in Prince George who exhibited her distaste for showering by getting into the shower on stage, shaving her legs, brushing her teeth, washing her hands, and douching, before she stomped off![65]

In spite of the new impulse for razzle-dazzle, not all club owners invested in expensive renovations, nor did strip clubs match the glitter of decades past. Still performing in Vancouver in her fifties, the unforgettable striptease queen Tempest Storm was interviewed in 1977 by a *Vancouver Sun* reporter about the disappearance of big production numbers. She sighed dejectedly: 'Oh yes, it has deteriorated. When I started there were big chorus lines. Big orchestras. Any type of staging you wanted. Needed a prop? They built it. Now, you are lucky to get a spotlight.'[66] The game had irrevocably changed for all of the players.

The shift towards small stages in peeler pubs equipped with poles and showers coincided with the gradual elimination of live music supplied by in-house professional musicians.In the heat and frenzy of the 1970s disco craze, the live musical accompaniment that striptease dancers had enjoyed for decades slowly faded away. To saxophone player Dave Davies, 'It was a gradual thing. I think a lot of the girls wanted music that the musicians couldn't or wouldn't play, so they'd bring in their own eight-track tapes. And the club owners loved it because they didn't have to pay musicians. So it was a win-win for them, and we had to find something else to do. The club owners weren't concerned with the quality of music, in terms of live versus canned music. They just wanted the right kind of music for the girls and not to have to pay any money for it. It was very Darwinian. Some musicians just stopped being musicians.' In fact, dancers had to start paying middlemen to assemble taped compilations of their favourite tunes. Music by disco stars Donna Summer, Gloria Gaynor, the Village People, Sister Sledge, and K.C. and the Sunshine Band became dancers' staples. By the late 1970s, the nightclub world had moved swiftly in the direction of fancy electronics, hyperkinetic DJs, a full disco slate, and, by the late 1970s, *Hockey Night in Canada* broadcasts on over-sized TV screens.

The sea-change in musical tastes, combined with the incorporation of new technology and club owners' belt-tightening, dealt a bitter blow to musicians who depended on and appreciated a weekly paycheque, and to their special bond with dancers. The final nail in the musicians' coffin, remembers drummer Gord Walkinshaw, was a legal action in 1978: 'The hotels went crying to the government to end the law that they had to have live music to get and keep their licence. And that killed it for us.' Though musicians rallied and lobbied to thwart the trend to taped music and the loss of their livelihood, the scale of transformation was insurmountable. The train was out of the station, as it were, and musicians were no longer welcome aboard.

Showing 'The Pink'

By the late 1970s, the transition to poles, showers, tape-recorded music, and bottomless dancing was broadened to include the practice of 'splitting' or 'spreading' one's undressed genitals on stage. Indeed, the practice was part and parcel of bigger changes in the production and promotion of ever-more graphic depictions of female sexuality in popular culture across North America. The launch of hardcore pornographic films such as *Deep Throat* (1972) and *Behind the Green Door* (1973), the inaugural issue of Larry Flynt's *Hustler* magazine in 1974 and Bob Guccione's *Penthouse* in 1977, and the arrival of new VCR technology announced the dawn of a triple-X-rated adult entertainment industry.[67] Matter-of-factly charting 'the ever-increasing brazenness of the flesh peddlers,' Robert Miller warned readers of *Maclean's* magazine about '[B]ody rub parlours, sleazy bookstores, nudie movie theatres, and "escort agencies" proliferating throughout urban Canada with the grim determination and frightening speed of lymphatic cancer.'[68] Barenaked ladies were fingered in the backlash as evidence of a debauched nation on the brink of moral collapse.

Located in large American cities such as Los Angeles and New York, the commercial sex industry, which included strip clubs, elevated the expectation of male consumers for live and photographed 'cunt shots.' In *Bound and Gagged*, Laura Kipnis argues that *Hustler*, with its working-class, anti-establishment focus on the lower half of the body, crusaded *for* explicitness (unprecedented for a mass-circulation magazine).[69] The textually mediated imperative to 'show the pink' meant heightened consciousness among erotic dancers of the need for geometric barbering of pubic hair, bikini waxes, and, for white women, tanning at salons or through acquisition of their own personal tanning beds. Unlike beautiful female models – both white and 'brown-skinned' – who were paid to sell consumer goods in *Vogue*, *Life*, and *Ebony* magazines,[70] striptease dancers sold their own hyper-feminine image (or brand), radically redefining the meaning of 'good grooming.' Years later, ex-stripper Diablo Cody mused about the penchant for 'pink' at the 'juice bars.' Emphasizing the democratic, non-discriminating assessment of exposed female genitalia, she explained, 'No one cares what you've got between your legs. Sloppy, tight, pierced, shaved, under-aged or "distinguished," it's still pussy and it's worth its depth in molten gold when you're a stripper.'[71]

The directive that dancers were to spread like cream-cheese in the 1970s touched off a firestorm of protest, especially among those dancers who had begun their careers with g-strings firmly in place. Headliner Bonnie Scott was distressed by the pattern she saw emerging across the commercial striptease scene:

The hotel bars opened up and there was this huge demand for girls. The girls would show up and just do anything. They didn't have any costumes, they didn't have shows, so they'd end up laying on the floor. There were places that wouldn't hire me, or they would fire me, because I would not lay down on the floor and spread my legs. It's like my art, and they were trying to taint that art. And that art was the truest expression of me. And they were trying to take that away from me, and I was angry and bitter about that. So it just went downhill. There was a time when the women who had the acts – me, Danielle, Michelle – got the most money. But it became that the women willing to show the most pussy were the highest-paid dancers.

Scott was not alone in either her criticism or her fear that A-grade features would be sidelined by the crush of novices eager to spread. To Princess Lillian, the only deaf dancer, the introduction of spreading jeopardized her livelihood and threatened her sense of herself as an independent professional: 'It happened in one year: everyone started splitting. I told them, "Leave me alone, I don't have to be changed that way. Don't ask me to do that, it's not your body, it's mine. I dance very good. I don't have to do this." They would say, "Goodbye then," and it hurt me. I wanted to leave the g-string on – more imagination, more exciting, and many of the spreaders were horrible dancers.' An unnamed journalist for the *Vancouver Sun* recorded the sentiments of one dancer in 1973:

Sunni Daye hates the bottomless trend among the girls appearing in various clubs. She is not liberated and she's not puritanical. She's just mad. She has a soft, round face, huge hazel eyes and shoulder-length champagne hair and she's a professional entertainer. 'A vocalist and exotic dancer.' She's been out of work for 8 weeks, because of girls who take it all off. 'I have eight or nine thousand dollars worth of costumes at home. I attended the Toronto Conservatory of Music. I worked and studied for four years to perfect an act. And I'm not alone. There's at least six of us in the same boat who've been put out of work because of this ... Suddenly they started bringing in girls from the U.S. who were not nearly as good as local talent. The club owners didn't mind if they wore nothing but contact lenses as long as it put a quick profit in the owner's pocket. They didn't care if it brought down the respect for the girls and the level of entertainment. Some owners even make suggestions to the girls to dance nude with a dummy. Many of these girls will do anything. Some will even pick out a male from the audience and undress him on the stage. The owners can hire three of these no-talent people for the price of a good entertainer and the good entertainers are out of work ... I will not go bottomless. It would upset my parents and I want to communicate with an audience on a different level than that.'[72]

Artistic autonomy extinguished, dancers were angry about the deterioration of their working conditions. In the mid-1970s, Miss Lovie joined a vocal group of white dancers to condemn what they perceived as the scourge of hotel beer parlours and the shift to gratuitous nudity: 'Those little tiny stages? Honey, where do you want me to dance? And it became too naked to be sensual. The respect was gone. Girls started to show ANYTHING to have this job and make this money. They hadn't practised and worked on it and got an act together. No costumes, no lighting, just terrible. They were prostitute-types. It was like stags had started coming on stage.' In his book *Behind the G-String*, David Scott dissected the magnetism of exposed female genitalia: 'The ability of the vulva to attract attention has few rivals. Because society demands that it be covered up, its appearance in public is an anomaly, and one that inspires a host of reactions. Its beauty, its mystery, its meaning, its desire, its danger and its intrigue – even an unappealing dancer will stop conversations and turn heads when she finally removes her g-string.'[73] Retired dancer Sarita Melita laughed when she recalled her cheeky response to men's genital fixation: 'A friend and I bought some plastic speculums, and we walked around gynaecology row, passing out the speculums, and latex examination gloves, to make a point. You know, "Why don't you really get in there, and dig?"'

Increasingly, dancers drew the line between good and bad stage-work, and good and bad dancers, on the basis of distinctions between art and smut. Tarren Rae spoke to the inevitability of the downward spiral:

I wasn't a spreader – I was naked for half of the last song. Even then, you didn't see anything except hair. Leanne was purely sexual. She was just a grinding machine on stage. She was really down and dirty. She was sweaty and in the doggie-style position, pure porno without a male actor ... There was no entertainment value in that to me, but there was a lot of entertainment value for men because they could picture themselves there doing it. It felt really degrading to me. It felt cheap, it felt sleazy, it felt like I was selling myself. That was the dividing line between self-denigration and being proud of what I did. It made me feel bad about myself ... It had to do with desensitization. After Leanne came Mitzi, the pinball shooter, and then the baby-oil acts. It was having live porno right in your face, and to many men it was very exciting, new, and different. It was a slippery slope that we'd already stepped upon, and once you got there, there was no turning back.

A fixture at the Drake Hotel, Lusty Leanne spurred a 'Pavlovian "Let's Go" reaction' in scores of fans, according to journalist Les Wiseman. *Rustler*, the Canadian men's magazine, ran a 'one-handed' article on her entitled the 'Hottest Stripper in the West.' Radio DJs urged their listeners to go down to the Drake. Wiseman added that, in addition to a twenty-four-bottle carton of baby oil, 'Men sent roses, and one group made her a crown out of cut-up $50 and $100 bills.'[74] Interviewed for *Vancouver Magazine* in 1982, Tarren Rae railed against the 'ego gratification of the spreaders,' and added that 'They'll be having animals up there soon, because baby oil isn't enough.'[75] April Paris, echoing Tarren Rae, blamed Leanne for triggering a destructive avalanche: 'In the late-1970s, we all hated her because she was a spreader. At that time, she threatened our livelihood, because no one ever did that. Those spreader-girls were *Hustler* and *Penthouse,* and we were *Playboy.* We referred to ourselves as dancers, never strippers. We thought what we did was dancing, we thought it was art. And when you started spreading your legs like that, that wasn't art any more, that was porn.' Being able to distinguish one's art and craft as a dancer from a prostitute or a porn model was pivotal to dancers who sought respectability and reputability for their profession. Implicitly, these dancers drew and redrew a class-specific boundary between respectable entertainer and disreputable 'ho.'[76]

A New Era Dawns

By the early 1970s, the striptease business had become more competitive, there was more money to be made, and the stakes were higher for all insiders. Dancers such as April Paris, Virginia, and Scarlett Lake toured, they were booked by (and beholden to) agents, and they performed topless – a development that rippled out from the epicentres of Paris, San Francisco, and Las Vegas. The most dramatic, irreversible change in dancers' working conditions followed the decriminalization of nudity in British Columbia in September 1972. Almost overnight, dancers faced a province-wide circuit of hotel peeler pubs, the loss of glamorous stages in independent nightclubs, and the growth of a seemingly insatiable appetite for full nudity and on-stage simulation of sex acts – both hetero- and homosexual. Similarly, at the Paradiso, the Bijou, and the Dolls' House in London, striptease dancers were required to do 'open leg work' on the floor.[77] Notwithstanding myriad objections to bottomless striptease tabled by politicians, police, clergy, and dancers (detailed in chapter 5), any campaign to stop the clock was unwinnable. Even booking agent Jack Card, a staunch advocate of old-school bump and grind, recognized the writing on the wall; only a fresh influx of profits eased his consternation.

Like many of the dancers who resented the shift to full nudity, jazz saxophonist Dave Davies disparaged the transition: 'The beer parlours that had nude dancers were an abomination. The whole concept was to get naked women and lots of guys in there to drink lots of beer. At the Penthouse and Isy's, there were real legitimate dancers who incidentally took their clothes off. They had routines, they rehearsed, they had acts, special costumes – it was extended foreplay. They'd drag it out on stage for half an hour – a glove comes off, there's feathers or balloons. Some of these girls would take forever to take their bra off. It used to drive me crazy.' In 1974, nightbeat columnist Jack Wasserman's mood was philosophical: 'Like everything else, including Rocky Road ice cream, or chopped chicken livers, too much of a good thing kills the taste.'[78]

To be solvent and 'bankable' in the business, dancers did what they could to stay fit, supple, fresh, innovative, and out of trouble (with the law, violent lovers, or drug/alcohol overuse). Using strategies familiar to beauty pageant contestants, dancers engaged in an intensive, Foucauldian regime of self-inspection: they monitored their appearance, diet, shape, size, colour, routines, punctuality, audiences, and competition (however friendly).[79] By the late 1970s, the drive to 'work out' reflected not only the growing fitness, yoga, and aerobics boom but the intensifying cultural obsession with youthful, lithe, but not overly muscled female bodies. Naked or near-naked floor and pole routines that highlighted the fruits of dancers' gym memberships substituted for large-scale, outmoded props, beaded gowns, feathered headpieces, and elaborately choreographed productions.

By the early 1980s, dancers made adjustments and embraced change, or they retired to seek alternative employment. Emphasis was increasingly placed on winning striptease competitions such as the 'Golden G-

String,' garnering the prestige of 'Miss Nude' titles, and landing roles in sexually provocative films and magazines. Each of these stints enhanced a dancer's profile, marketability, and profit-making potential. Shelinda witnessed the trend: 'Women started getting all these titles – "Miss Nude Calgary," "Miss Something-Something of Alberta," and that automatically got you more money. It became a three-ring circus to me.' Negotiating changes internal and external to the stage proper necessitated certain adaptations. For instance, dancers experienced unprecedented pressure to 'work the floor' before and after their shift on stage. Table dancing involved carting a small box from table to table, standing on it before a prospective customer, and soliciting a 'one-on-one' dance for a five-dollar fee. Shalimar bemoaned the trend: 'I never wanted to stand in some dark little corner with some guy's nose stuck in my ass.' Jasmine Tea likened the invention of table dancing to convenient yet unsatisfying fast food: 'It was like introducing a McDonald's drive-through window where you get this cheap meal in two minutes, as opposed to sitting down and ordering and having it come course by course, and enjoying every mouthful of it. It was like, "shove a hamburger in your face." It upset me.'

Lindalee Tracey (aka Fonda Peters), who danced in Montreal in the 1970s, argues that by the early 1980s television had swallowed imaginations, the corporate agenda had flattened dancers' individuality, and hard-core porn had leaked its numbing poison. 'After that,' she states, 'striptease became business-driven and mechanical and the genius of strippers disappeared under the tyranny of explicitness.'[80] Vancouver-based Shalimar put it this way: 'Before Joe [Philliponi] got shot at the Penthouse in 1983, dancing actually had some class and some taste. After Joe got shot, it turned into a bunch of anorexic, bleached-blond Barbie dolls with silicone boobs, tummy tucks, and hair extensions – for three thousand dollars any dumb bitch can look like that. It was plastic.' Working in nightclubs and hotels prior to the legendary Philliponi's death, dancers experienced multiple benefits on the job. In the next chapter, I explore how these same dancers navigated the choppy waters of a business replete with occupational hazards.

5 'Everyone Wanted to Date a Dancer, Nobody Wanted to Marry One':[1] Occupational Hazards in the Industry

It was always tricky explaining that I'd been a stripper once; it was startling to other sensibilities, as harsh a class distinction as one can make. People reacted with suspicion, pity or sometimes prurient fascination. They leaped into their assumptions, imagining me a whore, an idiot, a victim. I winced, not from my shame, because there really wasn't any, but from the shame people wanted to impose.

Lindalee Tracey, *Growing Up Naked*, 1997[2]

I told my mother I was going to be working as an erotic dancer and she was so excited. She thought that was marvellous. She even helped me make big capes and costumes thinking that I was a belly dancer at a Greek restaurant. Six months later I was on tour, went to the city where she lived and I said, 'This week I'm at the Lido.' And she goes, 'The Lido? That's a strip bar!' 'Yes, Mom, I'm a stripper, like an erotic dancer.' So the Catholic guilt hit the wall – it took years for her to recover from that. I was obviously up to no good if I was a stripper.

Klute, Interview, 1999[3]

The art of bump and grind has long conjured up negative stereotypes of female dancers as nymphomaniacs, survivors of broken homes and sexual abuse, degraded victims of predatory men, home-wreckers, and drug users dangerous to the social order, the family, and the nation.[4] Though my evidence contradicts this troublingly one-dimensional profile, a dancer was judged for refusing to confine her sexuality to the heterosexual, monogamous, nuclear family. Governed by the age-old Western dichotomy of asexual mother versus devouring whore, she was criticized for making a mockery of romantic love, fidelity, and dignified sexual propriety. To historian Robert C. Allen, the image of the mid-twentieth-century burlesque dancer is premised on the double-sided trope of the 'low other ... reviled by and excluded from the dominant social order as debased, dirty, and unworthy, but simultaneously the object of desire and/or fascination.'[5]

In this chapter, the retired dancers I interviewed convey myriad manifestations of the stripper stigma. They recount how they steeled themselves against harsh criticism from all quarters. True to sociologist Erving Goffman's conception of stigmatization, stripteasers were seen to embody an 'undesired differentness,' and were discounted and accorded discreditable status.[6] Working in spaces where recreational drugs and alcohol were as easy to obtain as lemon drops at Lee's Candies, they endeavoured to resist ever-present temptations. Dancers also remembered being vulnerable to violence, from catcalls to unwanted groping to sexual assault. Throughout the 1970s, amid country-wide drives by female workers to unionize, dancers made repeated attempts to bargain with club owners, though the barriers – structural and attitudinal – were entrenched. Moreover, the fear of police harassment, club raids, and arrests kept dancers (and club staff) on edge, wary of harm. And yet, ever gutsy, dancers swam against the current to make their own waves, on their own terms.

Stripper Stigma as Occupational Hazard

Both white and non-white dancers learned to cope with the stubborn contradiction: they were adored or rebuked. According to Tempest Storm, 'The stigma was one of my constant companions. No matter how successful I was to become, no matter how much class my act became known for, some people have never been able to deal with me. They can see nothing except their own image of a "stripper," and society has conditioned them to see that as a negative image.'[7] Dancers' bodies were insistently observed and administered by powers vested with the authority to adjudicate the 'healthy' versus the 'pathological.'[8] As a result, dancers were compelled to practise self-regulation and self-surveillance, at once balancing the threat of obscenity laws with, and against, nightclub owners' insistence on displays of more and more flesh.[9] Historian Lorraine Dong interviewed former showgirl Jadin Wong, who recalled that, 'Chinese people in San Francisco were ready to spit in our faces because we were nightclub performers. They wouldn't talk with us because they thought we were whores. We used to get mail at Forbidden City – "Why don't you get a decent job and stop disgracing the Chinese? You should be ashamed of yourselves, walking around and showing your legs!"'[10] To Vancouver-based show-girl Nena Marlene, deflecting moral judgment was simply part of the job in the 1950s:

> We had the censors, and the churches were always against us. They thought we were all going to hell in a basket. A lot of people had very narrow minds. A woman who lived nearby came and told my Mom, 'Your daughter's picture is outside the State Theatre,' and Mom says, 'So? She's working there.' Mom knew that the reason that I wanted to be there was so I could come home and look after her. She always had an open mind, and I told her, 'Mom, I would never do anything to make you ashamed.'[11]

In the late 1960s, sociologists, psychologists, and criminologists labelled striptease a 'deviant occupation.' James Skipper and Charles McCaghy conducted a sociological study of 119 'strippers' in 1969 and revealed that the 'girls displayed their bodies to gain attention they did not receive at home, especially from the father.'[12] They theorized that strippers experienced a form of arrested emotional development. In 1969, sociologists Jesser and Donovan interviewed 155 university students and 122 parents of students, all of whom assigned strip-teasers a lower occupational ranking than traditionally lower-status jobs: janitor, artist's model, and professional gambler.[13] Although half of the ex-dancers I interviewed identified as middle class, all dancers were attributed lower-class status by critics who disparaged their participation in the skin trade. As Beverly Skeggs claims, 'Respectability is one way in which sexual practice is evaluated, distinctions drawn, legitimated, and maintained between groups.'[14] Because disavowal of the sexual – a tactic necessary to secure hetero-feminine respectability – was impossible for stripteasers in the postwar era, they were measured as deficient *in relation to* the ideal of white, middle-class elegance, sophistication, and restraint. A regular club-goer in the 1960s, Megan Carvell Davis compromised her relaxed, hippie look to keep her job as a cocktail waitress. She explained, 'When I worked at the Shanghai Junk, which used to be the Kublai Khan, Stan [Chong] would tell me, "Get in that bathroom, take out that braid in your hair, put on your false eyelashes. Put on make-up." I hated wearing it, but I knew I had to do that to keep the job ... But I didn't have to dance on the stage with men looking at me. I would have felt humiliated to work as a dancer.'[15]

According to ex-dancer Margaret Dragu, all stripteasers were assumed to moonlight as prostitutes.[16] Whether or not they turned tricks, they were damned by those who disparaged nightclubs as the playgrounds of gangsters, bootleggers, bookies, pimps, hookers, and sex fiends. As a consequence, dancers often covered up what they did, or told family, friends, and lovers that they worked as waitresses, hostesses, travel agents, models, or modern dance instructors. To further 'closet' their identities,[17] they adopted stage names. Dancers, not their customers, were ticketed (as were prostitutes, folks receiving social assistance, and 'troubled' youth gangs) for conduct deemed intrinsically bad, wrong, or immoral.

The stripper stigma was especially hurtful for dancers who juggled child-rearing and a striptease career. I interviewed three retired dancers who, as mothers, recalled the painful judgment of other parents, day-care workers, coaches, and teachers who disapproved of their chosen field of work. In her autobiography, *Growing Up Naked*, Lindalee Tracey observed that, 'Women and men ... think it's an instinctive, swelling urge like nymphomania, something ferocious that drains the blood out of a woman's brain, leaving her feeble-minded and primitive. They don't recognize the performance elements, the business complexities, the guts it takes to manoeuvre around people's expectations every night.'[18] Later, Tracey tried to donate the proceeds from a large-scale strip-a-thon, 'Tits for Tots,' to help disabled kids in Montreal, only to face rejection from a series of agency spokespeople who explained they had 'reputations' to uphold.[19] Puerto-Rican Canadian Sarita Melita, who raised two children while dancing, felt she needed to hide her profession to protect them. When her children started school, Sarita remembered her fear: 'The neighbours didn't know what I did, the teachers didn't know what I did. They could have taken my kids away from me. People, they judged you very much. I almost lost my kids on several occasions for no good reasons, just because I was a stripper.' As Roxanne succinctly put it, 'Society has to have a scapegoat, and we were the bad girls.'

Choreographer and booking agent Jack Card summed up what he observed as the cruel, hypocritical stance towards striptease adopted by Vancouver's well-heeled: 'The upper class who saw strippers thought it was like going to the circus to see the clowns. "Oh, it's a little amusement for us." It was very bigoted. What about opera stars baring their breasts? Or first-class ballerinas raped on stage in a scene, and the "cream of society" is standing up shouting, "Bravo! Bravo!" It was a double standard.'[20] A half-century earlier, ballet was widely believed to be obscene. However, by the 1960s and 1970s, both opera and ballet were firmly established as respectable, high-class professions, sold as expensive, uplifting, and edifying events in the city's most lavish, uptown venues.[21] With fifteen years of ballet training, Christine Chipperfield became a professional jazz and contemporary dancer in Vancouver in the early 1970s. Familiar with the role of the 'totally clothed, virginal princess,' she later taught dance aerobics at Terpsichore Studio before a debilitating car accident derailed her career. Referencing her 'sheltered, uptight' childhood on the city's West Side, Christine explained that, 'No one I knew would ever work in a strip club to subsidize her dance classes. It wasn't the society you wanted to travel in. I thought the strippers were degraded and exploited ... It wasn't until later on, after I lost everything, and started really venturing into the world of poverty, disability, and falling between the cracks, that I started to understand these different subcultures.'[22] While Christine's accident instilled in her a more compassionate viewpoint, she continued to see exotic dancers as down on their luck and impoverished, with few options at their disposal.

A dancer and choreographer who worked with Jack Card, Patrick Kevin O'Hara was a cross-over artist who moved fluidly between the professional fields of classical ballet and exotic dancing, and between British Columbia and Europe. Sensitized to hypocrisy from having grown up in a working-class family, O'Hara recalled feeling exasperated by the adherence of many Vancouverites to foreign ideas of 'capital-C' Culture. Gesturing to the city's past as a 'raw resource colony for British and American imperialism,' he took pleasure in exposing the class-bound incommensurability between high and low art. Echoing the French theorist Pierre Bourdieu, O'Hara noted that 'People would underestimate the artistic merits of so-called strippers, or striptease dancers, by comparing them to ballet or modern dancers. This is a common mistake found in areas with a low cultural quotient and is indicative not so much of the quality of the artist but rather of the intellectual and cultural poverty of the evaluator. The notion of "legitimate dance" versus "exotic dance" is a provincial idea propagated by uncultured snobs.'[23] Drawing on years of work with erotic dancers in Vancouver and Paris, O'Hara turned the bourgeois claim to cultural competence on its head.

Conscious of the 'dominated' and 'degraded' aesthetic attached to their art form,[24] most ex-dancers I interviewed explained how their geographical distance from family and friends mitigated the humiliation of 'being caught' on stage. Indeed, physical separation from loved ones who lived outside Vancouver enabled their decision to enter commercial striptease in the first place. Yet even for those whose parents resided out of town, the risk of censure was ever-present. During her dancing career in the late 1950s and early 1960s, Choo Choo Williams's religious parents in Edmonton, Alberta, disapproved of the Harlem Nocturne – the club she operated with her husband, Ernie King. Choo Choo speculated that though her parents never said anything about their daughter's dancing 'with no clothes on,' they figured she was going to hell, and that the entertainment business was 'Satan's work.' Miss Lovie, originally from Chicago, shouldered the stigma no striptease dancer completely eluded: 'I upset my family, that's why I did it in Canada. And my step-dad's a minister! Women were not supposed to go out and be assertive – you were a hussy! Strippers were the low side of the totem pole, though we didn't feel that way. We felt wonderful and we made good money.'[25] Roxanne's mother disowned her, and to this day, her sister refuses to speak with her.[26] Filmed for a Vancouver-based television news spot on 'exotics' in the mid-1970s, Virginia was adamant that her identity be protected. However, as she explained, 'On the six o-clock evening newscast they gave my name, "a registered nurse from London with a three-month-old son, putting her husband through Simon Fraser University." They showed me performing at lunch time, high heels, bending over and looking at the audience upside-down between my legs. My husband's family were very straight-laced – they were told I was waitressing ... I never told my parents – my father was a church minister. They knew I go-go danced, that was it.' April Paris was not alone in defending her dancing career to parents by reassuring them that she was not 'working the streets.' She stated that, 'My mom wasn't thrilled. She thought any good girl shouldn't be doing that, but I explained that I wasn't a prostitute.'

For many critics, a stripper's career choice was abhorrent when compared to the gender-appropriate care-giving professions of nursing, teaching, and social work. Perceived as sexually loose and instantly available, Shelinda was reluctant to tell people what she did for a living. She rehearsed the adage: 'It was like, "If you were willing to take your clothes off in public, then why wouldn't you be willing to jump into bed with me?"' Similarly, Cascade told me how her genuine comfort with her dancing career was challenged by people whose impression of her changed drastically once they were apprised of her trade: 'I'd be astounded, especially the first few months, when I would tell somebody what I do, and somebody who'd been polite and gentle would become a raging animal! There was no respect.' Jasmine Tea identified the complex emotions she experienced while dancing – on the one hand, she gained a measure of professional and personal mastery and satisfaction on stage; on the other hand, she had trouble attracting a lover unencumbered by weighty stereotypes:

What little girl goes, 'Mummy, Daddy, when I grow up, I want to be a stripper.' They don't do that. It's not accepted. It's shunned. People have no respect for you. The hardest part of the business for me was the lack of respect ... It was like, 'You must not think very highly of yourself if you take your clothes off.' In a way, dancing gives you some self-esteem – people want to watch you dance, but it was hard. I was afraid that someone I knew would come in and see me and laugh at me because I wasn't good enough. And when they find out a woman dances in bars they think she's easy, an easy mark. No guy wants to bring you home and introduce you to their mother when you're a stripper. It's like, 'Where did you meet?' 'Well, actually, Mom, I met her in a bar, taking her clothes off.' I think that was the only time I was really, truly ashamed of what I did.

On themes of romance, cohabitation, commitment, and marriage, dancers told me that domesticity and striptease mixed poorly.[27] Few of the dancers I interviewed were married or engaged in long-term relationships during their dancing career. Bambi outlined her razor-sharp analysis of the dating scene:

Groupies were known as peeler pumpers or feature fuckers. They just wanted to tell their friends, 'Oh, I screwed a dancer,' and then you're one notch on their bedpost... It was really hard for a guy to bring a dancer home to his parents. Or if she's married and she's out late, her old man automatically thinks she's screwing around. I've never had one boyfriend that really thought this was a job. They don't classify it as a job. They think it's a party ... They think we're picking up guys and drinking all day. They'd have to do this job to see it as work.[28]

Knee-jerk criticism of striptease dancers and their craft oozed from business outsiders of all kinds, including lovers, family members, friends, clergy, police, 'square' employers, social scientists, politicians, feminists, and media pundits. In 1974, an unnamed reporter for *The*

Province newspaper, on assignment at the Penthouse nightclub, peppered his lurid exposé with elements of the well-worn captivity narrative: dancers were trapped, exploited victims. He warned: 'Mostly imports from Las Vegas, Tijuana, San Francisco and Fernie [B.C.], they're roughed up by contract men, promised the earth, and then brought here under contract to peel [for] anywhere from $250–$500 per week, 2 shows a night, no holds barred. Gimmicks run the gamut from A to Z, cups start at B, go as far as E plus and runneth over.'[29] Smug in his translation of 'underground scandal' to non-initiated readers, this reporter ignored the expanding presence of Vancouver-based dancers. In addition, he regurgitated tired stereotypes without interviewing dancers themselves.

Judged: 'In the Toilet of Show Business'

Negotiating the anti-stripper stigma required a thick skin, as rejection came packaged in myriad guises. Cascade applied to be an airline stewardess, noting on her application the nightclub where she had worked as an exotic dancer in the mid-1970s: she was angry and disappointed that 'they never called.' Toronto-based dancer Valerie Scott elected to travel west to work in the early 1970s, and endeavoured to protect her assets before she left: 'I approached my insurance company about getting my costumes insured for the trip to Vancouver. As soon as the company found out that I was a stripper, they tried to cancel my contract because in their eyes stripping was the same as prostitution and they didn't want to be insuring any sex-business thing.' Headliner Bonnie Scott was hired by the British Columbia Institute of Technology (BCIT) to perform as a stripper at the 'Woodchoppers' Ball.' She did her champagne glass show while the head of BCIT sat in the front row, and the next day 'The student union raised a big stink about me doing a strip show and they barred me from there for life.'

Booking agent Jeannie Runnalls noted that a dancer faced barriers to renting a nice apartment if she was not 'smart enough to say she's a typist, waitress, or bank clerk.' Moreover, Runnalls, added, 'Everyone from the maid to the manager treats her as an outcast. Joe Cool desk clerk, acting like he doesn't see her, hides her away in whatever room is left over. The maid won't supply towels. The bartender makes snide remarks and pats her bum ... There are two hundred people in that bar – all trained to disrespect the dancer. That's how the prejudice spreads.'[30] Again, though hotel and bar staff benefited financially from the business brought in by dancers, they could not be trusted to behave honourably.

Not one to mince words, Klute had a name for the harsh, external evaluation of her business and the tactics she adopted to protect herself and her co-workers upon exiting the scene: 'I was in the toilet of show business. Outside strip bars there's a stigma about what a stripper is. I had to doctor my résumé over the years to cover that five-year period. I'd say I was a nightclub entertainer. I did magic, I did mime, impersonation, black light. I just didn't say I did it while I took my clothes off. There's an unwritten code among ex-strippers: out of respect, you never tell another person about a retired stripper's former career.'

Dancers also encountered hostility from many feminists active during the late 1960s and 1970s in the context of second-wave women's liberation. Vancouver, like other cities across Canada and the United States, became fertile ground for feminist consciousness raising, organization building, and challenges to the sexism embedded in the institutions of family, mass media, law, advertising, health care, policing, religion, education, and the workplace, among others.[31] For instance, feminist activists initiated the Abortion Caravan in Vancouver in the spring of 1970 to raise awareness of barriers to full reproductive choice for women across Canada.[32] While ex-dancers told me that they believed in the movement's commitment to gender equality, none of them felt included or accepted by the front-line radicals who defined the terms of 'real' feminist debate, intervention, and identity.[33] As Tarren Rae commented, 'We would have called ourselves feminists – with a disclaimer. We believed in independence for ourselves and self-sufficiency and equal rights. But we also believed in femininity ... A lot of the women who were dancers, who are my friends, they came from backgrounds where they were taken advantage of and abused. And dancing was the one way to regain their sense of independence. A lot of women viewed dancing as a way of having power over men.' Though non-strippers similarly worked for 'the man' on many jobsites that required a highly feminized appearance and comportment, and some had histories of abuse, few were prepared to explore these points of connection with dancers.

Sex workers across the spectrum (in pornography, street-level prostitution, escort work, phone sex, massage, and striptease) were routinely viewed by women's liberationists with suspicion, if not disdain.[34] Perceived as part of the problem of patriarchal oppression, striptease dancers had few opportunities to speak out and be heard by their 'sis-

ters in struggle.' Instead, feminist leaders tended to condemn sex workers as disgraced, exploited pawns in ways that were reminiscent of
late-nineteenth-century campaigns by women (and allies) opposed to
prostitution and pornography.[35] Sociologist Alan Hunt argues that the
espousal of 'sexual purity' by Victorian maternal feminists bequeathed
a problematic legacy to twentieth-century feminism.[36] For example, in
the early 1900s in New York, bourgeois women reformers snitched on
the working women at Macy's department store who 'took to paint and
powder and peroxide and acting bold.'[37] Decades later, middle-class
and anti-male anxieties concerning the 'protection of women' from
(naturally) unscrupulous men stirred feminists in Vancouver (and elsewhere).[38] The assumption that femininity and feminism were mutually
exclusive and that dancers were falsely conscious, 'male-identified' re-
producers of normative heterosexuality prevailed. Dancing in Toronto in the 1970s, Gwendolyn was stung by the feminist credo that 'All
women like me really needed was protection from men and male sex.
And until I got it, or got out altogether, I was not welcome.'[39] When
feminist activists snubbed exotic dancers as non-feminists (in need of
rehabilitation), they governed themselves according to a strict moral
template.[40] Transgressive readings of striptease as mimicry, as 'female
clowning,' and as an enactment of hyper-femininity as a role, and not
a nature, were foreclosed by an essentialist attachment to belief in a
primary, authentic femaleness.[41]

In the early 1970s, Virginia recalled girding herself against the sting
of other women's misunderstanding, pity, and condescension: 'Most of
the criticism against what I did came from feminists. It was, "Poor you,
it must have been so tough, putting your husband through school. And
how could you have degraded yourself in that manner?" I hated that.
They had no idea. They'd say, "Look, look at her, she's dressing like a
stripper, she's a slut." It was a real put-down.' The former dancers I
interviewed deeply resented the middle-class feminist charge that they
were wholly controlled or owned by men in the business. Rather, as
Judith Butler might argue, stripteasers dramatized femininities, sometimes pleasurably and powerfully, always excessively, in ways that de-
naturalized gender as performative.[42] Exotic dancers knew that they
were not automatically less feminist, or less inclined to embrace tenets
of feminism, than telephone operators, daycare workers, or hairdressers. Both real and perceived class differences lay beneath what Michel
Foucault called 'dividing practices' – in this case, the middle-class
feminist distinction between 'good' and 'bad' behaviour that sidelined

erotic dancers as deserving of shame for acting overtly sexual.[43] In addition, unacknowledged white privilege likely impeded political and personal allegiance between white feminists and dancers of colour in the 1960s and 1970s. Not surprisingly, mutual distrust made formal alliances between dancers and non-dancers under one feminist umbrella virtually unthinkable.[44] Indeed, feminist organizers opposed to sex work (including pornography) found themselves uneasily aligned with other moralizing agents, such as the clergy, law enforcers, politicians, educators, and journalists, who defended (and disciplined) the virtues of decency, modesty, self-control, and 'family values' against what they defined as societal decline or degeneration.

Temptations of Drugs and Alcohol

Some dancers' indulgence, on and off the job, in a range of mood-altering substances was part coping strategy, part experimentation, and part recreation. Alcohol, marijuana, amphetamines, heroin, cocaine, MDA, and LSD were in plentiful supply at most Vancouver nightclubs and hotel pubs throughout the 1960s and 1970s.[45] Indeed, the club scene across North America and Europe was infamous for hard drinking and drug use by brilliant nightclub entertainers, including Charlie Parker, Dexter Gordon, Billie Holiday, John Coltrane, Lenny Bruce, Janis Joplin, and Jimi Hendrix – all of whom died of substance abuse. Of the nineteen retired dancers I interviewed, however, only two disclosed heavy use of alcohol and/or drugs during their careers, though all noted that it was a serious, ever-present temptation. Booking agent Jeannie Runnalls witnessed the 'party climate' in strip clubs and the toll it took on a small percentage of dancers hooked into the heady mix: 'A few of the women drank their money away. One could put away a twenty-sixer of Grand Marnier in two hours. Another drank so much she'd just fall off the stage. I'd fire her for a month, and then I'd let her back. Sometimes I let them go forever. It was the atmosphere – lots of booze, lots of pot around, lots of partying.' On the basis of a tight-knit group of dancers he met bartending at the No. 5 Orange Hotel in the late 1970s, Buddy offered a series of sombre observations: 'Some were very bad drug abusers. They all smoked cigarettes, they all drank alcohol, virtually all of them snorted cocaine. They got no exercise – well, they got lots of exercise on stage – but they got no fresh air or sunshine. Their skin colour looked pretty unhealthy to me. So they did not lead very healthy nor would I say happy lives.'

While the ex-dancers I interviewed objected strenuously to the judgment that they were 'unhealthy,' they stressed that those who became drug-dependent did not last long in a business that demanded punctuality, stage smarts, and top physical conditioning. Between stage shows, dancers often nursed free drinks from admirers for hours; several made arrangements with bartenders to minimize the alcohol content in mixed cocktails. As Shalimar noted with a chuckle, 'There is a trick so you don't get bombed – get the bartender to take the vodka and run it around the rim of glass, and then give me orange juice – if the guy smells it or tastes it, it tastes like booze, and the bartender keeps the extra money.' Jazz saxophonist Dave Davies remembers a 'James Dean attitude in those days. Don't worry about tomorrow, just get stoned tonight and have fun. You run out of wine, there were little Italian houses all up and down off Main Street. You could go and knock on the back door, slip them five bucks and get a bottle of the most awful vinegar you could imagine.'

Vancouver was (and is) well known as a hub for high-quality marijuana, or 'B.C. bud.' Musician Doug Cuthbert noted that, 'In the nineteen-sixties, everybody smoked pot in the clubs, and in the seventies, they smoked pot in the beer parlours.' Tarren Rae, among other dancers, appreciated the occupational benefits of a joint: 'Everyone used to smoke dope before their shows. It was the big thing. When you're stoned, and you've got music going and you've got a stage, you've got distance between you and the audience. You're in your own world.' Several ex-dancers stressed that dancing was entirely incompatible with the use of heroin, which became increasingly available in the 1970s. Others mentioned that a handful of club owners sold cocaine, including one who was infamous for selling it out of the safe in his hotel office and enticing dancers to snort lines on his desk in lieu of their weekly pay.

Foxy Lady noted that club owners expected dancers offstage to encourage patrons to buy booze. She explained: 'You are in an atmosphere where there's drinks available. A lot of the times you're bored, and if there's customers that you know, you end up sitting and having a few drinks and then you dance.' Bambi was well aware of the informal economy of 'drug supply and demand' in the clubs she worked. She openly admitted her need to 'smooth out the edges' of a job that had, at times, unsavoury components. She elaborated: 'The agents got some of the women hooked on coke, then their kids were taken away from them because they were seen as an "unfit mother." We all had a vice – more than seventy per cent did something. There wasn't one of us that got up there without a crutch. I loved dancing, but when you got some guy making funny noises and drooling and saying, "Stick it in, baby," you had to have a vice.' And yet dancers, especially those with feature billing, realized that securing marquee status was contingent on restraint; they either closely monitored their drug and/or alcohol consumption or simply refused to partake on the job site. In effect, professional stripping demanded intense concentration, focus, balance, and coordination – requirements that mixed poorly with chemical cocktails, whatever the recipe or method of ingestion.

The Toll of Sexual Harassment and Assault

The dancers I interviewed enjoyed the creativity of dancing, choosing music, and building routines; the flexible working hours; the joy of movement; and the 'high' of receiving applause. Every retired dancer identified striptease as an art form that stoked her desire for theatrical expression and served as a vehicle for sexual empowerment. However, paradoxically, dancers were revered for their sexiness *and* treated as objects to be harassed, sexually assaulted, pinched, verbally abused, and/or mocked, on and offstage. One male narrator who booked strippers for fraternity house parties on the campus of the University of British Columbia in the 1950s recalled that 'college boys could be monsters.' One evening, he escorted a dancer to a campus stag only to rescue her from 'an ugly scene,' and then 'drove her home along back alleys, with the headlights out, in order to lose crazy kids who were following us.'[46] Though stags offered a lucrative side-line venture, some dancers refused to work them under any circumstances; others hired security guards to accompany and protect them on the gig.

Sexual harassment was a problem experienced by many female workers across employment sectors during the postwar period, including erotic dancers. In the 1940s, female factory employees in Peterborough, Ontario, recalled suffering sexual harassment on the line, though these workers tended to accept this behaviour as 'part of the job,' or as an expression of 'male favouritism' in an era that predated feminist analysis of unwanted, intrusive male advances.[47] Writing in the early 1980s, Debbie Field found that female workers in traditionally male work sites were offended by men's sexist language, jokes, and pin-ups, and were outraged by more extreme forms of sexual coercion.[48] Though it is impossible to prove that striptease dancers were, in every instance, subject to a greater frequency and/or intensity of sexual innuendo, harassment, and assault than other workers, they laboured in an explicitly sexualized environment where these kinds of intrusions 'came with the territory.'

Choo Choo Williams, who worked the East End nightclubs in the 1960s, recalled one memorable evening at the Kublai Khan: 'The dance floor was surrounded by a fence. I was out there dancing one night, and this fool come up there and grabbed me! The bouncers came and got him out.' Some men who occupied front-row seats along gynaecology row or at the 'sushi bar' became sexually aroused and masturbated. Dancers had mixed opinions about this behaviour: several were upset, most did not find it offensive, and others pretended it didn't happen. Roxanne put it this way: 'If you looked down from the stage, and you actually looked, you'd catch a glimpse of an old guy taking it out, you know. And that would bother you. Especially me being brought up in a convent.' Tarren Rae, like most dancers, had good days and bad days in the business. On the bad days, she loathed the men who paid her bills: 'Sometimes you just resented every single man in the audience. You just thought they were all scum.'[49] Worn down from the accumulation of soul-destroying insults, Klute left the industry: 'I'd had it. Five years of having sexual innuendoes thrown at you, five years of having people cut your body down from your head to your toes, five years of harassment.' Some men in the company of other men, argues Pierre Bourdieu, construct 'manliness in front of and for other men and against femininity, in a kind of *fear* of the female,' firstly in themselves (emphasis in original).[50] For some men inside strip clubs, a 'frantic investment' in misogyny, born of their own vulnerability, may have served, symbolically, to certify their membership in the group of 'real men.'[51]

By necessity, dancers engineered multi-pronged strategies to fight against instances of abuse, large and small. They talked back to repugnant customers, refused to engage when baited, and solicited the help of bouncers, wait staff, and club managers. Pushed too far, some resorted to physical self-defence, taking satisfaction in their ability to ward off attackers. Cascade reached her boiling point one night at Gary Taylor's Show Lounge: 'I was performing on stage, and this guy was drinking and obnoxious and he took a run at the stage, and I just snapped. I got really angry. I hopped off the stage in my half-Danskin, and I hit him. My whole arm went numb. I was fed up with everything.' Jasmine Tea was clear that her occupation as a stripper put her at risk, compelling her to develop a set of life-saving skills. She described a series of disturbing encounters, and her quick-witted responses: 'This guy invited me out, to his place for coffee, and we got there and he tried to rape me. I was able to throw him off me. Another time I was stalked. Another time I was walking to get on the stage and a guy shoved his hand up my dress. I turned around and belted that guy so hard I knocked him out of his chair.'

In the context of late nights, shared states of undress, tiny change rooms, and personal disclosures, a collective awareness of their stigmatized and at times unsafe profession drew (some) dancers together. A headliner from the late 1960s to 1986, Bonnie Scott recalled the necessity for workplace reform, which included freedom from unwanted sexual advances. She articulated her critique at an organizing meeting in the late 1970s:

> The irony is that it's respectable enough that we have to pay taxes as strippers, but it's not respectable enough that we deserve the rights of the rest of the human race. We wanted better working conditions in the hotels. We didn't want harassment from these bartenders trying to manhandle us. We wanted the same right to say 'Keep your fucking hands off me or I'll sue your ass off.' We wanted a clean carpet on the stage. Like teachers, we wanted to be rewarded for seniority. We wanted some protection. I always remember the guy that screamed out to me, 'Who do you think you are? A fucking ballet dancer? Show us your cunt!'[52]

Sarita Melita was not the only dancer to suffer sexual assault on the job: 'I got raped once, by a Richmond fireman. He was a hero, and everybody loved him, but he was a dangerous and sick man.' She was angry about the lack of protection from either management or police, stating that, 'I had to take that one on the chin, because there was nothing that could be done: I was a stripper, and he was a fireman. Hello!'[53] In other words, dancers, like prostitutes, could not depend on the 'boys in blue' from the city's Police Department to serve and protect them. In 1985, an Ontario Supreme Court judge made a statement to a jury about Angelique Kennedy, a female striptease dancer who was raped three times by a pub customer. Justice John Bowlby opined that, 'She is from a particular class of women whose profession it is to promote lust.'[54] He also noted that Kennedy was not a virgin at the time of the attacks. Acutely conscious of the widespread caricature of sex workers as wanton, 'un-rapeable' deviants undeserving of legal support, dancers did whatever they could to maximize their own safety. Princess Lillian was traumatized by a sexual assault while on assignment in California. Her

suffering in pain and silence was bound up with the fact that her at-
tacker was female: 'I was raped in Los Angeles by a butch woman. I
went to the hospital, I didn't work for two weeks because of bruising.
I didn't tell anyone, I was too scared. That's why I came back home.
It was sick. She came over top of me with a knife.' When violated in
the business, dancers often confided in booking agent Jeannie Runnalls.
She told reporter Jim McDowell that dancers were vulnerable to men
who 'chucked quarters or beer glasses, or threw a German shepherd on
stage,' as well as to assault or rape in a club's parking lot, post-perfor-
mance.[55]

To Miss Lovie, most nightclub patrons in Vancouver and out of town
were 'wonderful gentlemen.' However, later in her interview, she related a harrowing experience that precipitated her decision to exit the
business: 'A guy tried to rape me after my show in Steveston. I unlocked my hotel room door and he was behind me, pushed me in. I
threw him over the bed. We wrestled, I wore his butt out! I was throwing everything I could see in that room. I was warmed up after my act.
I went downstairs, told them what happened. The bouncers tried to get
him but he got away. I got the police, and they didn't do anything. I
said, this guy tried ... and the police didn't care, 'cause you're a dancer,
right? So I said, "That's it for me."'

Strip clubs were well-known as recruiting grounds for men who
sought to 'turn girls out' for profit and prestige. Shelinda painted a picture of one of the city's most notorious pimps in the mid-1970s: 'Bob
Snider was a well-known pimp and drug-dealer. He married Dorothy
Stratten, and then killed her and himself in a murder-suicide. He came
into Gary Taylor's Show Lounge with his top girl – a beautiful redhead.
I thought he was gorgeous – he had a big long suede coat with a fox
collar. I was seventeen, and he tried to recruit me. I was scared to death
of him, I didn't know why. Years later, I saw this documentary and I
saw him at Dorothy Stratten's side and I almost fell on the ground.'
Black singer and MC Ron Small explained that white pimps like Snider
tended to work the Penthouse, Gary Taylor's, and Isy's in the 1960s
and 1970s, while the black pimps worked Vancouver's East End clubs:
'They were coming out of the service, others were coming up from
Seattle, and they'd bring their ladies across the border to make money
while they're up here. I guess they thought they were kings, and the
girls would fall right over them.'

While Scarlett Lake recounted a positive relationship with a pimp
who helped her establish a parallel career as an escort, one Vancouver-
based dancer retold her 'nightmare scenario': 'At the Shanghai Junk, a

pimp from Seattle picked me up, took me down to Seattle. I lived with him for two months and he tried to turn me out. I didn't make any money, so he beat me with a vacuum cleaner hose every day for two months. In Seattle, I stripped at a low-grade porno theatre – five shows a day, between dirty movies, seven days a week, noon to midnight.' The majority of dancers maintained a wariness of pimps and prospective boyfriends whose romantic pronouncements were rumoured to shield self-serving and unscrupulous conduct. Sarita Melita knew several dancers whose lives behind the 'glitz, glamour, and theatrics of a big stage' were marred by abusive relations with lovers at home. Sarita commented wryly: 'You imagine, "Wow, she must go home every night to have a milk-bath and eat bonbons." And it wasn't like that. A lot of these women would go home and they'd have an abusive boyfriend that was taking their money.'

Whether behind closed doors at home, on the street, or inside the confines of their workplaces, dancers were targets for behaviour that ran the gamut from the bizarre to the homicidal. Diane Middlebrook, author of *Suits Me: The Double Life of Billy Tipton*, quotes a male nightclub goer who recalled that in the 1960s across the United States, 'Guys would try to scrub out cigarettes or cigars on a stripper. Entice her over, use a cigarette to burn her leg, sometimes try to light their silken gowns on fire. I know one girl was burned to death when that happened, and many strippers carried burns on their bodies.'[56] At the most extreme end of the spectrum, retired booking agent Jeannie Runnalls was called to the Vancouver city morgue to identify the bodies of two strippers who had been murdered in downtown Vancouver nightclubs in the late 1960s. From links to other dancers' agents in eastern Canada, Runnalls learned that twenty-two dancers were murdered in Montreal in 1979.[57] In April 1983, Layla Underwood, a dancer for nine years in Vancouver, was brutally murdered in her apartment in Burnaby.[58] In September 1986, two Vancouver dancers – Darlinda Lee Ritchey and Karen Ann Baker – were murdered; their bodies were located only in 2002.[59] Indeed, the deaths of dancers must be registered alongside the murders of an estimated seventy female and trans sex workers in the city's Downtown Eastside between 1975 and 2002 – the majority of them Aboriginal.[60]

Women Make Waves in Unions Country-Wide

Facing not only sexual harassment but poor job security and unsafe, insecure working conditions, female workers, including striptease dancers, fought for workplace improvements throughout the twentieth century. The rich history of labour agitation across Canada attests to the resolve of workers to extract concessions from employers. Though men were at the forefront of union campaigns, by the 1940s women had achieved some successes in organizing workers in textiles, manufacturing, and waitressing. After World War II, few erotic dancers had union experience or knowledge of union structure and leadership; moreover, there was no consensus among dancers about the benefits of union certification.[61] Nevertheless, in the context of intensified union activity by women workers in the public sector across Canada in the 1960s and 1970s, Vancouver-based dancers instigated bold, spirited, though ultimately unsuccessful attempts to organize. Interviews with retired dancers, club owners, and booking agents reveal five central stumbling blocks to the formation of a dancers' union: (1) the small and transient workforce; (2) competition among dancers as independent contractors; (3) the resolute, combined efforts of club owners and agents to stymie agitation and punish 'ringleaders'; (4) the quasi-criminal character of the trade; and (5) barriers to organizing intrinsic to provincial labour law.

In 1961, only 29.5 per cent of women were employed in the Canadian labour force; by 1981, this figure had jumped to 50 per cent. While only 16 per cent of women were unionized in 1961, 30 per cent had achieved union representation by 1981.[62] In effect, women workers were increasingly attached to wage work, and they made important gains in securing union representation over a two-decade span.[63] As sociologist Linda Briskin discovered, between 1965 and 1980, the number of women unionists across Canada increased by 219 per cent.[64] Female employees in the public sector gained union leadership as municipal, provincial, and federal government workers (CUPE) in 1963, public service workers (PSAC) in 1966, postal workers (CUPW) in 1967, and B.C. government employees (BCGEU) in 1973.[65] Other female-dominated unions were formed in Vancouver, including, in 1972, the Association of University and College Employees and the Service, Office, and Retail Workers' Union of Canada.[66] In addition, emboldened by second-wave women's liberation, women workers won the right to form caucuses within unions, such as the Status of Women Committees in the B.C. Federation of Teachers in 1973 and the B.C. Government Employees' Union in 1975.[67] However, female workers were concentrated in the largely private sectors of sales, service, and clerical – 61.4 per cent in 1981, with a lowly 11 per cent rate of unionization in personal and/ or business services.[68] Striptease dancers were part of the expanding service sector, but on the periphery, uncounted, and in the shadows. Absent from Canada Census employment figures, and ungoverned by formal labour legislation, they were made invisible as real workers.

A Small-Scale, Transient Business

Striptease dancers across Canada and the United States belonged to a feisty tradition of showgirls in a business more notorious for the glamour of 'becoming a star' than for cutting-edge health and safety standards.[69] In the late 1940s, as one of a handful of Vancouver-born burlesque dancers, Nena Marlene endured both substandard dressing quarters and routine police busts for liquor and obscenity-related infractions. In the late 1950s, striptease dancer Choo Choo Williams and her contemporaries booked their own engagements at Vancouver's local nightspots. As mothers each would have benefited from maternity leave and childcare facilities, as well as workers' compensation, vacation pay, pensions, and freedom from nightly police harassment. However, there were too few dancers to constitute an active lobby. As greater numbers of Vancouver-based women entered the business of striptease in the mid-1960s, dancers made concerted efforts to unionize in order to improve their working conditions and, by extension, transform negative perceptions of 'strippers' and 'stripping.'

In 1967, according to an anonymous report in the *Vancouver Sun*, 'three fully-clothed topless dancers' staged a two-night picket at the Shanghai Junk at 442 Main Street in the city's East End near Chinatown.[70] Pearl Johnson, Betty Franklin, and Grace Jones demanded higher wages, staff privileges (including discounts on food), and a dressing-room heater. They had plans to organize dancers at six other nightclubs, but a day later, they settled for cheaper meals, a heater, and the same wages.'[71] A central difficulty facing all dancers was participation in a small, transient, and mobile workforce. From top-drawer headliners to 'B-level' second-stringers to 'novelties,' dancers toured for a living and regularly crossed the (permeable) U.S.-Canada border on a west coast, transnational circuit. Throughout the 1950s and 1960s, Vancouver's small East End nightclubs specialized in line-ups of imported 'exotics,' often women of colour; and the city's large, deluxe West End supper clubs became a favourite Canadian destination for white American striptease queens.[72] Vancouver jazz saxophonist Dave Davies noted that, 'A lot of the girls, especially the really fine dancers, came up from the U.S.A. and other parts of the world and circulated through Vancouver and then back down to wherever they were going so it wasn't really conducive to union thinking.'[73] Moreover, a handful of non-Canadian dancers who stayed past expired visas to work illegally in British Columbia lived with the persistent fear of deportation, as did other non-documented immigrant workers in the 1960s and 1970s.[74]

When increasing numbers of local Vancouver-based dancers joined the industry in the mid- to late 1960s, they became primarily self-supporting migrant labourers whose travel schedules meant they were on the move for weeks and months at a time.[75] While many dancers enjoyed the adventure of travel, the grind was not easily sustained, especially for those who were ambivalent about committing to career development over the long term. As Foxy Lady put it, 'Some dancers were just waiting to meet Mr Right and get married to a guy with lots of money. Nobody thought they'd be doing it for the rest of their lives. For many it was a transitional thing, and they would get out of it.'[76] Dancers saw other dancers as co-workers, though they rarely shared the same stage, and this frustrated efforts to organize across shifting, multiple geographies or 'territorial bases,' to cite Erving Goffman.[77]

Typically, only five to eight dancers shared a daily/nightly workplace, and by the late 1970s, approximately three hundred dancers were spread out in small clusters across thirty-five nightclubs in Vancouver and an estimated two hundred establishments across the Lower Mainland and the province.[78] Similar to garment workers doing piece-work at home, seasonal farmworkers, and live-in domestic workers isolated from one another, dancers not only moved in and out of the business, they were physically separated from one another, on the road, and out of touch.[79]

Unlike waitresses, who leveraged a tight-knit work culture and occupational pride into unionization for a quarter of the trade in the United States during the 1950s,[80] dancers lacked daily contact at a shared work site – what sociologist Julie White terms 'job fragmentation' – and this forestalled pro-union consciousness.[81] In fact, in the 1970s the overall rate of unionization in Canadian workplaces with fewer than twenty workers (such as nightclubs, laundries, hotels, hairdressing salons, and restaurants) was only 13 per cent.[82] Shelinda captured the particularities of her profession:

Every week you're with a different group of girls. We tried to form a union, but we held no power whatsoever. I don't know if it just was lack of persistence or lack of cooperation from enough dancers. We were too scattered. The lifestyle didn't necessarily lead you to want to go and have a business meeting with a couple of hundred women. A union is something that you do for your security and your future. And dancing's not something you did for the future. It was a state of mind. Dancers were not looking to tomorrow.[83]

Dancers Compete as Freelancers

Many retired dancers articulated the lack of cooperation among dancers as an impediment to workplace solidarity. Like other groups of wage earning women in the gender-segmented service, sales, and clerical sectors, dancers in the striptease business found that their employment encouraged both female friendship and intimacy and competition, jealousy, and distrust. Asked about dancers' relationships with co-workers, Roxanne maintained that women were conditioned 'to not like themselves and to compete with other women for men's attention.'[84] And Foxy Lady felt that women did not grow up learning how to trust each other.[85] In cramped, poorly equipped dressing rooms, dancers swapped stories, gossip, and make-up, but they also told tales of being back-stabbed, having costumes stolen, on-stage 'moves' appropriated, and lovers scooped by other dancers. In addition, Sarita Melita underscored what she experienced as a generational divide between dancers, the lack of mentorship, and the uppity disrespect of 'punk-assed young girls,' all of which thwarted the promise of 'sisterhood':

> Dancers did not adhere. There wasn't cohesiveness between the dancers. They all gave lip service to the idea of a union, but there were too many dancers that figured 'It's always like this, it's always the way.' The young ones said, 'We're rising stars and we're special and we're just going to keep on taking your jobs. And we're not going to adhere to your stupid rules or support you.' That lack of respect and the lack of support was unnerving. To me, it was like, 'Well, honey, someday you're going to be there. And who's going to support you? Who's going look after you?' They were not being supportive of other women.[86]

Dancers like Foxy Lady wanted to remain a 'free, independent agent,' willing to pit her skills, reputation, and drawing power against those of other dancers. A minority voice among those I interviewed, she explained that 'The difficulty was [dancing] was such an individual profession – you had your persona, your body type, your face, your dancing skills – you were your own ticket. You'd get the better gigs if you were the one that they wanted. So a union kind of was the lowest common denominator.'[87] Fearing a flatter wage scale and less money in her pocket, Foxy Lady was unconvinced by the alleged advantages of union organizing, instead stressing her entrepreneurial, 'go-it-alone' sensibility in keeping with the prevailing capitalist meritocracy of rugged individualism. Several other dancers were fuelled by individual dreams of 'making it big' in Las Vegas or Hollywood or on the cover of *Playboy* magazine – dreams that did not jibe with a collectivist vision for radical workplace reform.

'Making it big' was also contingent on maintaining a healthy, working body. Like many other professional performers, striptease dancers performed with minor injuries, and they were sidelined by serious back, ankle, and neck strains, sprains, and breaks. As freelancers, they had no extended health coverage and were ineligible for financial assistance from the Workers' Compensation Board. Therefore, injury on the job jeopardized their livelihood. By the mid-1970s, in the midst of a growing aerobics and fitness boom, the shift in striptease away from strutting to gymnastically inclined floor shows and pole routines put greater emphasis on a performer's overall strength and physical fitness, ramping up her risk of injury.[88] After fifteen years in stiletto heels, Bonnie Scott suffered from 'sway back' and eventually heeded her doctor's warning that she would not walk again were she to continue dancing. Jasmine Tea remembered her predicament one summer:

I used to do the splits and handstands against the wall ... I was dancing in Sooke [B.C.] and I pulled all the tendons in my ankle. I was on crutches for two weeks. I couldn't even walk, so I couldn't dance. I had no money coming in for two weeks. Though I was concerned about who might be making money off my dues, the one thing that did impress me about a union was the idea of having a health care plan, a dental plan and biggest of all, workers' compensation. There are injuries in the business. If you're the least bit acrobatic, you run the risk of pulling a hamstring, throwing your back out, sprained ankles, any kind of sport injury.[89]

The Anti-Union Resolve of Club Owners and Booking Agents

As was mentioned in chapter 4, when in peak condition, striptease dancers were well paid in comparison to other female service workers. According to ex-booking agent Jack Card, A-grade headliners or 'features' earned an average of $800 to $1,000 per week by the late 1970s, with the very best grossing $2,000 per week. B-grade and C-grade dancers who earned an average of $400 to $600 per week at the low end of the wage scale still pocketed more than twice as much as chambermaids, restaurant workers, office clerks, bank workers, drycleaners, and stewardesses.[90]

Throughout the 1970s, because Vancouver's commercial striptease scene seemed immune to the economic recession sweeping the rest of the country, dancers who complied with rigorously monitored directives from management enjoyed abundant opportunity for bookings. However, the flames of discontent were fanned by pro-union dancers keen to strategize for a better deal for all dancers across divisive designations of rank, age, race, breast size, and technique. In 1977 at another organizing meeting, Michelle argued that few clubs treated her as a human being.[91] In the mind of Tarren Rae, one of the biggest obstacles faced by dancers committed to forming a union was the fervent opposition by club owners and booking agents.

In formal and informal meetings, dancers swapped information about the arbitrary power of owners and agents to exact discipline and punishment by fining or firing a dancer for minor infractions, cutting a dancer's shifts, or demoting a dancer to 'B' or 'C' rank. Several owners were notorious for unsavoury recruitment tactics; others pressured dancers to 'put out' sexually and/or to exhibit more and more flesh on stage. In 1977, twenty-seven-year-old dancer Kandis Thompson claimed she had been unfairly dismissed from the Kings Castle pub on Granville Street for having tattoos on her left breast and right shoulder.[92] Largely unaccountable to dancers for decisions they made, owners and agents called the shots; as a result, dancers had little scope for airing complaints. During the 1960s and 1970s, Richard Walters worked for his father at Isy's Supper Club on Georgia Street. He spoke of his father's opposition to unions as well as his own:

Isy never liked unions. And I've never been a union man. We kicked out the union for waiters. We paid our people as well as they could be paid; we didn't take advantage of them. They always got paid as much as our budget would allow. Unions had no right to be in control of us. And they knocked a lot of businesses off because businesses couldn't handle the big wages. Maybe strippers would have benefited, but we wouldn't have had anything to gain. We might not have been able to keep our doors open if we got charged too much money.[93]

Well-versed in anti-union fear-mongering, and quick to foil a union drive on his premises, Walters grudgingly acknowledged that union membership might have helped dancers, but that he and his father had their eye firmly fixed on the bottom line. In fact, Walters noted that Isy, who died at work in 1976, made more money in the last five years of his life than he had in the previous three decades. In spite of Walters's claim that dancers' fortunes were tied to those of the club, there is no evidence that dancers shared in Isy's late career windfall.

Penthouse Cabaret owner Ross Filippone was unsympathetic to union activity in his nightclub: 'Naturally we were against it. Against it. With a union, the dancers would've put themselves out of business. You have A-girls, which is the top, you have the B-girls, C-girls. If you've got a good operation, you want all A-girls, but you've got to pay more for them. So all of a sudden, you've got a C-girl who expects to be paid A-prices. So if they start doing that to you, then they're just killing the goose that laid the golden egg.'[94] Rather than contemplate restructuring the ranking system itself, or taking seriously dancers' concerns about working conditions, Filippone expounded on his anti-union stance, re-inforcing the logic of stratification to defend his unwillingness to pay more. He argued that dancers would be to blame for destroying their own livelihood through unionizing, all the while that he manoeuvred to protect and expand his profit margin, his 'golden egg.'

In 1976, a union drive brought together black dancers Coco Fontaine, Tia Maria, and Miss Lovie and white dancers Lee Remmick, Tarren Rae, and Foxy Lady, among others. A mixed collective of 'A,' 'B,' and 'C' dancers, they articulated their demands for decent pay, renovated dressing rooms with showers, and an end to 'spreading,' recalled Coco Fontaine, 'because we were worth it.' Influenced by criticisms of sexism by second-wave women's liberationists, white and non-white dancers, both working class and middle class, carved out a gender-based alli-ance – though racialized pay scales, racist treatment, and stereotypes of idealized white female beauty were never raised, and the group never secured a first contract.[95] At one meeting, when it came to a vote in favour of a union, not enough dancers were willing to strike. Coco Fontaine remembered some dancers' concerns that were expressed that night:

Bonnie, Tia Maria, Lee Remmick, and I were pointed out as the trouble-makers. We wanted decent pay. We wanted to be treated like the rest of the staff. In some places we changed in the beer coolers. You worried about bringing your clothes and putting them on the side of the stage, hoping no one's going to take them. We wanted decent dressing rooms with a shower that worked. We realized what we paid for our costumes, our shoes, our hair, our make-up, cab fares. But we couldn't get solidarity. The girls were too afraid. Beer parlours said they wouldn't hire us if we formed a union.[96]

In contrast to their experiences of male club owners as powerful, overbearing figures, dancers recalled that most of these men fancied themselves as benevolent father figures who were in charge of one big, happy family. Yet this paternalism glossed over their cumulative record of injustice, indifference, and intransigence – the very factors that made so many dancers afraid of being sacked for speaking out. They also noted that club owners and staff tended to perceive (some) dancers as capricious, immature, and unprofessional. Aging dancers were especially vulnerable to nightclub owners' whims, as Coco Fontaine explained: 'By the late 1970s, you saw under-age girls coming in. I was told by agents when I was thirty-two that I was *old* and washed up. The club owners got caught up in the young blood.'

Agents and club owners/managers worked in cahoots, as both groups stood to gain from their monopoly. Ex-dancers Jeannie Runnalls and Katie Lynch were among the only women to own their own agencies in Vancouver, and they garnered more respect from dancers than male agents did. Runnalls revealed that she worked to set up a medical plan for dancers from London Life, only to be rejected by the insurance agent, who disliked 'exotic dancers.' She persevered and finally obtained a plan for a short while, but when she left the plan fell apart.[97] Notwithstanding Runnalls's advocacy, dancers were often critical of the role played by booking agents; Miss Lovie's comments were echoed by many others:

It was the agents who didn't want a union. As far as they were concerned, it was, 'Dancers? Are you kidding? You're not workers like truck drivers or construction workers.' So they didn't want it. We had a couple meetings but we didn't have enough to make a strong union. The agencies knew the dancers were going to take part of their money, so they kept us down. Club owners were not going to set it up. We had nobody to head it up. We would have had to stop dancing altogether, and nobody was willing to do that.[98]

Lindalee Tracey, who worked in Montreal in the 1970s, likened booking agents to 'bullies who muscle girls to work bad clubs, do free shows, con them into dependence. They have their tentacles in every part of the business: costumes, photos, dance lessons. A lot of them hone in on the small-town girls and runaways, convincing them they're on their way to Las Vegas if they just work one more scuz bar or sleep with one more owner.'[99] While agents had mixed reputations in Vancouver, they each needed a stable of dancers willing to disrobe and to push the parameters of 'community standards' without landing in jail.

Criminalized Labour Disavowed by Organized Labour

Unlike other female service workers, erotic dancers lived with the threat of criminal charges for staging a 'lewd and obscene public exhibition ... in any place open to the public where entertainments are given,' according to section 167 of the Criminal Code.[100] Without union backing, each dancer needed to learn, by hook or by crook, the implications of contravening municipal, provincial, and federal laws designed to protect the 'public good' from indecency. Whether they worked at the State Burlesque Theatre in the early 1950s, the Café Kobenhavn in 1972, Gary Taylor's Show Lounge in 1974, or the Penthouse in 1975, dancers became intimately familiar with the violent disruption of police raids and arrests. As retired dancer Bonnie Scott, who danced at Café Kobenhavn, recalled,

> My first job was dancing at the Kobenhavn – I was fourteen. It was on Main Street, down the street from the American Hotel. I worked there for a year and a half. It was a bottle club, and they had go-go dancers on the boxes – me and the biker chicks. We were paid seventeen-fifty a night. You'd dance on one box and then you'd dance on the other box and then you'd jump off until it was your turn again, and they rotated. It was the first bottomless club in Vancouver. Me and four other girls, we were the first girls that got busted for bottomless dancing. What used to happen is they'd bar the door twice a night, and we'd get up on the box without our panties on. When the show was over, they would unbar the door. If the cops came to the door, they'd press a little button and the red light went on. So we knew to put our panties back on. One night, the light goes on, we go to throw on our panties and these two undercover cops walk right up out of the audience and arrest us. They charged us with indecent exposure in a public place.

In 1973, the Supreme Court of Canada ruled (6 to 3) that Calgary-based exotic dancer Kelly Johnson was not guilty of an immoral performance. Justice Roland Ritchie, writing for the majority, disagreed with the Alberta courts in ruling that, 'The provisions of the Criminal Code do not stigmatize the display of the human form in its natural state as immoral.' Judge Ronald Martland, writing for the minority, decried Miss Johnson's striptease as 'prurient titillation of the all-male audience' without artistic merit, and staged for the purpose of gain.[101] In spite of the Supreme Court's ruling, obscenity charges continued to be laid and convictions sought in cities from coast to coast, though the policing of nudity and morality was wildly uneven. Dancer Linda Adams was charged with performing an 'immoral act' in Kamloops, in 1973.[102] Though striptease dancers were not convicted in nightclub busts of Gary Taylor's Show Lounge in 1974, or the Penthouse in 1975 (described in chapter 2), all dancers were hurt – economically they lost bookings and revenue, and psychologically they suffered from the chill of the obscenity law and the sharp reminder that they were associated with a shady, criminal underworld. At the same time, in keeping with the punitive, regulatory mood of the police, Vancouver city council voted to ban neon signs in the early 1970s. An internationally renowned symbol of Vancouver's night-time (and nightclub) razzmatazz for thirty years, neon was rejected as tawdry, cheap, and unsophisticated.[103]

Throughout the 1970s, the grip of the city's morality squad loosened and tightened in response to shifts in political climate and moral reformers' targets. In December 1976, the re-elected Social Credit provincial government granted municipalities and regional districts the jurisdiction, under new liquor regulations, to ban both erotic entertainment and hard liquor sales in beer parlours.[104] That month, charges were laid against Vancouver club owner Martin Roitman, club manager Paulette Depew, and dancer Virginia Scott for allowing and taking part in an indecent performance at Club Zanzibar.[105] Vancouver mayor-elect Jack Volrich maintained that 'matters had gone too far,' and that 'some cover-up would be desirable.'[106] Several influential media figures jumped into the bubbling controversy. Veteran night-beat columnist Jack Wasserman was concerned that dancers, who were legitimate workers, would lose their jobs, observing that, 'If the hotel beer parlours are stripped of nudity, the figures will turn up on the unemployment statistics. Manpower has been recruiting strippers for the clubs and bars in and out of Vancouver through notices on their bulletin boards.'[107] Reporter Christopher Dafoe opposed the tough talk designed to 'abolish sex' in drinking establishments. Instead, during lunch at the Crazy Horse, he found that the 'strangely innocent girls' were 'touchingly vulnerable in their nakedness and decidedly harmless … They seemed to enjoy their work, and there was no sign that any of them had been subjected to violence.'[108] At the same time, Vancouver alderman Harry Rankin called strip clubs 'exploiters of women,' and expressed his support for a clean-up of the city's entertainment district.[109] In effect, Rankin's abolitionist ideology mirrored that of the city fathers who initiated the campaign to clean up 'Toronto the good' after the death of shoeshine boy Emanuel Jaques on Yonge Street in 1977.[110] Similar efforts to erase signs of sin from cityscapes were underway on 'the Main' (St Laurent Boulevard) in Montreal, Halifax's Gottingen Street, Edmonton's Jasper Avenue and 107 Street, and Winnipeg's Kennedy Street.[111]

In response to the mounting moral panic in Vancouver, a meeting was convened at Isy's nightclub on Georgia Street by Jack Card in mid-December 1976. Card's agency, WaltCard, was the largest booking agency in the city at the time, representing more than 120 dancers. That night, sixty striptease dancers, including ten male strippers, voted to keep their g-strings on throughout their acts except for a final flash of total nudity at the end.[112] At the meeting, according to the *Vancouver Sun,* one woman was quoted as saying, 'I was fired because a girl before me was spreading her legs on stage, and I wasn't.' Also in mid-December, dancer Lisa Bishop expressed her fury towards new provincial liquor controls that granted B.C. municipalities and regional districts the right to prohibit nude dancing in beer parlours. In a letter to the *Vancouver Sun*, she defended her own and others' participation in the 'world's oldest form of theatre art.' She argued, 'We are professional dancers, and would love to be seen and rated as such. YOU are our public, after all. We work hard for you six days a week, 52 weeks a year' (emphasis in original).[113] Bishop painstakingly affirmed burlesque dancing as work in need of recognition and respect. Importantly, while dancers criticized hotel managers and owners for pressuring them to disregard their comfort zone on stage, they were horrified by politicians' pledges to clean up the striptease scene and snuff out their livelihood.

In the early 1980s, mayors and city officials chose, for the most part, to tolerate nudity in drinking establishments, though occasional transgressions made the news. In February 1980, undercover vice officers in Vancouver reported on a 'vulgar and improper act' by a female stripper, and an incident whereby a patron helped to remove the stripper's clothes at the Penthouse Cabaret.[114] In 1981, African American dancer Mitzi Duprée was arrested by the Royal Canadian Mounted Police

(RCMP) for performing an 'indecent act' with ping pong balls and a flute in Kamloops.[115] Found not guilty in 1982, Mitzi was deported to the United States from Vancouver in 1984 after a conviction in Calgary.[116] Exasperated by defenders of Duprée's act, the chief prosecutor opined, 'They try to make her out as some sort of Nadia Comaneci of the vagina for goodness sakes.'[117] In British Columbia, although charges, arrests, and fines were meted out sporadically after 1980, exotic dancing remained firmly under the gaze of politicians, police, the RCMP, and the provincial judiciary.[118]

Uninterested Male-Dominated Unions and Unreceptive Labour Law

The vulnerability of club owners, staff, and dancers to raids, arrests, and club closures reinforced the scene's reputation for scandal, dicey operations, and organized crime. While rumours of the Mafia remain unsubstantiated and the Hells Angels did not enter the business in Vancouver until after 1988, the hydra-headed stigma served as a potent disincentive to organizing initiatives by union bosses.[119] Sarita Melita explained her perspective: 'There's a saying: if the roots of the tree are rotten, the foundation is rotten. No building can stand, no tree is going to stand, if the roots are bad. The striptease business comes from shady roots, so it's never going to be socially acceptable. That's a drawback. No institutional coalition or union was going to take us seriously enough to cooperate.'[120]

The leadership of powerful unions in British Columbia was male-dominated, and brothers who might have assisted sisters by making striptease an organizing priority expressed little or no interest in doing so. This was not surprising, as the union movement in Canada had been a male bastion from its inception. For example, in 1980, of the 944 executive board members of international, government, and national unions in the country, only 160 (16.9 per cent) were women.[121] Dancers speculated that male unionists did not recognize striptease as skilled work or strippers as workers.[122] And widespread assumptions that dancers partook in lesbianism and/or prostitution – both harshly pathologized and criminalized behaviours – would have branded them as a serious liability in the eyes of male union leaders.[123] In addition, negative stereotypes of dancers as unstable and difficult to work with likely intensified male unionists' already jaundiced attitude towards collaboration.

Not surprisingly, given the elements of illegality and perceptions of gender treachery underpinning the stigma, support for erotic dancers never materialized from the B.C. Federation of Labour, nor from the Canadian Labour Congress. The most appropriate union in the hospitality sector – the Hotel, Restaurant, Culinary, and Bartenders' Union – had little success organizing nightclub and pub staff, and never pursued a mandate to reach striptease dancers. Neither the female-headed union of the Vancouver branch of the Service, Office, and Retail Workers' Union of Canada[124] nor the Association of University and College Employees made offers to share financial, educational, and human resources with dancers. Most notably, no alliances were forged between dancers who identified as feminists and feminist unionists who, like their sisters in the women's liberation movement in the 1970s, tended to define striptease as degraded and victimized objectification rather than *work* deserving of union representation. Dancers' lack of recognition as labourers underlines the extent to which union bodies (feminist and non-feminist) were invested in exclusionary regimes of moral and sexual regulation, unable or unwilling to extend respect and acceptance to erotic dancers.[125] At the same time, it is a curious paradox that some male unionists disavowed dancers as workers yet consumed dancers' services as customers.

As the 1970s came to a close, dancers were doubly frustrated by top-down management tactics and a lack of consensus among co-workers about how best to instigate change. In Toronto, the Canadian Association of Burlesque Entertainers (CABE) formed a local of the Canadian Labour Congress in the 1970s, though it did not survive long, nor did the American Guild of Variety Artists, which represented sex performers in central Canada until the early 1970s.[126] In 1973 in Sydney, Australia, the State Labour Council supported sixteen striking striptease dancers by cutting off supplies and services to several nightclubs – water, food, drinks, cigarettes, electricity, and mail – in an effort to secure better pay and fewer minutes per show of 'frontal nudity.'[127]

On top of the myriad barriers to organizing already mentioned, labour law in British Columbia banned certification and bargaining across a sector of work. As a result, dancers were forced to seek certification at each nightclub and pub separately (in the same way bank workers had to organize each branch). Moreover, club owners viewed dancers as mobile contract workers who lacked both the legal right to benefits packages and the right to union formation. In fact, in Toronto in 1981, the certification bid by CABE was rejected by the Ontario Labour Relations Board because the dancers were found to be self-employed.[128] While dancers in British Columbia periodically staged small-scale illegal pickets and threatened work stoppages during the 1960s and 1970s, they possessed neither sufficient clout nor sufficient militancy to force employers to negotiate voluntarily with them. In particular, dancers who were mothers and primary breadwinners (47 per cent of my sample) most acutely lacked the time and energy necessary for regular meetings and collective action. Thwarted by patriarchal, self-serving club owners and booking agents who felt threatened by labour unrest, as well as labour regulations unreceptive to independent contractors, dancers were unable to mount serious attempts at union certification and collective bargaining. For Bonnie Scott and others unhappy with the new direction, the powerful triumvirate of booking agents, club owners, and patrons who insisted on the evolution to 'cunt shows' constituted a formidable foe.

Directing Activist Energies Forward

The early 1980s heralded yet another group of dancers eager to harness their energies in a positive way. In 1981, Tarren Rae, Anne Gordon, and others formed the Vancouver Exotic Dancers' Alliance (VEDA): eighty members (of an estimated 120 dancers in Vancouver) signed up immediately. Tarren Rae recalled the nature of the debate around the table, and the compromise dancers struck: 'We didn't form a union because unions scared the pants off of hotel owners. They would drum you out of the business if you even mentioned a union. The owners would say, "Who do you think you are? We're the people who give you bread and butter!"'[129] Refusing to sit back and be 'grateful' for what they earned, VEDA members raised money for charities and supported dancers who were in financial trouble. While the alliance flourished until the late 1980s, not all dancers were involved in or supportive of its initiatives. Shalimar, who began dancing in the early 1980s, recalled being disillusioned by the 'messy women' she worked with in the business: 'You can't get a bunch of bitches to agree on anything because everybody was the "biggest and the best" ... VEDA was too many egos in the same room. Like I'm sorry, you think you're the centre of the universe and you're sitting there with eighteen other centres.'[130] Still, VEDA forged bravely ahead with a program of action, including plans to establish a scholarship for dancers to attend college upon retirement.

In December 1981, VEDA members organized a strip-a-thon, 'Burlesque 81,' at the Marr Hotel. Twenty-four dancers collected $3,000 from proceeds and a percentage of the bar sales for the Variety Club; they added that to the $3,500 they had raised at an earlier strip-a-thon at the Cecil Hotel for Timmy's Christmas Telethon.[131] In addition to its 'children's fund,' VEDA also held accounting, insurance, and investment seminars for dancers. And the organization bought a van for the Variety Club, though Tarren Rae ruefully remembered that club members permitted only the acronym VEDA to appear on the van's side panel, and not the words 'exotic dancers.' Gossip columnist Denny Boyd reported on the controversy in 1981:

> VEDA wants to donate to charities, but charities don't want to be publicly linked to the donors, the strippers. Prissiness is alive and blue-nosed in Vancouver. President Anne Gordon was told: '*Personally*, I don't have any hang-ups about your work, but the *committee* says, Blah, blah, blah ...' (That's just the subtle discrimination. The heavy stuff is being turned down for insurance, or on a credit-card application, simply because they list their occupation as exotic dancer.) They've had car washes, cuss boxes in dressing rooms where they pay two-bits when they utter a swear word. The dancers who shed it have set a target of $30,000.[132]

Having abandoned the dream of unionizing, VEDA members consciously endeavoured to rehabilitate the reputation of dancers and their business.[133] To counteract the perception that strippers were shady business risks, VEDA cleverly communicated the message that their members were upstanding, moral citizens and professionals with strong humanitarian interests, particularly concerning the well-being of children. Though fund-raising for kids was hardly a radical move, dancers were humiliated by the icy response from prospective recipients of their largesse. Close to twenty-five years later, in November 2004, striptease dancers raised $4,000 during their Christmas Strip-A-Thon for the Surrey Firefighters' Foundation and Charitable Society; however, the foundation declined the donation.[134]

Exotic dancers not only triggered disgust inside the leadership of local charities; they were excluded from applying to the Canada Council for funding to develop new artistic routines, props, and costumes. From the early 1970s onward, state subsidies to dancers in the 'legitimized' genres of modern, ballet, and jazz dance created the illusion that there was a significant difference between 'professional' dancers and striptease performers. As choreographer Patrick Kevin O'Hara shrewdly observed, 'Before 1980 [in Vancouver], dance was dance and if you wanted to work you took the job that was available. The Canada Council's funding distorted the market and helped create false divisions in the artistic hierarchy of the dance world.'[135] Again, striptease dancers confronted yet another troubling double standard: while they laboured to polish their skills they were nevertheless deemed ineligible for the prestigious, state-sanctioned prizes to which credentialled dancer-citizens were entitled. Attuned to class-specific markers of 'cultivated habitus' or 'cultural pedigree,' French theorist Pierre Bourdieu argued that, 'The most intolerable thing for those who regard themselves as possessors of legitimate culture is the sacrilegious reuniting of tastes which taste dictates shall be separated.'[136] So, to squelch the intolerable, Canadian arts adjudicators flexed their self-assured cultural competence to naturalize the separation of the (sacred) 'tasteful' dancer and the (profane) 'vulgar' stripper, thereby reinforcing the already intransigent stripper stigma.

Processes of Downsizing and Deskilling

In the 1950s, 1960s, and 1970s, striptease dancers based in Vancouver constituted a small, transient workforce who faced an emphasis on competitive entrepreneurship, the punishing stripper stigma linked to quasi-criminal facets of the business, and opposition from club owners and booking agents who hired and fired, issued arbitrary fines, threatened dissenters, and busted union drives.[137] These multiple factors, together with dancers' conflicting opinions about union membership and the vagaries of labour law combined to impede workers' solidarity and alliance-building. Without a unionized voice, striptease dancers were unable to halt the disappearance of fancy, Las Vegas-style costumes, MCs, innovative props and lighting, in-house musical accompaniment, choreography, and elaborate theme shows. In the summer of 1978, choreographer Jack Card spent $90,000 renovating Isy's Strip City, and then staging Folies-Bergère–style production numbers with $60,000 in costumes, props, and scenery, and a cast of twenty-two.[138] However, his burlesque revival, 'Girls à la Carte,' was a short-lived homage to an era already past.

As illustrated in chapter 4, the shift to full nudity and spreading on stage was in full swing by the mid- to late 1970s. While the No. 5 Orange, Drake, Marr, and Cecil Hotels renovated undersized, makeshift stages, most pubs in the city and throughout the province remained poorly equipped; dancers recalled deteriorating working conditions. Similarly in Ontario, dancers complained of changing in the offices of tavern bosses who demanded the door be left unlocked, or in basement change rooms that had earth floors and smelly bathrooms.[139] Toronto-based dancer Gwendolyn charted the transformation she witnessed: 'We were once part of a fine tradition – the burlesque tradition – with musicians, comics, and dancers all on one stage. First they took away the comics, then they took away the musicians – now they're taking away our stage.'[140] In effect, dancers across the country (and beyond) faced a deskilling process, though not one unique to dancing: women's work in manufacturing and clerical industries during this period underwent changes precipitated by new factory and office technologies that resulted not only in deskilling but also in mass layoffs and firings.[141] Like other non-unionized women, who flipped burgers, made hotel beds, served cocktails, processed data, handled bank customers, and cleaned toilets, striptease dancers possessed negligible ability to control or influence workplace transformations.[142]

Dancing in the 1980s: The 'Me Generation'

Another economic recession in the early 1980s meant layoffs in industrial and resource-based sectors, and, by extension, a decline in liquor sales. Philip Nowak, manager of the Drake Hotel, moaned that liquor sales fell between 25 and 30 per cent between the fall of 1981 and the summer of 1982.[143] In July 1982, International Artists, the largest and oldest agency for exotic dancers in Vancouver, implemented a wage cut across the board – $2 a show for all A-, B-, and C-ranked dancers. Booking agent Jeannie Runnalls warned dancers that if they did not accept the cut they would be out of a job. Tarren Rae, vice president of VEDA, was incensed: 'We were railroaded into accepting an across-the-board rollback across the province even at hotels where business was good.' Rae and other dancers pointed out that International had not reduced their 10 per cent commission.[144] Again in 1984, 130 dancers managed by International Artists (out of 300 in Vancouver) faced a 10 per cent rollback in salary. International partner Darcy Taylor cited the slack economy and a bus strike for the wage cut. In July, angry dancers, accustomed to between $18 and $22 for each fifteen-minute routine, set up an information picket at the Cecil Hotel on Granville Street.[145] Carrying placards that read 'Strippers Strapped' and 'Peelers Protest Price Cut,' they were furious that picketing dancer Louise

Figure 5.1 Dancers picket outside the Cecil Hotel, 12 July 1984, in Vancouver. The strike began when club owners cut the dancers' pay, citing reduced revenues from a transit strike.

LaVette was singled out and fired by Cecil Hotel manager Sam Sorich (fig. 5.1). When interviewed by reporter Terry Glavin, dancers on the picket line exposed the conflict of interest: International Agency was supposed to represent dancers in negotiating contracts with beer parlours, but it was controlled by three of the key hotels – the Drake, the Marr, and the Cecil.[146]

In the early 1980s, in the context of belt tightening by business brass and greater militancy by dancers, new trends sprang up like springtime crocuses. Club owners sponsored Tarren Rae and eleven other dancers to compete for the 'Golden G-String' at the Star '83 convention in Las Vegas. Filmmaker Jerome Gary (who had previously directed bodybuilders in the cult classic *Pumping Iron*) accompanied the Vancouver dancers to Vegas, and chronicled their quest for gold in his documentary film *Stripper* (1986).[147] According to Gary, Tarren Rae's sensational win as 'top exotic' put Vancouver on the map as 'the best

Figure 5.2 A 'duo' creates heat at Vancouver's Austin Hotel in 1985.

scene in the world.'[148] In 1984, Tom Longstaff, booking agent with International, repeated Gary's assertion by declaring Vancouver the 'striptease capital of Canada – maybe even the world.'[149] That same year, Longstaff and Jack Cooney, co-owner of the Marr Hotel, opened Image Studio on Alexander Street to train exotic dancers in pole work, floor work, and choreography.[150] In an interview with reporter Len Bacchus, Cooney favourably compared strippers to athletes and reckoned that dancers needed a 'farm system' or 'minor league' akin to those in men's professional baseball, hockey, and football. To that end, he boasted about how the city's first strip school had attracted twenty-five regular students, including six men, all of them exotic dancers, or potential exotic dancers. Competitions such as 'Exotica '84' at the Drake Hotel became regular events on a headliner's schedule.[151] In 1985, 350 gallons of raspberry Jello filled the four-by-eight-metre 'pit' at the Austin Hotel's 'Jello Olympics' on Friday nights. Exotic dancers shimmied across the pool, horizontally, along a greased pole.[152] That same year, commercial photographer Theodore Wan, known as Theo, shot an erotic 'duo' in action on stage at the Austin Hotel against a backdrop of signed promotional stills of dancers (fig. 5.2).

Historian Greg Potter argues that Vancouver's striptease business boomed throughout the 1980s, inspiring Bon Jovi's 1986 mega-platinum album *Slippery When Wet* and Mötley Crüe's 1987 chart-topper 'Girls, Girls, Girls.'[153] Jane Jones fanned the flames of seduction with her dazzling tiger and fire acts (see plate 6). New trends in the business translated into new challenges, pressures, and contradictions. By the early 1980s, the Smilin' Buddha had become a venue for punk rock bands, leaving live striptease acts to hotel pubs and the Penthouse Cabaret.[154]

6 'You Started to Feel Like a Dinosaur':[1] Exiting and Aging in the Business

Table dancing signalled the end of my career. The features had nowhere else to go. Standing on a two-by-two box, in high heels, in a customer's face, for three songs, was totally degrading and humiliating. Table dancing brought younger people who would arrive with a duffel bag full of clothing, as opposed to the features, who had carloads of stuff. And let's face it, at a foot away, a thirty-year-old body doesn't look anywhere near as smooth as a seventeen-year-old does.

Klute, Interview, 1998[2]

It was hard to constantly regard [my body] as a big deal, and the only reason it was one, the only reason it was anything other than the comfortable thing I lived in, was because of the way people looked at it. I imagined a world with no clothing, mirrors or photographs, and I wondered if my body would be such a big deal then.

Elisabeth Eaves, Bare: The Naked Truth about Stripping, 2002[3]

The Pleasures and Perils of Risky Business

Prior to 1980, the industry of professional female striptease flourished, pinned in place by contradictions. Tourism Vancouver never promoted striptease in the port city as legitimate entertainment, yet member organizations (restaurants, cab companies, hotels) reaped handsome revenues from vacationers and conventioneers who frequented the famed nightspots of 'Las Vegas North.' Liquor inspectors refused to license bottle clubs like the Penthouse, Café Kobenhavn, and New Delhi until 1969, but club owners turned the tables by peddling bootlegged booze and line-ups of 'exotics.' Police officers were paid to patrol, raid, and bust the same strip clubs that they patronized as customers. While many of the top jazz men disparaged the striptease scene as beneath them – an affront to their 'real' talent – they relied on gigs accompanying dancers. Nervy dancers earned lucrative incomes yet were chided for lacking a 'real' job. Dancers who objected to the trend towards 'spreading' also benefited from the crush of flush customers after bottomless acts were decriminalized in 1972. Some vocal feminists, including influential Canadian filmmaker Bonnie Sherr Klein, dismissed erotic dancers as dupes of a debasing, misogynist plot, while dancers redefined and embraced feminism on their own terms.[4] Symptomatic of what Chris Gudgeon calls 'our entrenched neurotica,'[5] these paradoxes were part and parcel of a business that straddled arenas of vice and popular entertainment: striptease was not prostitution, but near it; it was not pornography, but near it; it was not consummated sex, but near it.[6] And therein lay its enduring genius for tapping collective anxieties about gender, sexuality, class mobility, and racial difference.

The ex-dancers interviewed for this book enjoyed flouting societal taboos that prohibited female sexual display. They felt enormous pride in putting on a good show, they loved the applause, and they relished the challenge of developing new routines, costumes, and props. Local Vancouver strippers (and many Americans who landed bookings) believed that the city's strip clubs were 'the best in the West,' in part because they were paid a weekly salary, in cash; they did not need to rely on either tips or physical contact with club patrons.[7] Well-paid, glamorous entertainers, they earned, on average, more than other female workers in the service sector's pink ghetto. Like miners, loggers, and Mohawk ironworkers, dancers commanded a premium wage for doing a high-risk job, making considerably more money than most women, and as much as (or more than) some men. In her memoir, *Candy Girl*, Diablo Cody compares her work as a stripper with her role as a 'glorified steno bitch' at an advertising agency: 'A single good night of stripping could elevate my sense of self to Kilimanjaro altitudes. That was real approval, the assurance that Me the Brand was fit for sale. No middle manager could accurately put a price on my intellect or work ethic, but I knew precisely how much my body was worth per pound on any given night in the all-girl charcuterie. This concrete information was reassuring, much more so than the bogus corporate praise I'd garnered in the past.'[8]

Price per kilogram aside, while not in danger of dying in an underground mine-shaft or falling to death from a skyscraper or tree-top, erotic dancers risked perpetual outsiderness for breaching what I call the decency covenant.[9] By striking a bargain with the patriarchal devil, they were denied the respectability granted to straight, married, maternal, and monogamous women who observed the rules of the social order. Paid well to compensate for the stain of the stripper stigma, dancers were subjected to criminal and social sanctions that pressured them to be ashamed of their work, pretend that they did something else for a living, or abandon their profession altogether.

From the late 1940s to the early 1980s, the erotic dancers I interviewed bravely eschewed full-time marriage and stay-at-home motherhood. Harshly judged, they were presumed incapable of meaningful relationships and families. Rendered ineligible for rental housing, credit at banks, and life insurance, they could never take for granted the fundamental constituents of substantive citizenship such as inclusion, belonging, equity, and justice.[10] Despite social reverence towards motherhood, no dancer who raised children was ever honoured for her role as mother and moral guardian. Several retired dancers explained to me that they had never disclosed details of their former career to their adult children. Because strippers were commonly perceived as anti-family, they were presumed to possess no maternal honour worth protecting. Rather than being extended dignity, security, and safety, they (and their children) were scorned as a menace to the stability and health of the nation.[11]

In *Imperial Leather*, Anne McClintock argues that 'abject peoples are those whom industrial imperialism rejects but cannot do without ... the abject returns to haunt modernity as its constitutive, inner repudiation: the rejected from which one does not part.'[12] Simply put, the polarized categories of abject stripteaser versus self-sacrificing mother were mutually constitutive: one term depended on the other for its meaning. All women's bodies and psyches were disciplined and haunted by negative perceptions of the stripper. Female sexual civility was contingent on the repeated avowal of erotic dancers' uncivil, carnal disobedience, and the repeated disavowal of strippers' humanity. The multifaceted penalties meted out to dancers reminded all women of the steep cost of stepping out of line. The adage 'desperate women did desperate things' stuck to strippers like contact cement. Moreover, the potent moral discourse of sleazy club owners and sex-crazed customers in odious strip joints reinforced the imperative of the upstanding, straight-laced company man, devoted husband, and active father.

Business outsiders in Vancouver (and elsewhere) assured themselves that good, genteel white ladies would never undress in public unless coerced and/or drugged by pimps or mobsters, as popular lore would have it. Spectators – both men and women – cleaved to racial and sexual stereotypes that 'coloured girls' on stage embodied what Yvette Abrahams calls a primordial foreignness in a city visibly governed by white, Anglo-Canadian elites.[13] Patrons desired *and* repudiated stripteasers of colour, whose bodies carried the weight of white cultural projections and preoccupations with difference and deviance. Until Vancouver's beer parlour boom in the early to mid-1970s, non-white dancers were largely confined to the city's East End stages, where opportunities to attain marquee status, top salaries, and prime working conditions were notably constrained. African, Latina, and Asian Canadian dancers such as Miss Lovie, Coco Fontaine, Sarita Mileta, and Suzie Wong negotiated racist and sexist expectations with humour, anger, courage, and irony. White dancers Lili St Cyr, Nena Marlene, and Shelinda appropriated symbols of the racial 'other' as erotic spectacle or played up the pageantry of Hollywood glamour, though white privilege never fully immunized them against stigma. Even waves of non-Anglo immigrants to the city in the early 1970s did little to alter the common-sense racism internal to the business, though the skin trade was hardly unique among employment sectors.[14]

Former feature dancer Tarren Rae relished the open, sexualized atmosphere that surrounded stripping in the 1970s: 'You never thought about AIDS. You thought about syphilis or crabs or herpes. You never thought about something that could kill you. It was so free, you could do whatever you wanted, sleep with whoever you wanted.' Lesbian and bisexual dancers, gay choreographers and costume designers, male-to-female transsexuals, and female and male impersonators worked under cover in the city's strip clubs. Queers had long been expected to gravitate to sexualized occupations; the flagrantly heterosexual sensibility of the strip club afforded them a welcome measure of protection. Similarly, straight women found some measure of empowered sexual subjectivity while capitulating, as all dancers did, to employers' and customers' demands for fantasy fulfilment. Like all entertainers, erotic dancers cleverly catered to what they perceived customers wanted, using boundary-setting rules (such as never dating a customer) to protect themselves and their self-concept as artistic professionals.[15] However, the 'nudity imperative' differentiated dancers from other professional female entertainers of the postwar era, including singers, tennis players, golfers, actors, ballet dancers, and figure skaters.[16]

The Respectability Sweepstakes

Barbara Ann Scott, a champion figure skater from Ottawa, was known for her stunning beauty, as well as her grace and finesse on the ice (plate 7). She pioneered impressive athletic feats after years of exhausting training, winning Olympic gold for Canada in 1948, and two world championships in 1948 and 1949. A media darling, Scott enjoyed a short, glitzy career with the Hollywood Ice Revue in Chicago in the early 1950s, followed by lucrative product endorsements in retirement. In a sexist photograph from 1950 that erases Scott's skating prowess, she coquettishly fellates an ice cream cone, stripped down to little more than the costumes favoured by stripteasers of her era. Notwithstanding the cheesecake imagery, it was Scott who was attributed national, iconic status, not the dazzling Lili St Cyr, 'Queen of the Strippers,' who garnered notoriety and devoted fans in Vancouver, and internationally.

The triumphant 'blond beauty on blades,' Barbara Ann Scott embodied Canadian hopes and dreams for success. The conventions of her sport – ladylike charm, refinement, self-discipline, and artistry – mirrored postwar ideals of white, heterosexual femininity commensurate with women's future vocation in the service of 'better homes and gardens.' According to historian Michelle Kaufman, during Barbara Ann Scott's career, figure skaters sifted through hundreds of pieces of music and spent thousands of dollars per year on the perfect beaded and sequined gowns.[17] Though immersed in the heady world of glamour and stardom, Scott was not expected to own, or exhibit, jewelled pasties and g-strings. Her respectability was contingent on the context of her athletic and aesthetic performances – community arenas, not the local burlesque theatre or strip club. Her victories were spread across the pages of mainstream sports and women's magazines, not the centrefold of *Playboy*. Unlike Scott or other high-profile female athletes, no marquee striptease dancer was offered lucrative endorsement fees, invitations to ribbon-cutting ceremonies, a commemorative stamp, a street or park named in her honour, a doll manufactured in her image (fig. 6.1), public-speaking engagements, or the Order of Canada.[18] No striptease dancer was ascribed the status of nationally sanctioned heroine esteemed by adoring girls across the nation.

What distinguished striptease from 'family-oriented' entertainment like figure skating was dancers' self-conscious intention to sell sexual fantasy to voyeurs in the already excessively sex-saturated spaces of burlesque halls, strip clubs, and summer carnivals. The State Burlesque

Figure 6.1 Barbara Ann Scott doll, circa 1953

Theatre, the Penthouse, Harlem Nocturne, and New Delhi clubs, and the Pacific National Exhibition supplied venues that were, in the eyes of many, notorious emporiums of sleaze. Criticized for what they did, and for where, why, when, and for whom they did it, erotic dancers were assigned outlaw status. Even in the context of second-wave women's liberation in the early 1970s and the relaxation of some gender and sexual mores, erotic dancers provoked shock, anxiety, and moralizing judgment. At the same time, the dancers I interviewed spurned the label of degraded, powerless victim. While employed, they inhabited a liminal state between awareness of the limits of their racist, patriarchal business and determination to be self-possessed sexual agents.

Exiting and Aging

Retired dancers were articulate, thoughtful, and candid about how the occupation afforded them substantial income, ego gratification, rigorous exercise, the opportunity to travel, and a more flexible work schedule than that of a nine-to-five switchboard operator, clerk, or nurse. Dancing stoked the rebellious spirit of both working-class and middle-class young women who sought adventure. Many retirees told me how they missed the camaraderie, the paid workouts, and the intoxicating chant from animated customers: 'We love you! We love you!' For Cascade, her craft fed her self-esteem; she enjoyed a standing ovation but she noted that the business made her vulnerable to flattery, to looking outside herself rather than feeling good about herself. Similarly, former headliner Bonnie Scott turned outward to please her audiences for fifteen years: 'It was a profession. I worked very hard to be very good at what I thought was a reasonably respectable job. Whether other people thought so or not didn't really matter to me. To me it was an art, and I was an artist ... One of the things that really makes me sad is that I had no knowledge of my own beauty.' One of the stars of the Vancouver scene, Tarren Rae, won the Golden G-String Award in Las Vegas in 1983 at the mid-way point of her fourteen-year career. She soaked up the spoils of victory, knowing that fame would not last forever:

> I had a very good show ... like I had the music, I had a theme, I had costumes, and I had pluck. I did a show to *Cabaret*'s 'Money, Money, Money.' I had all this American fake money, and threw it all over the place. My last song was 'Maybe this time I'll be lucky, maybe this time I'll win.' I was very animated, I smiled a lot. There were more than a thousand people in the audience. First prize was five thousand American dollars, and a little silver trophy I still have. I did some commercials after that, I worked on a TV series for nine months. There was lots of media interest, but I really didn't want to make a big deal out of it. I didn't want everyone to know me as Tarren the Stripper. I think subconsciously I knew that I had another life yet to come.[19]

While few former dancers frequented strip clubs in retirement, they remarked on the homogenization of their former art in the twenty-first century. Miss Lovie was amused by recent developments: 'Now, it cracks me up because I look on TV and every dancer's a stripper, and nobody keeps no clothes on nowadays. I said, "My lord, they shock me! Why don't they leave something for the bedroom?"' Honey Rider danced in the mid-1980s, leaving before the trend to sameness on stage had fully taken hold: 'Now, I don't see anybody that looks different. There used to be the rock 'n' roll girls, the girls that were retro and burlesque, the goth-looking girls, the girls with really short hair. There was something for everybody. We were just like snowflakes, no two were alike. And now, you can't tell the difference ... It's all platforms and boobs.'[20]

An added pressure for every dancer was the time-sensitive character of her career – a by-product of the cultural premium on young, smooth, wrinkle-free bodies. It was rare for dancers to work past the age of thirty-five; in my research, they exited after an average of ten years in the trade. Stripteasers, like most female television journalists, actors, ballerinas, singers, and models extracted what fame and fortune they could during their short-term employment. As Wendy Chapkis argues, all beautiful women are tightly fettered to time.[21] Some dancers endeavoured to extend and enrich their careers by plastic surgeries, aggressive dieting, exercise programs, and copious non-surgical enhancements, with mixed results.[22] To survive in the business, Marissa Crazytrain, a Cree ex-dancer from Saskatchewan, advised, 'You have to possess the three Bs: beauty, brains, and balls.'[23]

Asked about retirement from the business, each ex-dancer recalled her desire to remain self-employed, to be her own boss. Upon leaving dancing, the women I interviewed pursued an array of occupations, including magician, restaurant manager, professional translator, accountant, photographer, house cleaner, metal worker, professional dominatrix, belly-dancing instructor, owner of an escort agency, social worker, professor, retail worker, and inventor. Several dancers went back to school. One relied on welfare payments, while another supplemented her monthly disability cheques by making jewellery and crafts. April Paris explained that upon her move to Italy after marrying a marquis in the 1970s, she became 'the Marquise' – a rank 'one under a princess,' as well as a baronessa, but, she stated wryly, 'That's even lower, so the girls called me "the Cuntessa."' Miss Lovie shifted her career from stripteaser to MC to nightclub owner (in Powell River on the Sunshine Coast). Today, she thrills audiences with her electric vocals as a gospel singer and stage performer. In the mid-1970s, Virginia managed her earnings wisely, saved, sought investment advice, and after three years dancing, became a successful realtor. Many echoed the trepidation Foxy Lady felt upon exiting:

And you always did worry what you were going to do after. I mean, you knew you didn't want to have a job that you had to get paid less. You got spoiled being in the entertainment business. It's just more flexible, you don't have so many rules, you can kind of be your own boss, it's exciting.

· I danced twelve years, and left when I was thirty-six. I knew I wanted to be out of it before I was sent out. Today, I just love my profession! We make expensive railings for pubs, we also make dancers' poles. But I never breathe a word that I used to be one. It just wouldn't work there.

Ex-dancers were determined to find equally well-paying work, shake the stigma, and make pragmatic moves forward. These goals were more easily met by some than others. Jasmine Tea tried to leave erotic dancing on several occasions, once to teach aerobics, but she earned only one-third of her dancer's weekly income. She offered a clue to the challenge of moving out of the stripper-world: 'I got into modelling for a couple of years – Sears catalogues, Avon, Keri Lotion, Bata shoes, fitness equipment. I was still dancing a little bit on the side, but it was dangerous. I shot one ad, and the guys came into the bar afterwards, and there I am dancing. I got in trouble for that. They didn't want the girl advertising Keri lotion being a stripper. The Keri girl isn't in the bar taking her clothes off!' Klute also found the transition out of dancing eye-opening and sobering: ·

> I had seen too many girls die from drugs, get shot and killed, some in biker-related incidents. And it was truly such a hard business to quit. I started waitressing for two hundred and fifty a week and I was used to fifteen hundred a week … One day I went to my closet took all my costumes out, took kitchen shears, sat down in the middle of my apartment and cut all my costumes to shreds and put them all in a green garbage bag. That was it.

Many dancers noted that exiting the business meant freedom from work in smoky bars, an end to late nights surrounded by drunks, and escape from the insidious pressure of having always to look gorgeous on stage. For years, Tarren Rae experienced panic dreams where she was ready to go on stage but unable to find her tape, shoes, or costume. Carson Lee, an erotic dancer in Vancouver a decade later, from 1990 to 1998, captured mixed feelings about leaving the business, ones that were shared by other dancers. Having danced all over British Columbia, as well as in Japan, England, and Iceland, she was wistful about her departure:

> When you're up on stage, you know that you can only look that good for eighteen minutes. At the end of eighteen minutes, you're all falling apart.

You're dressed from head to toe in sequins and you're looking the best you can look. The lights are designed to make your body look better than it is, you're moving to music that you love – it *is* a sensual experience … I never wear lipstick anymore, I never wear nail polish, I don't own anything sequined. I don't even wear make-up to work anymore. I do miss the aspect of knowing that you look incredible, you look inhuman, you just look so pretty. I miss the dance moves. You just hear a song, and it makes you move in a certain way. I don't twirl at work anymore (laughs). I don't do back bends. I never kick my legs up. Dancing, doing four shows a day you feel healthy, you feel alive, you get an adrenaline rush: it's like you're breathing different oxygen. Now at the end of a day, I don't have that.[24]

The men who owned and operated Vancouver's nightclubs enjoyed long careers in show business; they were among the most animated, larger-than-life characters ever to call the port city home. Former club owners have since died: Isy Walters (in 1976), Joe Philliponi (in 1983), Ernie King (in 2004), and Ross Filippone (in 2007). Richard Walters is semi-retired, in his mid-eighties, and lives in Palm Desert, California. Journalist Patrick Nagle died in 2006 at seventy-one, and night-beat columnist Denny Boyd died in 2007 at seventy-six. Now sixty-seven, Gary Taylor – notorious club manager, drummer, and recruiter of 'female talent' – works as a music promoter. Choreographer Jack Card is retired and lives in Vancouver, while Patrick Kevin O'Hara, at sixty-eight, is an active force in the professional modern dance scene in Paris. Buddy, the ex-bartender, is a lawyer employed by the federal government. Ex-MC Ron Small combines singing with cameo roles in the film industry. Musicians Dave Davies, Doug Cuthbert, Gord Walkinshaw, Gerry Palken, Sean Gunn, and Mike Kalanj still perform professionally, though nights of rousing accompaniment to exotic dancers are long behind them. Once pivotal players, the men I interviewed contend that they barely recognize, let alone partake in, the striptease industry as it exists today.

Post-1980 Changes in the Business

Beginning in the early 1980s across North America, professional female striptease underwent dramatic changes. It is now synonymous with table dancing, lap and couch dancing, slick merchandising, conventions and contests, private booths, strip shows on the Internet, the Hells Angels' involvement, and the global movement of migrant 'burlesque entertainers.'[25] Women from the former Soviet Union, including Moldova, Russia, Belarus, and Ukraine, are on the move, working as exotic dancers on six-month contracts in Turkey. Rather than being 'trafficked' as 'sex slaves,' these women deliberately cross borders in search of money, independence, and a better way of life.[26] Leaving the sexual repression of the Cultural Revolution behind, Chinese women are moving from neighbouring villages to work for wages in the rapidly expanding sex industry – including fancy, neon-lit strip clubs – in Shanghai and Beijing. The sexual strategies adopted by these migrant women are linked to broader patterns of global economic restructuring, new forces of tourism, the loosening of state regulations, and stubborn tenets of sexism in a host of national contexts.

In her memoir, *Strip City*, Lily Burana describes twenty-first-century stripping as a 'full-contact sport.'[27] Criminologist Chris Bruckert, also a former dancer, notes that female strippers in Ontario increasingly engage in deskilled, de-professionalized fee-for-service arrangements with male customers who demand one-on-one erotic and emotional labour.[28] In other words, exotic dancers are paid for selling table dances and lap dances offstage to individual customers. In addition to the shift away from onstage work, dancers in many clubs are required to pay 'stage fees' – $30 to $40 a night – to the 'house' (which includes DJs, bouncers, and bartenders) for the 'privilege' of earning a decent night's wage. In Toronto, dancers must obtain a licence and photo-identification from the Metro Licensing Board for an initial fee of $186, and must pay another $85 every six months.[29] Many dancers hire drivers who drive them to and from gigs, carry their bags, and escort them from the dressing room to the car. Today, the required payouts push dancers to hustle hard, sometimes in ways that threaten, or at least unsettle, their otherwise firm rules about what they will or will not do to 'bank.'

Upon interviewing thirty-six dancers in a mid-sized city in the United States, Bernadette Barton found that in relation to male customers, 'Dancers read racial preferences much like they do a client's interest in breast size or legs: as information they can manipulate to make more money.'[30] In broad terms, Barton says, all dancers learn to read a customer's desire and perform his gendered and racial fantasies. However, dancers (actors and models) of colour know that performing on an uneven playing field means uneven access to dividends, and vulnerability to race-based discrimination that continues to render them 'less marketable.'

In the new world of economic insecurity, dancers compete with other dancers for clients and tips, much like other service workers reliant on the 'tipping system.'[31] Diablo Cody, Academy Award-winning screenwriter for *Juno* (2007), worked in strip clubs around Minneapolis, Minnesota, for one year. Having achieved sufficient success to make her a target for 'stripperly ire,' she reflected on the cross-generational friction inside strip joints: 'A new girl might as well don veal underwear and dance the Watusi through a gauntlet of jackals. Most veteran strippers are punch-drunk on Haterade, and they'd sooner dredge their Vuitton clutch in a cow pie before mustering a pixel of common courtesy toward their fellow woman.'[32] At the same time, the strip club staff in southern Ontario interviewed by Jacqueline Lewis (much like those in Bruckert's study) engaged in an 'informal economy of favours' (e.g., dancers tipped doormen who ignored infractions of club rules; waitresses tipped doormen who sat a 'big shooter' in their section) to enhance cooperative income-generating in 'an ever more exploitive working environment.'[33]

While lap dances in champagne rooms or adjacent 'bedrooms' offer dancers more money than working the stage, issues of dancers' safety, security, consent, and workplace control remain unresolved.[34] In clubs where intimate, one-on-one interaction between dancers and customers is mandatory, worker-client relations are more complicated than ever. From her interviews with dancers in the United States, sociologist Bernadette Barton found that, over time, they became more and more cynical, jaded, and ill as a result of working conditions, the motivations of men, and sacrifices they have made in their personal lives.[35] Whether all dancers currently experience this cumulative, negative toll is a worthy question for future research.[36] What seems clear is that the retired dancers I spoke with improvised possibilities for expressions of gender and sexuality onstage (and off), always under conditions of constraint. And as Judith Butler theorizes, possibility was not then, nor is it now, a luxury; it is as crucial as bread.[37]

In 2000, Brandy Sarionder became the first woman to own a strip club in downtown Vancouver – Brandi's Show Lounge at Dunsmuir and Hornby Streets.[38] Nine years later, hers is only one of three venues still specializing in exotic dancing; thirty years ago, there were more than thirty stripperies.[39] The No. 5 Orange Hotel on Main Street still specializes in 'adult entertainment.[40] And the third strip club, the Penthouse Cabaret on Seymour Street, chugs along after sixty-two years, more a stage set for movies, TV crime-dramas, video shoots, new music concerts, sexpos, and neo-burlesque extravaganzas than bona fide strip

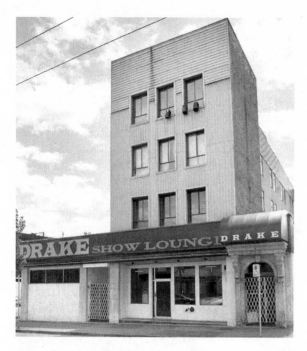

Figure 6.2 The Drake Show Lounge closed in June 2007, marking the end of an era in show business in Vancouver.

shows.[41] Though the owner, Danny Filippone, claims that business has never been better, the Penthouse may one day join the long list of once naughty, neon-lit nightspots buried under the weight of Vancouver's swanky glass-sided condominiums, upscale coffee bars, doggie day-cares, hot yoga studios, and urban spas.[42] In June 2007, the City of Vancouver purchased the Drake Hotel and Show Lounge as a future site of social housing, ending its thirty-five-year run as an internationally renowned venue for erotic entertainment (fig. 6.2).[43] This trend is not confined to Vancouver: on the same day that the Drake was sold, the pastor at the Queensway Cathedral bought the twenty-five-year-old Casino Gentlemen's Lounge at the corner of Queensway and Kipling Avenue in Toronto.[44] The substitution by Pentecostal congregants of a holy cross for a stripper's pole seems like a perversely ironic twist of postmodernity.

For strip clubs still in operation across Canada and the United States, debates swirl around lap dancing, peep shows, live sex acts on stage, the geographical location of exotic dance, and the role of nightclubs as venues for prostitution. Lap dancing was declared 'indecent and illegal' in 1997 by the Supreme Court of Canada in *R v. Mara*; however, municipalities have inconsistently enforced the law, which specified the 'attitudinal harm' caused to male spectators as perceived through the eyes of the national community.[45] The combination of old-fashioned police pressure, residents' associations dedicated to the protection of family values, and media sensationalism, plus the manipulation of zoning ordinances, has imperilled what remains of strip club culture. According to anthropologist Judith Lynne Hanna, more than sixty-two communities across the United States have enacted laws to restrict striptease, including Seattle, Tacoma, Fort Lauderdale, Syracuse, and Phoenix.[46] In 2005, in Seattle, Washington, city councillors voted to ban lap dances and private rooms, placing dollar bills in a dancer's g-string, and standing less than 1.2 metres from a dancer. While city council meetings drew protests from more than 100 of the city's 554 licensed dancers, councillors enacted among the strictest regulations on erotic entertainment of any big city in North America.[47]

In October 2006, the application for a licence to run a strip club in Lunenburg, Nova Scotia, was met by ferocious opposition from city officials determined to keep bump and grind at bay. The mayor and councillors were clear that a strip club 'borders on the risqué' and did not fit the uniqueness of the quaint seaside town. Council member Jamie Myra is quoted as saying, 'I think it's obviously common sense you wouldn't want it in your community.'[48] Throughout the spring of 2007, dancers in Vancouver circulated a petition to protest a flurry of scare tactics and police harassment in strip clubs. Afraid of losing jobs and stable incomes, dancers blew the whistle on intimidating cops and liquor inspectors who checked licence plates in parking lots, searched customers without cause, and entered dressing rooms unannounced.[49] And in August 2008, the Chamber of Commerce of Chilliwack, British Columbia, made public their support for a city by-law to 'ban strippers' from the downtown core. Interviewed on CBC radio, Chamber of Commerce CEO Sue Attrill argued that 'revitalization' efforts, orchestrated by the Business Improvement Association, did not include strip joints such as the Vault in the definition of a 'safe, family-friendly environment.' Rather, she insisted that the city's 'hub of action' was the 'wrong place' for a business 'better suited to an outside, industrial area.'[50] In Chilliwack, a loose consortium of city councillors and corporate captains has made it their goal to deny dancers and club owners access to legitimate commerce on their own terms. More than sixty years after the raid on Vancouver's State Burlesque Theatre for purveying 'indecency,' dancers were subjected to a rude reminder of how legal and political pressure works to expel bodies and transactions labelled contaminating.

While communities continue to debate the pros and cons of adult entertainment, mechanisms of surveillance inside clubs train a disciplinary gaze on bodies 'most likely to offend.' In a move that conjures up Jeremy Bentham's nineteenth-century theory of the all-seeing panopticon, police routinely install cameras in clubs and dressing rooms to record criminal activity – a tactic that engenders hyper self-consciousness and self-discipline among dancers.[51] At the same time, cameras positioned inside the performance space are capable of transmitting live strip shows to viewers via the Internet – a move that satisfies the needs of at-home consumers, blurs public and private boundaries, and deposits little or no extra cash in the hands of working women. Still, not to be outdone, some former strippers stream digitalized sexual images of their own onto the Internet in exchange for healthy annual revenues. For example, no longer beholden to strip club managers or booking agents, ex-dancer Danni Ashe is the proprietor and star of Danni's Hard Drive, a website that profitably brands on-line sex for Ashe and her staff.[52]

Repudiations Recur

In the world of live strip acts, *plus ça change* ... In February 1999, Leilani Rios, a twenty-one-year-old Latina track star for California State, Fullerton, was purged from the university's track and field team. Several members of the male baseball team at Fullerton had witnessed Rios's striptease act at the Anaheim Flamingo Theater, and reported her performance to authorities. Handed an ultimatum by her coach, John Elders, to choose between her sport and her job as a stripteaser, Rios elected to keep dancing because, as a non-scholarship athlete of colour, she needed the money. In a written statement, Coach Elders said: 'I determined that Ms. Rios' decision to remain an exotic dancer would detract from the image and accomplishments of her team-mates, the athletics department, and the university.'[53]

The male baseball players at Fullerton were neither reprimanded nor expelled – their consumption of striptease did not besmirch the university's reputation. Rather, the tired adage 'boys will be boys' not only afforded them protection from rebuke, but also, paradoxically, authenticated their status as 'real' men. Rios, by contrast, was deployed by university brass in the service of boundary-maintenance: good, white, obedient girls who keep their noses clean, their shorts on, and their loyalties straight secure team membership, praise, and the promise of future dividends. Bad, non-white, disloyal girls like Rios who are seen to embarrass an entire school and state get jettisoned as unscrupulous trespassers and traitors – Satan's wicked harlots. Her 'secret' disclosed, Rios was publicly humiliated: her athletic body, once revered for its speed, grace, and pure form, was subordinated to sexist claims that she embodied all that was grotesque and infectious. To university officials, Leilani Rios had broken the law and was duly punished. Her case conveys a sobering message: all female entertainers are haunted by the punishing discursive logic of the whore stigma. More recently, lurid mass media reports of nipple and crotch flashing by celebrities Janet Jackson (2004) and Britney Spears (2007) exploited the juicy 'scandals' by relentlessly smearing each woman for 'sex crimes' unbecoming of her stature as a pop icon. In Santiago, Chile, in 2008, Monserrat Morilles, 'La Diosa del Metro,' or Subway Goddess, was arrested for dancing on the poles of subway trains.

Since the early 1990s, capitalist globalization has spurred migrant sex workers to travel to Canada from Eastern Europe, Japan, Thailand, the Philippines, Australia, and Latin America. Those awarded a short-term 'burlesque entertainer' visa face formidable barriers to labour and immigration rights, as well as the threat of deportation and criminal charges, particularly in Ontario, if caught dancing without a licence. Between 1993 and 2009, Canada's Immigration Department has granted thousands of temporary six-month work permits to women from Romania, the Czech Republic, Hungary, and Poland. Some of these women (and men) exercise more employment options than others. During rancorous debates in November 2004 about the 'Exotic Dancers' Visa Program' precipitated by the alleged improprieties of Immigration Minister Judy Sgro, dancers were never consulted.[54] Instead, the largely Romanian 'girls' were portrayed as sexually exploited, 'trafficked' victims in need of rescue from unsavoury men.[55] That dancers recruited to fill the labour shortage were muzzled during 'Strippergate' while media pundits, lawyers, and politicians scurried to slam shut the nation's door is testament to both the disenfranchisement of (all) migrant workers and the potency of a wrong-headed, protectionist strategy. In May 2007, in a move to mollify their right-wing voters, the Conservative government vowed to tighten already stringent immigration guidelines for exotic dancers.[56] Though the number of non-citizen dancers permitted entry has dropped off considerably (from sixty-seven in 2004 to ten in 2005), I argue that those who are still quietly recruited deserve acknowledgment for contributions to the socio-economic growth and development of Canada, not discriminatory violation of their international labour rights. If dancers are deemed 'good enough' to work in Canada, why not extend to them the rights and responsibilities of full citizenship?[57]

In February 2007, the Breast Cancer Society of Canada rejected the offer of a sizeable donation from the Exotic Dancers for Cancer in British Columbia. Reminiscent of past rejection from children's hospitals and firefighters' organizations, the society's censure exposed the pernicious clout of corporate conservatism.[58] In a letter to the Exotic Dancers of British Columbia, the female executive director of the Breast Cancer Society, Rany Xanthopoulo, wrote: 'Unfortunately we will have to decline your kind offer as we have certain major donors that are not in favour of this connection. This decision came as a result of donor disgruntlement and together with the board of directors we have decided not to accept any donations from what donors consider controversial sources.'[59] Dancers and supporters, including me, were outraged by the society's vicious attack. What, they asked, made them and their pledge 'controversial'? Weren't dancers, like other women, at risk of breast cancer? Didn't dancers, like other women, have friends and loved ones battling breast cancer? What, exactly, made dancers' hard-earned dollars so repulsive to the self-styled guardians of moral rectitude? Again, all exotic dancers were dealt a debilitating blow: they were meant to skulk off into the shadows, ashamed of their seemingly audacious desire to make themselves, their labour, and their generosity, visible. Interviewed by a host of (largely supportive) media outlets in Vancouver, organizer and former dancer Annie Temple insisted that 'cancer does not discriminate.'[60] Showing his support, cartoonist Dan Murphy depicted the society's stance as an out-dated no-brainer (plate 8). After the actual strip-a-thon in early March, Temple and fellow dancers donated some of the $7,000 raised to a dancer living with cancer, while the rest went to 'Rethink Breast Cancer' – a feminist organization specializing in cancer prevention and education.

Striptease Spin-offs: The Burlesque Revival

While professional striptease continues to arouse the ire of critics, neo-burlesque dancers are determined to conjure the magic of mid-twentieth-century burlesque.[61] As part of a trend that began in New York and London in the mid- to late 1990s, Catherine D'Lish, Immodesty Blaize, Fanny Fitztightlee, Scarlette Fever, Dirty Martini, and Diamond Minx (plate 9), among others, have since sought to re-imagine what it means to tease while stripping. Blending sly raunchiness and comedic timing with inventive costuming and satirical send-ups of female archetypes (e.g., balloon girl, Wonder Woman, cowgirl, mermaid), retro burlesquers often draw on traditions of vaudeville, performance art, modern dance, comedy, and circus performance, as well as elements of goth, rockabilly, punk, and 1940s lounge culture.[62]

Several years ago, I attended an evening of 'the new bump and grind' by Cecilia Bravo's (now defunct) Fluffgirl Burlesque Society at the Commodore Ballroom in Vancouver.[63] Provoking appreciative gasps – and later, martini-soaked screams – women in soft pink negligées, ermine stoles, fishnet stockings, lacy garter belts, gold lamé, satin gloves, feathered mules, shiny black vinyl, fringed buckskin, Spanish headdresses, sequined g-strings, chiffon dusters, and leather corsets shook, shimmied, and flashed their way to near nudity. A plethora of tattoos dispelled any illusion that we were reliving the burlesque boom of the 1930s.

A straight male friend commented breathily that the show at the Commodore 'was far more sexy and exciting than beaver shots.' Whether jaded by *Hustler* magazine's explicitness or hungry for saucy displays of female sexuality, women, men, and trans folks savoured the foxy shenanigans of Betty Bijou, Misty Vine, and Kitten Coquette. Cowgirl Mia Moré (my favourite) sashayed in suede jacket, chaps, and rhinestone-studded g-string. Blaze, covered in strategically placed balloons, offered guests a hatpin to poke her latex protuberances. Headliner Dita von Teese, the Los Angeles import and *Playboy Lingerie* poseur, coyly unhinged corset after corset, then slyly manipulated black ostrich plumes – a peek-a-boo fan dance, vintage Fay Bacon. During the intermissions, patrons jumped up to crowd the hardwood dance floor in a flurry of interactivity unknown to peeler pubs and gentlemen's clubs. In fact, the gender-mixed, age-diverse, and vintage-adorned crowd has become a staple feature of neo-burlesque events and on-line community-building.

Today, Vancouver's Sweet Soul burlesque troupe arranges its own bookings, promotion, photography, music, and venues. In the spring of 2008, relying heavily on Facebook technology to advertise, the troupe co-organized the second Vancouver International Burlesque Festival.[64] In contrast to professional exotic dancers, members of Sweet Soul do not face pressure from the 'boss' to couch dance, lose weight, augment their tits, perform six nights a week, and sell as much booze as possible. Sweet Soul's members are not heckled by louts who belch out 'show me the pink' from gyno-row. Nor have their shows been raided for purveying 'indecent acts.' Unlike professional, full-time strippers, neo-burlesque performers have not made unionization a priority, nor do they contend with *Hockey Night in Canada* broadcasts and video porn while on stage. What they champion is a collective commitment to size-acceptance inspired by a broad redefinition of female beauty. As aficionado Miss Astrid explains, 'Different shapes, different sizes, tall, short, fat, thin are all beautiful.'[65] Most importantly, however, the vast majority do not earn a living wage from their passion for costuming, vamping, and wowing spectators; they pursue interpretation of strip-tease as a hobby, a side-line venture. In the land of patriarchal payout, the money is still contingent on a pussy's full disclosure.

Pole Dancing Goes to College, Fitness Clubs, and the Bedroom

Into the trendy world of urban fitness scamper young women in search of their inner vixen and eager to register for pole-dancing classes at local gyms, fitness studios, and the University of British Columbia.[66] Pole-dancing parties are staged all over North America in the tradition of home-marketed Tupperware products. Contests like the 'B.C. Pole Dance Challenge' have sprung up, reminiscent of the wet t-shirt contests of thirty years ago. In Vancouver, ex-stripper Tammy Morris (formerly known as Portia) offers striptease cardio at her Tantra Fitness studio to females who range in age from seventeen to sixty-two, while 'burlesque yoga' instructor Little Woo adds 'minx-like energy' and feather boas to classic poses.[67] Curiously, once a staple of strip club raunchiness, the pole has assumed a newly polished, almost wholesome appeal. Morris maintains that the pole was originally used in the circus and is used today by the world-famous Cirque du Soleil.[68]

Commenting on interpersonal dynamics at her club, Flirty Girl Fitness, co-owner Kerry Knee observed that, 'It's the only class I've ever been in where women are clapping and cheering for each other. It's an absolute high after leaving a class; they just feel great about themselves.'[69] It seems that women who sign up for pole dancing and strip-percise classes are genuinely excited about developing sexualized moves in a supportive, gyno-centred milieu.[70] In my view, anything that undermines the pernicious hierarchy that divides women from one another is a positive step towards sexual liberation for all women. Here's wishing it were that simple!

Like exotic dancers who headline at Brandi's Show Lounge, both pole dancers and new burlesquers employ skills, talent, and creativity in the service of erotic fantasy. Some, like professional peelers, fund-raise for charitable organizations, including anti-war initiatives. Without a doubt, all groups of dancers spark anxiety about traditional feminine roles through their openly public sexual display. However, pole dancers and neo-burlesquers tend to harbour apprehension about the slippery line that divides them from the 'prick-teasers' who 'get down and dirty' in strip clubs. I ask: are age-old divisions between the Madonna and the whore, the risqué and the respectable, simply being recast in ways that echo many exotic dancers' claim to a higher moral standing than those perceived as 'no-talent hookers'?

In 2007, anthropologist Oralia Gómez Ramírez found that female students in pole dancing classes confronted the stripper stigma by distinguishing 'sexy' from 'slutty,' by dancing fully clothed for charity, and by locating pole dancing strictly within the realm of sport and fitness. In addition, participants in pole dancing competitions were explicitly warned against stripping, feigning sexual arousal, wearing g-strings, simulating masturbation on stage, and participating in the pornography industry.[71] Laura Herbert, from Exotic World Museum, separates neo-burlesque dancers from 'transaction oriented humpers who hump poles and hump laps.'[72] To many erotic 'non-strippers,' it seems important to elaborate their real and symbolic investment in smut-free performance, though I argue that *stripping* is precisely what they share with the pros. The presence or absence of a g-string constitutes pretty skimpy grounds for definitive differentiation. In fact, I see evidence of feminist self-awareness, exaggerated femininity as drag performance, and diversely gendered fans as points of commonality, not things over which neo-burlesque and pole dancers have a monopoly.[73] Exotic dancers, new burlesquers, and pole dancers past and present embody the reality that femininity is not reducible to a single object or practice; rather, as Judith Butler reminds us, femininity may offer an array of identificatory sites opposed to, or transcendent of, dominant relations of discipline, regulation, and punishment.[74] Stripping bodies expose the regulatory norm of hetero-femininity as unstable, 'never quite carried out according to expectation,' hence productive of its own insubordinations.[75]

As I see it, the cross-fertilization between genres of pole dancing, neo-burlesque, and professional striptease suggests the possibility for solidarity rather than acrimony among exhibitionist women. In my view, these forms of female entertainment give fleshy substance to resident-architect Bing Thom's praise for Vancouver's unique 'experimentalism' – a site of 'alternative culture, on the edge ... A farm-team place for the cultural inventions of other cities.'[76] All erotic performers, regardless of historical period, venue, audience, or degree of nudity, embody the Latin definition of burlesque, which is to lampoon societal morals and introduce risqué themes into the public arena. As I show in *Burlesque West*, burlesque did not die, at least not entirely, in the 1950s with the advent of television and mass communication. The flame of rebellion that burned for pre-war burlesque queens and postwar striptease artists burns today for professional strippers, pole dancers, and new burlesquers, who are smartly aware, as were their stripper-forebears, of the power of disrobed female flesh as desired commodity. In effect, refuting false distinctions permits new ways of appreciating continuity and overlap across otherwise disparate forms of erotic display. To widen this claim further, we might add the scantily costumed, oiled, and painted self-presentations of female bodybuilders, ice dancers, synchronized swimmers, ballroom dancers, and competitors in beauty pageants across the world.[77]

In her book *Undressed for Success*, Brenda Foley posits a clever parallel between beauty queens and strippers: 'The beauty contestant's cheerleader image is frequently appropriated by strippers, to play upon the heterosexual fantasy of the "good girl gone bad," just as the stripper's harem dance, with its pelvic thrust and shimmy, is utilized by the beauty contestant to suggest the potential for misbehaviour underneath her controlled reserve.'[78] In spite of cultural attempts to segregate variant forms of female performance, the performers themselves, at different times, have endeavoured to break through oppressive assumptions that divide the moral from the immoral, the socially acceptable from the perverse. That those on the erotic stage continue to encounter capitalist, patriarchal, and racist imperatives that tether them to a limited theatrical repertoire does not diminish the fact that they both mime and interrupt exacting standards of proper feminine comportment.[79]

Olympian Beauty Games

Today, notwithstanding some neo-burlesque and pole dancers' efforts to pluralize and elasticize what it means to act and feel sexy, simulation of a narrowly cast beauty ideal has spilled out beyond the traditional glamour-based sectors of stripping, modelling, beauty pageantry, and acting. In effect, consumption of new self-improvement techniques seems infinite: women in ever-expanding numbers (and at younger ages) seek 'designer selves' through vaginal rejuvenation, liposuction, collagen injections, and labiaplasty.[80] Eager copy-cats enlist pictures of 'perfect pussies' belonging to strippers and porn actresses as inspiration. Demand for breast implants has increased seven-fold in the past ten years; an estimated 350,000 women in North America alone opted for an enlarged cup size in 2007. The spate of reality TV shows – 'Extreme Makeover,' 'The Swan,' and 'America's Top Model' – reinforces the magic of medicine to offer (all) women aesthetic upgrades and, by extension, upgraded marriageability and employability. The burgeoning industries of hymen reconstruction in Iran, double-eyelid and nose-bridge surgery in Asia, and the marketing of skin-lightening creams in Africa attest to the global reach of patriarchal, capitalist markets governed by new, Westernized standards for what counts as heterosexy.[81] Compelled to navigate the ever-shifting line that divides the 'tasteful' from the 'vulgar,' women the world over are reminded that sexiness is a culturally contingent ascription that carries both costs and benefits.

Hypocritically, for more than a century, striptease dancers were (and are) held to the highest beauty standard, while also being punished for being too forthrightly sexy. Trendsetters rather than followers, risk takers rather than bench sitters, dancers continue to push the bounds of propriety, testing the limits of a dominant discourse that reviles the skanky and reveres the innocent. Today, women who strip for a living – the rule busters – are still misrepresented and misunderstood by the media, clergy, politicians, residents' groups, some feminists, employers, police, lawyers, and judges. At the same time, many exotic dancers' innovations in performance, music, and fashion (onstage and off) have been sold, in less provocative forms, to a mass consumer market. That the ex-dancers I spoke with recalled their experiences with such humour, courage, passion, and urgency is a sign of their desire to talk back. That dancers' voices in general are rarely solicited or heard is a bitter reminder, as Lesley Ann Jeffrey and Gayle MacDonald note, that the figure of the sex worker 'stands as moral outrage, a damned spot to be cleansed from the public psyche, a non-woman who is, at the same time, Everywoman.'[82]

Contemporary Organizing

Erotic dancers who dance for a living full time want their skilled, innovative work to be appreciated *as work*. The fact that it has rarely been treated this way has inspired dancers to sex activism at various points over the past four decades. In 1997, female peep show dancers at Lusty Lady, an adult theatre in San Francisco, organized a successful union drive represented by the Service Employees' International Union (SEIU), Local 790.[83] Dancers fought for a first collective agreement, and with it, the right to health insurance, sick pay, an end to firings without just cause, implementation of health and safety standards, and the abolition of scheduling practices based on race/ethnicity and breast size. Dancers of colour had been routinely allotted fewer shifts or blocked altogether from the lucrative 'Private Pleasures' booth because management classified them as less 'marketable' than their white peers – a tactic with deep historical roots.[84] After five months of difficult negotiation and compromises, dancers ratified the first strippers' union in the United States. Seven years later, in May 2003, Lusty Lady's workers – dancers, cashiers, and janitors – bought the club from the previous owners and, in unprecedented fashion, restructured it as a cooperative.[85]

In 2009, some organizations operate as a collective voice for dancers, including Dancers' Equal Rights Association in Ottawa, Exotic Dancers for Cancer in British Columbia, Exotic Dancers' Alliance of Ontario in Toronto, and the Oregon-based Danzine. The Vancouver-based website nakedtruth.ca is a powerful vehicle for dancers' activism, as is the monthly newsletter *Yoni*. Sex workers, including some dancers, are unionized in five countries: the London-based International Union of Sex Workers in England; the Red Thread in the Netherlands; the Association of Women Prostitutes in Argentina; the Exotic Dancers' Union representing Lusty Lady strippers in San Francisco; and Salli, the United Sex Professionals of Finland in that country.[86] In Toronto, prostitutes, strippers, private escorts, phone sex operators, and other sex industry workers may soon join forces under the Canadian Guild for Erotic Labour. Meanwhile, 'house dancers' who work exclusively for one strip club may seek status as 'dependent contractors' under the Labour Relations Act in order to exercise their rights to organize and bargain.[87] In Vancouver, a coalition of sex workers, including dancers, has initiated a business cooperative akin to those formed by credit unions, artists, and farmers, with the aim of pooling resources, offering health and safety services, and providing job training.[88]

Though under-resourced, sex activists globally – like other service workers in the airline industry, retail outlets, call centres, hotels, and restaurants – are determined to fight oppressive state regulation, unsafe workplaces, and the criminalization of their labour. Vulnerable to whore-bashing, poverty, and lethal violence, hundreds of survival sex workers, including erotic dancers, have been murdered across Canada over the past thirty years.[89] In addition, for countless young women and men in the global South whose participation in sexual labour is less an occupational choice than a dire economic necessity, the risk of exploitation must be weighed continually against the reality of few viable alternatives.[90] When legal avenues of migration are choked off, hopeful migrants may be pressured to rely on traffickers and smugglers, thereby increasing the potential for coercion. Beyond the pitched battles over sex work, debates percolate world-wide, under the broad banner of sexual politics, about topics such as abortion, contraception, sex education, HIV/AIDS, marriage, pornography, polyamory, homosexuality, and transsexuality. As an academic attuned to current affairs, British sociologist Jeffrey Weeks points out how so-called 'fundamentalists,' whether Christian, Islamic, Jewish, or Hindu, have positioned the body and its pleasures at the core of efforts to reconstruct neo-traditional societies marked by rigid gender roles and the severe punishment of transgressors.[91]

The Steel-Shafted Stiletto: A Museum Artefact in the Offing?

In the end, what does the future hold for the skin trade? For many, the mystery, illusion, and secrecy of strip*tease* disappeared long ago. Yet the rebellious stripper still freights contemporary cachet: she pops up regularly in films, on TV talk-shows and cable programming, in autobiographies, and on dancers' blogs. The Ultimate Strip Club List website tallies the numbers of clubs around the globe: the United States: 2,778; Mexico: 115; Europe: 248; Asia: 31; Africa: 6; South America: 32; and Canada: 275.[92] This list is a sign that the business is resilient and profitable. And yet, with the spike in virtual nudity on the Internet, the revival of 1950s burlesque by never-naked 'performance artists,' and the demise of strip clubs across Canada, the demand for *live* nude girls in nightclubs appears to be waning. Compounding this trend are the rising costs of licensing and operating strip clubs, the ban on smoking in clubs, the rising price of a night out, the gentrification of downtown cores, and the changing appetites of (some) young feminist men. Even the storied Tropicana nightclub in Havana, Cuba, is replacing its famed showgirls with spectacles sans strippers that emphasize theatricality, fancy technology, and new stage sets.[93]

To ex-dancer Annie Temple, the recent rash of strip club closures in Vancouver – the Drake Show Lounge, the Fraser Arms Hotel, and the Marble Arch Pub and Showroom – is heartbreaking. On her blog in May 2007, she wrote: '[British Columbia] is one of the few provinces left where dancers are consistently paid for their stage shows, and women who need options for financial independence can work without crossing any physical barriers.' Stressing 'no-contact' exotic dancing as a safe sex-work option for women, Temple added that the loss of precious stages means 'one less place to work, one less option for women not born for the straight life ... Abracadabra, the strip club becomes a strip mall.'[94] Another irony: as exotic dancers today seek to participate in the century-long tradition of doffing one's clothes in public for a decent return, the business appears to be hurtling towards extinction.

Mindful of Temple's poignant lament, I wonder: will dancers dance for dollars at clubs while customers pay for fantasy in twenty years' time? Since we are still in the grip of a puritan ideology that is at once fascinated and repulsed by female nudity and sexuality, a full-scale disappearance of marquees announcing 'Live nude girls!' seems unlikely. Yet across North America, only a few headlining dancers make lots of money over a short period of time; the rest weigh the unpredictable, sometimes skinny wages against the feminized, poorly paid, and insecure alternatives – at Safeway, Journey's End motels, or Tim Horton's – available to those without better options.

If strip clubs endure, will exotic dancer ever rate as a desirable, reputable career choice for little girls growing up? Not in my lifetime. As long as striptease conjures up popular associations of worthless, diseased, lazy, drug-addicted, oversexed, and dangerous bodies, the erotic labour performed by dancers, past and present, will never be appreciated as labour: it will be forever figured as something else. Age-old struggles by dancers for improved working conditions, union certification, destigmatization of their art form, and respect for their skills will continue in the absence of a titanic transformation in the cultural meanings attached to bump and grind.

Notes

Preface: Beginnings, Backlash, and Brazenness

1 See an interview with Gwendolyn by Shannon Bell in her book *Whore Carnival*, 69–82.
2 Ken MacQueen, 'Sociologist in Search of the Naked Truth,' and Dene Moore, 'Historian Studying Erotic Entertainment.'
3 My favourite is the interview done by Vancouver-based writer Ellen Schwartz, 'The Striptease Project: Uncovering the Bare Truth about Vancouver's Past.'
4 On this history, see Frances Backhouse, *Women of the Klondike*; Rich Mole, *Rebel Women of the Klondike: Extraordinary Achievements and Daring Adventures*; Lael Morgan, *Good Time Girls of the Alaska-Yukon Gold Rush*; and Jennifer Duncan, *Frontier Spirit:The Brave Women of the Klondike*.
5 Rafe Mair show, guest-hosted by Peter Warren, 19 June 2000.
6 John Geddes, 'Saving Ms. Stewart.'
7 See Linda Tuhiwai Smith, *Decolonizing Methodologies: Research and Indigenous Peoples*.

1. Uncloaking the Striptease Past

1 Male striptease dates back to the 1920s; it resurfaced in the late 1970s with the emergence of the popular 'Chippendales.' An under-researched trend, there is evidence of an appetite for male strippers in the British hit film *The Full Monty* (1998) and in gay nightclubs in most North American, British, and European cities. In the fall of 2003, Bravo! screened episodes of *Strip Search!* Their reality-TV show tells the story of creating a touring revue of male strippers. See Rebecca Caldwell, 'Wanted: Canucks in the Buff.' For

an academic account, see Joseph DeMarco, 'Power and Control in Gay Strip Clubs.'

2 Laszlo Buhasz, 'Leer Jet.'

3 Sarah Hampson, 'And Now, the Nudes.'

4 Kerry Gold, 'Strip and Tell, Sort Of.'

5 See William Weintraub, *Crazy about Lili*, and Billie Livingston, *Cease to Blush*. Livingston and I became friends while researching our 'burlesque projects,' and I chuckled (and blushed) when I discovered that I 'made an appearance' in her novel as Samantha Barnes – a 'sleek dyke of the urban designer-wear, Annie Lennox variety, in the midst of writing a big fat book on the history of strippers in Vancouver for which she'd received a hefty government grant, making her a target for neo-conservatives across the country' (6).

6 For the website, see www.burlesquehall.com.

7 See Michelle Baldwin, *Burlesque (and the New Bump-n-Grind)*, and Debra Ferreday, '"Showing the Girl": The New Burlesque.'

8 See Adam Gopnik, 'The Naked City'; Kim Izzo, 'Rattle, Shake and Roll'; and Ken MacQueen, 'Undressing Up.' On the prevalence of neo-burlesque in Las Vegas, see Tara Weingarten, 'I'm a Dancer, Not a Stripper.'

9 Brenda Whitehall, 'Stilettos and Strap-Ons: Infusing Burlesque with Queer Femme Flair,' 19.

10 Daphne Bramham, 'Long-Stemmed Lovelies Play On.'

11 See Mireille Silcoff, 'Dita Von Teese: International Queen of Burlesque.'

12 See Michel Foucault, *The History of Sexuality, Volume I* (New York: Vintage Books, 1980).

13 Ibid., 36.

14 Ibid., 40. On the rise of heterosexuality as norm and privileged social institution, see Jonathon Ned Katz, *The Invention of Heterosexuality*, and Mary Louise Adams, *The Trouble with Normal: Postwar Youth and the Making of Heterosexuality*.

15 For an excellent summary of major debates, see Angus McLaren, *Twentieth-Century Sexuality: A History*.

16 Oliver Moore, 'Swingers' Clubs Hope Ruling Will Help to Stimulate Their Business.'

17 Editorial, 'Just Like That, There Go Community Standards.' Also, see Moore, 'Swingers' Clubs.'

18 Margaret Dragu and A.S.A. Harrison, *Revelations: Essays on Striptease and Sexuality*, 53–7.

19 In this book, I use the term 'dancer,' rather than 'stripper,' in keeping with my narrators' preference.

20 See Lucinda Jarrett, *Stripping in Time: A History of Erotic Dancing*, 2–6.

21 See Robert Allen, *Horrible Prettiness: Burlesque and American Culture.*

22 Jarrett, *Stripping in Time*, 59–83.

23 Ibid., 68.

24 On Maud Allen, see ibid., 89.

25 Robert Allen, *Horrible Prettiness*, 248.

26 See Angela Latham's analysis in *Posing a Threat: Flappers, Chorus Girls, and Other Brazen Performers of the American 1920s*, 113.

27 Alexander John Baptiste Parent-Duchatelet, *De la prostitution dans la Ville de Paris, Vol. I*. Trans. by Jill Harsin, as *Policing Prostitution in Nineteenth Century Paris*, 205–35; and Havelock Ellis, *Sex in Relation to Society: Studies in the Psychology of Sex*, 277.

28 See Andrea Stuart, *Showgirls*, 1.

29 Latham, *Posing a Threat*, 115.

30 Allen, *Horrible Prettiness*, 282.

31 Charlene Kish, 'A Knee Is a Joint and Not an Entertainment: The Moral Regulation of Burlesque in Early Twentieth-Century Toronto,' 2–4.

32 Ibid., 18.

33 Ibid., 19.

34 See Lael Morgan, *Good Time Girls of the Alaska-Yukon Gold Rush*, 12–32, and Bay Ryley, *Gold Diggers of the Klondike: Prostitution in Dawson City, Yukon, 1898–1908*, 9–14.

35 Andrea Friedman, *Prurient Interests: Gender, Democracy, and Obscenity in New York City, 1909–1945*, 67. Vancouver-based choreographer Jack Card recalls that Sally Rand performed several times in the 1950s and 1960s in Vancouver. She was known to say, 'I dare anyone to say that they can see any of my body parts at the end of my act or during my act.' Card affirmed Rand's declaration: 'Except at the very end she climbed this long staircase and the lights went down to a deep blue, with a lavender light on her face, washed from the sides, the front was all shadowed in deep blue, and she'd lift her fans like this, boom, and the curtains would close. You never a saw a thing.' Interview with Jack Card, Vancouver, 28 January 2000.

36 Ann Corio with Joseph DiMona, *This Was Burlesque*, 175.

37 Beatrix Zumsteg, 'Promoting Censorship in the Name of Youth: The Council of Women's Activism against Vaudeville in the 1920s and 1930s in Vancouver,' 2.

38 Cited in Ivan Ackery, *Fifty Years on Theatre Row*, 127.

39 See Rachel Shteir, 'LaGuardia Kicks Striptease Out of New York,' in *Striptease: The Untold History of the Girlie Show*, 156–76.

40 See Andrea Friedman, 'Habitats of Sex-Crazed Perverts: Campaigns against Burlesque,' in her *Prurient Interests*, 91.

41 Marilyn Hegarty, 'Patriot or Prostitute: Sexual Discourses, Print Media, and American Women during World War II,' 122. Also see her *Victory Girls, Khaki-Wackies, and Patriotutes: The Regulation of Female Sexuality during World War II.*

42 Robert Campbell, in *Demon Rum or Easy Money: Government Control of Liquor in British Columbia from Prohibition to Privatization*, 50–5, argues that the B.C. Liquor Control Board enforced a 'no food, no entertainment, no dancing' policy in Vancouver's beer parlours (in hotels), until 1954. Campbell points out that the chief inspector for the B.C. Liquor Control Board rejected applications for a liquor licence from Chinese in Vancouver, as it 'has been found that Chinese are not able to handle this type of business' (123).

43 Carolyn Strange, *Toronto's Girl Problem: The Pleasures and Perils of the City*, 106.

44 'Police Revert to One O'Clock Cabaret Closing.'

45 'Drunken, Immoral Conduct in Cabarets: Church, Temperance Heads Related Visits to Night Spots.'

46 'Reformers to Fight Night Club License.'

47 After it closed in 1952, the State Burlesque Theatre became the Avon Theatre, and then the Everyman Theatre.

48 Owen A. Aldridge, 'American Burlesque at Home and Abroad: Together with the Etymology of Go-Go Girl,' 568.

49 This is stripteaser Ann Corio's phrase, cited in Joseph Smith, 'Ann Corio Brings Back Burlesque,' 3.

50 Interview with Norman Young, Vancouver, B.C., 13 December 1999. See advertisement for Tom Farmer, Stinky Mason, and Zandra, famous exotic dancers, and two screen features, *Vancouver Sun*, 15 June 1946.

51 Charlene Kish, 'A Knee Is a Joint and Not an Entertainment,' 46.

52 'Arrests May Cost Theatre License.' On the use of the Wales Padlock Law to close down a theatre if it produced an 'indecent' production featuring 'sex degeneracy' or 'sex perversion,' see Rachel Shteir, *Striptease*, 106.

53 Ray Gardner, 'Jails Manager.'

54 Letter from A. Moore to Chairman and Members of the Licenses and Claims Committee, City Hall, 5 September 1946, Vancouver City Archives, 28-D, File 20, City Clerk fonds, Series 27.

55 William Best, 'Police, Night Club Eyes Bulge as Sally Rand Strains Corset.'

56 Also in 1951, Lili St Cyr was arrested and subjected to a trial for giving an obscene and immoral performance; she was arrested again in 1967 before tourists arrived for Expo.

57 'Burlesque Show Gets Okay for Just Little Sex Appeal: Alderman Debate Bare Facts.'

58 'Bumps, Sex Shows are Taboo.'
59 'Burlesque Theatre Closed.'
60 '"Exotic Dancers" to Give Free Show Tuesday Night.'
61 '5 Convicted of Indecent Stage Show.'
62 'Burlesque Show Closed: Appeal Next.'
63 On shifting conceptions of gender and sexuality in the post-World War II era, see Mary Louise Adams, *The Trouble with Normal*; Doug Owram, *Born at the Right Time: A History of the Baby Boom Generation*; Joan Sangster, 'Doing Two Jobs: The Wage-Earner Mother, 1945–1970'; and Joanne Meyerowitz ed., *Not June Cleaver: Women and Gender in Postwar America, 1945–1960*.
64 Pat Armstrong, 'The Welfare State as History,' 52.
65 F.H. Lacey, ed., *Historical Statistics of Canada*, H50, F83, F1, F82.
66 See Ernie Crey and Suzanne Fournier, *Stolen from Our Embrace: The Abduction of First Nations and the Restoration of Aboriginal Communities*; and Tamara Kulusic, 'The Ultimate Betrayal: Claiming and Re-Claiming Cultural Identity.'
67 Dionne Brand, '"We Weren't Allowed to Go into Factory Work until Hitler Started the War": The 1920s to the 1940s.'
68 See Franca Iacovetta, 'Making Model Citizens: Gender, Corrupted Democracy, and Immigrant and Refugee Reception Work in Cold War Canada'; and Iacovetta, *Gatekeepers: Reshaping Immigrant Lives in Cold War Canada*.
69 See Reg Whitaker and Gary Marcuse, *Cold War Canada: The Making of a National Insecurity State, 1945–1957*; Larry Hannant, *The Infernal Machine: Investigating the Loyalty of Canada's Citizens*; and Julie Guard, 'Women Worth Watching: Radical Housewives in Cold War Canada.'
70 See Mona Gleason, 'Safeguarding the Family: Psychology and the Construction of Normalcy,' in *Normalizing the Ideal: Psychology, Schooling, and the Family in Postwar Canada*, 80–96.
71 Owram, *Born at the Right Time*, 18.
72 See Karen Dubinsky, *The Second Greatest Disappointment: Honeymooning and Tourism at Niagara Falls*.
73 On Kinsey's research, see McLaren, *Twentieth-Century Sexuality*, 145–7.
74 For selected work on the sexualization of postwar commercial culture, see McLaren, *Twentieth-Century Sexuality*, 143–92; Adams, *The Trouble with Normal*; Andrea Friedman, 'Sadists and Sissies: Anti-Pornography Campaigns in Cold War America'; and Jonathan Gathorne-Hardy, *Kinsey: A Biography*.
75 McLaren, *Twentieth-Century Sexuality*, 143.

76 On the genealogy of 'bombshells,' see Kristina Zarlengo, 'Civilian Threat, the Suburban Citadel, and Atomic Age American Women.'

77 Valerie Korinek, *Roughing It in the Suburbs: Reading Chatelaine Magazine in the Fifties and Sixties*, 336–40.

78 See Adams, *The Trouble with Normal*.

79 Gary Kinsman, 'Constructing Gay Men and Lesbians as National Security Risks, 1950–1970'; and his 'The Canadian Cold War against Queers: Sexual Regulation and Resistance.' Also see Gary Kinsman and Patrizia Gentile, *The Canadian War on Queers: National Security as Sexual Regulation*.

80 See Patricia Roy, *Vancouver: An Illustrated History*, 129–36.

81 On the history of colonial occupation and the making of Stanley Park, see Renisa Mawani, 'Imperial Legacies, (Post)Colonial Identities: Law, Space and the Making of Stanley Park, 1859–2001'; and Jean Barman, *Stanley Park's Secret: The Forgotten Families of Whoi Whoi, Kanaka Ranch and Brockton Point*.

82 Interview with Norman Young by Becki Ross, 13 December 1999, Vancouver. Hugh Pickett died in Vancouver on 13 February 2006 at the age of ninety-two. For obituaries, see Tom Hawthorn, 'Hugh Pickett, Impresario, 1913-2006'; John Mackie, 'Mr. Showbiz – Promoter Hugh Pickett – Dies at 92'; and John Mackie, 'Famous Friends: Impresario Hugh Pickett's Wit and Charm Won over a Long List of Celebrities.'

83 See Graeme Wynn, 'The Rise of Vancouver,' 70.

84 To date, Vancouver's postwar striptease scene has been conspicuously absent from historical writing. For instance, Douglas Cole erases 'bump and grind' from the city's cultural traditions – opera, the symphony, radio, visual and literary artists, poetry, theatre, architecture, modern dance, and professional and recreational sports in Vancouver. See his chapter 'Leisure, Taste and Tradition in British Columbia,' in Johnston, ed., *The Pacific Province*.

85 Roy, *Vancouver*, 144, n35.

86 On postwar Vancouver's lively and profitable downtown, see Robert North and Walter Hardwick, 'Vancouver since the Second World War: An Economic Geography,' 207; and Sherry McKay, 'Urban Housekeeping and Keeping the Modern House,' 35. On American downtowns, see Michael Johns, *Moment of Grace: The American City in the 1950s*, 42; and Jane Jacobs, *The Death and Life of Great American Cities*.

87 Vancouver hosted the British Empire Games at the Empire Stadium in 1954 and later that year acquired a professional football team, the B.C. Lions. A National Hockey League franchise, the Vancouver Canucks, followed in 1970. The Queen Elizabeth Theatre (1959), the Vancouver Playhouse (1963), the Agrodome exhibition hall (1963), the Arts Club Theatre (1964),

the Pacific Ballet Theatre (1969), and the Vancouver East Cultural Centre (1973) were built to showcase live performances of drama, music, opera, comedy, and ballet. Movie theatres – the Maple Leaf, Globe, Capital, Orpheum, Dominion, Paramount, Lyric, Colonial, and Strand – brought silver screen pleasures to throngs in the downtown core, though screening movies on Sundays was illegal until 1963. In the world of theatre, Hugh Pickett and Ivan Ackery were the city's star impresarios, handling celebrities, booking acts, staging zany promotions, and courting the media with flash and pizzazz. The Orpheum Theatre became a popular movie house; after a major renovation in 1977, it housed the Vancouver Symphony Orchestra. 'Mr. Music,' saxophonist and band leader Dal Richards, led his orchestra's hugely successful swing repertoire, and accompanied his wife, singer Lorraine McAllister, every week for loyal, dance-crazy guests at the upscale Panorama Roof at the Hotel Vancouver from 1940 to 1965. Younger audiences lined up by the thousands to hear Elvis Presley at Empire Stadium (1957), the Beatles at Empire Stadium (1964), and the Rolling Stones at the Pacific National Exhibition (PNE) and Agrodome (1965). Evelyn Ward opened her famous Dance Academy and trained thousands of professional jazz and tap dancers, many of whom appeared in local and touring productions at the PNE and the Queen Elizabeth Theatre. As well, in 1962, former showgirl Paula Ross formed her own modern dance company, and Mimi Ho opened the Strathcona Chinese Dance Company in 1973. See Ivan Ackery's memoir, *Fifty Years on Theatre Row*, and Greg Potter and Red Robinson, *Backstage Vancouver: A Century of Entertainment Legends*.

88 See Brandon Yip, 'Rockin' Back the Clock.'

89 Johns, *Moment of Grace*, 24–5.

90 See Eric Nichol, *Vancouver*, 236.

91 Jack Wasserman, 'Saloon Crawler's Notebook.' On the history of Vancouver's 'cosmopolitan' character, see Michelle Swann, 'Hiding Hot Topics: Science, Sex and Schooling in British Columbia, 1910–1916,' 17–28.

92 For selected readings in Canadian labour history, see Bryan Palmer, *Working Class Experience: The Rise and Reconstitution of Canadian Labour, 1800–1980*; Craig Heron and Bob Storey, *On the Job: Confronting the Labour Process in Canada*; Greg Kealey, *Workers and Canadian History*; David Bercuson and David Bright, eds, *Canadian Labour History: Selected Readings*; Franca Iacovetta, *Such Hard-Working People: Italian Immigrants in Postwar Toronto*; Joy Parr, *The Gender of Breadwinners: Women, Men, and Change in Two Industrial Towns*; and Helen Smith and Pamela Wakewich, '"Beauty and the Helldivers": Representing Women's Work and Identities in a Warplant Newspaper.'

93 An important exception is David Scott's *Behind the G-String: An Exploration of the Stripper's Image, Her Person, and Her Meaning*. Though not
focused on Vancouver, per se, Scott's book introduces significant Canadian
content. For a sampling of urban histories that feature Vancouver, see
Graeme Wynn and Timothy Oke, *Vancouver and Its Region*; Jean Barman,
The West beyond the West: A History of British Columbia; Gillian Creese
and Veronica Strong-Boag, eds, *British Columbia Reconsidered: Essays on
Women*; and Chuck Davis, ed., *The Greater Vancouver Book: An Urban Ency-
clopaedia*.

94 Contributors to the field of sex history include Gary Kinsman, *The Regulation of Desire: Homo and Hetero Sexualities*; Steven Maynard, '"Horrible
Temptations": Sex, Men, and Working Class Male Youth in Urban Ontario,
1890–1935'; Adams, *The Trouble with Normal*; Dubinsky, *The Second Greatest
Disappointment*; and Line Chamberland, *Mémoires lesbiennes: Le lesbianisme
à Montréal entre 1950 et 1972*.

95 See Daniel Francis, *Red Light Neon: A History of Vancouver's Sex Trade*; and
Trina Ricketts, Susan Davis, Stacey Grayer, Candice Hansen, Jennifer
Allan, and Chanel Martin, *History of Sex Work: Vancouver*. Knowledge of
the history of striptease – the commodification of sexual arousal – is not
chronicled in either text.

96 Jarrett, *Stripping in Time*, and Shteir, *Striptease*. Here, I would also like to
mention A.W. Stencell's excellent book on the American history of 'girlie
shows' at travelling summer-time exhibitions: *Girl Show: Into the Canvas
World of Bump and Grind*.

97 My thanks to Kim Greenwell who assisted me in assessing these films'
portrayals of burlesque and striptease entertainers. Other films with
striptease-related content include Helen Morgan in *Applause* (1929), Sally
Rand in *Bolero* (1934), Greta Garbo in *Mata Hari* (1931), Josephine Baker
in *Princess Tam Tam* (1935), Vera Zorina in *On Your Toes* (1939), Gypsy
Rose Lee in *Stage Door Canteen* (1943), Susan Hampshire in *Expresso Bongo*
(1959), Rita Hayworth in *Gilda* (1946), Leslie Caron in *Glory Alley* (1954),
Brigitte Bardot in *Mlle Striptease (Please Mr. Balzac)* (1956), Marilyn Monroe
in *Bus Stop* (1956), Jayne Mansfield in *Too Hot To Handle* (1960), Valerie Per-
rine in *Lenny* (1974), and Lolita Davidovich in *Blaze* (1989). Additional film
titles are: *Ladies of the Chorus* (1949), *King of Burlesque* (1935), *Panama Hattie*
(1942), *Bring on the Girls* (1945), *Lady of Burlesque* (1943), *The Trouble with
Women* (1947), *Playgirl* (1954), *The Travelling Saleswoman* (1950), *Let's Do It
Again* (1953), *So This Is Love* (1953), *Pal Joey* (1965), *Girl Happy* (1965), and
Meet Me in Las Vegas (1956). My sincere thanks to historian Lisa Davis and
writer/activist Michael Bronski for helping me to compile this list.

98 More recently, a handful of rich documentary films tell stories about the history of striptease. See *This Was Burlesque* (2002), *Anatomy of Burlesque* (2003), and *Pretty Things* (2005).

99 For a sampling of scholarship uncritically rooted in the 'sociology of deviance' in the 1970s and 1980s, see James Skipper and Charles Mc-Caghy, 'Stripteasers: The Anatomy and Career Contingencies of a Deviant Occupation,' 'Stripping: Anatomy of a Deviant Lifestyle,' and 'Stripteasing: A Sex-Oriented Occupation'; Charles McCaghy and James Skipper, 'Lesbian Behavior as an Adaptation to the Occupation of Stripping'; and Sandra Harley Carey, Robert Peterson, and Louis Sharpe, 'A Study of Recruitment and Socialization in Two Deviant Female Occupations.' For more contemporary scholarship informed by the 'deviance' framework, see Craig Forsyth and Tina Deshotels, 'A Deviant Process: The Sojourn of the Stripper'; G.E. Enck and J.D. Preston, 'Counterfeit Intimacy: A Drama-turgical Analysis of an Erotic Performance'; and William Thompson and Jackie Harred, 'Topless Dancers: Managing Stigma in a Deviant Occupa-tion.' Charles McCaghy has donated his extensive 'striptease archive,' en-titled the Charles H. McCaghy Collection of Exotic Dance from Burlesque to Clubs, to the University of Ohio's Jerome Lawrence and Robert E. Lee Theatre Research Institute, Columbus, Ohio.

100 Skipper and McCaghy, 'Stripping,' 368.

101 See Parent-Duchatelet, *De la prostitution dans la Ville de Paris*, and Skipper and McCaghy, 'Stripteasing,' 278.

102 For a sampling of feminist writing that equates sex work with women's exploitation, see Kathleen Barry, *Female Sexual Slavery*, Andrea Dworkin, *Pornography: Men Possessing Women*, Sheila Jeffreys, *Anticlimax: A Femi-nist Perspective on the Sexual Revolution*, and Catharine MacKinnon, *Only Words*.

103 Nickie Roberts, quoted in Jarrett, *Stripping in Time*, 208.

104 Gwendolyn, quoted in Shannon Bell, *Reading, Writing and Rewriting the Prostitute Body*, 168.

105 Lindalee Tracey, *Growing Up Naked: My Years in Bump and Grind*, 191, 202, 204.

106 See Magda Fahrni and Robert Rutherdale, 'Introduction,' in *Creating Post-war Canada: Community, Diversity and Dissent, 1945–75*, 2.

107 Pierre Bourdieu, *Distinction: A Social Critique of the Judgement of Taste*, 76.

108 Shteir, *Striptease*, 6.

109 Here, I borrow from, and stretch forward, Greg Marquis's observation of earlier decades in, 'Vancouver Vice: The Police and the Negotiation of Morality, 1904–1935,' 243.

110 Murray Campbell, 'Memories of Montreal's Skin Queen.'

111 See Eric Nichol, *Vancouver*, 207.

112 This phrase appeared in the title of Earle C. Westwood's speech to the Greater Vancouver Tourist Association in 1957, cited in Michael Dawson's wonderful book *Selling British Columbia: Tourism and Consumer Culture, 1890–1970*, 153.

113 Estimate cited in Robert Collier, 'Downtown: Metropolitan Focus,' 160.

114 Wreck Beach has been the focus of debate and contest for four decades. Recently, members of the Wreck Beach Preservation Society mounted a protest against the development of three residential towers on the campus of the University of British Columbia, overlooking the nude beach. See Jonathan Woodward, 'The Battle to Keep B.C. Beach Bare.' In July 2008, members of the Royal Canadian Mounted Police stepped up patrols against 'indiscriminate sex' in the bushes on the beach. See, Jeremy Hainsworth, 'RCMP Targets Gay Cruisers at Wreck Beach.' Also see Carellin Brooks's lovely book *Wreck Beach*.

115 Stephen Brown, 'Myth Shattered: We Win One!,' 25.

116 See Kathy Tait, 'Wreck Beach Skinny-Dippers Raided'; Paul Manning, 'Gawkers Flock to View Nude-In'; and 'Sunbather Convicted for Nudity.' From the 1920s to the 1950s, Doukhobors in southeastern British Columbia engaged in stripping of another kind to protest compulsory schooling and resocialization to 'Canadian ways.' In 1953, 144 adult Sons of Freedom were convicted of public nudity under section 205A of the Criminal Code and sentenced to jail terms. See John McLaren, 'The State, Child Snatching, and the Law: The Seizure and Indoctrination of Sons of Freedom Children in British Columbia, 1950–1960.' Vancouver has had a lively 'nudist' culture dating back to the 1940s. See Peter Thompson, 'Nudism Soaring in Popularity as Club Membership Doubles.'

117 Kevin Griffin, '30 Years Ago, a Pot Smoke-In Sparked the Gastown Riot.'

118 Robert Hunter, *The Greenpeace to Amchitka: An Environmental Odyssey*, 16.

119 On the careers of the Canadian Ice Fantasy skaters, from 1952 to 1954, see Michael Scott, 'The Original Blade Runners,' *Vancouver Sun*, 2 February 2002: I8.

120 Lindalee Tracey, *Growing Up Naked*, 210. Sadly, Lindalee Tracey died of breast cancer at the age of forty-nine in Toronto on 19 October 2006.

121 Four of the six interviews with musicians were conducted by my research assistants, Kim Greenwell and Michelle Swann.

122 Catharine MacKinnon, 'Defamation or Discrimination,' in *Only Words*, 3–41; Jill Dolan, *The Feminist Spectator as Critic*; Kate Millett, *The Prostitution Papers*; Kathleen Barry, *The Prostitution of Sexuality*; Susan Griffin,

Pornography and Silence: Culture's Revenge against Nature; Andrea Dworkin, *Pornography: Men Possessing Women*; Sara Wynter, 'WHISPER: Women Hurt in Systems of Prostitution Engaged in Revolt'; and M. Farley, '"Bad for the Body, Bad for the Heart": Prostitution Harms Women Even if Legalized or Decriminalized.'

123 For theorizing sex workers' feminist insiderness, I thank Margo St James, 'The Reclamation of Whores'; and Jill Nagle, 'Introduction,' in *Whores and Other Feminists*, 3. I also applaud Kay Armatage's film *Striptease*, made in 1980 with the cooperation of the Canadian Association of Burlesque Entertainers (CABE).

124 Merri Lisa Johnson, 'Stripper-Bashing: An Autovideography of Violence against Strippers,' 161.

125 Leslie Roman, 'Double Exposure: The Politics of Feminist Materialist Ethnography.'

126 Carol Queen, *Real Live Nude Girl: Chronicles of Sex-Positive Culture*, 45.

127 On hostility towards femme lesbians, see Joan Nestle, *A Restricted Country*; Alice Echols, *Daring to Be Bad: Radical Feminism in America, 1967–1975*, 215–19; Joan Nestle, ed., *The Persistent Desire: A Femme-Butch Reader*; Sally Munt, ed., *Butch/Femme: Inside Lesbian Gender*; Amber Hollibaugh, *My Dangerous Desires: A Queer Girl Dreaming Her Way Home*; and Chlöe Brushwood Rose and Anna Camilleri, eds, *Brazen Femme: Queering Femininity*.

128 Judith Stacey, 'Can There Be a Feminist Ethnography?'

129 Geoffrey Cubitt, *History and Memory*, 76.

130 Joan Sangster, 'Telling Our Stories: Feminist Debates and the Use of Oral History.'

131 Alessandro Portelli, 'What Makes Oral History Different?,' 21.

132 Sangster, 'Telling Our Stories,' 22–3.

133 For contemporary research on exotic dancing, see David A. Scott, *Behind the G-String*; Carol Rambo-Ronai, 'Sketching with Derrida: An Ethnography of a Researcher/Erotic Dancer'; Jacqueline Lewis, 'Controlling Lap Dancing: Law, Morality, and Sex Work'; Jacqueline Lewis, '"I'll Scratch Your Back if You'll Scratch Mine": The Role of Reciprocity, Power and Autonomy in the Strip Club'; Chris Bruckert, *Taking It Off: Putting It On: Women in the Strip Trade*; Katherine Liepe-Levinson, *Strip Show: Performances of Gender and Desire*; Katherine Frank, *G-Strings and Sympathy: Strip Club Regulars and Male Desire*; Wendy Chapkis, *Live Sex Acts: Women Performing Erotic Labour*; Siobhan Brooks, 'Dancing toward Freedom'; Danielle Egan, *Dancing for Dollars and Paying for Love*; Bernadette Barton, *Stripped: Inside the Lives of Exotic Dancers*; R. Danielle Egan, Katherine Frank, and Merri Lisa Johnson, eds, *Flesh for Fantasy: Producing and Con-*

suming Exotic Dance; Brenda Foley, *Undressed for Success: Beauty Contestants and Exotic Dancers as Merchants of Morality*; and Katherine Frank, 'Thinking Critically about Strip Club Research.'

134 Autobiographies include Ann Corio, *This Was Burlesque* (1968), Margaret Dragu and A.S.A. Harrison, *Revelations: Essays on Striptease and Sexuality* (1988), Janet Feindel, *A Particular Class of Women* (1988), Diana Atkinson, *Highways and Dancehalls* (1995), Lindalee Tracey, *Growing Up Naked* (1997), Lily Burana, *Strip City: A Stripper's Farewell Journey across America* (2001), Elisabeth Eaves, *Bare: the Naked Truth about Stripping* (2002), Lillian Faderman, *Naked in the Promised Land* (2003), and Diablo Cody, *Candy Girl: A Year in the Life of an Unlikely Stripper* (2006).

135 Cody, *Candy Girl*, 211.

136 See Dorothy E. Smith, *The Everyday World as Problematic: A Feminist Sociology*.

2. 'I Ain't Rebecca, and This Ain't Sunnybrook Farm': Men behind the Marquee

1 Quotation attributed to Joe Philliponi by his brother Ross Filippone, interviewed in Vancouver, 15 June 2000.

2 Interview with Ross Filippone.

3 Sean Gunn, 'Kublai Khan Ten,' unpublished poem, Vancouver (2000), 1.

4 Dennis Barker, 'King of Soft Porn Became the Richest Man in Britain.'

5 The exception appears to be California, where some nightclubs were owned and managed by women. According to historian Rachel Shteir, Sally Rand managed two clubs in San Francisco, stripper Ginger Britton owned the Follies in Los Angeles in the mid-1940s, and Lillian Hunt managed the El Rey Theater in Oakland. See Shteir, *Striptease: The Untold History of the Girlie Show*, 255.

6 Jack Wasserman, 'Saloon Crawler's Notebook.'

7 Interview with Patrick Nagle, Victoria, British Columbia, 28 July 2000. Sadly, Patrick Nagle died suddenly at the age of seventy-one in Sooke, British Columbia, on 10 January 2006. See Sandra McCulloch, 'Patrick Nagle, Journalist, Dead at 71.'

8 For selected histories of class and racial/ethnic clashes in Vancouver, see Robert McDonald, *Making Vancouver: 1863–1913*, 3–32, 149–74; Cole Harris, *Making Native Space: Colonialism, Resistance, and Reserves*; Patricia Roy, *The Oriental Question: Consolidating a White Man's Province, 1914–1941*; and Adele Perry, *On the Edge of Empire: Race, Gender and the Making of British Columbia, 1849–1871*.

9 In 1951, the total population of British, French, and other Europeans in British Columbia was 93.2 per cent, the Asian population was 2.4 per cent, and the Aboriginal population was 2.2 per cent (other: 2.2 per cent); in 1961, British/French/other European was 93.4 per cent, Asian was 2.5 per cent, and Aboriginal was 2.4 per cent (other: 1.7 per cent); in 1971, British/French/other European was 92.4 per cent, Asian was 3.5 per cent, and Aboriginal was 2.4 per cent (other: 1.7 per cent). Cited in Veronica Strong-Boag, 'Society in the Twentieth Century,' 276.

10 See the 1998 documentary film directed by Meilan Lam, *Show Girls: Celebrating Montreal's Legendary Black Jazz Scene.*

11 See Greg Potter and Red Robinson, *Backstage Vancouver: A Century of Entertainment Legends.*

12 Jack Wasserman, 'Tale of a City.'

13 On prohibitions against entertainment in Vancouver beer parlours, see Robert Campbell, *Sit Down and Drink Your Beer: Regulating Vancouver's Beer Parlours, 1925–1954*, 15, 24, 36, 132.

14 Jack Wasserman, 'City Cabarets Facing "Ruin."'

15 The history of postwar striptease dancers and shows in famous Las Vegas clubs near and on 'The Strip' – Tropicana, Dunes, Stardust, Caesars Palace, Desert Inn, and the Sands – remains unwritten. Clues can be found in Robert McCracken, *Las Vegas: The Great American Playground*, 69-86. At the Sands, the main showroom featured the Copa Girls, 'the most beautiful girls in the world,' to quote the resort's own promotion (73).

16 I borrow 'horrible prettiness' from Robert C. Allen's book of the same name, *Horrible Prettiness: Burlesque and American Culture.*

17 For a pictorial history of Vancouver's Cave Supper Club (1937–81), see Claire Hurley, *Remember the Cave.*

18 Interview with Denny Boyd, West Vancouver, 2 August 2001. Sadly, Denny Boyd died of cancer in Vancouver, on 27 October 2006 at the age of seventy-six. For moving obituaries, see Pete McMartin, 'The Sun's Voice Who Spoke to Readers Has Fallen Silent,' and Jenny Lee and Doug Ward, 'Beloved Columnist Will Always Be Known as the: "Voice of the Little Guy."'

19 'City Cafés Get Wine Licenses'; and '102 B.C. Liquor Licenses Issued.'

20 Mariana Valverde, *Diseases of the Will: Alcohol and the Dilemmas of Freedom*, 97.

21 Ibid.

22 Len Carlyle, 'The Show Business Phenomenon Called the Cave,' 47.

23 Ibid., 45.

24 Isy Walters interviewed by Meyer Freedman, 1975, at Isy's Supper Club.

My thanks to Della Walters for access to this tape recording from her personal collection.

25 Jewish Canadian fashion icon Harry Rosen was raised by a father who arrived in Canada (northern Ontario) from Poland in 1925, 'hardly employable.' Like Isy Walters, Harry's father got a push cart and collected scrap to provide a livelihood for his family. According to Harry, some Jewish men found that the salvage business 'permitted them to take Friday afternoon and Saturday off to observe the Sabbath.' Personal correspondence with Harry Rosen, 18 May 2005.

26 Interview with Richard Walters, Vancouver, 8 July 2000. For more on striptease at travelling carnivals, see A.W. Stencell, *Girl Show: Into the Canvas World of Bump and Grind*, and Susan Meiselas, *Carnival Strippers*.

27 In 2000, Hugh Pickett rudely refused to be interviewed by me for this book. He haughtily claimed that he was 'writing his own book.' Dead six years later (2006) at age ninety-two, Pickett never completed his autobiography. For an introduction to his career as Vancouver's 'agent to the stars,' see the documentary film *Hugh Pickett: A Portrait*, directed by Moyra Rodger (2003). See obituaries by Tom Hawthorn, 'Hugh Pickett, Impresario, 1913-2006'; and John Mackie, 'Mr. Showbiz – Promoter Hugh Pickett – Dies at 92,' and 'Famous Friends.'

28 Isy Walters, interviewed by Meyer Freedman, 1975.

29 Female dancers booked by Isy Walters at the Cave include: Terry True Dancers (1954), Joy Healy Dancers (1954), DuVarney Dancers (1954), Patty Kay Dancers (1955), Japanese Can Can Dancers (1955), Coronet Dancers (1956), Strachen Dancers (1956), and the Balladines Dancers (1958).

30 My thanks to Richard Walters, Isy Walters's son, for lending me his father's booking diary.

31 Interview with Richard Walters.

32 Jack Wasserman, 'Night Spotter's Notebook.'

33 Interview with Jack Card, Vancouver, 28 January 2000.

34 See obituary for Isy Walters by Jack Wasserman, 'The Passing Parade.'

35 'Jack Wasserman's World.'

36 Ibid.

37 Jack Wasserman, 'Along the Triviera.'

38 In an article for *Vancouver* magazine, Ric Mazerennie acknowledged that the 600 block of Hornby Street was designated 'Wasserman's Beat'; a bronze plaque was remounted on the site of the new Cathedral Place in 1991; and his ashes were spread over Cathedral Place's garden courtyard. See Mazerennie's 'The Beat Goes On.'

39 Interview with Richard Walters.

40 Interview with Della Walters, Vancouver, 20 September 2001.
41 Interview with Jeannie Runnalls, Coquitlam, British Columbia, 21 June 2000.
42 Mike McRanor, *Vancouver Sun*, 12 March 1976: 3A.
43 Interview with Della Walters. For an obituary, see 'Memorial Service Set for Showman Walters.'
44 Interview with Jack Card.
45 Ibid.
46 E-mail interview with Patrick Kevin O'Hara, 18 June 2007.
47 Interview with Richard Walters.
48 When Joe (the eldest) and his parents arrived in British Columbia from San Nicola, Italy, in 1929, a racist immigration officer anglicized Filippone to Philliponi. Joe's siblings were given the original surname, Filippone.
49 Interview with Ross Filippone. One of the last connections to Vancouver's 'golden era' of nightclubs in the 1950s and 1960s, Ross Filippone died on 28 October 2007. See John Mackie's tribute, 'Ross Filippone Was Classic Rags-to-Riches Story.'
50 Interview with Ross Filippone.
51 Denny Boyd, 'Legend Larger Than the Man.'
52 Interview with Doug Cuthbert, Vancouver, 5 July 2000.
53 Maida Price, 'Oh, It Was Athletic: Life and Times at the Penthouse Nightclub.'
54 Alex MacGillivray, *Vancouver Sun*, Leisure Section, 27 December 1968: 2A.
55 Denny Boyd, *Vancouver Sun*, 9 March 1978: B3.
56 Rachel Shteir, *Striptease: The Untold History of the Girlie Show*, 317.
57 'Rathie Tackles "Topless" Issue,' and George Peloquin, 'Go-Go Cabarets Can't Go Topless.' Also in 1966, Vancouver city councillors imposed a ban on topless waitresses at the Bunkhouse restaurant on Davie Street, stating that the trend was 'in poor taste and offensive to the community.' See 'Council Tells Girls to Cover.'
58 'Topless Dancer and Boss Fined.'
59 One reporter claimed that the Cat's Whiskers in suburban Surrey, British Columbia, boasted the first bare-bosom go-go dancer, Bonnie Rish, in the province. See 'B.C. Nightspot has Topless Show.' According to Patrick Nagle, Jeffrey and Peter Barnett ran a popular topless go-go joint in a converted chicken hatchery in Langley in the late 1960s.
60 Interview with Bob Stork, Abbottsford, British Columbia, 29 January 2000.
61 'Advertisement,' *Vancouver Sun*, 17 April 1969: 27.

62 *Household Facilities and Equipment,* Table 25: Telephones, Radios, Television Receivers, by Province, September 1955, 18; and *Household Facilities and Equipment* Table 29: Black and White TV Sets, by Province, April 1975, 23.

63 Ian Todd, 'Liquor Laws Unrealistic, Says Booth.'

64 Ibid.

65 'Obey Liquor Law or Else, Chief Warns.'

66 Larry Rose, 'Cabaret Policing "Will Get Tougher."'

67 Jack McCaugherty, 'It's Fun, It's Accepted … But Illegal.'

68 See Chuck Poulsen, 'Penthouse "Hangout for Mafia."'

69 See Les Wiseman, 'Not Your Average Joe,' 64.

70 Cited in Lucinda Jarrett, *Stripping in Time: A History of Erotic Dancing,* 136.

71 Interview with Ross Filippone.

72 See Allan Fotheringham, *Vancouver Sun,* 22 December 1977, and Daniel Wood, 'The Naked and the Dead: Truth Isn't the Only Victim in the 50-year Penthouse Saga,' 104.

73 Interview with Larry Wong and Sean Gunn, Vancouver, 18 March 2004.

74 Campbell, *Sit Down and Drink Your Beer,* 51–77. Campbell makes the salient point that parlour operators and liquor officials were never successful in stamping out the sex trade; indeed, they provided additional revenue for some hotels, which rented them rooms.

75 Interview with Doug Cuthbert.

76 Interview with Ron Small, Vancouver, 22 September 2000.

77 'An End to Class Distinction.'

78 See Edward Said, *Orientalism,* 71. On Chinatown as tourist destination, see Kay Anderson, *Vancouver's Chinatown: Racial Discourse in Canada, 1875–1980,* 144–77; and Graeme Wynn, 'The Rise of Vancouver,' 141–42.

79 Anderson, *Vancouver's Chinatown,* 206.

80 In the early 1980s, the Smilin' Buddha became ground zero to the thriving punk scene in Vancouver.

81 Alex Louie interviewed by Bernice Chan, aired on CBC radio, 14 May 2004.

82 On racialized entertainment in postwar Montreal, Quebec, see Meilan Lam's film *Show Girls: Celebrating Montreal's Legendary Black Jazz Scene.* On slumming, see George Chauncey, *Gay New York: Gender, Urban Culture and the Making of the Gay Male World, 1890–1940,* 246–7; Kevin Mumford, *Interzones: Black/White Sex Districts in Chicago and New York in the Early Twentieth Century,* 135–56; and Benson Tong, *The Chinese Americans.*

83 Mumford, *Interzones,* 135.

84 On contact zones, see Mary Louise Pratt, *Imperial Eyes: Travel Writing and Transculturation,* 4.

85 In Montreal, Quebec, in the 1940s and 1950s, the city was similarly racial-ized, with white folks attending nightclubs 'uptown,' and black folks relegated to downtown nightspots. See Meilan Lam's film *Show Girls*.

86 E-mail interview with Patrick Kevin O'Hara.

87 Eric Nichol, *Vancouver*, 229.

88 Sean Gunn remembers the bad reputation of one police officer who patrolled outside the Kublai Khan nightclub: 'Because the hookers were hanging around, he would hail a taxi and then force them into a cab, give the driver ten bucks, and say, "Drive her as far as this ten bucks will go and let her off." The girls were pretty mad about that.' Interview with Sean Gunn, Vancouver, 18 March 2004.

89 Cited in Veronica Strong-Boag, 'Society in the Twentieth Century,' 273.

90 See Jeff Sommers, 'Men at the Margin: Masculinity and Space in Down-town Vancouver, 1950–1986,' 287.

91 Alex Louie and Harvey Lo, interviewed for CBC radio by Bernice Chan, Vancouver, 15 December, 2003.

92 Interview with Sean Gunn.

93 Sean Gunn, 'Kublai Khan Ten,' unpublished poem, Vancouver (2000), 1.

94 Advertisement, *Vancouver Sun*, 21 February 1964: 23.

95 Advertisement, *Vancouver Sun*, 26 July 1969: 12.

96 Advertisement, *Vancouver Sun*, 3 October 1969: 38.

97 Interview with Ron Small.

98 Interview with Mike Kalanj, Vancouver, 5 July 2000.

99 See Maxwell Smith, 'The Downtown Scene,' 24.

100 See 'All Star Imported Show: Advertisement.'

101 Interview with Gerry Palken, Vancouver, 18 February 2002.

102 Interview with Ernie King, Vancouver, 14 February 2002.

103 See Bruce Shepard, *Deemed Unsuitable: Blacks from Oklahoma Move to the Canadian Prairies in Search of Equality in the Early Twentieth Century Only to Find Racism in Their New Home*.

104 Interview with Ernie King.

105 See 'Negro Band Barred from Hotel Here'; Mac Reynolds, 'City Asked to "Go It Alone" in Fight on Racial Bans'; and Bruce Constantineau, 'Cabaret Guilty of Turning away Blacks.'

106 Interview with Megan Carvell Davis, Vancouver, 20 July 2000.

107 See the video *Remember Africville*, directed by Shelagh Mackenzie, Na-tional Film Board of Canada, 1991; and Jennifer Nelson, 'The Space of Africville: Creating, Regulating and Remembering the Urban "Slum."'

108 See the 1994 video *Hogan's Alley*, directed by Andrea Fatona and Cornelia

Wyngaarden; and Wayde Compton's 2002 edited collection *Bluesprint: Black British Columbian Literature and Orature*. In February 2003, to correspond with Black History Month, the Hogan's Alley Memorial Project staged the exhibit 'Hogan's Alley Revisited' at the Roundhouse Community Centre in Vancouver. Interestingly, the first Georgia Street viaduct replaced a thriving area known as the 'Red Light District' or 'The Restricted Area' near what is now East Georgia and Main Streets. On this point, see Michael Kluckner, *Vancouver: The Way It Was*, 34.

109 In October 1959, the city prosecutor, Stewart McMorran, asked the city licence inspector to suspend the licences of three cabarets – the New Delhi, the Club Utopia, and the Harlem Nocturne, quick on the heels of the suspension of the MayLing Cabaret's licence. The Harlem Nocturne was singled out as 'an example of poor management.' See 'Shut 3 More Cabarets, Prosecutor Tells City.'

110 Jack Wasserman, 'About Now: Gypsy Takes Off for Jack – on Various Topics, That Is.'

111 Jack Wasserman, 'Tale of a City,' *Vancouver Sun*, 13 August 1959: 25.

112 Jack McCaugherty, 'It's Fun, It's Accepted … But Illegal.'

113 Jack Wasserman, 'The Booze Who.'

114 Interview with Ernie King.

115 Poet and writer Peter Trower notes that Vancouver was home to a black club in the early 1950s, the New Orleans Club, off Granville Street. Cited in Greg Potter and Red Robinson, *Backstage Vancouver*, 87.

116 George Peloquin, 'Go-Go Cabarets Can't Go Topless.'

117 Michel Foucault, *The History of Sexuality, Vol. I*, 68.

118 Liquor Control Board, 47th Annual Report, 1 April 1967–31 March 1968, L.R. Peterson, Attorney General, 26 Sept 1968, B.C. Archives, GR-0560, Box 16, File 40, F22; Liquor Control Board, 48th Annual Report, 1 April 1968–31 March1969, L.R. Peterson, Attorney General, 3 October 1969, B.C. Archives, GR-0560, Box 16, File 40, F1.

119 Not unique to Vancouver during this period; white police carried out even more brutal and outrageously racist acts against black residents in Philadelphia, Chicago, Detroit, Atlanta, Oakland, and New York.

120 'Peelers Picket Police.'

121 Jack Wasserman, 'Saloon Crawler's Notebook.'

122 Ibid.

123 'Peterson Wants to Wrap Up Naked Nightclub Dancers.'

124 Stan Shillington, 'Nude Nightspot Operators Charged.'

125 Ed Simons, 'Nude Shows Acceptable – Court Plea.' Ironically, on 28 August 1972, the Liquor Control Board banned topless waitresses from local

cabarets and dining lounges – a directive that did not apply to dancers or other performers. See 'Cover Up Tops, LCB Tells Girls.'

126 Chris Bird, 'Strip Clubs Taking Off as Court Okays Nudity'; and 'Club Acquitted in Nudity Case.'

127 Jim Fairley, 'Fake Hanky-Panky in Nude Obscene – Judge.'

128 'Nude Dancing Ruled Obscene but Club Operator Acquitted.'

129 See Campbell, *Sit Down and Drink Your Beer*, 53.

130 Paul Raugust, 'Vancouver Goes Boom in the Night.'

131 Interview with Gary Taylor, Vancouver, 22 June 2007.

132 Interview with Gord Walkinshaw, Vancouver, 27 June 2000.

133 Cited in Eve Johnson, 'Money, Music, and Sleaze.'

134 Interview with Gary Taylor.

135 Interview with Ross Filippone.

136 Interview with Jack Card, Vancouver, 14 March 2000. In his book *The Night They Raided Minsky's*, Rowland Barber tells a similar tale of a stilt walker hired by the Minsky brothers to walk up and down Forty-second Street wearing a billboard with strippers' names on it. The stilt walker's nose, cigar butt, and shirt buttons lit up as he strode through the neighbourhood (341–2).

137 Roy Shields, 'Can't a Man Have a Beer without Sex?'

138 Interview with Jeannie Runnalls.

139 I would like to thank Erin Bentley for helping me to prepare these tables.

140 Les Wiseman, 'Young, Sexy and Well Heeled,' 30.

141 Sorich quoted in ibid., 31.

142 'Firm, 2 Men Fined $5,500 for Selling Obscene Books'; Michael McCardell, 'Super-Hardcore Porn Flooding City'; and 'Mayor Eyes Playboy in Porn Crackdown.'

143 Paul Raugust, 'LCL Cracks Down on Nude Clubs Here.'

144 Eve Johnson, 'Money, Music and Sleaze.'

145 'Delta Takes Off on Strippers.'

146 'Square-Minded Surrey Moves to Ban Strippers.'

147 'Show Not Obscene.'

148 Interview with Gary Taylor.

149 See Dick MacLean, *Dick MacLean's Guide*, 113.

150 Brian Salmi, 'Hooker History: 125 Years of Illegal Sex and the City,' 21. Salmi expands on the infamous Penthouse bust: 'The basis of the crown's case was that the Philliponis were adding a 20 per cent surcharge to credit-card advances given to amorous patrons in those days before ATMs. The Philipponis never denied taking the 20 per cent but they claimed that it was none of their business what the gentlemen did with

the money ... Even after the acquittal, the city refused for months to grant the Philliponis a business licence, contrary to another Supreme Court decision that ruled that municipal councils could not deny business licences on the grounds that they were attempting to protect public morality.'

151 Interview with Denny Boyd.

152 Larry Still, 'Philliponi Says Nudity Was Banned at His Club.'

153 Larry Still, 'Penthouse "Love Affair" with Vancouver Soured with Age.'

154 Larry Still, 'Cabaret "Kind of Union Shop" for Hookers.'

155 Denny Boyd, *Vancouver Sun*, 9 March 1978: B3.

156 Larry Still, 'Crown Calls the Penthouse "A Scandal in This Community."'

157 Ibid.

158 See Denny Boyd, *Vancouver Sun*, 14 September 1978: B3. John Lowman, a criminologist at Simon Fraser University, claims that the closure of the Penthouse Cabaret in 1975, combined with the closure of other off-street prostitution venues in Vancouver, played a decisive role in the spread of street prostitution. After 1978, outdoor sex workers, pushed out of the city's West End, became increasingly vulnerable to violence and murder. See John Lowman, 'Street Prostitution in Vancouver: Some Notes on the Genesis of a Social Problem,' and 'Violence and the Outlaw Status of (Street) Prostitution in Canada.' Deborah Brock charts a similar process in Toronto in 1977 following the crackdown on Yonge Street massage parlours. See her book *Making Work, Making Trouble: Prostitution as a Social Problem*. Between 1978 and 2002, more than seventy survival sex workers went 'missing' and presumed dead. Coquitlam pig farmer, Robert (Willie) Pickton was charged with murdering twenty-six of these women. In December 2007, he was convicted of second-degree murder in six cases, and sentenced to twenty-five years in prison without parole. See Mark Hume, 'The Downtown Eastside: A Haunting Ground for Many, a Hunting Ground for One,' and Robert Matas, 'Pickton Shows No Emotion to Guilty Verdict.'

159 Larry Still, 'Penthouse Drama a $2 Million Morality Play.'

160 Denny Boyd, *Vancouver Sun*, 14 September 1978: B3.

161 Allan Fotheringham, *Vancouver Sun*, 22 December 1977: B1.

162 Interview with Della Walters.

163 The exception is Joe Philliponi, a self-declared playboy and bachelor his entire life.

164 Here I borrow from the wonderful title of Michael Dawson's book *Selling British Columbia: Tourism and Consumer Culture, 1890–1970*.

165 To consult obituaries for Joe Philliponi, see Denny Boyd, 'Legend Larger Than the Man,' and Boyd, 'Joe Draws His Last Crow – and It's a Full

House'; Jes Odam, 'Man of Many Faces Ran a Mixed Empire'; Jack Brooks, '800 Mourners Gather to Remember Slain Joe'; and Keith Morgan and Ann Rees, 'Tears, Smiles, Raised Glasses Mark Sendoff for Joe.'

166 On twentieth-century raids and closures of burlesque and striptease venues, see Andrea Friedman, *Prurient Interests: Gender, Democracy, and Obscenity in New York City, 1909–1935*; and Becki Ross, 'Striptease on the Line: Investigating Trends in Erotic Entertainment.' On the policing of striptease in North America during the 1980s and 1990s, see Judith Lynne Hanna, 'Undressing the First Amendment and Corseting the Striptease Dancer.'

167 Hugh Adami, 'Strippers Continue to Take It Off, Despite Goulbourn's New Bylaw.'

168 'Police Frown on Strip Acts.'

169 On mid-twentieth-century prostitution in Vancouver see Michaela Freund, 'The Politics of Naming: Constructing Prostitutes and Regulating Women in Vancouver, 1939–1945.'

170 Interview with Patrick Nagle.

171 Interview with Lynn Ross, Abbotsford, British Columbia, 29 January 2000.

172 Scott Macrae, 'Tints and Tones of the Penthouse Trial.'

173 Les Wiseman, 'Not Your Average Joe.'

174 On the formation of Vancouver's 'High Society,' and the role played by private networking clubs, most of which were men-only in the early twentieth century, see Robert McDonald, *Making Vancouver: 1863–1913*, 149–74.

3. 'We Were Like Snowflakes – No Two Were Alike': Dancers and Their Gimmicks

1 Interview with Honey Rider, Vancouver, 8 December 2004.

2 Interview with Choo Choo Williams, Vancouver, 4 February 2002.

3 Sean Rossiter, 'They Call Her Fox.'

4 Rachel Shteir, *Striptease: The Untold History of the Girlie Show*, 8.

5 Michael Johns, *Moment of Grace: The American City in the 1950s*, 24.

6 In the late 1950s, Canadian singer and TV personality Juliette (born Juliette Augustina Sysak) was said to slim down her 'homey solidity' to a 'showgirl shape.' See Barbara Moon, 'Why Should Juliette Knock Them Dead?'

7 See comments made in the late 1940s by trumpeter and bandleader Joy Cayler about how she was promoted in the 'glossies,' cited in Sherry

Tucker, *Swing Shift: 'All Girl' Bands of the 1940s*, 58–9. Striptease dancers – both white and non-white – were not the only female performers to be rewarded for pandering to the titillation factor. On the image of glamour constructed by and for white elite figure skaters Sonja Henie, Barbara Ann Scott, and Janet Lynn, see Michelle Kaufman, 'Gaining an Edge.' For parallels between female striptease stars and female professional golfers, tennis players, and figure skaters, see Becki Ross, 'Entertaining Femininities: Embodied Exhibitions of Female Striptease and Sport, 1950–1975.'

8   Lois Browne, *Girls of Summer*.

9   Shteir, *Striptease*, 323–4.

10 Interview with Jack Card, Vancouver, 28 January 2000.

11 William Weintraub, 'Show Business: Lili St Cyr's Town – and Al's and Oscar's,' 116–40.

12 Steve Sullivan, *Bombshells: Glamour Girls of a Lifetime*, 274.

13 Murray Campbell, 'Memories of Montreal's Skin Queen.'

14 Cited in Steve Sullivan, *Va Va Voom: Bombshells, Pin-ups, Sexpots, and Glamour Girls*, 280.

15 Cited in ibid., 281.

16 'Advertisement,' *Vancouver Sun*, 29 June 1947.

17 Interview with Jack Card.

18 Interview with Nena Marlene, Vancouver, 27 February 2002.

19 Ann Corio, with Joseph DiMona, *This Was Burlesque*.

20 Kristina Zarlengo, 'Civilian Threat, the Suburban Citadel, and Atomic Age American Women,' 946.

21 Liz Goldwyn, 'Diva in Disguise.'

22 M. Alison Kibler, *Rank Ladies: Gender and Cultural Hierarchy in American Vaudeville*, 116, 142.

23 See Linda Mizejewski, *Ziegfeld Girl: Image and Icon in Culture and Cinema*, 11.

24 On how circus spectacles featuring 'Indian subjects' glorified British imperialism, see Janet Davis, 'Spectacles of South Asia at the American Circus, 1890–1940,' 125.

25 Edward Said, *Orientalism*, 71.

26 Ray Gardner, 'After Dark.'

27 Interview with Nena Marlene.

28 *Vancouver Sun*, 6 May 1963: 23.

29 In 1962, American jazz musician Billy Tipton – a biological female who passed successfully as a man all his adult life – 'married' stripteaser Kitty Kelly. Because striptease demanded public display of exaggerated heterofemininity, Kitty's occupation surely enhanced Billy's masquerade as a

red-blooded heterosexual male. See Diane Wood Middlebrook, *Suits Me: The Double Life of Billy Tipton*, 220–32.

30 Sullivan, *Va Va Voom*, 274.

31 Though Shalimar began dancing in 1982, I include her in this sample because she located her act/s in the earlier performative tradition of elaborate costumes, props, and self-conscious humour. In the interest of further understanding shifts in the business over time, I interviewed four additional women – Shawna Black, Honey Ryder, Tiana, and Carson Lee – who worked as exotic dancers in the 1980s and 1990s.

32 Interview with Nena Marlene.

33 With Johnny Maylo and Kay, Nena Marlene developed a 'sporting comedy act' where she and Kay would dance together with Johnny on stage, and then engage in a faux boxing match after having torn each other's breakaway dresses off to reveal satin underwear, and after donning real boxing gloves. Nena Marlene reminisced about sharing the bill with upwards of fifteen strippers and about playing countless men's clubs across the United States and Canada in the early 1950s.

34 On Janis Joplin, see Alice Echols, *Scars of Sweet Paradise: The Life and Times of Janis Joplin*, and Tim Powis, 'Electric Lady,' 82. Joplin died, tragically, of an overdose of heroin in 1970 at the age of twenty-seven.

35 Lindalee Tracey, *Growing Up Naked: My Years in Bump and Grind*, 153–6.

36 Ann Thomson, *Winning Choice on Abortion: How British Columbian and Canadian Feminists Won the Battles of the 1970s and 1980s*.

37 See Rachel Shteir, 'Stormy Weather: How a Climate of Rebellion, in Theatre and Society, Wrought the Death of Burlesque in 1969.'

38 Pierre Bourdieu, *Distinction: A Social Critique of the Judgement of Taste*, 202, 206.

39 Before his untimely death from cancer in 1987, at age thirty-four, Theodore Wan was a Chinese Canadian photographer and conceptual artist based in Vancouver. Showgirls hired 'Theo' to take publicity photos for club marquees. In the 1980s, he also photographed dancers' performances and competitions in nightclubs and hotels. Thank you to Scott Watson and Christine Conley for alerting me to Wan's exceptional oeuvre in the Vancouver Art Gallery collection.

40 See Liz Goldwyn, *Pretty Things: The Last Generation of American Burlesque Queens*, 30.

41 E-mail interview with Patrick Kevin O'Hara, 18 June 2007.

42 Gord Walkinshaw interview with Michelle Swann and Kim Greenwell, Vancouver, 27 June 2000. For a rich depiction of a singing burlesque dancer, see Billie Livingston's novel *Cease to Blush*.

43 Kathy Hassard, 'Making the Sweat Pay Off.'

44 I have found reference to only one other disabled striptease dancer, Jenine Hodgson, who won second prize at the Drake Hotel's amateur striptease contest in June 1984. See 'Jenine "All-Round Gutsy Lady."'

45 Interview with Princess Lillian, Burnaby, British Columbia, 26 January 2001.

46 Rossiter, 'They Call Her Fox,' 70.

47 Advertisement, 'Night Life' section, Dick MacLean, *Dick MacLean's Leisure Magazine* 6, 8 (August 1973): 90.

48 Interview with Tarren Rae, Vancouver, 5 December 2000.

49 Christopher Dafoe, *Vancouver Sun*.

50 John Masters, 'The Grind Is Gone.'

51 Interview with Scarlett Lake, Vancouver, 25 February 2005.

52 See June Sochen, *From Mae to Madonna: Women Entertainers in Twentieth-Century America*, 25. In Meilan Lam's Canadian National Film Board documentary *Showgirls* (1998), black burlesque dancers in Montreal recalled that they 'worked the line' as the 'show and dance girls' behind the featured white stripper.

53 See Mizejewski, *Ziegfeld Girl*, 8–9.

54 Andrea Stuart, *Showgirls*, 82.

55 See Patricia Hill Collins, *Black Sexual Politics*, 98.

56 On anachronistic space, see Anne McClintock, *Imperial Leather: Race, Gender and Sexuality in the Colonial Contest*, 40.

57 Stuart, *Showgirls*, 76, and Phyllis Rose, *Jazz Cleopatra: Josephine Baker in Her Time*, 12.

58 See Karen Dalton and Henry Louis Gates, Jr, 'Josephine Baker and Paul Colin: African American Dance Seen through Parisian Eyes,' 911. In *Dishing It Out: Waitresses and Their Unions in the Twentieth Century*, historian Dorothy Sue Cobble notes that in the 1940s and 1950s, few African American women were permitted entry to waitress in white-owned restaurants because of racist standards of white female beauty and (hetero)sexiness (23). Black women and other women of colour were prohibited from being 'sky girls' or stewardesses in the same era. See Georgia Panter Nielson, *From Sky Girl to Flight Attendant: Women and the Making of a Union*, 81–2, 98–9.

59 April Paris, interview with Becki Ross, Vancouver, 30 August 2000.

60 See Robert Bogdan, *Freak Show: Presenting Human Oddities for Amusement and Profit*. For her inspiration, I am grateful to Helen Humphreys, whose historical research for her prize-winning novel, *Leaving Earth*, turned up evidence of women stripping underwater on the fairgrounds of the Canadian National Exhibition in Toronto in the 1930s (96).

61 According to A.W. Stencell in *Girl Show: Into the Canvas World of Bump and Grind*, in the 1860s it was said that in the various saloons and parlours, girls pretending to be can-can dancers, as practised in Parisian cabarets in Montmartre and Montparnasse, would do private dances without clothes for a dollar (4).

62 Ibid., 4.

63 Official histories of the PNE include David Breen and Ken Coates, *The Pacific National Exhibition: An Illustrated History* and *Vancouver's Fair: An Administrative and Political History of the Pacific National Exhibition*. Details about the detention of Japanese people on the fairgrounds are found in *Vancouver's Fair*, 98–100. Surprisingly, neither book offers more than a cursory mention of the long-standing presence of the 'girl show' at this annual August fair.

64 For more on the Japanese internment in the 1940s, see Ken Adachi, *The Enemy That Never Was*, Peter Ward, *White Canada Forever*, Joy Kogawa's novel *Obasan*, and Roy Miki, *Redress: Inside the Japanese Canadian Call for Justice*.

65 Interview with Jack Card.

66 In her book *Striptease*, Rachel Shteir notes that strippers of colour during the Depression in the United States were limited to 'torrid dances' or Mammy acts, often under names like Aloha and Naomi Dusk (204).

67 Interview with Jack Card.

68 Interview with Della Walters, Vancouver, 20 September 2001.

69 A review of the first PNE in Vancouver, printed in the *Vancouver Daily News-Advertiser* on 16 August 1910 lists the week's highlights: 'Petrified women, sacrificial crocodiles from the sacred river of Ganges; chickens that lay eggs and dusky negroes who dodge swiftly thrown baseballs, to say nothing of the numerous Salomé dancers, Spanish Carmens, Dutch comedians and chorus girls are some of the attractions ... see the dancing attractions, throw baseballs at each of the African dodgers, ride the merry-go-rounds.' Cited in Chuck Davis, ed., *The Greater Vancouver Book: An Urban Encyclopedia*, 724. Representations of 'dusky negroes' and 'African dodgers' in Vancouver were shaped by pernicious racial stereotypes that pitted 'savagery' against 'civilization.' See Bernth Lindfors, 'Circus Africans.'

70 See Bruce Shepard, *Deemed Unsuitable: Blacks from Oklahoma Move to the Canadian Prairies in Search of Equality Only to Find Racism in Their New Home*.

71 Interview with Choo Choo Williams.

72 Ibid.

73 Interview with Ernie King, Vancouver, 4 February 2002.

74 Interview with Choo Choo Williams.

75 Interviews with Ernie King and Choo Choo Williams. On black histories

in Vancouver, see Wayde Compton, ed., *Bluesprint: Black British Columbian Literature and Orature*, 95–120.

76 In addition to Lena Horne, Louis Armstrong, Marian Anderson, and the Will Mastin Trio were among the African American performers denied hotel accommodation in Vancouver in the 1940s and 1950s.

77 Similarly, in 1973, Nickie Roberts earned the equivalent of $500 Canadian working as a stripper in England, which was three or four times the wage of a skilled working-class man and seven times the wage she had earned as a factory worker in Lancashire before she moved to London in 1969. See Lucinda Jarrett, *Stripping in Time*, 198.

78 Interview with Miss Lovie, Vancouver, 22 September 2000.

79 In the 1940s and 1950s, prior to Fidel Castro's 1959 revolution, the Tropicana's sexy, theatrical stage shows and showgirls rivalled those at the Moulin Rouge in Paris. See Vanessa Arrington, 'Tropicana Trades Sex for Theatrics.'

80 Advertisement in *Vancouver Sun*, 14 March 1969: 40.

81 See Nancy Spencer, 'Sister Act IV: Venus and Serena Williams at Indian Wells: "Sincere Fictions" and White Racism'; Jacqueline Brady, 'Pumping Iron with Resistance: Carla Dunlap's Victorious Body'; and Lexi Boyle, 'Female Bodybuilding and the Politics of Muscle: How Female Bodybuilders Negotiate Race, Gender, and (Hetero)sexuality in Bodybuilding Competition,' 89–118.

82 Jacqueline Brady argues that in the pseudo-documentary *Pumping Iron II*, African American bodybuilder Carla Dunlap's routines open and close to a 'jungle soundtrack with blaring elephant noises and roaring tiger sounds.' See Brady's chapter 'Pumping Iron with Resistance: Carla Dunlap's Victorious Body,' 265.

83 Interview with Ernie King.

84 See the documentary film *Standing in the Shadows of Motown*, directed by Paul Justman, 2002.

85 Interview with Dave Davies by Kim Greenwell and Michelle Swann, Vancouver, 27 June 2000.

86 An unnamed Vancouver police officer remembers Mitzi's act in 1982 this way: 'I was with a group of deputy sheriffs from the Court House, and they managed to get [a ping pong ball] autographed by Mitzi. A sheriff named Ron Hoskins made a little wooden trophy and mounted the ball on top ... Hoskins claimed that the sheriffs' ping pong team had won it in a tournament. It sat in the trophy case for years.' Thank you to historian Aaron Chapman for this delicious anecdote.

87 Interview with Klute, Vancouver, 19 September 1998.

88 In the early 1950s, Parisian club owner Alain Bernardin renamed dancers who performed at the Crazy Horse Saloon. Abe Weinstein, owner of the infamous Colony Club in Dallas, Texas, in the 1950s, gave Juanita Slusher the stage name of Candy Barr, and Barr rose to fame as a stripper and choreographer. Barr was linked romantically to Jack Ruby, the Dallas nightclub owner found guilty of shooting and killing Lee Harvey Oswald, the man convicted of assassinating U.S. president John F. Kennedy. Barr died of pneumonia on 30 December 2005 at the age of seventy. See 'Candy Barr: Exotic Dancer, 1935–2005.'

89 Paige Raibmon makes a similar point in 'Theatres of Contact: The Kwakwaka'wakw Meet Colonialism in British Columbia and at the Chicago World's Fair.'

90 Interview with Jeannie Runnalls, Coquitlam, British Columbia, 21 June 2000.

91 Interview with Gerry Palken, Delta, British Columbia, 18 February 2002.

92 On the imperialist exhibition of Sara Bartman, an African woman captured by Dutch colonizers in the early nineteenth century, see Yvette Abrahams, 'Images of Sara Bartman: Sexuality, Race, and Gender in Early Nineteenth Century Britain,' 227. Also, see Zine Magubane, 'Which Bodies Matter? Feminism, Poststructuralism, Race, and the Curious Theoretical Odyssey of the "Hottentot Venus,"' 816; and Evelynn Hammonds, 'Towards a Genealogy of Black Female Sexuality: The Problematic of Silence,' 173. For links made between female sexual degeneracy and the landscapes of early-twentieth-century dance halls and cabarets, see Hazel V. Carby, 'Policing the Black Woman's Body,' 32.

93 See Patricia Hill Collins, *Black Feminist Thought: Knowledge, Consciousness and the Politics of Empowerment*, and her *Black Sexual Politics*, 87–116.

94 According to Karen Flynn, black nurses who immigrated to Canada from the Caribbean in the 1950s and 1960s, were similarly exoticized, rarely seen as a threat because they were so few in number. See her chapter, 'Experience and Identity: Black Immigrant Nurses to Canada, 1950–1980,' 396.

95 On Hattie McDaniel, see Jill Watts, *Hattie McDaniel: Black Ambition, White Hollywood*, and Hilton Als' review of Watts, 'Mammy for the Masses'; on Raven Wilkinson, see Sarah Hampson, 'A Trailblazer in Life and Ballet'; and on Jennie LeGon, see Alexandra Gill, 'Maverick of the Dance.'

96 Bob Smith, 'Oriental Dolls Lace Dance with Spice.'

97 Advertisement in *Vancouver Sun*, 18 October 1953: 39; Advertisement in *Vancouver Sun*, 5 July 1955: 8.

98 On Noel Toy and other Chinese American postwar stripteasers, see

Lorraine Dong, 'The Forbidden City Legacy and Its Chinese American Women'; Judy Yung, *Unbound Feet: A Social History of Chinese Women in San Francisco*; and Arthur Dong's 1989 video documentary *Forbidden City, USA*. On stereotyping of Asian women, see Linda Xiao Jia Chen, 'Laundresses and Prostitutes: Deconstructing Stereotypes and Finding an Asian Feminist Voice.'

99 Sean Gunn, 'Kublai Khan Ten,' unpublished poem, Vancouver (2000): 2.
100 Ibid.
101 See Kathleen M. Barry, *Femininity in Flight: A History of Flight Attendants*, 115.
102 Interview with Sarita Melita, Vancouver, 15 December 2004.
103 On the negative stereotyping of Asian golfers on the LPGA since the late 1990s, see Eui Hang Shin and Edward Adam Nam, 'Culture, Gender Roles and Sport: The Case of Korean Players on the LPGA.'
104 See Frances Negrón-Muntaner, 'Feeling Pretty: *West Side Story* and Puerto Rican Identity Discourses,' 85.
105 See Jean Barman, 'Taming Aboriginal Sexuality: Gender, Power, and Race in British Columbia, 1850–1900.' On histories of racism towards First Nations in British Columbia, see Cole Harris, *The Resettlement of British Columbia: Essays on Colonialism and Geographical Change*; Adele Perry, *On the Edge of Empire: Gender, Race, and the Making of British Columbia, 1849–1871*; and Mary-Ellen Kelm, *Colonizing Bodies: Aboriginal Health and Healing in British Columbia, 1900–50*.
106 See Marissa Crazytrain, 'Dances for Dollars,' 155.
107 See Robert Campbell, '"A Fantastic Rigmarole": Deregulating Aboriginal Drinking in British Columbia, 1945–62.'
108 See the 1994 documentary film *Hogan's Alley*, directed by Andrea Fatona and Cornelia Wyngaarden.
109 It was not until 1984 that an African American woman – Vanessa Williams – was crowned Miss America.
110 Lorraine Dong, 'The Forbidden City Legacy,' 140.
111 On the racist, anti-Asian discourse of 'yellow peril,' see Patricia Roy, 'The "Oriental Menace" in British Columbia'; Roy, 'A Choice between Two Evils: The Chinese and the Construction of the Canadian Pacific Railway in British Columbia'; and Peter Ward, *White Canada Forever: Popular Attitudes and Public Policy toward Orientals in British Columbia*.
112 Interview with Klute.
113 Elizabeth Kennedy and Madeline Davis, in *Boots of Leather, Slippers of Gold: The History of a Lesbian Community*, note that in the 1940s and 1950s, femmes in Buffalo, New York, typically had steady paid employment

while their butch lovers struggled with long stretches of unsteady, spo-
radic labour and financial uncertainty as car jockeys, elevator operators,
and couriers (278–322). Striptease dancers were more likely to identify
as femme, and to embrace femininity, particularly given the tendency of
butches to bind their breasts, wear men's clothing, and spurn feminine
artifice. In 'The Butch as Drag Artiste: Greenwich Village in the Roaring
Forties,' historian Lisa Davis notes that in New York's Greenwich Village
in the 1940s, nightclubs operating under protection of the mob employed
'gorgeous femme' strippers who embodied showgirl glamour (45).

114 Cited in Lucinda Jarrett, *Stripping in Time*, 119.
115 See Lillian Faderman, *Naked in the Promised Land*.
116 David Ward and Gene Kassebaum, *Women's Prison: Sex and Social Structure*, 75.
117 James Skipper and Charles McCaghy, 'Stripteasing: A Sex-Oriented Occupation,' 292.
118 Marilyn Salutin, 'Stripper Morality,' 16.
119 In 1983, two Vancouver-based female dancers claimed that they had been
legally married in 1980; they invented the 'Pain and Passion' routine
using whips, torches, shackles, and S/M themes. See 'Hewitt Eyes Ban
against Kinky Acts.'
120 The same point is made about the contemporary context of female strippers in Christine Bruckert and Sylvie Frigon, '"Making a Spectacle of
Herself": On Women's Bodies in the Skin Trades,' 58-9.
121 Gunn, 'Kublai Khan Ten,' 2.
122 Interview with Coco Fontaine, Vancouver, 20 September 2000.
123 See George Chauncey, *Gay New York: Gender, Urban Culture, and the Making of the Gay Male World*, especially the introduction and chapter 9.
124 Interview with Klute.
125 Interview with Scarlett Lake, Vancouver, 25 February 2005.
126 See Tom Warner, *Never Going Back: A History of Queer Activism*.
127 A.W. Stencell, *Girl Show: Into the Canvas World of Bump and Grind*, 97.
128 Ibid., 92.
129 Ibid., 93.
130 Don Paulson with Roger Simpson, *An Evening at the Garden of Allah:
Seattle's Gay Cabaret*, 127–34.
131 See Viviane Namaste, 'Beyond Leisure Studies: A Labour History of Male
to Female Transsexuals and Transvestite Artists in Montreal, 1955–1985,'
6. In 2007, in Pattaya, Thailand, male-to-female cross-dressers and transsexuals, or 'lady boys,' earned a living performing at the gay cabaret
Tiffany.

132 See Lisa Davis, 'The Butch as Drag Artiste,' 45, and 'Back in Buddy's Day: Drag's Original Lesbians Reflect on their Heyday.'

133 Tom Hazlitt, 'Legal or Illegal: City's Night Life Roars Wide Open.'

134 See Claudia Shoppmann, *Days of Masquerade: Life Stories of Lesbians during the Third Reich*.

135 See Donna Penn, 'The Sexualized Woman: The Lesbian, the Prostitute, and the Containment of Female Sexuality in Postwar America,' 372.

136 Interview with Princess Lillian.

137 In her book *Mother Camp: Female Impersonators in America*, Esther Newton argues that 'Drag strip differs from its female counterpart only in the difficulty of creating the illusion of femininity with little body covering. Drag strippers shave off all body hair, and they particularly avoid heavy labour in order to minimize muscular development, especially in the arms' (44).

138 Gunn, 'Kublai Khan Ten,' 2.

139 For violence against trans sex workers, see two documentary films, *Screaming Queens*, directed by Victor Silverman and Susan Stryker (2005), and *Hookers on Davie*, directed by Holly Dale and Janis Cole (1984).

140 Facing discrimination in virtually all other labour markets, trans women worked in the sex industry across North America. Some of their stories from San Francisco are told in the documentary film *Screaming Queens: The Riot at Compton's Cafeteria* (2005) directed by Victor Silverman and Susan Stryker.

141 Interview with Tricia Foxx, Vancouver, 27 September 2006.

142 Peter Trower, *Dead Man's Ticket*, 210.

143 Interview with Tricia Foxx.

144 Judith Butler, *Excitable Speech*, 159. Leila J. Rupp and Verta Taylor make a similar claim about gender and sexual transgressions in their work with and for drag queens and 'girlie shows' at the 801 Cabaret in Key West, Florida. See Leila J. Rupp and Verta Taylor, *Drag Queens at the 801 Cabaret*.

145 See Julia Creet, 'A Test of Unity: Lesbian Visibility in the British Columbia Federation of Women, 1974–5'; and Becki Ross, *The House That Jill Built: A Lesbian Nation in Formation*.

146 See Harvey Oberfeld, 'City "Gay" Clubs Losing Red Tape Battle.' For news coverage of police harassment, see articles in *Gay Tide*, including 'Editorial: Police Entrapment on the Upswing' (August 1975): 1; David Rand and Robert Cook, 'Community Unites to Voice Anger,' 16 (1977): 1; and Don Hann and Rob Joyce, 'City Police Record: Smash Hit!' 16 (1977): 4.

147 Roland Barthes, 'Striptease,' in *Mythologies*, 86.

4. 'Peelers Sell Beer, and the Money Was Huge': The Shifting Conditions of Selling Fantasy

1 Interview with Tarren Rae, Vancouver, 5 December 2000.
2 Interview with Shalimar, Vancouver, 2 July 2000.
3 I borrow this wonderful line from Lindalee Tracey, *Growing Up Naked: My Years in Bump and Grind*, 5.
4 Interview with Nena Marlene, Vancouver, 27 February 2002.
5 Interview with Foxy Lady, Vancouver, 12 July 2000.
6 Interview with Bonnie Scott, Vancouver, 19 June 2000.
7 Interview with Miss Lovie, Vancouver, 22 September 2000.
8 Interview with Shelinda, Vancouver, 6 July 2000.
9 Jack Wasserman, 'Flesh Tones,' *Vancouver Sun*, 1 October 1974: 19.
10 Interview with Choo Choo Williams, Vancouver, 4 February 2002.
11 For working-class lesbian stories of the Vanport and the New Fountain, see the documentary film *Forbidden Love: The Unashamed Stories of Lesbian Lives*, directed by Aerlyn Weissman and Lynne Fernie.
12 Interview with Gord Walkinshaw by Michelle Swann and Kim Greenwell, Vancouver, 27 June 2000.
13 Interview with Coco Fontaine, Vancouver, 20 September 2000.
14 See Robert Campbell, *Sit Down and Drink Your Beer: Regulating Vancouver's Beer Parlours, 1925–1954*, 76.
15 Interview with Cascade, Kelowna, British Columbia, 24 July 2000.
16 Seeking to reinvent itself, the Cobalt has become home to a Softcore Comedy Night complete with musical performance, neo-burlesque dancers, sketch and improv comedy acts, and a clown. See Kevin Chong, 'From Peelers and Punks to Stand-Up.'
17 Interview with April Paris, Vancouver, 30 August 2000.
18 Steve Sullivan, *Va Va Voom: Bombshells, Pin-ups, Sexpots, and Glamour Girls*, 280–1.
19 For insights into the economic agency of early-twentieth-century prostitutes, I am indebted to Lindsey McMaster, *Working Girls in the West: Representations of Wage-Earning Women*, 104-5.
20 On male strippers in Vancouver, see Dona Crane, 'Vancouver's Male Strippers Let It All Hang Out.' On male strippers in the United States, see David Petersen and Paula Dressel, 'Equal Time for Women: Social Notes on the Male Strip Show,' and for a more contemporary account, Clarissa Smith, 'Shiny Chests and Heaving G-Strings: A Night Out with the Chippendales.'
21 Rachel Shteir, *Striptease: The Untold History of the Girlie Show*, 235.

22 On ever-single women who were self-employed in Victoria and Vancouver in the early twentieth century, see Jenéa Tallentire, 'Everyday Athenas: Strategies of Survival and Identity for Ever-Single Women in British Columbia, 1880–1930.'

23 Interview with Choo Choo Williams.

24 Les Wiseman, 'Young, Sexy and Well Heeled.'

25 Interview with Jack Card, Vancouver, 14 March 2000.

26 See Women's Council, *Women in the Labour Force, 1971, Facts and Figures*, 65.

27 In 1980, female teachers in Canada earned an average of $20,693. See Statistics Canada, *Population Worked in 1980 – Employment Income by Occupation*, Census 1981, Statistics Canada, Catalogue 92-930.

28 Diana Ricardo, 'Stripping: It Sure Beats the Steno Pool.'

29 Tracey, *Growing Up Naked*, 149.

30 Rick Ouston, 'Rivals Had Nothing on City Stripper Rae.'

31 Interview with Roxanne, Vancouver, 19 April 2000.

32 African American jazz singer Teri Thornton, who died in May 2000 of cancer, found work as the intermission pianist for striptease dancers at the Red Garter nightclub in Chicago in the 1950s. See Ben Ratliff's obituary, 'Singer Was a Favourite of Ella Fitzgerald.' Thornton performed in Vancouver at Isy's Supper Club in January 1967, though it is unclear whether or not she accompanied strippers at that gig.

33 See Hess, quoted in Rachel Shteir's *Striptease*, 116.

34 Bernard Primeau was a jazz drummer from Montreal who began his career in 1956 doing drum rolls at the Rodeo, a Montreal strip club. He died of cancer on 9 October 2006.

35 Sean Gunn, 'Kublai Khan Ten,' unpublished poem, Vancouver (2000): 3.

36 Nickie Roberts, quoted in Lucinda Jarrett, *Stripping in Time*, 203.

37 See Jennie Livingston's documentary film *Paris Is Burning* (1990). Also see Judith Butler's reading of the film, in *Bodies That Matter: On the Discursive Limits of 'Sex,'* 121–37.

38 Focusing on five strip clubs in a major urban centre in the American South during the late 1990s, Katherine Frank excavates the complexities of spectatorship by male 'regulars' in her wonderfully rich ethnography *G-Strings and Sympathy: Strip Club Regulars and Male Desire*.

39 Though Egan conducted her study from 1996 to 2000, her findings echo mine. See her book *Dancing for Dollars and Paying for Love: The Relationship between Exotic Dancers and Their Regulars*, 145.

40 Arlie Hochschild, *The Managed Heart: Commercialization of Human Feeling*, 7. Though Hochschild focused on flight attendants and bill collectors, her

analysis of emotional work is highly applicable to striptease performers, particularly in the 1990s and 2000s as exotic dancers entered a business highly dependent on interactive 'banking' through offstage sales to individual clients.

41 Here, I adapt the insight of Hochschild in *Managed Heart*, 19. Also see Kathleen M. Barry, *Femininity in Flight: A History of Flight Attendants*.

42 'Nude Dancers Bare Welfare Fears.'

43 Wiseman, 'Young, Sexy and Well Heeled,' 35.

44 Ibid., 45.

45 Diana Atkinson, *Highways and Dancehalls*, 92.

46 Denny Boyd, 'Something Is Lost with Beef Dip and Beer.'

47 Interview with Denny Boyd, West Vancouver, 2 August 2001.

48 On the careers of the Canadian Ice Fantasy skaters, from 1952 to 1954, see Michael Scott, 'The Original Blade Runners.'

49 In an interview with Deborah Brock, former erotic dancer Valerie Scott recalled her own experience of dancing in small northern Ontario towns in the late 1970s: 'You didn't want to go out because in these small towns everyone knew you were the stripper ... When you'd go into a restaurant all the men would ogle you and alternately make rude comments. The women all looked at you with stiletto eyes, like they wanted to kill you.'

50 Interview with Sarita Melita, Vancouver, 15 December 2004.

51 Valerie Scott, unpublished interview by Deborah Brock, Toronto, 2000.

52 See Tracey, *Growing Up Naked*, 125.

53 For more on the life and death of Dorothy Stratten, see Darah Hansen, 'Death of a Playmate.' Vancouver-born Barbara Parkins became a *Playboy* pin-up in the 1960s, and later an actress in the series *Peyton Place* and in the film, *Valley of the Dolls* (1967). Other playmates from British Columbia include Heidi Sorenson (July 1981), Kelly Tough (October 1981), Kimberley Conrad, playmate of the year in 1989, and Pamela Anderson (October 1979).

54 Ian Haysom, 'Getting Down to the Bare Essentials.'

55 Dr David Reid was a well-known plastic surgeon who performed breast augmentation for women, many of them erotic dancers, beginning in the late 1970s in Princeton, British Columbia, a four-hour drive east of Vancouver. See Jeff Lee, 'How Princeton Became a Breast-Enhancement Centre.'

56 Jarrett, *Stripping in Time*, 173.

57 See Gretchen Edgren, *The Playmate Book: Six Decades of Centerfolds*.

58 Klute recalls a conversation she had with Chesty Morgan: 'She said, "When I retire, I'm getting these cut off." She had had her chest enlarged

like three or four times and she said, "This is what makes me money, that's all. And when I quit, I'm having them removed."'

59 Rick Ouston, 'Putting the Tease Back into Strip.'

60 Valerie Scott, interviewed by Deborah Brock.

61 See Pierre Bourdieu, *Distinction: A Social Critique of the Judgement of Taste*, 206.

62 Dorothy E. Smith, *Texts, Facts, and Femininity: Exploring the Relations of Ruling*, 190, 193.

63 Ibid., 193.

64 A.W. Stencell makes this claim about the stripper-pole's debut in his book *Girl Show: Into the Canvas World of Bump and Grind*, 81.

65 Interview with Tiana, 6 December 2004. Tiana danced in Vancouver and around the province from 1981 to 2000.

66 'Still Kicking Up a Storm.'

67 On the explosion of XXX-rated pornography, see Eric Schlosser, *Reefer Madness: Sex, Drugs and Cheap Labor in the American Black Market*, 148. American filmmaker Russ Meyer was called 'king of the nudies' for writing, directing, and producing a string of porn films in the 1960s and 1970s, including *Vixen*, *Wild Gals of the Naked West*, and my favourite, *Faster Pussycat, Kill! Kill!*, starring the mesmerizing Tura Satana, a raven-haired stripper-cum-dominatrix-cum-murderer. Meyer died at eighty-two in 2004. For a detailed obituary, see Myrna Oliver, 'Skin-Flick King Russ Meyer Dies of Pneumonia at 82.'

68 Robert Miller, 'Mean Streets,' 18.

69 Laura Kipnis, *Bound and Gagged: Pornography and the Politics of Fantasy in America*, 129. Larry Flynt's magazine *Hustler* originated as a two-page newsletter for Flynt's go-go bars in Ohio, called the Hustler Clubs.

70 See Laila Haidarali, 'Polishing Brown Diamonds: African American Women, Popular Magazines, and the Advent of Modeling in Early Postwar America.'

71 Diablo Cody, *Candy Girl: A Year in the Life of an Unlikely Stripper*, 138.

72 'Leisure's Sound Off … on Bottomless Dancing in Clubs.'

73 David G. Scott, *Behind the G-String: An Exploration of the Stripper's Image, Her Person, and Her Meaning*, 26.

74 Wiseman, 'Young, Sexy and Well Heeled,' 33.

75 Ibid., 45.

76 See Esther Bott, 'Pole Position: Migrant British Women Producing "Selves" through Lap Dancing Work,' 37.

77 Jarrett, *Stripping in Time*, 191.

78 Wasserman, 'Flesh Tones,' *Vancouver Sun*, 17 December 1974: 41.

79 For compelling comparisons drawn between beauty contests and striptease, see Brenda Foley, *Undressed for Success: Beauty Contestants and Exotic
   Dancers as Merchants of Morality.*
80 Tracey, *Growing Up Naked*, 210.

5. 'Everyone Wanted to Date a Dancer, Nobody Wanted to Marry One': Occupational Hazards in the Industry

1 Interview with Bambi, Vancouver, 21 June 2001.
2 Lindalee Tracey, *Growing Up Naked: My Years in Bump and Grind*, 209.
3 Interview with Klute, Vancouver, 19 September 1998.
4 In northern British Columbia, the Yukon, and Alaska, dance hall girls
   were routinely assumed to work as prostitutes, and both dancers and sex
   workers were regarded as fallen, wanton women. See Lael Morgan, *Good
   Time Girls of the Alaska-Yukon Gold Rush*, 12–32, and Bay Ryley, *Gold Diggers of the Klondike: Prostitution in Dawson City, Yukon, 1898–1908*, 9-14. In
   the blockbuster film *Moulin Rouge* (2001), Nicole Kidman plays a cabaret
   dancer who is also a much-desired courtesan. On stereotypes of burlesque
   dancers, see Robert Allen, *Horrible Prettiness: Burlesque and American
   Culture*, and Charlene Kish, 'A Knee Is a Joint and Not an Entertainment:
   The Moral Regulation of Burlesque in Early Twentieth-Century Toronto,'
   1–15. For details about the stigma attached to chorus girls in the 1920s,
   see Angela Latham, *Posing a Threat: Flappers, Chorus Girls and Other Brazen
   Performers of the American 1920s*, 113–18.
5 Allen, *Horrible Prettiness*, 26.
6 Erving Goffman, *Stigma: Notes on the Management of Spoiled Identity*, 3-4.
7 Tempest Storm, *The Lady Is a Vamp*, 119.
8 Michel Foucault, *The History of Sexuality, Vol. I*: 44.
9 In *The Desirable Body*, drawing from Freud and Lacan, Jon Stratton argues
   that in striptease, women sell the visibility of their body in the larger
   cultural context of the fetishism of the female body. He says, 'striptease
   commodifies the scopophilic concern with the sight of the female body.
   In striptease, the female body is consumed by men as a spectacle. The act
   climaxes in the revelation of what is not there – that is, the absence of the
   penis – whilst the body itself is eroticised as a phallic substitute' (101).
10 Quoted in Lorraine Dong, 'The Forbidden City Legacy and Its Chinese
   American Women,' 138.
11 Interview with Nena Marlene, Vancouver, 27 February 2002.
12 See James Skipper and Charles McCaghy, 'Stripteasers: The Anatomy and
   Career Contingencies of a Deviant Occupation.' For other work in the

'sociology of deviance,' see Craig Forsyth and Tina Deshotels, 'A Deviant
Process: The Sojourn of the Stripper'; G.E. Enck and J.D. Preston, 'Counterfeit Intimacy: A Dramaturgical Analysis of an Erotic Performance'; and
William Thompson and Jackie Harred, 'Topless Dancers: Managing Stigma
in a Deviant Occupation.'

13 C. Jesser and L. Donovan, 'Nudity in the Art Training Process,' 356. American comedian Chris Rock commented in a recent routine that having a
daughter who is a stripper is the ultimate failure for a father. See Katherine
Frank's critique of Rock's anti-stripper shtick in her chapter 'Keeping Her
Off the Pole? Creating Sexual Value in a Capitalist Society.'

14 Beverley Skeggs, *Formations of Class and Gender: Becoming Respectable*, 118.

15 Interview with Megan Carvell Davis, Vancouver, 20 July 2000.

16 Margaret Dragu and A.S.A Harrison, *Revelations: Essays on Striptease and
Sexuality*, 23. And on the construction of the stripper as sex deviant, see
Skipper and McCaghy, 'Stripteasers.' Also see, David Scott, *Behind the
G-String: An Exploration of the Stripper's Image, Her Person, and Her Meaning*,
37–8, 132–3.

17 On 'closeting,' see Goffman, *Stigma*, 79.

18 Tracey, *Growing Up Naked*, 149. In her autobiography, Tracey criticizes the
Canadian feminist film director Bonnie Sherr Klein, who used and distorted her experience to tell an anti-stripper and anti-pornography parable
in *Not a Love Story* for the National Film Board of Canada, 1981.

19 Ibid., 163.

20 Interview with Jack Card, Vancouver, 28 January 2000.

21 The Canada Council for the Arts began funding members of ballet companies and modern dance troupes beginning in 1967. Striptease was not then,
nor is it now, eligible for state-sanctioned subsidy.

22 Interview with Christine Chipperfield, Vancouver, 8 November 1999.

23 E-mail interview with Patrick Kevin O'Hara in Paris, France, 18 June 2007.
In another example of French openness towards nudity, historian Rachel
Shteir notes that in Paris in 1955, the Académie du Striptease was formed
to promote and disseminate knowledge about the genre to an eager public.
See her book *Striptease: The Untold History of the Girlie Show*, 280.

24 See Pierre Bourdieu, *Distinction: A Social Critique of the Judgement of Taste*,
41.

25 Interview with Miss Lovie, Vancouver, 22 September 2000.

26 Ex-dancer Marissa Crazytrain, a Cree woman from Saskatchewan, recounted that her mother believes that stripping is immoral and robs one of
one's spirit. She elaborated: 'My other critics, non-Aboriginal and especially Aboriginal, are on the same page with this one: stripping is wrong, and

if you've ever stripped, you're a bad person with no scruples who should be scorned. Period.' See her thoughtful essay 'Dances for Dollars,' 151.

27 In her book *Striptease,* Rachel Shteir notes that the much-married Gypsy Rose Lee, Sally Rand, and Lili St Cyr ended up alone (244).

28 Interview with Bambi.

29 'No Game to Roulette.'

30 Runnalls, cited in Jim McDowell, 'Strippers Seek Women's Rights,' 4.

31 See Marylee Stephenson, 'Being in Women's Liberation: A Case Study in Social Change.'

32 See Ann Thomson, *Winning Choice on Abortion: How British Columbian and Canadian Feminists Won the Battles of the 1970s and 1980s,* 41–50.

33 See Laurie Bell, 'Introduction,' in *Good Girls/Bad Girls: Sex Trade Workers and Feminists Face to Face;* and Jill Nagle, 'Introduction,' in *Whores and Other Feminists.*

34 See, for example, Kate Millett, *The Prostitution Papers;* Robin Morgan, *Going Too Far: The Personal Chronicle of a Feminist;* Andrea Dworkin, *Pornography: Men Possessing Women;* and Catharine MacKinnon, *Toward a Feminist Theory of the State.* An important exception to feminists' rebuke of dancers is Kay Armatage's 1980 film *Striptease,* and her 1981 article 'Striptease: Work, Peformance, Sexuality.'

35 See Mariana Valverde, *The Age of Light, Soap and Water: Moral Reform in English Canada, 1885–1925;* and Alan Hunt, *Governing Morals: A Social History of Moral Regulation.*

36 Hunt, *Governing Morals,* 141.

37 Quoted in Val Marie Johnson's excellent article '"The Rest Can Go to the Devil": Macy's Workers Negotiate Gender, Sex, and Class in the Progressive Era.' Johnson argues that Macy's working women also fortified social hierarchies by using moral judgment to define 'bad' women (inside and outside the store) as immoral, therefore impeding class and feminist solidarity.

38 See my work on feminist debates about sex work in the 1970s in *The House That Jill Built: A Lesbian Nation in Formation,* 133–4.

39 Gwendolyn, quoted in Becki Ross, *The House That Jill Built,* 133.

40 I appreciate Alan Hunt's elucidation of self-governance in his book *Governing Morals,* 1–27.

41 Here, I adapt the work of S. Sawhney, 'Feminism and Hybridity Round Table,' and Carol-Ann Tyler, *Female Impersonation,* 23. The fabulous term 'female clowning' is Gwendolyn's. See her interview in Shannon Bell's *Whore Carnival,* 70.

42 See Judith Butler, *Undoing Gender,* 42–55.

43 See Michel Foucault, 'The Subject and Power.'
44 On conflicts between sex workers and feminist activists, see Laurie Bell, 'Introduction,' in *Good Girls/Bad Girls.*
45 See Green Thumb, *Georgia Straight.*
46 Telephone interview with George Paidy, Vancouver, 19 June 2000.
47 Female factory employees recalled suffering sexual harassment on the line in the 1940s, though clerical staff at Quaker Oats (in Ontario) tended to accept this behaviour as 'part of the job' in an era that predated feminist analysis of unwanted, intrusive male advances. See Joan Sangster, 'Telling Our Stories: Feminist Debates and the Use of Oral History,' and her *Earning Respect: The Lives of Working Women in Small-Town Ontario, 1920–1960.* For an important feminist critique of workplace sexual harassment, see Susan Attenborough, 'Sexual Harassment: An Issue for Unions.'
48 See Debbie Field, 'Coercion or Male Culture: A New Look at Co-Worker Harassment.'
49 Bambi noted that when the Canadian loonie was introduced to replace the one-dollar bill, 'Eighteen-year-old guys in Calgary would heat them up with lighters and throw them at your pussy. They thought that was fun.'
50 Pierre Bourdieu, *Masculine Domination,* 53.
51 Ibid., 51–2.
52 Interview with Bonnie Scott, Vancouver, 19 June 2000.
53 Interview with Sarita Melita, Vancouver, 15 December 2004.
54 'Judge Angers Raped Stripper,' and Janet Feindel, *A Particular Class of Women.*
55 McDowell, 'Strippers Seek Women's Rights,' 4.
56 Diane Wood Middlebrook, *Suits Me: The Double Life of Billy Tipton,* 221.
57 Runnalls, cited in McDowell, 'Strippers Seek Women's Rights,' 4.
58 Rick Ouston, 'The Life and Death of Layla, a Stripper,' and Rick Ouston, 'Ashes, Silver Dollar Cast into Water in Rite for Murdered Stripper.'
59 See Gerry Bellett, 'Slain Stripper's Boyfriend Accused in 1986 Death.'
60 See Maggie De Vries, *Missing Sarah: A Vancouver Woman Remembers Her Vanished Sister;* Daniel Wood, 'Missing'; Trevor Greene, *Bad Date: The Lost Girls of Vancouver's Low Track;* Lauren Carter, 'Where Are Canada's Disappeared Women?'; and Patrick Moores, '(Re)Covering the Missing Women: News Media Reporting on Vancouver's Disappeared.' For an insightful novel informed by the murders, see Nancy Richler, *Throwaway Angels.*
61 Rachel Shteir reports that striptease dancers represented by the American Guild of Variety Artists (AGVA) won higher wages in 1957, but the President Follies in San Francisco could not afford to pay them. She argues that

in 1958 a group of strippers in Los Angeles demanded a raise, which put many burlesque theatres out of business. See her book *Striptease*, 294.

62 Department of Labour Canada, *Women at Work in Canada: A Fact Book on the Female Labour Force, 1964*, Table 1, page 10; Statistics Canada, *1971 Census of Canada*, Vol. 3, Part 2, Labour Force, Table 8l (cited in Julie White, *Sisters and Solidarity: Women and Unions in Canada*, 46).

63 In British Columbia in 1980, almost 50 per cent of male workers were unionized; this number reflected, in part, the province's largest industry, timber, which at that time was unionized and employed very few women. See Linda Briskin, 'Women and Unions in Canada: A Statistical Overview,' 30.

64 Ibid., 34.

65 See Linda Briskin and Lynda Yanz, eds, *Union Sisters: Women in the Labour Movement*, and Linda Briskin and Pat McDermott, *Women Challenging Unions: Feminism, Democracy, and Militancy*.

66 Betty Griffin and Susan Lockhart, *Their Own History: Women's Contribution to the Labour Movement of British Columbia*, 155.

67 Ibid., 157.

68 White, *Sisters and Solidarity*, 48.

69 See Linda Mizejewski, *Ziegfeld Girl: Image and Icon in Culture and Cinema*; June Sochen, *From Mae to Madonna: Women Entertainers in Twentieth-Century America*; and Angela Latham, *Posing a Threat: Flappers, Chorus Girls and Other Brazen Performers of the American 1920s*.

70 'Topless Dancers Don Coats to Picket City Nightclub.'

71 'Dancers End Picket at Club: Deal Reached.'

72 On discourse and practices of racialization, see Becki Ross and Kim Greenwell, 'Spectacular Striptease: Performing the Sexual and Racial Other in Vancouver, B.C., 1950–1975.'

73 Interview with Dave Davies by Michelle Swann and Kim Greenwell, Vancouver, 27 June 2000.

74 See Makeda Silvera, *Silenced: Talks with Working Class West Indian Women about Their Lives and Struggles as Domestic Workers in Canada*.

75 On parallels between stripteasers and female professional athletes, see my chapter 'Entertaining Femininities: The Embodied Exhibitions of Striptease and Sport, 1950–1975.'

76 Interview with Foxy Lady, Vancouver, 12 July 2000.

77 Goffman, *Stigma*, 23.

78 Jack Wasserman, *Vancouver Sun*, 6 December 1976: 23.

79 In Canada, the International Ladies Garment Workers Union (ILGWU) set up a homeworkers' association in Toronto as a local branch of the

union in 1992, though homeworkers have yet to form their own union. See Jane Tate, 'Organizing Homeworkers in the Informal Sector: Canada'; on domestic workers' efforts to organize prior to 1980, see Rachel Epstein, 'Domestic Workers: The Experience in B.C.,' and Audrey Macklin, 'On the Outside Looking In: Foreign Domestic Workers in Canada.' And see Laura Johnson, *The Seam Allowance: Industrial Home Sewing in Canada.*

80 Dorothy Sue Cobble, *Dishing It Out: Waitresses and Their Unions in the Twentieth Century*, 60.

81 Julie White, *Women and Unions*, 46.

82 White, *Sisters and Solidarity*, 168.

83 Interview with Shelinda, Vancouver, 6 July 2000.

84 Interview with Roxanne, Vancouver, 20 April 2000.

85 Interview with Foxy Lady, Vancouver, 12 July 2000.

86 Interview with Sarita Melita, 15 December 2004.

87 Interview with Foxy Lady.

88 On the emergence of the fitness/aerobics boom across North America, see Benjamin Rader, 'The Quest for Self-Sufficiency and the New Strenuosity: Reflections on the Strenuous Life of the 1970s and 1980s.'

89 Interview with Jasmine Tea, Kelowna, British Columbia, 24 July 2000.

90 In 1980, stewardesses in Canada earned an average of $269 per week. In Vancouver in 1981, secretarial salaries averaged $292 for a junior clerk, and $340 for a senior clerk, all of which were significantly lower than the average weekly salary earned by striptease dancers. See Women's Bureau, Labour Canada, *Women in the Labour Force*, 33, 53.

91 Carol Volkart, 'City's Strippers Hint Strike over Pay, Working Conditions.'

92 Clive Jackson, 'They Fired Tattooed Lady.'

93 Interview with Richard Walters, Vancouver, 8 July 2000.

94 Interview with Ross Filippone, Vancouver, 15 June 2000.

95 In addition, the predominantly white workforces of waitresses and 'sky girls' (flight attendants) in the United States were complicit in similar racist exclusions and barriers to anti-racist solidarity during this period. See Cobble, *Dishing It Out*, 122–4, and Georgia Panter Nielson, *From Sky Girl to Flight Attendant: Women and the Making of a Union*, 81–2, 98–9.

96 Interview with Coco Fontaine, Vancouver, 20 September 2000.

97 Interview with Jeannie Runnalls, Coquitlam, British Columbia, 21 June 2000.

98 Interview with Miss Lovie, Vancouver, 22 September 2000.

99 Tracey, *Growing Up Naked*, 123.

100 On Criminal Code prohibitions against nude dancing, see June Ross, 'Nude Dancing and the Charter.'

101 'Supreme Court Clears Dancer of Giving Immoral Exhibition.'

102 'Court Goes to Cabaret to Check Stripper's Act.'

103 Michael Turner, 'Fred and Ethel,' 144.

104 See Jamie Lamb, 'New Liquor Laws Threat to Strippers, Some B.C. Hotels'; and Tom Barrett, 'Beer Parlour Managers Cry in Their Brew.'

105 'Cabaret Charged.'

106 'McKita Determined to Ban Strippers.'

107 Jack Wasserman, *Vancouver Sun*, 6 December 1976: 23.

108 Christopher Dafoe, *Vancouver Sun*, 10 December 1976: 23.

109 Lamb, 'New Liquor Laws,' 25.

110 Deborah Brock, *Making Work, Making Trouble: Prostitution as a Social Problem*, 35–43.

111 See Chris Gudgeon, *The Naked Truth: The Untold Story of Sex in Canada*, 137.

112 'Strippers Vote to Clean Up Their Acts.'

113 'G-Strings, Cheap Gimmicks Out.'

114 Lisa Bishop, 'Police Frown on Strip Acts.'

115 '"Incredible" Stripper Charged with Indecency'; 'Ingenious Mitzi Stirs Up Strippers'; and Damian Wood, 'Ping-Pong Prowess Is Making Mitzi Rich.'

116 Wyng Chow, 'Busted Stripper Hopes for Ping Pong Diplomacy.'

117 Cited in Scott, *Behind the G-String*, 130. According to Scott, the original complaint in Calgary was filed by a self-described feminist who was 'disturbed and very, very sad that Miss Dupree ... used her body in such a way that was degrading to women.'

118 Martin Taylor of the B.C. Supreme Court subsequently ruled that the Liquor Control Board Licensing Act forbids 'disorderly conduct – a euphemism for immoral or indecent behaviour,' and concluded that strippers must refrain from 'audience participation.' See Larry Still, 'Strippers Must Keep "Hands Off"'; and 'Hewitt Eyes Ban against Kinky Acts.'

119 The Hells Angels formed chapters in Vancouver in 1983 and became involved in the striptease industry through ownership of clubs and booking agencies that continues to the present. See Julian Sher and William Marsden, 'B.C. Bonanza.'

120 Interview with Sarita Melita.

121 Briskin, 'Women and Unions in Canada,' 37.

122 Long-time union organizer Laurel Ritchie underlined the stubborn myth that women were still 'secondary' income earners and therefore second-

ary members of the paid labour force. See Ritchie's chapter 'Why Are So Many Women Unorganized?,' 201.

123 In 1969, American sociologists James Skipper and Charles McCaghy claimed that 50 to 75 per cent of the stripteasers they interviewed engaged in 'homosexual liaisons' in the business. See 'Stripteasing: A Sex-Oriented Occupation,' 292. In 1971, Canadian journalist Marilyn Salutin made the same claim, in 'Stripper Morality,' 16.

124 More empirical investigation is needed of the priorities of the Service, Office and Retail Workers Union of Canada, Vancouver branch (1972–86). See the Union's fonds archived at the University of British Columbia, Special Collections. Also see Bank Book Collective, *An Account to Settle*.

125 Judith Butler, *Undoing Gender*, 13–14.

126 See Amber Cooke, 'Stripping: Who Calls the Tune?'; Mary Johnson, 'CABE and Strippers: A Delicate Union'; and 'Strippers' Union Expanding to B.C. with Support from Labor Congress.'

127 'More Pay, Less Peeling, Ask Striking Strippers.'

128 'Stripper Bid Fails.'

129 Interview with Tarren Rae, Vancouver, 5 December 2000.

130 Interview with Shalimar, Vancouver, 2 July 2000.

131 Eve Johnson, 'Stripping for Charity.'

132 Denny Boyd, 'The Ladies Will Take It Off for Charity.'

133 While not published by VEDA, the short-lived bi-monthly *Spotlight: Western Canada's Original Magazine of Exotic Entertainment*, launched in 1982, regularly carried news of VEDA's events. Thanks to Gordy Walker for sending me a copy.

134 Pete McMartin, 'When Charity Comes with a G-String,' B1.

135 For his insights into state funding for 'legitimate dance,' I am indebted to Patrick Kevin O'Hara, e-mail interview, 18 June 2007. The issue here is not to emphasize the generosity of federal arts funding for 'legitimate' dance over the past forty years. On the contrary, artists in Canada have never made a comfortable living from grants bestowed by government bodies. Rather, I am making a point about how adjudicating the 'deserving' and the 'undeserving' is a fraught exercise in moral regulation.

136 Bourdieu, *Distinction*, 56–7, 63, 66.

137 In 1984, dancers picketed the Cecil Hotel to protest a 10 per cent wage cut imposed by the booking agency International Artists, and one dancer was fired by Cecil manager, Sam Sorich, for picketing and 'bitching' about the wage cut. See Terry Glavin, 'Protesting Peeler Stripped of Her Job.'

138 Denny Boyd, *Vancouver Sun*, 23 June 1978: B3; Don Stanley, 'For the Burlesque Hungry, Isy's Offers Girls à la Carte.'

139 'Seedy Job Conditions behind Strippers' Bid for Union Protection.'
140 Gwendolyn, quoted by Chris Bearchell, 'No Apologies: Strippers as the Upfront Line in a Battle to Communicate,' 27. For more about Gwendolyn, 'a postmodern burlesque performer,' see Shannon Bell, *Reading, Writing and Rewriting the Prostitute Body*, 157–70.
141 See Heather Menzies, *Women and the Chip: Case Studies of the Effects of Informatics on Employment in Canada*; Maria Pollack, 'Women, Unions, and Microtechnology'; Marcie Cohen and Margaret White, *Taking Control of Our Future: Clerical Workers and the New Technology*; and Pat Armstrong, *Labour Pains: Women's Work in Crisis*.
142 Esther Reiter, *Making Fast Food: From the Frying Pan into the Fryer*; Eric Schlosser, *Fast Food Nation: The Dark Side of the All-American Meal*; and Barbara Ehrenreich, *Nickel and Dimed. On (Not) Getting By in America*.
143 Anne Mullens, 'Wage-Cut Strippers Just Grin and Bare It.'
144 Ibid.
145 See Holly Horwood, 'Strippers Bare Their Ire'; and Terry Glavin, 'Dancers Protest Pay Cut.'
146 Glavin, 'Protesting Peeler Stripped of Her Job.'
147 See John Lekich's review of the film *Stripper* by Jerome Gary (1986) in 'Jerome Gary's Documentary Tries to Erase Some Clichés: *Stripper* More Than Skin Deep.'
148 Ted Laturnus, 'How 12 Strippers from Vancouver … Conquered the Competition in Vegas.'
149 Jon Ferry, 'All Bust in This Boom.'
150 Len Bacchus, 'School for Strippers.'
151 Jeani Read, 'Stripping Away Concepts.'
152 Len Bacchus, 'Shower Power Flowers as Pubs Offer Patrons "Good Clean Fun."'
153 Greg Potter and Red Robinson, *Backstage Vancouver: A Century of Entertainment Legends*, 12.
154 Brian Kieran, 'Buddha Grins and Bears It,' *Vancouver Sun*, 6 June 1980: 6.

6. 'You Started to Feel Like a Dinosaur': Exiting and Aging in the Business

1 Interview with Klute, Vancouver, 19 September, 1998.
2 Ibid.
3 Elisabeth Eaves, *Bare: The Naked Truth about Stripping*, 23.
4 See Bonnie Sherr Klein's film *Not a Love Story: A Film about Pornography*.
5 Chris Gudgeon develops his compelling theory of neurotica in his book *The Naked Truth: The Untold Story of Sex in Canada*, 130.

6 Here, I borrow Rachel Shteir's wonderful 'near principle,' developed in *Striptease: The Untold History of the Girlie Show*, 5–6.

7 See Bernadette Barton, 'Managing the Toll of Stripping: Boundary Setting among Exotic Dancers'; and Chris Bruckert, *Taking It Off, Putting It On: Women in the Strip Trade*.

8 Diablo Cody, *Candy Girl: A Year in the Life of an Unlikely Stripper*, 148–9.

9 I develop this idea in my chapter 'Entertaining Femininities: Embodied Exhibitions of Striptease and Sport, 1950–1975.'

10 Jeffrey Weeks, 'The Sexual Citizen,' 35–9.

11 Nora Räthzel, 'Nationalism and Gender in West Europe: The German Case,' 168.

12 In *Imperial Leather: Race, Gender and Sexuality in the Colonial Contest* (72), Anne McClintock, borrowing from French feminist Julia Kristeva, theorizes the paradox of abjection: 'Abject peoples are those whom industrial imperialism rejects but cannot do without: slaves, prostitutes, the colonized, domestic workers, the insane, the unemployed, and so on.'

13 Yvette Abrahams, 'Images of Sara Bartman: Sexuality, Race, and Gender in Early Nineteenth Century Britain,' 227.

14 On the racism faced by black immigrant nurses in Canada from 1950 to 1980, see Karen Flynn, 'Experience and Identity: Black Immigrant Nurses to Canada, 1950–1980.'

15 Barton, 'Managing the Toll of Stripping,' 584–6. Here, Barton describes the boundary-setting practices to manage the 'toll' of stripping in the late 1990s and early 2000s in the United States.

16 Betsy Rawls, a top female professional golfer from the late 1940s to the mid-1970s, remembers that 'we were conscious of needing to dress properly and look and act ladylike, and we always did.' See Betsy Rawls, quoted in Michele Kort, *Dinah!: Three Decades of Sex, Golf, and Rock 'n' Roll*, 15. Similarly, historians Patricia Vertinsky and Gwendolyn Captain show that African American athletes Wilma Rudolph (track and field) and Althea Gibson (tennis/golf) were coached to cultivate an attractive, feminine image. See their article 'More Myth Than History: American Culture and Representations of the Black Female's Athletic Ability,' 545.

17 Michelle Kaufman, 'Gaining an Edge,' 166.

18 In 1948, after having won the Olympic gold medal for figure skating at St Moritz, Switzerland, Barbara Ann Scott became the inspiration for a 'Barbara Ann Scott Doll' manufactured by the Reliable Toys Company in the United States. In 1996, Canada Post Corporation issued a stamp honouring Fanny 'Bobbie' Rosenfeld as a past Olympic champion.

19 Interview with Tarren Rae, Vancouver, 5 December 2000.

20 Interview with Honey Rider, Vancouver, 8 December 2004.

21 Wendy Chapkis, *Beauty Secrets: Women and the Politics of Appearance*, 14.

22 In 1977, Karen Petty had plastic surgery to remove excessive loose skin and fat from her stomach. Because the operation was a failure and marked the end of her career as an exotic dancer, she sued Vancouver plastic surgeon Peter Mackay. In 1979, Judge Richard Anderson dismissed Petty's case. See Clive Jackson, 'Scarred Dancer Loses Case against Surgeon.'

23 See Marissa Crazytrain, 'Dances for Dollars,' 155.

24 Interview with Carson Lee, Vancouver, 25 February 2002.

25 Estanislao Oziewicz, 'Canada's Bare Essentials,' and Daphne Bramham, 'Foreign Strippers Are Teased with Work Visas.' Inside some up-scale strip clubs in the United States, dancers have access to tanning beds, studios with free weights, practice poles, workout machines, and private whirlpools.

26 See Alexia Bloch, 'Victims of Trafficking or Entrepreneurial Women? Narratives of Post-Soviet Entertainers in Turkey.' Also see Kamala Kempadoo, 'From Moral Panic to Global Justice: Changing Perspectives on Trafficking.'

27 Lily Burana, *Strip City: A Stripper's Farewell Journey across America*, 68. Burana also notes that the Pure Talent School of Dance in Clearwater, Florida, offers a five-day course in stripper training for $750 (U.S.), as well as instruction in make-up, financial planning, diet, and fitness.

28 See Bruckert, *Taking It Off, Putting It On*, 153. Bruckert notes that, 'a dancer might work eight hours and make no money, even losing bar and driver fees, or she might earn $300 during a four-hour period' (93). Danielle Egan argues that a culture of patriarchal entitlement in strip clubs remains premised on a basic equation: men are at leisure to command sexual services while female dancers are at work. See her book *Dancing for Dollars and Paying for Love: The Relationship between Exotic Dancers and Their Regulars*.

29 Gudgeon, *The Naked Truth*, 134.

30 Barton, 'Managing the Toll of Stripping,' 14.

31 In her book *Stripped: Inside the Lives of Exotic Dancers*, Bernadette Barton notes that dancers at Lusty Lady peep show in San Francisco tend to develop closer relationships with other dancers because they do not compete for clients and tips (136). On the 'tipping system' in the service sector, see Jeffrey Sallaz, 'House Rules: Autonomy and Interests among Service Workers in the Contemporary Casino Service Industry.'

32 Cody, *Candy Girl*, 188.

33 Jacqueline Lewis, '"I'll Scratch Your Back, If You'll Scratch Mine": The Role of Reciprocity, Power and Autonomy in the Strip Club,' 310.

34 Jacqueline Lewis, 'Controlling Lap Dancing: Law, Morality, and Sex Work.'
35 Bernadette Barton, 'Managing the Toll of Stripping,' 572.
36 Much more research is needed to understand how racism is embedded in contemporary exotic dancing. See Siobhan Brooks, 'Dancing toward Freedom,' and her 'Exotic Dancing and Unionizing: The Challenges of Feminist and Antiracist Organizing at the Lusty Lady Theater.'
37 See Judith Butler, *Undoing Gender*, 29.
38 Wyng Chow, 'A Principal of Brandi's Plans a Facility in Palm Springs.' In 2007, in a disturbing show of intimidation, Vancouver police and the Liquor Control Board attempted to suspend Brandi's liquor licence, claiming that gang violence within the club could endanger the public. See Gerry Bellett, 'LCB Wants Strip Club Shut, Fears Gang Violence.'
39 The Marble Arch closed on 15 February 2002. For his reminiscences, see Alex Waterhouse-Hayward, 'Closing Time: A Fan Bids a Fond Farewell to the Marble Arch Pub and Showroom.'
40 The Cecil Hotel on Granville Street is earmarked for demolition. See Janet Mackie, 'Goodbye to Great Vancouver Nights at the Cecil Hotel.'
41 Aaron Chapman, 'Strip Off the Old Block.'
42 Danny Filippone, cited in John Mackie, 'Surviving on the Strip: Penthouse Reaches 60.' Also see Kevin Chong, 'Stripped Down.'
43 Jeff Lee, 'City Pays $3.2m for Hotel Linked to Hells Angels.'
44 Unnati Gandhi, '"Pastorization" Cleans up Strip Club.'
45 Lewis, 'Controlling Lap Dancing.' Also see Mariana Valverde, *Law's Dream of a Common Language*, 42–3.
46 Judith Lynne Hanna, 'Undressing the First Amendment and Corsetting the Striptease Dancer,' 40.
47 Gene Johnson, 'Keeping Strippers, Customers at Arm's Length.'
48 Shawna Richer, 'Planned Strip Club May Bring More Fishnets to Lunenburg.' By contrast, in Paris, France, where Parisians have perfected a seen-it-all, done-it-all approach to sex, two strip clubs – Stringfellows and Pink Platinum – instantly became the hottest outposts of 'erotic-chic' when they opened in 2002.
49 See Prostitution Alternatives, Counselling, Education (PACE), 'Petition to Keep Safe Working Spaces for Exotic Dancers.'
50 Sue Attrill, interviewed by Cameron Phillips, CBC radio, 27 August 2008.
51 See Danielle Egan, 'Eyeing the Scene: The Uses and (Re)uses of Surveillance Cameras in an Exotic Dance Club.'
52 Peter Cheney, 'Is Pornography Out of Control?'
53 On the controversy, see Judy Lin, 'Three Strips and She's Out of Here.' 2001. In 2002, a Christian school in Sacramento, California, expelled a child

from kindergarten, claiming her mother was an exotic dancer who was told she 'did the wrong thing wilfully' by the head pastor. See 'Five-Year-Old Expelled Because Mom's a Stripper.'

54 On news coverage of 'strippergate,' see Colin Freeze and Marina Jiménez, 'Strippers Put Ottawa Program at Centre Stage'; Jeff Sallot and Colin Freeze, 'Exotic-Dancer Program on Sgro Hit List'; and Margaret Wente, 'Why Is Canada Pimping?'

55 Robert Fife, 'Feds Stop Giving Visas to Strippers,' and Marina Jiménez and Campbell Clark, 'Volpe Ends Exotic-Dancer Program.' According to Jiménez and Clark, Human Resources Minister Joe Volpe told reporters that not all Canadians support the program, and that there was no justification for it.

56 Alex Dobrota, 'Tories Rapped over Crackdown on Strippers.' Concerned with the alleged 'trafficking of women,' the Canadian Conservative government proposed Bill C-17 to give immigration officers the power to refuse temporary work permits to non-Canadian dancers judged to be 'at risk of exploitation.' See Editorial, 'Less Than Meets the Eye,' *Globe and Mail*, 25 April 2008: A14.

57 On the struggles facing 'undocumented' migrant labourers across Canada, see Nandita Rani Sharma, *Home Economics: Nationalism and the Making of 'Migrant Workers' in Canada*, and Daiva K. Stasiulis and Abigail B. Bakan, *Negotiating Citizenship: Migrant Women in Canada and the Global System*.

58 It is reported that Gypsy Rose Lee auctioned off the leaves from her leotard in a charity strip in the 1930s, only to learn that the money she made was refused. See Laura Jacobs, 'Taking It All Off,' 207.

59 Cited in Sandra Thomas, 'Strippers' Money Not Good Enough.' Also see Stuart Hunter, 'Exotic Dancers' Money Not Welcome.'

60 Thomas, 'Strippers' Money Not Good Enough,' 9.

61 On the burlesque revival, see Michelle Baldwin, *Burlesque (and the New Bump-n-Grind)*, 32; and Debra Ferreday, '"Showing the Girl": The New Burlesque.'

62 Baldwin, *Burlesque*, 32.

63 In the past ten years, neo-burlesque troupes have come and gone, including the Fluffgirl Burlesque Society and Empire Burlesque Follies in Vancouver, and the Dangerettes in Toronto. This ever-changing sub-culture deserves its own detailed chronicle.

64 The first festival was held in February 2006. For a report, see Vanessa Richards, 'Burlesque Keeps Gathering Steam.' In late April 2008, as part of the second Vancouver International Burlesque Festival, I was honoured to deliver a workshop on my striptease research to twenty-five burlesque

dancers and fans at the Chicken Coup, a small performance space on East Hastings.

65 Miss Astrid, cited in Michelle Baldwin, *Burlesque*, 55.

66 See Karen Gram, 'Sexy Moves for a Fit Form.'

67 Lucy Hyslop, 'Burlesque Yoga Draws Out Inner Sass.' Also see www.burlesqueyoga.com, and Kerry Gold, 'Strip and Tell, Sort Of.'

68 Tammy Morris, cited in Marilisa Racco, 'Good Girls Do.'

69 Kerry Knee, cited in Racco, 'Good Girls Do.'

70 See Oralia Gómez Ramírez, 'Swinging around the Pole: Sexuality, Fitness, and Stripper Stigma in Erotic Dancing Classes.'

71 Ibid., 44.

72 Laura Herbert, quoted in Baldwin, *Burlesque*, 50.

73 Here, I am quibbling with Debra Ferreday, who recuperates the excess, queer parody, and sexual self-awareness of new burlesque performers as feminist, all the while remaining strangely mute about the significant parallels between these women and professional strippers. See her article '"Showing the Girl,"' 60–2.

74 Judith Butler, *Bodies That Matter: On the Discursive Limits of 'Sex,'* 239.

75 Ibid., 231, 237.

76 Bing Thom is quoted in Victor Dwyer, 'Vancouver "Doesn't Try to Be Other Places."'

77 Asked about performing, a Vancouver-based female bodybuilder was emphatic about the negative influence of striptease: 'I am appalled to see bodybuilders pose as if they were about to perform a lap dance. I've seen far too many women do the "bump and grind" on stage and I am embarrassed for our sport. Bodybuilding is a family affair ... I am utterly disgusted to see the sexual degradation of flaunting one's body in such a manner that belongs solely in a closed-door bedroom.' Sadly, a woman whose own barely clad, oiled, and hyper-muscled body publicly transgresses the bounds of conventional femininity feels the need to scorn strippers as a way to prop up the respectability of her own sport. Quoted in Lexi Boyle, 'Female Bodybuilding and the Politics of Muscle: How Female Bodybuilders Negotiate Race, Gender, and (Hetero)sexuality in Body building Competition,' 87. Also, see Sarah Banet-Weiser, *The Most Beautiful Girl in the World: Beauty Pageants and National Identity*.

78 See Brenda Foley, *Undressed for Success: Beauty Contestants and Exotic Dancers as Merchants of Morality*, 9. I find Foley's uncritical genuflection to Roland Barthes's critique of striptease as 'insignificant' both inexplicable and disingenuous. See her reference to Barthes, 171.

79 Again, I borrow from Judith Butler's *Bodies That Matter*, 232.

80 See Virginia Braun, 'In Search of (Better) Sexual Pleasure: Female Genital "Cosmetic" Surgery.'

81 See Eugenia Kaw, 'Medicalization of Racial Features: Asian American Women and Cosmetic Surgery.'

82 Lesley Ann Jeffrey and Gayle MacDonald, *Sex Workers in the Maritimes Talk Back*, 7.

83 On experiences at Lusty Lady, in San Francisco, see Tawnya Dudash, 'Peepshow Feminism'; Vicki Funari, 'Naked, Naughty, Nasty: Peep Show Reflections'; and Siobhan Brooks, 'Exotic Dancing and Unionizing: The Challenges of Feminist and Antiracist Organizing at the Lusty Lady Theater.' Also see the website www.lustyladysf.com.

84 See Julia Query and Vicky Funari's documentary film *Live Nude Girls Unite!*, released in 2000.

85 Tad Friend, 'Naked Profits: The Employees Take Over a Strip Club.'

86 Gregor Gall, *Sex Worker Union Organizing: An International Study*.

87 According to legal scholar Adrienne Couto, 'freelance' dancers in Canada may gain access to collective bargaining rights through a statutory scheme similar to that of the Status of the Artist Act, in which artists are extended the right to collective bargaining rights as independent contractors. See Couto, 'Clothing Exotic Dancers with Collective Bargaining Rights.'

88 Stephanie Levitz, 'Group of Sex Workers Seeking to Go Legit.'

89 See Elianna Lev, 'For Those Selling Sex, Little Has Changed'; and Lori Culbert, 'Nothing's Changed: Women Continue to Go Missing in the Downtown Eastside.'

90 For feminist research that explores the limitations of 'trafficking' discourse, see Kamala Kempadoo, ed., with Jyoti Sanghera and Bandana Pattanaik, *Trafficking and Prostitution Reconsidered: New Perspectives on Migration, Sex Work, and Human Rights*.

91 Jeffrey Weeks, *Sexuality*, 2.

92 See www.tuscl.com/.

93 Vanessa Arrington, 'Tropicana Trades Sex for Theatrics.'

94 Annie Temple, 'R.I.P. the Drake Showlounge.'

Bibliography

Abrahams, Yvette. 'Images of Sara Bartman: Sexuality, Race, and Gender
  in Early Nineteenth Century Britain.' In Ruth Roach Pierson and Nupur
  Chaudhuri, eds, with assistance from Beth McCauley, *Nation, Empire,
  Colony: Historicizing Gender and Race*, 220–36. Bloomington: Indiana
  University Press, 1998.
Ackery, Ivan. *Fifty Years on Theatre Row*. North Vancouver, BC: Hancock
  House, 1980.
Adachi, Ken. *The Enemy That Never Was*. Toronto: McClelland and Stewart,
  1976.
Adami, Hugh. 'Strippers Continue to Take It Off, Despite Goulbourn's New
  Bylaw.' *Ottawa Citizen*, 3 November 1982: 29.
Adams, Mary Louise. *The Trouble with Normal: Postwar Youth and the Making of
  Heterosexuality*. Toronto: University of Toronto Press, 1997.
'Advertisement.' *Vancouver Sun*, 29 June 1947.
'Advertisement.' *Vancouver Sun*, 17 April 1969: 27.
Aldridge, A. Owen. 'American Burlesque at Home and Abroad: Together with
  the Etymology of Go-Go Girl.' *Journal of Popular Culture* 5, 3 (1971): 565–75.
'All Star Imported Show: Advertisement.' *Vancouver Sun*, 11 January 1964: 13.
Allen, Robert C. *Horrible Prettiness: Burlesque and American Culture*. Chapel
  Hill: University of North Carolina Press, 1991.
Als, Hilton. 'Mammy for the Masses.' *The New Yorker*, 26 September 2005:
  148–51.
Ample, Annie. *The Bare Facts: My Life as a Stripper*. Toronto: Key Porter, 1988.
Anderson, Kay. *Vancouver's Chinatown: Racial Discourse in Canada, 1875–1980*.
  Montreal and Kingston: McGill-Queen's University Press, 1991.
Armatage, Kay. *Striptease*. Documentary film. Distributed by the Canadian
  Film Distribution Centre. Toronto, 1980.

- 'Striptease: Work, Performance, Sexuality.' *Canadian Woman Studies* 3, 2 (1981): 32–5.
Armstrong, Jane. 'Police Alter Missing-Women Theory.' *Globe and Mail*, 21 August 2001: A3.
Armstrong, Pat. *Labour Pains: Women's Work in Crisis*. Toronto: Women's Press, 1984.
- 'The Welfare State as History.' In Raymond Blake, ed., *The Welfare State in Canada: Past, Present, and Future*. Toronto: Irwin Publishing, 1997.
'Arrests May Cost Theatre License.' *Vancouver Sun*, 10 July 1946: 2.
Arrington, Vanessa. 'Tropicana Trades Sex for Theatrics.' *Globe and Mail*, 17 November 2004: T6.
Atkinson, Diana. *Highways and Dancehalls*. Toronto: Vintage, 1995.
Attenborough, Susan. 'Sexual Harassment: An Issue for Unions.' In Linda Briskin and Lynda Yanz, eds, *Union Sisters: Women in the Labour Movement*, 136–43. Toronto: Women's Press, 1983.
Bacchus, Len. 'School for Strippers.' *Vancouver Sun*, 7 July 1984: C2.
- 'Shower Power Flowers as Pubs Offer Patrons "Good Clean Fun."' *Vancouver Sun*, 9 February 1985: A3.
Backhouse, Frances. *Women of the Klondike*. Vancouver: Whitecap Books, 1995.
Baldwin, Michelle. *Burlesque (and the New Bump-n-Grind)*. Denver: Speck Press, 2004.
Banet-Weiser, Sarah. *The Most Beautiful Girl in the World: Beauty Pageants and National Identity*. Los Angeles: University of California Press, 1999.
Bank Book Collective. *An Account to Settle*. Vancouver: Press Gang, 1979.
Barber, Rowland. *The Night They Raided Minsky's*. New York: Simon and Schuster, 1960.
Barker, Dennis. 'King of Soft Porn Became the Richest Man in Britain.' *Globe and Mail*, 10 March 2008: S10.
Barman, Jean. *Stanley Park's Secret: The Forgotten Families of Whoi Whoi, Kanaka Ranch and Brockton Point*. Madeira Park, BC: Harbour Publishing, 2005.
- 'Taming Aboriginal Sexuality: Gender, Power, and Race in British Columbia, 1850–1900.' *BC Studies* 115/116 (1997–8): 237–66.
- *The West beyond the West*. Toronto: University of Toronto Press, 1991.
Barrett, Tom. 'Beer Parlour Managers Cry in Their Brew.' *Vancouver Sun*, 6 December 1976: 21.
Barry, Kathleen. *Female Sexual Slavery*. Englewood Cliffs, NJ: Prentice Hall, 1979.
- *The Prostitution of Sexuality*. New York: New York University Press, 1995.
Barry, Kathleen M. *Femininity in Flight: A History of Flight Attendants*. Durham and London: Duke University Press, 2007.

Barthes, Roland. *Mythologies.* Trans. Annette Lavers. New York: Hill and Wang, 1972.

Barton, Bernadette. 'Managing the Toll of Stripping: Boundary Setting among Exotic Dancers.' *Journal of Contemporary Ethnography* 35, 5 (October 2007): 571–96.

– *Stripped: Inside the Lives of Exotic Dancers.* New York: New York University Press, 2006.

'B.C. Nightspot Has Topless Show.' *Daily Colonist,* 26 July 1966: 13.

Bearchell, Chris. 'No Apologies: Strippers as the Upfront Line in a Battle to Communicate.' *The Body Politic* 123 (February 1986): 26–9.

Bell, Laurie. 'Introduction.' In Laurie Bell, ed., *Good Girls / Bad Girls: Sex Trade Workers and Feminists Face to Face,* 5–15. Toronto: Women's Press, 1987.

Bell, Shannon. *Reading, Writing and Rewriting the Prostitute Body.* Bloomington: Indiana University Press, 1994.

– *Whore Carnival.* Brooklyn, NY: Autonomedia, 1995.

Bellett, Gerry. 'LCB Wants Strip Club Shut, Fears Gang Violence.' *Vancouver Sun,* 13 January 2007: A10.

– 'Slain Stripper's Boyfriend Accused in 1986 Death.' *Vancouver Sun,* 16 November 2000: B3.

Bercuson, David, and David Bright, eds. *Canadian Labour History: Selected Readings.* 2nd ed. Toronto: Copp Clark Pitman, 1994.

Best, William. 'Police, Night Club Eyes Bulge as Sally Rand Strains Corset.' *Vancouver Sun,* 26 June 1946: 1.

Bhopal, Kalwant. 'Women and Feminism as Subjects of Black Study: The Difficulties and Dilemmas of Carrying Out Research.' *Journal of Gender Studies* 4, 2 (1995): 153–68.

Bird, Chris. 'Strip Clubs Taking Off as Court Okays Nudity.' *The Province,* 13 September 1972: 1–2.

Bishop, Lisa. 'Police Frown on Strip Acts.' *Vancouver Sun,* 2 February 1980: A7.

Bloch, Alexia. 'Victims of Trafficking or Entrepreneurial Women? Narratives of Post-Soviet Entertainers in Turkey.' *Canadian Woman Studies* 22, 3–4 (2003): 152–8.

Bogdan, Robert. *Freak Show: Presenting Human Oddities for Amusement and Profit.* Chicago: University of Chicago Press, 1988.

Bornstein, Kate. *Gender Outlaw: On Men, Women, and the Rest of Us.* New York and London: Routledge, 1994.

Bott, Esther. 'Pole Position: Migrant British Women Producing "Selves" through Lap Dancing Work.' *Feminist Review* 83 (2006): 23–41.

Bourdieu, Pierre. *Distinction: A Social Critique of the Judgement of Taste.* Trans. Richard Nice. Cambridge, MA: Harvard University Press, 1984.

- *Masculine Domination*. Trans. Richard Nice. Stanford, CA: Stanford University Press, 2001.
Boyd, Denny. 'Joe Draws His Last Crow – and It's a Full House.' *Vancouver Sun*, 23 September 1983: A3.
- 'The Ladies Will Take It Off for Charity.' *Vancouver Sun*, 27 August 1981: A3.
- 'Legend Larger Than the Man.' *Vancouver Sun*, 20 September 1983: A3.
- 'Something Is Lost with Beef Dip and Beer.' *Vancouver Sun*, 22 February 1980: A3.
- *Vancouver Sun*, 9 March 1978: B3.
- *Vancouver Sun*, 23 June 1978: B3.
- *Vancouver Sun*, 14 September 1978: B3.
Boyle, Lexi. 'Female Bodybuilding and the Politics of Muscle: How Female Bodybuilders Negotiate Race, Gender, and (Hetero)sexuality in Bodybuilding Competition.' MA thesis, Women's Studies and Gender Relations, University of British Columbia, 2003.
Brady, Jacqueline. 'Pumping Iron with Resistance: Carla Dunlap's Victorious Body.' In Michael Bennett and Vanessa Dickerson, eds, *Recovering the Black Female Body: Self-Representations by African American Women*, 253–78. New Brunswick, NJ: Rutgers University Press, 2001.
Bramham, Daphne. 'Canada's Complicity in Human Trafficking.' *Vancouver Sun*, 17 June 2006: C5.
- 'Foreign Strippers Are Teased with Work Visas.' *Vancouver Sun*, 15 May 2004: C7.
- 'Long-Stemmed Lovelies Play On.' *Vancouver Sun*, 10 February 2001: A16.
Brand, Dionne. '"We Weren't Allowed to Go into Factory Work until Hitler Started the War": The 1920s to the 1940s.' In Peggy Bristow, ed., *We're Rooted Here and They Can't Pull Us Up: African Canadian Women's History*, 171–92. Toronto: University of Toronto Press, 1994.
Braun, Virginia. 'In Search of (Better) Sexual Pleasure: Female Genital "Cosmetic" Surgery.' *Sexualities* 8, 4 (2005): 407–24.
Breen, David, and Ken Coates. *The Pacific National Exhibition: An Illustrated History*. Vancouver: University of British Columbia Press, 1982.
- *Vancouver's Fair: An Administrative and Political History of the Pacific National Exhibition*. Vancouver: University of British Columbia Press, 1982.
Briskin, Linda. 'Women and Unions in Canada: A Statistical Overview.' In Linda Briskin and Lynda Yanz, eds, *Union Sisters: Women in the Labour Movement*, 28–43. Toronto: Women's Press, 1983.

Briskin, Linda, and Pat McDermott. *Women Challenging Unions: Feminism, Democracy, and Militancy*. Toronto: University of Toronto Press, 1993.

Brock, Deborah. *Making Work, Making Trouble: Prostitution as a Social Problem*. Toronto: University of Toronto Press, 1998.

Brock, Deborah, Kara Gillies, Chantelle Olier, and Mook Sutdhibhasilp. 'Migrant Sex Work: A Roundtable Analysis.' *Canadian Woman Studies Journal* 20, 2 (2000): 84–91.

Brooks, Carellin. *Wreck Beach*. Vancouver: New Star Books, 2007.

Brooks, Jack. '800 Mourners Gather to Remember Slain Joe.' *Vancouver Sun*, 22 September 1983: A1.

Brooks, Siobhan. 'Dancing toward Freedom.' In Jill Nagle, ed., *Whores and Other Feminists*, 252–5. New York: Routledge, 1997.

– 'Exotic Dancing and Unionizing: The Challenges of Feminist and Antiracist Organizing at the Lusty Lady Theater.' In France Winddance Twine and Kathleen M. Blee, eds, *Feminism and Antiracism: International Struggles for Justice*, 59–70. New York and London: New York University Press, 2000.

Brown, Stephen. 'Myth Shattered: We Win One!' *Georgia Straight*, 24 September – 1 October 1969. Reprinted in Naomi Pauls and Charles Campbell, eds, *The Georgia Straight: What the Hell Happened?*, 25. Vancouver: Douglas and McIntyre, 1997.

Browne, Lois. *Girls of Summer*. Toronto: HarperCollins, 1993.

Bruckert, Chris. *Taking It Off, Putting It On: Women in the Strip Trade*. Toronto: Women's Press, 2002.

Bruckert, Christine, and Sylvie Frigon. '"Making a Spectacle of Herself": On Women's Bodies in the Skin Trades.' *Atlantis* 28, 1 (Fall 2003): 58–65.

Buhasz, Laszlo. 'Leer Jet.' *Globe and Mail*, 3 April 2003: T5.

'Bumps, Sex Shows are Taboo.' *Vancouver News Herald*, 19 September 1951: 1.

Burana, Lily. *Strip City: A Stripper's Farewell Journey across America*. New York: Hyperion, 2001.

'Burlesque Show Closed; Appeal Next.' *Vancouver Sun*, 19 January 1952: 6.

'Burlesque Show Gets Okay for Just Little Sex Appeal: Alderman Debate Bare Facts.' *Vancouver Sun*, 19 September 1951: 9.

'Burlesque Theatre Closed.' *The Province*, 18 January 1952: 21.

Burnham, Christine Wg, with Patricia Diewold. *Gender Change Employability Issues: Including Transitional Employment Survey Results*. Vancouver: Perceptions Press, 1994.

Butler, Judith. *Bodies That Matter: On the Discursive Limits of 'Sex.'* New York: Routledge, 1993.

– *Excitable Speech*. New York: Routledge, 1997.

– *Undoing Gender*. New York: Routledge, 2004.

'Cabaret Charged.' *Vancouver Sun*, 10 January 1977: 31.

Caldwell, Rebecca. 'Wanted: Canucks in the Buff.' *Globe and Mail*, 20 May 2003: R3.

Campbell, Murray. 'Memories of Montreal's Skin Queen.' *Globe and Mail*, 3 February 1999: A3.

Campbell, Robert. *Demon Rum or Easy Money: Government Control of Liquor in British Columbia from Prohibition to Privatization*. Ottawa: Carleton University Press, 1991.

– '"A Fantastic Rigmarole": Deregulating Aboriginal Drinking in British Columbia, 1945–62.' *BC Studies* 141 (Spring 2004): 81–104.

– 'Managing the Marginal: Regulating and Managing Decency in Vancouver's Beer Parlours, 1925–1954.' *Labour / Le travail* 44 (1999): 109–27.

– *Sit Down and Drink Your Beer: Regulating Vancouver's Beer Parlours, 1925–1954*. Toronto: University of Toronto Press, 2001.

'Candy Barr: Exotic Dancer, 1935-2005.' *Globe and Mail*, 3 January 2006: S9.

Carby, Hazel, V. 'Policing the Black Woman's Body.' In *Cultures in Babylon*. London and New York: Verso, 1999.

Carey, Sandra Harley, Robert Peterson, and Louis Sharpe. 'A Study of Recruitment and Socialization in Two Deviant Female Occupations.' *Sociological Symposium* 11 (1974): 11–24.

Carlyle, Len. 'The Show Business Phenomenon Called the Cave: Why Stars like Berle, Berman, Damone and Carter Go Out of Their Way to Play Vancouver.' *Vancouver Life* 1, 10 (July 1966): 44–7.

Carter, Lauren. 'Where Are Canada's Disappeared Women?' *Herizons* (Fall 2005): 20–3, 45–6.

Carter, Sarah. 'First Nations Women of Prairie Canada in the Early Reserve Years, the 1870s to the 1920s: A Preliminary Inquiry.' In Christine Miller and Patricia Churchryk, eds, *Women of the First Nations: Power, Wisdom, and Strength*, 51–76. Winnipeg: University of Manitoba Press, 1996.

Chamberland, Line. *Mémoires lesbiennes: Le lesbianisme à Montréal entre 1950 et 1972*. Montreal: Editions du Remue-ménage, 1996.

Chapkis, Wendy. *Beauty Secrets: Women and the Politics of Appearance*. Boston: South End Press, 1986.

– *Live Sex Acts: Women Performing Erotic Labour*. New York: Routledge, 1997.

Chapman, Aaron. 'Strip off the Old Block.' *Vancouver Courier*, 6 February 2008: 1, 4–7.

Chauncey, George. *Gay New York: Gender, Urban Culture and the Making of the Gay Male World, 1890–1940*. New York: Basic Books, 1994.

Chen, Linda Xiao Jia. 'Laundresses and Prostitutes: Deconstructing

Stereotypes and Finding an Asian Feminist Voice.' *Resources for Feminist Research* 20, 3/4 (1992): 88–90.

Cheney, Peter. 'Bordertown Canada $et for $uper $unday.' *Globe and Mail*, 28 January 2006: A14.

– 'Is Pornography out of Control?' *Globe and Mail*, 2 December 2004: F4, F5.

Chong, Kevin. 'From Peelers and Punks to Stand-Up.' *Globe and* Mail, 19 January 2007: R5.

– 'Stripped Down.' *Vancouver Magazine*, 1 January 2009: 1–4 www. vanmag.com/News_and_Features/Stripped_Down.

Chow, Wyng. 'Busted Stripper Hopes for Ping Pong Diplomacy.' *Vancouver Sun*, 28 July 1984: A15.

– 'A Principal of Brandi's Plans a Facility in Palm Springs.' *Vancouver Sun*, 2 January 2002: C1, C5.

'City Cafés Get Wine Licenses.' *Vancouver Sun*, 22 April 1954: 1.

'Club Acquitted in Nudity Case.' *Vancouver Sun*, 13 September 1972: 6.

Cobble, Dorothy Sue. *Dishing It Out: Waitresses and Their Unions in the Twentieth Century*. Urbana and Chicago: University of Illinois Press, 1991.

Cody, Diablo. *Candy Girl: A Year in the Life of an Unlikely Stripper*. New York: Penguin, 2006.

Cohen, Marcy, and Margaret White. *Taking Control of Our Future: Clerical Workers and the New Technology*. Vancouver: Press Gang, 1987.

Cole, Douglas. 'Leisure, Taste and Tradition in British Columbia.' In Hugh Johnston, ed., *The Pacific Province: A History of British Columbia*, 344–81. Vancouver and Toronto: Douglas and McIntyre, 1996.

Collier, Robert. 'Downtown: Metropolitan Focus.' In L.J. Evenden, ed., *Vancouver: Western Metropolis*, 159–77. Victoria, BC: University of Victoria Press, 1978.

Collins, Patricia Hill. *Black Feminist Thought: Knowledge, Consciousness and the Politics of Empowerment*. New York: Routledge, 1990.

– *Black Sexual Politics*. New York: Routledge, 2004.

Compton, Wayde, ed. *Bluesprint: Black British Columbian Literature and Orature*. Vancouver: Arsenal Pulp Press, 2002.

Constantineau, Bruce. 'Cabaret Guilty of Turning Away Blacks.' *Vancouver Sun*, 26 October 1979: 1.

Cooke, Amber. 'Stripping: Who Calls the Tune?' In Laurie Bell, ed., *Good Girls / Bad Girls: Sex Trade Workers and Feminists Face to Face*, 92–9. Toronto: Women's Press, 1987.

Corio, Ann, with Joseph DiMona. *This Was Burlesque*. New York: Madison Square Press, 1968.

Corrigan, Philip. 'On Moral Regulation: Some Preliminary Remarks.' *Sociological Review* 29, 2 (1981): 313–37.

Corrigan, Philip, and Derek Sayer. *The Great Arch: English State Formation as Cultural Revolution*. London: Oxford University Press, 1985.

Cosco, Vanessa. 'Obviously Then I'm Not Heterosexual: Lesbian Identities, Discretion, and Communities.' MA thesis, Department of History, University of British Columbia, 1997.

'Council Tells Girls to Cover.' *The Province*, 5 October 1966: 25.

Coupland, Douglas. *City of Glass: Douglas Coupland's Vancouver*. Vancouver: Douglas and McIntyre, 2000.

'Court Goes to Cabaret to Check Stripper's Act.' *The Province*, 7 March 1973: 9.

Couto, Adrienne. 'Clothing Exotic Dancers with Collective Bargaining Rights.' *Ottawa Law Review* 38, 1 (2006–7): 37-63.

'Cover Up, Says A-G.' *Vancouver Sun*, 31 August 1976: A5.

'Cover Up Tops, LCB Tells Girls.' *The Province*, 1 September 1972: 1–2.

Crane, Dona. 'Vancouver's Male Strippers Let It All Hang Out.' *Georgia Straight*, 21–8 July 1977. Reprinted in Naomi Pauls and Charles Campbell, eds, *The Georgia Straight: What the Hell Happened?*, 68–70. Vancouver: Douglas and McIntyre, 1997.

Crazytrain, Marissa. 'Dances for Dollars.' In Drew Hayden Taylor, ed., *Me Sexy: An Exploration of Native Sex and Sexuality*, 150–9. Vancouver: Douglas and McIntyre, 2008.

Creese, Gillian, and Veronica Strong-Boag, eds. *British Columbia Reconsidered: Essays on Women*. Vancouver: Press Gang, 1992.

Creet, Julia. 'A Test of Unity: Lesbian Visibility in the British Columbia Federation of Women, 1974–5.' In Sharon Stone, ed., *Lesbians in Canada*, 183–97. Toronto: Between the Lines, 1990.

Crey, Ernie, and Suzanne Fournier. *Stolen from Our Embrace: The Abduction of First Nations and the Restoration of Aboriginal Communities*. Vancouver: Douglas and McIntyre, 1997.

Cubitt, Geoffrey. *History and Memory*. Manchester: Manchester University Press, 2007.

Culbert, Lori. 'City, Police Investigate Eastside Bawdy House.' *Vancouver Sun*, 22 July 2000: A8.

– 'Nothing's Changed: Women Continue to Go Missing in the Downtown Eastside.' *Vancouver Sun*, 26 February 2008: B1, B4.

Dafoe, Christopher. *Vancouver Sun*, 10 December 1976: 23.

Dale, Holly, and Janis Cole, dirs. *Hookers on Davie*. Spectrum Films, 1984.

Dalton, Karen, and Henry Louis Gates, Jr. 'Josephine Baker and Paul Colin:

African American Dance Seen through Parisian Eyes.' *Critical Inquiry* 24 (1998): 903–34.

'Dancers End Picket at Club: Deal Reached.' *Vancouver Sun,* 19 October 1967: 22.

Dank, Barry, and Roberto Refinetti, eds. *Sex Work and Sex Workers.* New Brunswick, NJ: Transaction Publishers, 1999.

Davis, Chuck, ed. *The Greater Vancouver Book: An Urban Encyclopedia.* Surrey, BC: Linkman Press, 1997.

Davis, Janet. 'Spectacles of South Asia at the American Circus, 1890–1940.' *Visual Anthropology* 6 (1993): 121–38.

Davis, Lisa. 'Back in Buddy's Day: Drag's Original Lesbians Reflect on their Heyday.' *Xtra! West,* 2 March 2005: 14–15.

– 'The Butch as Drag Artiste: Greenwich Village in the Roaring Forties.' In Joan Nestle, ed., *The Persistent Desire: A Femme/Butch Reader,* 45–53. Boston: Alyson Publications, 1992.

Dawson, Michael. *Selling British Columbia: Tourism and Consumer Culture, 1890–1970.* Vancouver: University of British Columbia Press, 2004.

De Vries, Maggie. *Missing Sarah: A Vancouver Woman Remembers Her Vanished Sister.* Toronto: Penguin Canada, 2003.

Delacoste, Frederique, and Priscilla Alexander, eds. *Sex Work: Writings by Women in the Sex Industry.* Pittsburgh: Cleis Press, 1987.

'Delta Takes Off on Strippers.' *Vancouver Sun,* 10 December 1974: 1, 2.

DeMarco, Joseph. 'Power and Control in Gay Strip Clubs.' *The Journal of Homosexuality* 53, 1/2 (2007): 111–27.

Department of Labour, Canada. *Women at Work in Canada: A Fact Book on the Female Labour Force, 1964,* Table 1: 10. Ottawa, 1965.

Derko, Kim. 'A High-Heeled Point of View.' *Independent Eye* 12, 3 (1991): 1–8.

DeWitt, Clyde. 'Legal Commentary.' *Adult Video News* (1995): 112–27.

Didon, Pino. 'A Candid Interview: Philliponi Disapproves of Nudity.' *L'Eco d'Italia,* 20 January 1978: 1–3, 8.

Dobrota, Alex. 'Tories Rapped over Crackdown on Strippers.' *Globe and Mail,* 17 May 2007: A7.

Dolan, Jill. *The Feminist Spectator as Critic.* Ann Arbor: University of Michigan Research Press, 1988.

Dominion Bureau of Statistics. *Household Facilities and Equipment,* Table 25 and Table 29. Ottawa: Statistics Canada, 1955.

Dong, Arthur, dir. *Forbidden City, USA.* Video recording. 1989.

Dong, Lorraine. 'The Forbidden City Legacy and Its Chinese American Women.' In *Chinese America: History and Perspectives,* 125–48. San Francisco: Chinese Historical Society of America, 1992.

'Douk Woman Strips in Nelson City Hall.' *Vancouver Sun*, 9 May 1945: 13.

Dragu, Margaret, and A.S.A Harrison. *Revelations: Essays on Striptease and Sexuality*. London: Nightwood Editions, 1988.

Dreyfus, Herbert, and Paul Rabinow. *Michel Foucault: Beyond Structuralism and Hermeneutics*. Chicago: University of Chicago Press, 1982.

'Drunken, Immoral Conduct in Cabarets: Church, Temperance Heads Related Visits to Night Spots.' *Vancouver News Herald*, 13 December 1941: 10.

Dubinsky, Karen. *The Second Greatest Disappointment: Honeymooning and Tourism at Niagara Falls*. Toronto: Between the Lines, 1999.

Dudash, Tawnya. 'Peepshow Feminism.' In Jill Nagle, ed., *Whores and Other Feminists*, 98–118. New York: Routledge, 1997.

Duncan, Jennifer. *Frontier Spirit: The Brave Women of the Klondike*. Toronto: Doubleday, 2003.

Dworkin, Andrea. *Pornography: Men Possessing Women*. New York: Plume, 1989.

Dwyer, Victor. 'Vancouver "Doesn't Try to Be Other Places."' *Globe and Mail*, 10 May 2008: T5.

Eaves, Elisabeth. *Bare: The Naked Truth about Stripping*. Emeryville, CA: Seal Press, 2002. Originally published as *Bare: On Women, Dancing, Sex, and Power*. New York: Knopf, 2002 .

Echols, Alice. *Daring to Be Bad: Radical Feminism in America, 1967–1975*. Minneapolis: Minnesota University Press, 1989.

– *Scars of Sweet Paradise: The Life and Times of Janis Joplin*. New York: Metropolitan Books, Henry Holt and Company, 1999.

Edgren, Gretchen. *The Playmate Book: Six Decades of Centerfolds*. New York: Taschen, 2006.

Editorial. 'Just Like That, There Go Community Standards.' *Globe and Mail*, 22 December 2005: A16.

Editorial. 'Less Than Meets the Eye.' *Globe and Mail*, 25 April 2008: A14.

Editorial. 'Police Entrapment on the Upswing.' *Gay Tide* (August 1975): 1.

Egan, R. Danielle. *Dancing for Dollars and Paying for Love: The Relationship between Exotic Dancers and Their Regulars*. New York: Palgrave Macmillan, 2006.

– 'Eyeing the Scene: The Uses and (RE)uses of Surveillance Cameras in an Exotic Dance Club.' *Critical Sociology* 30, 2 (2004): 300–19.

Egan, R. Danielle, Katherine Frank, and Merri Lisa Johnson, eds. *Flesh for Fantasy: Producing and Consuming Exotic Dance*. New York: Thunder's Mouth Press, 2006.

Ehrenreich, Barbara. *Nickel and Dimed. On (Not) Getting By in America*. New York: Henry Holt, 2002.

Ellis, Havelock. *Sex in Relation to Society: Studies in the Psychology of Sex, Vol. VI*. Philadelphia: F.A Davis, 1910.

Enck, G.E., and J.D. Preston. 'Counterfeit Intimacy: A Dramaturgical Analysis of an Erotic Performance.' *Deviant Behaviour* 9 (1988): 360–81.

'An End to Class Distinction.' *Vancouver Sun*, 14 December 1964: 4.

Epstein, Rachel. 'Domestic Workers: The Experience in B.C.' In Linda Briskin and Lynda Yanz, eds, *Union Sisters: Women in the Labour Movement*, 222–37. Toronto: Women's Press, 1983.

'"Exotic Dancers" to Give Free Show Tuesday Night.' *Vancouver Sun*, 22 January 1952: 1.

Faderman, Lillian. *Naked in the Promised Land*. Boston: Houghton Mifflin, 2003.

Fahrni, Magda, and Robert Rutherdale, eds. *Creating Postwar Canada: Community, Diversity and Dissent, 1945–75*. Vancouver: University of British Columbia Press, 2008.

Fairley, Jim. 'Fake Hanky-Panky in Nude Obscene – Judge.' *The Province*, 15 February 1974: 8.

'The Farce of Liquor in Public ...' *The Province*, 5 November 1959: 4.

Farley, M. '"Bad for the Body, Bad for the Heart": Prostitution Harms Women even if Legalized or Decriminalized.' *Violence against Women* 10, 10 (2004): 1087–1125.

Fatona, Andrea, and Cornelia Wyngaarden, dirs. *Hogan's Alley*. Documentary film. Distributed by Video Out, Vancouver. 1994.

Fausto-Sterling, Anne. 'Gender, Race and Nation: The Comparative Anatomy of "Hottentot" Women in Europe, 1815–1817.' In Jennifer Terry and Jacqueline Urla, eds, *Deviant Bodies*, 19–48. Bloomington: Indiana University Press, 1995.

Feindel, Janet. *A Particular Class of Woman*. Vancouver: Lazara Publications, 1988.

Ferreday, Debra. '"Showing the Girl": The New Burlesque.' *Feminist Theory* 9, 1 (April 2008): 47–66.

Ferry, Jon. 'All Bust in This Boom.' *The Province*, 15 June 1984: 6.

Field, Debbie. 'Coercion or Male Culture: A New Look at Co-worker Harassment.' In Linda Briskin and Lynda Yanz, eds, *Union Sisters: Women in the Labour Movement*, 144–60. Toronto: Women's Press, 1983.

Fife, Robert. 'Feds Stop Giving Visas to Strippers.' *Vancouver Sun*, 2 December 2004: A5.

'Firm, 2 Men Fined $5,500 for Selling Obscene Books.' *The Province*, 2 November 1972: 8.

'5 Convicted of Indecent Stage Show.' *Vancouver Sun*, 18 January 1952: 25.

'Five-Year Old Expelled Because Mom's a Stripper.' *Vancouver Sun*, May 17 2002: A12.

Flynn, Karen. 'Experience and Identity: Black Immigrant Nurses to Canada, 1950–1980.' In Marlene Epp, Franca Iacovetta, and Frances Swyripa, eds, *Sisters or Strangers? Immigrant, Ethnic, and Racialized Women in Canadian History*, 381–98. Toronto: University of Toronto Press, 2004.

Foley, Brenda. *Undressed for Success: Beauty Contestants and Exotic Dancers as Merchants of Morality*. New York: Palgrave Macmillan, 2005.

Forsyth, Craig, and Tina Deshotels. 'A Deviant Process: The Sojourn of the Stripper.' *Sociological Spectrum* 18 (1998): 77–92.

Fotheringham, Allan. *Vancouver Sun*, 22 December 1977: B1.

Foucault, Michel. *Discipline and Punish: The Birth of the Prison*. New York: Vintage Books, 1979.

– *The History of Sexuality, Vol. I*. New York: Vintage Books, 1980.

– 'The Subject and Power.' In Hubert Dreyfus and Paul Rabinow, *Michel Foucault: Beyond Structuralism and Hermeneutics*, 208–26. Chicago: University of Chicago Press, 1982.

Francis, Daniel. *Red Light Neon: A History of Vancouver's Sex Trade*. Vancouver: Subway Books, 2006.

Frank, Katherine. *G-Strings and Sympathy: Strip Club Regulars and Male Desire*. Durham, NC: Duke University Press, 2002.

– 'Keeping Her Off the Pole? Creating Sexual Value in a Capitalist Society.' In R. Danielle Egan, Katherine Frank, and Merri Lisa Johnson, eds, *Flesh for Fantasy: Producing and Consuming Exotic Dance*, 203–11. New York: Thunder's Mouth Press, 2006.

– 'Thinking Critically about Strip Club Research.' *Sexualities* 10, 4 (2007): 502–17.

Freeze, Colin, and Marina Jiménez. 'Strippers Put Ottawa Program at Centre Stage.' *Globe and Mail*, 27 November 2004: A1, A4

Freund, Michaela. 'The Politics of Naming: Constructing Prostitutes and Regulating Women in Vancouver, 1939–1945.' In John McLaren, Robert Menzies, and Dorothy Chunn, eds, *Regulating Lives: Historical Essays on the State, Society, the Individual, and the Law*, 231–58. Vancouver: University of British Columbia Press, 2002.

Friedman, Andrea. *Prurient Interests: Gender, Democracy, and Obscenity in New York City, 1909–1935*. New York: Columbia University Press, 2000.

– 'Sadists and Sissies: Anti-Pornography Campaigns in Cold War America.' *Gender and History* 15, 2 (2003): 201–27.

Friend, Tad. 'Naked Profits: The Employees Take Over a Strip Club.' *The New Yorker*, 12 and 19 July 2004: 56–61.

Funari, Vicki. 'Naked, Naughty, Nasty: Peep Show Reflections.' In Jill Nagle, ed., *Whores and Other Feminists*, 19–35. New York: Routledge, 1997.

Furniss, Elizabeth. 'Pioneers, Progress and the Myth of the Frontier: The Landscape of Public History in Rural B.C.' *BC Studies* 115/116 (1997–8): 7–44.

Gall, Gregor. *Sex Worker Union Organizing: An International Study*. New York: Palgrave Macmillan, 2006.

Gandhi, Unnati. '"Pastorization" Cleans up Strip Club.' *Globe and Mail*, 22 June 2007: A3.

Gardner, Ray. 'After Dark,' *Vancouver Sun*, 12 May 1945: 6.

– 'Jails Manager.' *Vancouver Sun*, 10 July 1946: 2.

Gathorne-Hardy, Jonathan. *Kinsey: A Biography*. London: Pimlico, 2005.

Geddes, John. 'Saving Ms. Stewart.' *Maclean's*, 14 February 2000: 14–19.

Gibson, Margaret. 'Clitoral Corruption: Body Metaphors and American Doctors' Constructions of Female Homosexuality, 1870–1900.' In Vernon Rosario, ed., *Science and Homosexualities*, 118–21. New York: Routledge, 1997.

Gill, Alexandra. 'Maverick of the Dance.' *Globe and Mail*, 28 October 2006: R11.

Gilman, Sander. *Difference and Pathology: Stereotypes of Sexuality, Race and Madness*. Ithaca, NY: Cornell University Press, 1985.

Glavin, Terry. 'Dancers Protest Pay Cut.' *Vancouver Sun*, 30 July 1984: A10.

– 'Protesting Peeler Stripped of Her Job.' *Vancouver Sun*, 31 July 1984: A3.

Gleason, Mona. *Normalizing the Ideal: Psychology, Schooling, and the Family in Postwar Canada*. Toronto: University of Toronto Press, 1999.

Goffman, Erving. *Stigma: Notes on the Management of Spoiled Identity*. New York: Simon and Schuster, 1963.

Gold, Kerry. 'Strip and Tell, Sort Of.' *Vancouver Sun*, 2 July 2005: F1, F17.

Goldwyn, Liz. 'Diva in Disguise.' *FQ* (Summer 2006): 26.

– *Pretty Things: The Last Generation of American Burlesque Queens*. New York: HarperCollins, 2006.

Gopnick, Adam. 'The Naked City.' *The New Yorker* 23 July 2000: 30–4.

Gram, Karen. 'Sexy Moves for a Fit Form.' *Vancouver Sun*, 15 November 2004: C1, C5.

Green Thumb, *Georgia Straight*, 19 May 1967. Reprinted in Naomi Pauls and Charles Campbell, eds, *The Georgia Straight: What the Hell Happened?*, 11–12. Vancouver: Douglas and McIntyre, 1997.

Greene, Trevor. *Bad Date: The Lost Girls of Vancouver's Low Track*. Toronto: ECW Press, 2001.

Griffin, Betty, and Susan Lockhart. *Their Own History: Women's Contribution to the Labour Movement of British Columbia*. New Westminster, BC: United Fishermen and Allied Workers' Union/CAW Seniors' Club, 2002.

Griffin, Kevin. '30 Years Ago, a Pot Smoke-In Sparked the Gastown Riot.' *Vancouver Sun*, 7 August 2001: B1, B4.

Griffin, Susan. *Pornography and Silence: Culture's Revenge against Nature*. New York: Harper and Row, 1981.

Groneman, Carol. *Nymphomania: A History*. New York: W.W. Norton, 2000.

– 'Nymphomania: Historical Construction of Female Sexuality.' In Jennifer Terry and Jacqueline Urla, eds, *Deviant Bodies*, 219–49. Bloomington: Indiana University Press, 1995.

'G-Strings, Cheap Gimmicks Out.' *Vancouver Sun*, 17 December 1976: 6.

Guard, Julie. 'Women Worth Watching: Radical Housewives in Cold War Canada.' In Gary Kinsman, Dieter Buse, and Mercedes Stedman, eds, *Whose National Security? Canadian State Surveillance and the Creation of Enemies*, 73–90. Toronto: Between the Lines, 2000.

Gudgeon, Chris. *The Naked Truth: The Untold Story of Sex in Canada*. Vancouver: Greystone Books, 2003.

Gwendolyn. 'Nothing Butt: The Truth about the Sex Trade.' In Janine Marchessault, ed., *Toward the Slaughterhouse of History: Working Paper on Culture*, 16–23. Toronto: YYZ Gallery, 1992.

Haidarali, Laila. 'Polishing Brown Diamonds: African American Women, Popular Magazines, and the Advent of Modeling in Early Postwar America.' *Journal of Women's History* 17, 1 (Spring 2005): 10–37.

Hainsworth, Jeremy. 'RCMP Targets Gay Cruisers at Wreck Beach.' *XTRA! West*, 3 July 2008: 7.

Hammonds, Evelynn. 'Toward a Genealogy of Black Female Sexuality: The Problematic of Silence.' In M. Jacquie Alexander and Chandra T. Mohanty, eds, *Feminist Genealogies, Colonial Legacies, Democratic Futures*, 170–92. New York: Routledge, 1997.

Hampson, Sarah. 'And Now, the Nudes.' *Globe and Mail*, 25 January 2001: R1, R4.

– 'A Trailblazer in Life and Ballet.' *Globe and Mail*, 17 December 2005: R3.

Hann, Don, and Rob Joyce. 'City Police Record: Smash Hit!' *Gay Tide* 16 (1977): 4.

Hanna, Judith Lynne. 'Undressing the First Amendment and Corsetting the Striptease Dancer.' *The Drama Review* 42 (1998): 38–69.

Hannant, Larry. *The Infernal Machine: Investigating the Loyalty of Canada's Citizens*. Toronto: University of Toronto Press, 1995.

Hansen, Darah. 'Death of a Playmate.' *Vancouver Sun*, 13 August 2005: B2, B3.

Harris, Cole. *Making Native Space: Colonialism, Resistance, and Reserves*. Vancouver: University of British Columbia Press, 2002.

– *The Resettlement of British Columbia: Essays on Colonialism and Geographical Change*. Vancouver: University of British Columbia Press, 1997.

Harvey, Brett. *The Fifties: A Woman's Oral History*. New York: HarperCollins, 1993.

Hassard, Kathy. 'Making the Sweat Pay Off.' *Vancouver Sun*, 6 May 1971: 44.

Hawthorn, Tom. 'Hugh Pickett, Impresario, 1913–2006.' *Globe and Mail*, 14 March 2006: S9.

Haysom, Ian. 'Getting down to the Bare Essentials.' *Vancouver Sun*, 22 January 1982: C4.

Hazlitt, Tom. 'Legal or Illegal: City's Night Life Roars Wide Open.' *The Province*, 9 January 1965: 5.

Hegarty, Marilyn. 'Patriot or Prostitute: Sexual Discourses, Print Media, and American Women during World War II.' *Journal of Women's History* 10, 2 (1998): 112–36.

– *Victory Girls, Khaki-Wackies, and Patriotutes: The Regulation of Female Sexuality during World War II*. New York and London: New York University Press, 2008.

Heron, Craig, and Bob Storey. *On the Job: Confronting the Labour Process in Canada*. Montreal and Kingston: McGill-Queen's University Press, 1986.

'Hewitt Eyes Ban against Kinky Acts.' *The Province*, 26 June 1983: B5.

High Risk Society. *Finding Our Place. Transgender Law Reform*, 1–44. Vancouver: Author, 1996.

Highcrest, Alexandra. *At Home on the Stroll: My Twenty Years as a Prostitute in Canada*. Toronto: Knopf, 1997.

Hochschild, Arlie. *The Managed Heart*. Berkeley, CA: University of California Press, 1983.

Hollibaugh, Amber. *My Dangerous Desires: A Queer Girl Dreaming Her Way Home*. Durham, NC: Duke University Press, 2000.

Horwood, Holly. 'Strippers Bare Their Ire.' *The Province*, 30 July 1984: 4.

Household Facilities and Equipment. Telephones, Radios, Television Receivers, by Province, September 1955. Ottawa: Dominion Bureau of Statistics, 1955.

– Black and White TV Sets, by Province, April 1975. Ottawa: Statistics Canada, 1975.

Hume, Mark. 'The Downtown Eastside: A Haunting Ground for Many, a Hunting Ground for One.' *Globe and Mail*, 10 December 2007: A1, A12.

Humphreys, Helen. *Leaving Earth*. Toronto: HarperCollins, 1997.

Hunt, Alan. *Governing Morals: A Social History of Moral Regulation*. Cambridge: Cambridge University Press, 1999.

Hunter, Robert. *The Greenpeace to Amchitka: An Environmental Odyssey.* Vancouver: Arsenal Pulp Press, 2004.

Hunter, Stuart. 'Exotic Dancers' Money Not Welcome.' *The Province,* 8 February 2007: 7.

Hurley, Claire. *Remember the Cave.* Vancouver: Goalgetter Publications Ltd., 1982.

Hyslop, Lucy. 'Burlesque Yoga Draws Out Inner Sass.' *Vancouver Sun,* 19 June 2006: C1, C5.

Iacovetta, Franca. *Gatekeepers: Reshaping Immigrant Lives in Cold War Canada.* Toronto: Between the Lines, 2006.

– 'Making Model Citizens: Gender, Corrupted Democracy, and Immigrant and Refugee Reception Work in Cold War Canada.' In Gary Kinsman, Dieter Buse, and Mercedes Stedman, eds, *Whose National Security? Canadian State Surveillance and the Creation of Enemies,* 154–67. Toronto: Between the Lines, 2000.

– *Such Hard-Working People: Italian Immigrants in Postwar Toronto.* Montreal and Kingston: McGill-Queen's University Press, 1992.

'"Incredible" Stripper Charged with Indecency.' *Vancouver Sun,* 1 October 1981: A14.

'Ingenious Mitzi Stirs Up Strippers.' *The Province,* 4 October 1981.

Izzo, Kim. 'Rattle, Shake and Roll.' *Fashion,* Vancouver Edition (May 2000): 86–90.

'Jack Wasserman's World.' *Vancouver Life,* 19 February 1966: 37-40.

Jackson, Clive. 'Scarred Dancer Loses Case against Surgeon.' *Courier,* 14 June 1979: 1–2.

– 'They Fired Tattooed Lady.' *The Province,* 29 September 1977: 29.

Jacobs, Jane. *The Death and Life of Great American Cities.* New York: Modern Library, 1961.

Jacobs, Laura. 'Taking It All Off.' *Vanity Fair* (March 2003): 207.

Jagose, Anne Marie. *Queer Theory: An Introduction.* New York: New York University Press, 1996.

Jarrett, Lucinda. *Stripping in Time: A History of Erotic Dancing.* London: HarperCollins, 1997.

Jeffrey, Lesley Ann, and Gayle MacDonald. *Sex Workers in the Maritimes Talk Back.* Vancouver: University of British Columbia Press, 2006.

Jeffreys, Sheila. *Anticlimax: A Feminist Perspective on the Sexual Revolution.* London: Women's Press, 1990.

'Jenine "All-round Gutsy Lady."' *The Province,* 15 June 1984: 6.

Jesser, C., and L. Donovan. 'Nudity in the Art Training Process.' *Sociological Quarterly* 10 (1969): 355–71.

Jiménez, Marina, and Campbell Clark. 'Volpe Ends Exotic-Dancer Program.' *Globe and Mail*, 2 December 2004: A4.

Johns, Michael. *Moment of Grace: The American City in the 1950s*. Berkeley and Los Angeles: University of California Press, 2003.

Johnson, Eve. 'Money, Music and Sleaze.' *Vancouver Sun*, 20 March 1981: L3.

– 'Stripping for Charity.' *Vancouver Sun*, 16 December 1981: C1.

Johnson, Gene. 'Keeping Strippers, Customers at Arm's Length.' *Vancouver Sun*, 3 October 2005: A3.

Johnson, Karle E. 'Police–Black Community Relations in Postwar Philadelphia: Race and Criminalization in Urban Social Spaces, 1945–1960.' *The Journal of African American History* 89, 2 (Spring 2004): 118–33.

Johnson, Laura. *The Seam Allowance: Industrial Home Sewing in Canada*. Toronto: Women's Educational Press, 1982.

Johnson, Mary. 'CABE and Strippers: A Delicate Union.' In Laurie Bell, ed., *Good Girls / Bad Girls: Sex Trade Workers and Feminists Face to Face*, 109–13. Toronto: Women's Press, 1987.

Johnson, Merri Lisa. 'Pole Work: Autoethnography of a Strip Club.' In Barry Dank and Roberto Refinetti eds, *Sex Work and Sex Workers*, 149–58. New Brunswick, NJ: Transaction Publishers, 1999.

– 'Stripper-Bashing: An Autovideography of Violence against Strippers.' In Danielle Egan, Katherine Frank, and Merri Lisa Johnson, eds, *Flesh for Fantasy: Producing and Consuming Exotic Dance*, 159–88. New York: Thunder's Mouth Press, 2006.

Johnson, Val Marie. '"The Rest Can Go to the Devil": Macy's Workers Negotiate Gender, Sex, and Class in the Progressive Era.' *Journal of Women's History* 19, 1 (2007): 32–57.

Johnston, Hugh, ed. *The Pacific Province: A History of British Columbia*. Vancouver and Toronto: Douglas and McIntyre, 1996.

'Judge Angers Raped Stripper.' *Vancouver Sun*, 8 February 1985: A17.

Justman, Paul, dir. *Standing in the Shadows of Motown*. Video recording. 2002.

Katz, Jonathan Ned. *The Invention of Heterosexuality*. New York: Dutton, 1995.

Kaufman, Michelle. 'Gaining an Edge.' In Lissa Smith, ed., *Nike Is a Goddess: The History of Women in Sports*, 159–68. New York: Atlantic Monthly Press, 1998.

Kaw, Eugenia. 'Medicalization of Racial Features: Asian American Women and Cosmetic Surgery.' *Medical Anthropology Quarterly* 7, 1 (1993): 74–89.

Kealey, Greg. *Workers and Canadian History*. Montreal and Kingston: McGill-Queen's University Press, 1995.

Kempadoo, Kamala. 'From Moral Panic to Global Justice: Changing Perspectives on Trafficking.' In Kamala Kempadoo, ed., *Trafficking and*

Prostitution Reconsidered: New Perspectives on Migration, Sex Work, and Human Rights, vii–xxxiv. Boulder, CO: Paradigm Publishers, 2005.

Kennedy, Elizabeth Lapovsky, and Madeline Davis. *Boots of Leather, Slippers of Gold: The History of a Lesbian Community*. New York: Routledge, 1993.

Kibler, M. Alison. *Rank Ladies: Gender and Cultural Hierarchy in American Vaudeville*. Chapel Hill and London: University of North Carolina Press, 1999.

Kieran, Brian. 'Buddha Grins and Bears It.' *Vancouver Sun*, 6 June 1980: 6.

King, Mike. 'Canadian Sex-Trade Workers Could Soon Be Joining a Guild.' *Vancouver Sun*, 9 October 2004: A8.

Kinsman, Gary. 'The Canadian Cold War against Queers: Sexual Regulation and Resistance.' In Richard Cavell, ed., *Love, Hate, and Fear in Canada's Cold War*, 108–32. Toronto: University of Toronto Press, 2004.

– 'Constructing Gay Men and Lesbians as National Security Risks, 1950–1970.' In Gary Kinsman, Dieter Buse, and Mercedes Stedman, eds, *Whose National Security: Canadian State Surveillance and the Creation of Enemies*, 143–53. Toronto: Between the Lines, 2000.

– *The Regulation of Desire: Homo and Hetero Sexualities*. 2nd ed. Montreal: Black Rose Books, 1996.

Kinsman, Gary, and Patrizia Gentile. *The Canadian War on Queers: National Security as Sexual Regulation*. Vancouver: University of British Columbia Press, forthcoming, 2010.

Kipnis, Laura. *Bound and Gagged: Pornography and the Politics of Fantasy in America*. New York: Grove Press, 1996.

Kish, Charlene. 'A Knee Is a Joint and Not an Entertainment: The Moral Regulation of Burlesque in Early Twentieth-Century Toronto.' MA thesis, Department of History, York University, 1997.

Klein, Bonnie Sherr. *Not a Love Story: A Film about Pornography*. Distributed by the National Film Board of Canada, 1981.

Kluckner, Michael. *Vancouver: The Way It Was*. Vancouver: Whitecap Books, 1984.

Kogawa, Joy. *Obasan*. Toronto: Lester and Orpen Dennys, 1981.

Korinek, Valerie. *Roughing It in the Suburbs: Reading Chatelaine Magazine in the Fifties and Sixties*. Toronto: University of Toronto Press, 2000.

Kort, Michele. *Dinah!: Three Decades of Sex, Golf, and Rock 'n' Roll*. Los Angeles: Alyson Publications, 2005.

Kulusic, Tamara. 'The Ultimate Betrayal: Claiming and Re-Claiming Cultural Identity.' *Atlantis* 29, 1 (Spring-Summer 2005): 23–8.

Lacey, F.H., ed. *Historical Statistics of Canada*. 2nd ed., H50, F83, F1, F82. Ottawa: Statistics Canada, 1983.

Lam, Meilan, dir. *Show Girls: Celebrating Montreal's Legendary Black Jazz Scene.* Documentary film. Distributed by the National Film Board of Canada. 1998.

Lamb, Jamie. 'New Liquor Laws Threat to Strippers, Some B.C. Hotels.' *Vancouver Sun,* 4 December 1976: 25.

Latham, Angela. *Posing a Threat: Flappers, Chorus Girls and Other Brazen Performers of the American 1920s.* Hanover, NH: University Press of New England [for] Wesleyan University Press, 2000.

Laturnus, Ted. 'How 12 Strippers from Vancouver … Conquered the Competition in Vegas.' *The Province* (magazine), 3 July 1983: 10.

Leblanc, Daniel. 'Ottawa Gives Free Ad Space to Strip Club.' *Globe and Mail,* 22 August 2001: A5.

Lee, Jeff. 'City Pays $3.2m for Hotel Linked to Hells Angels.' *Vancouver Sun,* 22 June 2007: A1, A3.

– 'How Princeton Became a Breast-Enhancement Centre.' *Vancouver Sun,* 6 March 2002: A1, A6.

Lee, Jenny, and Doug Ward. 'Beloved Columnist Will Always Be Known as the "Voice of the Little Guy."' *Vancouver Sun,* 28 October 2006: A4.

'Leisure's Sound Off … on Bottomless Dancing in Clubs.' *Vancouver Sun,* 13 July 1973: L8.

Lekich, John. 'Jerome Gary's Documentary Tries to Erase Some Clichés: *Stripper* More Than Skin Deep.' *Globe and Mail,* 2 September 1983: E5.

Lev, Elianna. 'For Those Selling Sex, Little Has Changed.' *Globe and Mail,* 31 December 2007: A8.

Levitz, Stephanie. 'Group of Sex Workers Seeking to Go Legit.' *Globe and Mail,* 24 March 2007: 3.

Lewis, Jacqueline. 'Controlling Lap Dancing: Law, Morality, and Sex Work.' In Ronald Weitzer, ed., *Sex for Sale: Prostitution, Pornography and the Sex Industry,* 203–16. New York: Routledge, 2000.

– '"I'll Scratch Your Back if You'll Scratch Mine": The Role of Reciprocity, Power and Autonomy in the Strip Club.' *Canadian Review of Sociology and Anthropology* 43, 3 (August 2006): 297–312.

– 'Lap Dancing: Personal and Legal Implications for Exotic Dancers.' In J.E. Elias and V.L. Bullough, eds, *Prostitution: Whores, Hustlers, and Johns,* 376–89. Amherst, NY: Prometheus Books, 1998.

Liepe-Levinson, Katherine. *Strip Show: Performances of Gender and Desire.* London and New York: Routledge, 2002.

– 'Striptease: Desire, Mimetic Jeopardy, and Performing Spectators.' *The Drama Review* 42, 2 (1998): 9–37.

Lin, Judy. 'Three Strips and She's Out of Here.' *Vancouver Sun,* 30 March 2001: F4.

Lindfors, Bernth. 'Circus Africans.' *Journal of American Culture* 6, 2 (1983): 9–14.

Liquor Inquiry Commission. *Proceedings*. Archives of British Columbia, GR-0560, Vol. 3, 9 June 1969.

Livingston, Billie. *Cease to Blush*. Toronto: Random House Canada, 2006.

Livingston, Jennie, dir. *Paris Is Burning*. Documentary film. 1990.

Lowman, John. 'Street Prostitution in Vancouver: Some Notes on the Genesis of a Social Problem.' *Canadian Journal of Criminology* 28 (1986): 1–16.

– 'Violence and the Outlaw Status of (Street) Prostitution in Canada.' *Violence against Women* 6, 9 (2000): 987–1011.

MacGillivray, Alex. *Vancouver Sun*, Leisure Section, 27 December 1968: 2A.

Mackenzie, Shelagh, dir. *Remember Africville*. Documentary film. Distributed by the National Film Board of Canada. 1991.

Mackie, Janet. 'Goodbye to Great Vancouver Nights at the Cecil Hotel.' *Georgia Straight*, 28 May 2008. Available at www.straight.com.

Mackie, John. 'Famous Friends: Impresario Hugh Pickett's Wit and Charm Won over a Long List of Celebrities.' *Vancouver Sun*, 18 February 2006: F3.

– 'Mr. Showbiz – Promoter Hugh Pickett – Dies at 92.' *Vancouver Sun*, 14 February 2006: A3.

– 'Ross Filippone Was Classic Rags-to-Riches Story.' *Vancouver Sun*, 1 November 2007: A12.

– 'Set 'Em Up, Ross.' *Vancouver Sun*, 10 March 2001: E5.

– 'Surviving on the Strip: Penthouse Reaches 60.' *Vancouver Sun*, 29 September 2007: F14.

MacKinnon, Catharine. *Only Words*. Cambridge, MA: Harvard University Press, 1993.

– *Toward a Feminist Theory of the State*. Cambridge, MA: Harvard University Press, 1989.

Macklin, Audrey. 'On the Outside Looking In: Foreign Domestic Workers in Canada.' In Wenona Giles and Sedef Arat-Koc, eds, *Maid in the Market*, 13–39. Halifax: Fernwood, 1994.

MacLean, Dick. *Dick MacLean's Guide: The Fortnightly Restaurant Magazine* (Vancouver), 4–18 October 1978.

– *Dick MacLean's Leisure Magazine* (Vancouver), August 1973.

MacQueen, Ken. 'Sociologist in Search of the Naked Truth.' *Vancouver Sun*, 10 June 2000: A1, A2.

– 'Undressing Up.' *Maclean's*, 18 February 2002: 52–3.

Macrae, Scott. 'Tints and Tones of the Penthouse Trial.' *Vancouver Sun*, Leisure Section, 22 October 1976: 2A.

Magubane, Zine. 'Which Bodies Matter? Feminism, Poststructuralism, Race, and the Curious Theoretical Odyssey of the "Hottentot Venus."' *Gender and Society* 15, 6 (2001): 816–34.

Manning, Paul. 'Gawkers Flock to View Nude-In.' *The Province*, 24 August 1970: 1.

Marquis, Greg. 'Vancouver Vice: The Police and the Negotiation of Morality, 1904–1935.' In John McLaren and Hamar Foster, eds, *The Legal History of British Columbia and the Yukon: Essays in the History of Canadian Law*, 242–73. Toronto: University of Toronto Press, 1995.

Mason, Gary. 'Web Hoax Dispels Implant Myths.' *Globe and Mail*, 22 April 2006: S1, S3.

Masters, John. 'The Grind Is Gone.' *The Province*, 23 December 1979: 6.

Matas, Robert. 'Pickton Shows No Emotion to Guilty Verdict.' *Globe and Mail*, 10 December 2007: A1, A12.

Mawani, Renisa. 'Imperial Legacies, (Post)Colonial Identities: Law, Space and the Making of Stanley Park, 1859–2001.' *Law Text Culture* 7 (2003): 98–141.

Maynard, Steven. '"Horrible Temptations": Sex, Men, and Working Class Male Youth in Urban Ontario, 1890–1935.' *Canadian Historical Review* 78, 2 (1997): 191–235.

'Mayor Eyes Playboy in Porn Crackdown.' *The Province*, 24 March 1977: 1.

Mazerennie, Rick. 'The Beat Goes On.' *Vancouver* 25 (September 1992): 106.

McCaghy, Charles, and James Skipper. 'Lesbian Behaviour as an Adaptation to the Occupation of Stripping.' *Social Problems* 17 (Fall 1969): 262–70.

McCardell, Michael. 'Super-Hardcore Porn Flooding City.' *Vancouver Sun*, 28 July 1976: 1–2.

McCaugherty, Jack. 'It's Fun, It's Accepted ... But Illegal.' *The Province*, 14 August 1965: 1, 5.

McClintock, Anne. *Imperial Leather: Race, Gender and Sexuality in the Colonial Contest*. New York: Routledge, 1995.

McCracken, Robert. *Las Vegas: The Great American Playground*. Reno: University of Nevada Press, 1996.

McCulloch, Sandra. 'Patrick Nagle, Journalist, Dead at 71.' *Vancouver Sun*, 11 January 2006: A8.

McDonald, Robert A.J. *Making Vancouver, 1863–1913*. Vancouver: University of British Columbia Press, 1996.

McDowell, Jim. 'Strippers Seek Women's Rights.' *The Vancouver Free Press*, 5–11 October 1979: 1, 4.

McKay, Sherry. 'Urban Housekeeping and Keeping the Modern House.' *BC Studies* 140 (2003-4): 11–38.

'McKita Determined to Ban Strippers.' *Vancouver Sun*, 14 December 1976: 17.

McLaren, Angus. *Twentieth-Century Sexuality: A History.* Oxford: Blackwell Publishers, 1999.

McLaren, John. 'The State, Child Snatching, and the Law: The Seizure and Indoctrination of Sons of Freedom Children in British Columbia, 1950–1960.' In John McLaren, Robert Menzies, and Dorothy E. Chunn, eds, *Regulating Lives: Historical Essays on the State, Society, the Individual, and the Law*, 259–93. Vancouver: University of British Columbia Press, 2002.

McMartin, Pete. 'The Sun's Voice Who Spoke to Readers Has Fallen Silent.' *Vancouver Sun*, 28 October 2006: B1, B8.

– 'When Charity Comes with a G-String.' *Vancouver Sun*, 11 December 2004: B1, B10.

McMaster, Lindsey. *Working Girls in the West: Representations of Wage-Earning Women.* Vancouver: University of British Columbia Press, 2008.

McPherson, Kathryn. *Bedside Matters: The Transformation of Canadian Nursing 1900–1990.* Toronto: Oxford University Press, 1996.

McRanor, Mike. *Vancouver Sun*, 12 March 1976: 3A.

Meiselas, Susan. *Carnival Strippers.* New York: Whitney Museum of American Art, 1976.

'Memorial Service Set for Showman Walters.' *Vancouver Sun*, 8 March 1976: 30.

Menzies, Heather. *Women and the Chip: Case Studies of the Effects of Informatics on Employment in Canada.* Montreal: The Institute for Research on Public Policy, 1981.

Meyerowitz, Joanne, ed. *Not June Cleaver: Women and Gender in Postwar America, 1945–1960.* Philadelphia: Temple University Press, 1994.

Middlebrook, Diane Wood. *Suits Me: The Double Life of Billy Tipton.* Boston and New York: Houghton and Mifflin, 1998.

Miki, Roy. *Redress: Inside the Japanese Canadian Call for Justice.* Vancouver: Raincoast, 2004.

Miller, Robert. 'Mean Streets.' *Maclean's*, 5 September 1977: 18–20.

Millett, Kate. *The Prostitution Papers.* New York: Avon Books, 1973.

Misty. *Strip!* Toronto: New Press, 1973.

Mizejewski, Linda. *Ziegfeld Girl: Image and Icon in Culture and Cinema.* Durham and London: Duke University Press, 1999.

Mole, Rich. *Rebel Women of the Klondike: Extraordinary Achievements and Daring Adventures.* Canmore, AB: Altitude, 2007.

Moon, Barbara. 1958. 'Why Should Juliette Knock Them Dead?' *Maclean's*, 26 April 1958: 26–7, 46, 48–50.

Moore, Dene. 'Historian Studying Erotic Entertainment.' *Globe and Mail*, 12 June 2000: A3.

Moore, Oliver. '"Swingers" Clubs Hope Ruling Will Help to Stimulate Their Business.' *Globe and Mail*, 23 December 2005: A10.

Moores, Patrick. '(Re)Covering the Missing Women: News Media Reporting on Vancouver's "Disappeared."' MA thesis, Department of Sociology, University of British Columbia, 2006.

'More Pay, Less Peeling, Ask Striking Strippers.' *Vancouver Sun*, 4 December 1973: 64.

Morgan, Keith, and Ann Rees. 'Tears, Smiles, Raised Glasses Mark Sendoff for Joe.' *The Province*, 23 September 1983: 5.

Morgan, Lael. *Good Time Girls of the Alaska-Yukon Gold Rush*. Fairbanks, AL: Epicenter Press, 1998.

Morgan, Robin. *Going Too Far: The Personal Chronicle of a Feminist*. New York: Vintage Books, 1978.

Mullens, Anne. 'Wage-Cut Strippers Just Grin and Bare It.' *Vancouver Sun*, 24 July 1982: B1.

Mumford, Kevin. *Interzones: Black/White Sex Districts in Chicago and New York in the Early Twentieth Century*. New York: Columbia University Press, 1997.

Munt, Sally, ed. *Butch/Femme: Inside Lesbian Gender*. London: Cassell, 1998.

Nagle, Jill, ed. 'Introduction.' In *Whores and Other Feminists*, 1–15. New York: Routledge, 1997.

Namaste, Viviane. 'Beyond Leisure Studies: A Labour History of Male to Female Transsexuals and Transvestite Artists in Montreal, 1955–1985.' *Atlantis: A Woman's Studies Journal* 9, 1 (Fall/Winter 2004): 4–11.

'Negro Band Barred from Hotel Here.' *Vancouver Sun*, 9 July 1947: 7.

Negrón-Muntaner, Frances. 'Feeling Pretty: *West Side Story* and Puerto Rican Identity Discourses.' *Social Text* 18, 2 (Summer 2000): 83–106.

Nelson, Jay. '"A Strange Revolution in the Manners of the Country": Aboriginal-Settler Intermarriage in Nineteenth-Century British Columbia.' In John McLaren, Robert Menzies, and Dorothy E. Chunn, eds, *Regulating Lives: Historical Essays on the State, Society, the Individual and the Law*, 23–62. Vancouver: University of British Columbia Press, 2002.

Nelson, Jennifer. 'The Space of Africville: Creating, Regulating and Remembering the Urban "Slum."' In Sherene Razack ed., *Race, Space, and the Law: Unmapping a White Settler Society*, 211–32. Toronto: Between the Lines, 2002.

Nestle, Joan. *A Restricted Country*. Ithaca, NY: Firebrand Books, 1987.

– *The Persistent Desire: A Femme/Butch Reader*. Boston: Alyson Publications, 1992.

Newton, Esther. *Mother Camp: Female Impersonators in America*. Englewood Cliffs, NJ: Prentice-Hall, 1972.

Nichol, Eric. *Vancouver*. Toronto: Doubleday Canada, 1970.

Nielson, Georgia Panter. *From Sky Girl to Flight Attendant*: *Women and the Making of a Union*. New York: School of Industrial and Labour Relations, ILR Press, 1982.

Nilsen, Deborah. 'The "Social Evil": Prostitution in Vancouver, 1900–1920.' In Barbara Latham and Cathy Less, eds, *Selected Essays on Women's History in B.C.*, 205–28. Victoria, BC: Camosun College, 1980.

'No Game to Roulette,' *Province*, 31 January 1974: 38.

North, Robert, and Walter Hardwick. 'Vancouver since the Second World War: An Economic Geography.' In Graeme Wynn and Timothy Oke, eds, *Vancouver and Its Region*, 200–33, Vancouver: University of British Columbia Press, 1992.

'Nude Dancers Bare Welfare Fears.' *Vancouver Sun*, 31 December 1971: 12.

'Nude Dancing Ruled Obscene but Club Operator Acquitted.' *Vancouver Sun*, 14 February 1974: 84.

Oberfeld, Harvey. 'City "Gay" Clubs Losing Red Tape Battle.' *Vancouver Sun*, 31 December 1974: 48.

'Obey Liquor Law or Else, Chief Warns.' *The Province*, 28 September 1965: 25.

Odam, Jes. 'Man of Many Faces Ran a Mixed Empire.' *Vancouver Sun*, 20 September 1983: A3.

Oikawa, Mona. 'Cartographies of Violence: Women, Memory, and the Subject(s) of the "Internment."' In Sherene Razack, ed., *Race, Space, and the Law: Unmapping a White Settler Society*, 71–98. Toronto: Between the Lines, 2002.

Oliver, Myrna. 'Skin-Flick King Russ Meyer Dies of Pneumonia at 82.' *Vancouver Sun*, 22 September 2004: F10.

'102 B.C. Liquor Licenses Issued.' *Vancouver Sun*, 22 April 1954: 1-2.

Osler, Rebecca. 'Peekaboo Girls Revive the Pin-Up.' *Vancouver Sun*, 29 April 2006: F1, F4.

Ouston, Rick. 'Ashes, Silver Dollar Cast into Water in Rite for Murdered Stripper.' *Vancouver Sun*, 17 May 1983: 11.

– 'The Life and Death of Layla, a Stripper.' *Vancouver Sun*, 9 April 1983: A13.

– 'Putting the Tease Back into Strip.' *Vancouver Sun*, 20 October 1982: D17.

– 'Rivals Had Nothing on City Stripper Rae.' *Vancouver Sun*, 21 June 1983: A16.

Owram, Doug. *Born at the Right Time: A History of the Baby Boom Generation*. Toronto: University of Toronto Press, 1996.

Oziewicz, Estanislao. 'Canada's Bare Essentials.' *Globe and Mail*, 19 February 2000: A11.

Palmer, Bryan. *Working Class Experience: The Rise and Reconstitution of Canadian Labour, 1800–1980.* Toronto and Vancouver: Butterworth and Co., 1983.

Parent-Duchatelet, Alexander John Baptiste. *De la prostitution dans la Ville de Paris, Vol. I* (1836). Trans. Jill Harsin as *Policing Prostitution in Nineteenth Century Paris.* Princeton: Princeton University Press, 1985.

Parmar, Neil. 'Masculinity on the Move.' *Check Up: The Magazine for Optimal Health* 25 (2006): 20–2.

Parr, Joy. *The Gender of Breadwinners: Women, Men and Change in Two Industrial Towns.* Toronto: University of Toronto Press, 1990.

–, ed. *Diversity of Women, Ontario 1945–1980.* Toronto: University of Toronto Press, 1995.

Paulson, Don, with Roger Simpson. *An Evening at the Garden of Allah: Seattle's Gay Cabaret.* New York: New York University Press, 1996.

'Peelers Picket Police.' *Vancouver Sun,* 27 November 1971: 8.

Peloquin, George. 'Go-Go Cabarets Can't Go Topless.' *Vancouver Sun,* 19 September 1966: 44.

Pendleton, Eva. 'Love for Sale: Queering Heterosexuality.' In Jill Nagle, ed., *Whores and Other Feminists,* 73–82. New York: Routledge, 1997.

Penn, Donna. 'The Sexualized Woman: The Lesbian, the Prostitute, and the Containment of Female Sexuality in Postwar America.' In Joanne Meyerowitz, ed., *Not June Cleaver: Women and Gender in Postwar America, 1945–1960,* 358–81. Philadelphia: Temple University Press, 1994.

Perry, Adele. *On the Edge of Empire: Gender, Race, and the Making of British Columbia, 1849–1871.* Toronto: University of Toronto Press, 2001.

Persky, Stan. *The House (Convention Centre, Stadium, Rapid Transit System, Etc.) That Jack Built: Mayor Jack Volrich and Vancouver Politics.* Vancouver: New Star Books, 1980.

Petersen, David, and Paula Dressel. 'Equal Time for Women: Social Notes on the Male Strip Show.' *Urban Life* 11 (1982): 185–208.

'Peterson Wants to Wrap Up Naked Nightclub Dancers.' *Vancouver Sun,* 30 December 1971: 1–2.

Pheterson, Gail. *The Prostitution Prism.* Amsterdam: University of Amsterdam Press, 1996.

– *A Vindication of the Rights of Whores.* Seattle: Seal Press, 1989.

'Police Frown on Strip Acts.' *Vancouver Sun,* 2 February 1980: A7.

'Police Revert to One O'clock Cabaret Closing,' *Vancouver News Herald,* 13 December 1941: 3.

Pollack, Maria. 'Women, Unions, and Microtechnology.' *Resources for Feminist Research* 10, 2 (1981): 21–2.

Portelli, Alessandro. 'What Makes Oral History Different?' In Robert Perks and Alistair Thomson, eds, *The Oral History Reader*, 32–42. New York and London: Routledge, 2006.

Potter, Greg. 'Closing Time.' *BC Business* (June 2005): 31–3.

Potter, Greg, and Red Robinson. *Backstage Vancouver: A Century of Entertainment Legends*. Vancouver: Harbour Publishing, 2004.

Poulsen, Chuck. 'Penthouse "Hangout for Mafia."' *The Province*, 11 September 1976: 45.

Powis, Tim. 'Electric Lady.' *FQ* (Fall 2005): 82–3.

Pratt, Mary Louise. *Imperial Eyes: Travel Writing and Transculturation*. New York: Routledge, 1992.

Price, Maida. 2002. 'Oh, It Was Athletic: Life and Times at the Penthouse Nightclub.' *Heritage Vancouver Newsletter*, 1 November 2002: 3.

Prostitution Alternatives, Counselling, Education (PACE). 'Petition to Keep Safe Working Spaces for Exotic Dancers.' P.O. Box 73537, 1014 Robson St., Vancouver, BC, V6E 1A7.

Queen, Carol. *Real Live Nude Girl: Chronicles of Sex-Positive Culture*. Pittsburgh: Cleis Press, 1997.

Query, Julia, and Vicky Funari, dirs. *Live Nude Girls Unite!* Documentary film. Distributed by First Run Features, New York. 2000.

Racco, Marilisa. 'Good Girls Do.' *Globe and Mail*, 8 April 2006: L2.

Rader, Benjamin. 'The Quest for Self-Sufficiency and the New Strenuosity, 1991: Reflections on the Strenuous Life of the 1970s and 1980s.' *Journal of Sport History* 18, 2 (1991): 255–66.

Raibmon, Paige. 'Theatres of Contact: The Kwakwaka'wakw Meet Colonialism in British Columbia and at the Chicago World's Fair.' *Canadian Historical Review* 81, 2 (2000):186–90.

Rambo-Ronai, Carol. 'Sketching with Derrida: An Ethnography of a Researcher/Erotic Dancer.' *Qualitative Inquiry* 4, 3 (1998): 405–20.

Ramírez, Oralia Gómez. 'Swinging around the Pole: Sexuality, Fitness, and Stripper Stigma in Erotic Dancing Classes.' MA thesis, Department of Anthropology, University of British Columbia, 2007.

Rand, David, and Robert Cook. 'Community Unites to Voice Anger.' *Gay Tide* 16 (1977): 1.

'Rathie Tackles "Topless" Issue.' *Vancouver Sun*, 27 September 1966: 11.

Räthzel, Nora. 'Nationalism and Gender in West Europe: The German Case.' In Helma Lutz, Ann Phoenix, and Nira Yuval-Davis, eds, *Crossfires: Nationalism, Racism and Gender in Europe*, 161–89. London: Pluto Press, 1995.

Ratlif, Ben. 'Singer Was a Favourite of Ella Fitzgerald.' *Globe and Mail*, 8 May 2000: R6.

Raugust, Paul. 'The Grind Is Gone.' *The Province* (magazine), 23 December 1980: 6.
– 'LCL Cracks Down on Nude Clubs Here.' *The Province*, 28 June 1973: 31.
– 'Vancouver Goes Boom in the Night.' *The Province*, 13 March 1974: 13.
Read, Jeani. 'Stripping away Concepts.' *The Province*, 16 September 1984: 54.
'Reformers to Fight Night Club License.' *Vancouver Sun*, 28 June 1945: 5.
Reid, Scott, Jonathon Epstein, and D.E. Benson. 'Does Exotic Dancing Pay Well but Cost Dearly?' In A. Thio and T. Calhou, eds, *Readings in Deviant Behaviour*, 284–8. New York: HarperCollins, 1995.
Reiter, Esther. *Making Fast Food: From the Frying Pan into the Fryer.* Montreal: McGill-Queen's University Press, 1996.
Reynolds, Mac. 'City Asked to "Go It Alone" in Fight on Racial Bans.' *Vancouver Sun*, 6 August 1959: 1–2.
Ricardo, Diana. 'Stripping: It Sure Beats the Steno Pool.' *Vancouver Sun*, 4 February 1972: 29.
Richards, Vanessa. 'Burlesque Keeps Gathering Steam.' *Globe and Mail*, 3 February 2006: R5.
Richer, Shawna. 'Planned Strip Club May Bring More Fishnets to Lunenburg.' *Globe and Mail*, 17 October 2006: A1, A4.
Richler, Nancy. *Throwaway Angels*, Vancouver: Press Gang Publishers, 1996.
Ricketts, Trina, Susan Davis, Stacey Grayer, Candice Hansen, Jennifer Allan, and Chanel Martin. *History of Sex Work: Vancouver.* Vancouver: Continuing Studies, Simon Fraser University, 2007.
Ritchie, Laurel. 'Why Are So Many Women Unorganized?' In Linda Briskin and Lynda Yanz, eds, *Union Sisters: Women in the Labour Movement*, 200–11. Toronto: Women's Press, 1983.
Roberts, Nickie. *Whores in History: Prostitution in Western Society.* London: HarperCollins, 1992.
Rodger, Moyra, dir. *Hugh Pickett: A Portrait.* Documentary film. 2003.
Roman, Leslie. 'Double Exposure: The Politics of Feminist Materialist Ethnography.' *Educational Theory* 43, 3 (1993): 279–308.
Rose, Chlöe Brushwood, and Anna Camilleri, eds. *Brazen Femme: Queering Femininity.* Vancouver: Arsenal Pulp Press, 2002.
Rose, Larry. 'Cabaret Policing "Will Get Tougher."' *Vancouver Sun*, 28 September 1965: 14.
Rose, Phyllis. *Jazz Cleopatra: Josephine Baker in Her Time.* New York: Doubleday, 1989.
Rosen, Ruth. *The Lost Sisterhood: Prostitution in America, 1900–1918.* Baltimore and London: Johns Hopkins University Press, 1982.

Ross, Becki. 'Bumping and Grinding on the Line: Making Nudity Pay.' *Labour /
Le travail* 46 (Fall 2000): 221–50.
– 'Destaining the (Tattooed) Delinquent Body: Moral Regulatory Practices
at Toronto's Street Haven, 1965–1969.' *Journal of the History of Sexuality* 8,
1(1997): 561–95.
– 'Entertaining Femininities: The Embodied Exhibitions of Striptease and
Sport, 1950–1975.' In Jennifer Hargreaves and Patricia Vertinsky, eds,
Physical Culture, Power, and the Body, 121–41. New York: Routledge, 2006.
– *The House That Jill Built: A Lesbian Nation in Formation*. Toronto: University of
Toronto Press, 1995.
– 'Men behind the Marquee: Greasing the Wheels of Vansterdam's Striptease
Scene, 1950–75.' In Robert Rutherdale and Magda Fahrni, eds, *Creating
Post-War Canada: Diversity, Community, and Dissent*, 318–49. Vancouver:
University of British Columbia Press, 2007.
– 'Striptease on the Line: Investigating Trends in Female Erotic Entertain-
ment.' In Deborah Brock ed., *Making Normal: Social Regulation in Canada*,
146–78. Toronto: Thomson Nelson, 2003.
– 'Troublemakers in Tassels and G-Strings: Striptease Dancers and the Union
Question, Vancouver, B.C., 1960–1980.' *Canadian Review of Sociology and
Anthropology* 43, 3 (August 2006): 307–22.
Ross, Becki, and Erin Bentley. 'Gold-Plated Footballs and Orchids for Girls, A
"Palace of Sweat" for Men.' In Patricia Vertinsky and Sherry McKay, eds,
Disciplining Bodies in the Gymnasium: Memory, Monument, and Modernism,
99–116. New York: Routledge, 2004.
Ross, Becki, and Kim Greenwell. 'Spectacular Striptease: Performing the
Sexual and Racial Other in Vancouver, B.C., 1950–1975.' *Journal of Women's
History* 17, 1 (2005): 137–64.
Ross, June. 'Nude Dancing and the Charter.' *Review of Constitutional Studies* 1,
2 (1994): 298–355.
Rossiter, Sean. 'They Call Her Fox.' *Vancouver* 12, 6 (June 1979): 56, 70–5.
Rotenberg, Lori. 'The Wayward Worker: Toronto's Prostitute at the Turn of the
Century.' In J. Acton, P. Goldsmith, and B. Shephard, eds, *Women at Work
1850–1930*, 33–70. Toronto: Canadian Women's Educational Press, 1974.
Rothe, Len. *The Queens of Burlesque: Vintage Photographs from the 1940s and
1950s*. Atglen, PA: Schiffer Publishing, 1997.
Roy, Patricia. 'A Choice between Two Evils: The Chinese and the Construction
of the Canadian Pacific Railway in British Columbia.' In *The CPR West:
The Iron Road and the Making of a Nation*, 13–34. Vancouver: Douglas and
McIntyre, 1984.

- 'The "Oriental Menace" in British Columbia.' In J. Friesen and H. Ralston, eds, *Historical Essays on British Columbia*, 243–55. Toronto: Gage, 1980.
- *The Oriental Question: Consolidating a White Man's Province, 1914–1941*. Vancouver: University of British Columbia Press, 2003.
- *Vancouver: An Illustrated History*. Toronto: James Lorimer and Co., 1981.

Rupp, Leila J., and Verta Taylor. *Drag Queens at the 801 Cabaret*. Chicago: University of Chicago Press, 2003.

Ryley, Bay. *Gold Diggers of the Klondike: Prostitution in Dawson City, Yukon, 1898–1908*. Toronto: Watson Dwyer, 1997.

Said, Edward. *Orientalism*. New York: Vintage Books, 1979.

St James, Margo. 'The Reclamation of Whores.' In Laurie Bell, ed., *Good Girls / Bad Girls: Sex Trade Workers and Feminists Face to Face*, 81–7. Toronto: Women's Press, 1987.

Sallaz, Jeffrey. 'House Rules: Autonomy and Interests among Service Workers in the Contemporary Casino Service Industry.' *Work and Occupations* 29, 4 (2002): 394–427.

Salmi, Brian. 'Hooker History: 125 Years of Illegal Sex and the City.' *Georgia Straight* 34 (November 2000): 2–9, 17–19, 21.

Sallot, Jeff, and Colin Freeze. 'Exotic-Dancer Program on Sgro Hit List.' *Globe and Mail*, 24 November 2004: A9.

Salutin, Marilyn. 'Stripper Morality.' *Trans-Action* 8, 8 (1971): 12–23.

Sangster, Joan. 'Doing Two Jobs: The Wage-Earner Mother, 1945–1970.' In Joy Parr, ed., *Diversity of Women, Ontario 1945–1980*, 98–134. Toronto: University of Toronto Press, 1995.

- *Earning Respect: The Lives of Working Women in Small-Town Ontario, 1920–1960*. Toronto: University of Toronto Press, 1995.
- 'Incarcerating "Bad Girls": The Regulation of Sexuality through the Female Refuges Act in Ontario, 1920–1945.' *Journal of the History of Sexuality* 7, 2 (1996): 239–75.
- 'Telling Our Stories: Feminist Debates and the Use of Oral History.' *Women's History Review* 3, 1 (November 1994): 5–28.

Sasha. 'Taking It Off Is One Thing …' *Globe and Mail*, 22 January 2000: A15.

Sawhney, S. 'Feminism and Hybridity Round Table.' *Surfaces* 7, 113 (2006): 3–12.

Saxby, Jessie M. 'Women Wanted.' In S. Jackel, ed., *A Flannel Shirt and Liberty: British Emigrant Gentlewomen in the Canadian West, 1880–1914*, 68–74. Vancouver: University of British Columbia Press, 1982.

Schlosser, Eric. 'The Business of Pornography.' *U.S. News and World Report* 10 (February 1997): 44.

- *Fast Food Nation: The Dark Side of the All-American Meal.* New York: Perennial, 2002.
- *Reefer Madness: Sex, Drugs and Cheap Labour in the American Black Market.* Boston: Houghton Mifflin Co., 2003.
Schwartz, Ellen. 'The Striptease Project: Uncovering the Bare Truth about Vancouver's Past.' *Trek: The Magazine of the University of British Columbia* (Spring 2001): 21–6.
Scott, David A. *Behind the G-String: An Exploration of the Stripper's Image, Her Person, and Her Meaning.* Jefferson, NC: McFarland and Company, 1996.
Scott, Michael. 'The Original Blade Runners.' *Vancouver Sun*, 2 February 2002: I8.
Scott, Valerie. 'I Love Sex and I'm Good at It.' *Globe and Mail*, 17 March 2001: R14.
Scott, Valerie, Peggy Miller, and Ryan Hotchkiss. 'Realistic Feminists.' In Laurie Bell, ed., *Good Girls / Bad Girls: Sex Trade Workers and Feminists Face to Face*, 204–17. Toronto: Women's Press, 1987.
'Seedy Job Conditions behind Strippers' Bid for Union Protection.' *Vancouver Sun*, 29 January 1981: A15.
Sharma, Nandita Rani. *Home Economics: Nationalism and the Making of 'Migrant Workers' in Canada.* Toronto: University of Toronto Press, 2006.
- 'Race, Class, Gender and the Making of Difference.' *Atlantis: A Women's Studies Journal* 24, 2 (2000): 5–15.
Shepard, Bruce. *Deemed Unsuitable: Blacks from Oklahoma Move to the Canadian Prairies in Search of Equality in the Early Twentieth Century Only to Find Racism in Their New Home.* Toronto: Umbrella Press, 1997.
Sher, Julian, and William Marsden. 'B.C. Bonanza.' In *To Hell: How the Biker Gangs Are Conquering Canada*, 304–31. Toronto: Alfred Knopf, 2003.
Shields, Roy. 'Can't a Man Have a Beer without Sex?' *The Province*, 10 January 1975: 27.
Shillington, Stan. 'Nude Nightspot Operators Charged.' *Vancouver Sun*, 12 April 1972: 2.
Shin, Eui Hang, and Edward Adam Nam. 'Culture, Gender Roles and Sport: The Case of Korean Players on the LPGA.' *Journal of Sport and Social Issues* 28, 3 (August 2004): 223–44.
Shoppmann, Claudia. *Days of Masquerade: Life Stories of Lesbians during the Third Reich.* Trans. Allison Brown. New York: Columbia University Press, 1996.
'Show Not Obscene.' *Vancouver Sun*, 28 June 1974: 12.
Shteir, Rachel. 'Stormy Weather: How a Climate of Rebellion, in Theatre and

Society, Wrought the Death of Burlesque in 1969.' *American Theatre* 20, 4 (April 2003): 28–31, 71–6.
- *Striptease: The Untold History of the Girlie Show*. New York: Oxford University Press, 2004.
'Shut 3 More Cabarets, Prosecutor Tells City.' *Vancouver Sun*, 16 October 1959: 30.
Silcoff, Mireille. 'Dita Von Teese: International Queen of Burlesque.' *Toro: Canada's Magazine for Men* (October 2004): 68–72.
Silvera, Makeda. *Silenced: Talks with Working Class West Indian Women about Their Lives and Struggles as Domestic Workers in Canada*. Toronto: Sister Vision Press, 1989.
Silverman, Victor, and Susan Stryker, dirs. *Screaming Queens*. Documentary film. 2005.
Simons, Ed. 'Nude Shows Acceptable – Court Plea.' *The Province*, 1 September 1972: 21.
Skeggs, Beverley. *Formations of Class and Gender: Becoming Respectable*. London: Sage Publications, 1997.
Skipper, James, and Charles McCaghy. 'The Stripper.' *Sexual Behaviour* 1, 3 (June 1971): 78–81.
- 'Stripping: Anatomy of a Deviant Lifestyle.' In S.D. Feldman and G.W. Theilbar, eds, *Life Styles: Diversity in American Society*, 362–73. Boston: Little Brown, 1972.
- 'Stripteasers: The Anatomy and Career Contingencies of a Deviant Occupation.' *Social Problems* 17, 3 (1970): 391–405.
- 'Stripteasing: A Sex-Oriented Occupation.' In James Henslin, ed., *Studies in the Sociology of Sex*, 275–96. New York: Meredith and Co., 1971.
Smith, Bob. 'Oriental Dolls Lace Dance with Spice.' *Vancouver Sun*, 22 July 1969: 25.
Smith, Clarissa. 'Shiny Chests and Heaving G-Strings: A Night Out with the Chippendales.' *Sexualities* 5, 1 (2002): 67–89.
Smith, Dorothy E. *The Everyday World as Problematic: A Feminist Sociology*. Boston: Northeastern University Press, 1987.
- *Texts, Facts, and Femininity: Exploring the Relations of Ruling*. London and New York: Routledge, 1990.
Smith, Helen, and Pamela Wakewich. '"Beauty and the Helldivers": Representing Women's Work and Identities in a Warplant Newspaper.' *Labour / Le travail* 44 (1999): 71–107.
Smith, Joseph. 'Ann Corio Brings Back Burlesque.' *Vancouver Sun* (Weekend Magazine), 19 May 1962: 3.

Smith, Linda Tuhiwai. *Decolonizing Methodologies: Research and Indigenous Peoples*. London and New York: Zed Books, 1999.

Smith, Maxwell. 'The Downtown Scene.' *Vancouver Life* 3, 4 (January 1968): 24, 25, 35, 52.

Snowden, Lynn. *Nine Lives: From Stripper to Schoolteacher: My Year Long Odyssey in the Work World*. New York: W.W. Norton and Co., 1994.

Sochen, June. *From Mae to Madonna: Women Entertainers in Twentieth-Century America*. Lexington: University of Kentucky Press, 1999.

Sommers, Jeff. 'Men at the Margin: Masculinity and Space in Downtown Vancouver, 1950–1986.' *Urban Geography* 19, 4 (1998): 287–310.

Spencer, Nancy. 'Sister Act IV: Venus and Serena Williams at Indian Wells: "Sincere Fictions" and White Racism.' *Journal of Sport and Social Issues* 28, 2 (May 2004): 115–35.

'Square-Minded Surrey Moves to Ban Strippers.' *Vancouver Sun*, 17 December 1974: 22.

Stacey, Judith. 'Can There Be a Feminist Ethnography?' In Sherna Gluck and Daphne Patai, eds, *Women's Words: The Feminist Practice of Oral History*, 111–19. New York: Routledge, Chapman and Hall, 1992.

Stanley, Don. 'For the Burlesque Hungry, Isy's Offers Girls à la Carte.' *Vancouver Sun*, 29 June 1978: B3.

Stasiulis, Daiva K., and Abigail B. Bakan. *Negotiating Citizenship: Migrant Women in Canada and the Global System*. Toronto: University of Toronto Press, 2005.

Statistics Canada. *1971 Census of Canada*. Vol. 3, Part 2, Labour Force, Table 8l. Ottawa: Statistics Canada, 1971.

– *Population Worked in 1980 – Employment Income by Occupation*. Census, Catalogue 92-930. Ottawa: Statistics Canada, 1981.

Stencell, A.W. *Girl Show: Into the Canvas World of Bump and Grind*. Toronto: ECW Press, 1999.

Stephenson, Marylee. 'Being in Women's Liberation: A Case Study in Social Change.' PhD diss., Department of Anthropology and Sociology, University of British Columbia, 1975.

Still, Larry. 'Cabaret "Kind of Union Shop" for Hookers.' *Vancouver Sun*, 18 September 1976: 21.

– 'Crown Calls the Penthouse "A Scandal in This Community."' *Vancouver Sun*, 25 February 1977: 21.

– 'Penthouse Drama a $2 Million Morality Play.' *Vancouver Sun*, 21 December 1977: A1, A2.

– 'Penthouse "Love Affair" with Vancouver Soured with Age.' *Vancouver Sun*, 23 April 1977: 15.

– 'Philipponi Says Nudity Was Banned at His Club.' *Vancouver Sun*, 2 December 1976: 12.
– 'Strippers Must Keep "Hands Off."' *Vancouver Sun*, 2 April 1982: C13.
'Still Kicking Up a Storm.' *Vancouver Sun*, 5 August 1977: L7.
Stoler, Ann Laura. *Race and the Education of Desire: Foucault's History of Sexuality and the Colonial Order of Things*. Durham and London: Duke University Press, 1997.
Storm, Tempest. *The Lady Is a Vamp*. Atlanta: Peachtree Publishers, 1987.
Strange, Carolyn. 'Bad Girls and Masked Men: Recent Works on Sexuality in U.S. History.' *Labour / Le travail* 30 (1997): 261–75.
– *Toronto's Girl Problem: The Pleasures and Perils of the City*. Toronto: University of Toronto Press, 1995.
Strange, Carolyn, and Tina Loo. *Making Good: Law and Moral Regulation in Canada, 1867–1939*. Toronto: University of Toronto Press, 1997.
– 'Spectacular Justice: The Circus on Trial, and the Trial as Circus, Picton, 1903.' *Canadian Historical Review* 77, 2 (1996): 159–84.
Stratton, Jon. *The Desirable Body*. Manchester and New York: Manchester University Press, 1996.
'Stripper Bid Fails.' *Vancouver Sun*, 12 August 1981: A9.
'Strippers' Union Expanding to B.C. with Support from Labor Congress.' *The Province* 8 May 1980: A10.
'Strippers Vote to Clean Up Their Acts.' *Vancouver Sun*, 13 December 1976: 3.
Strong-Boag, Veronica. 'Society in the Twentieth Century.' In Hugh Johnston, ed., *The Pacific Province: A History of British Columbia*, 273–312. Vancouver: Douglas and McIntyre, 1996.
Stuart, Andrea. *Showgirls*. London: Jonathan Cape, 1996.
Sugiman, Pamela. 'Memories of Internment: Narrating Japanese Canadian Women's Life Stories.' *Canadian Journal of Sociology* 29, 3 (2004): 359–87.
Sullivan, Steve. *Bombshells: Glamour Girls of a Lifetime*. New York: St Martin's Griffin, 1998.
– *Va Va Voom: Bombshells, Pin-ups, Sexpots, and Glamour Girls*. Los Angeles: General Publishing Group, 1995.
'Sunbather Convicted for Nudity.' *Vancouver Sun*, 17 September 1970: 10.
'Supreme Court Clears Dancer of Giving Immoral Exhibition.' *The Province*, 3 October 1973: 6.
Swann, Michelle. 'Hiding Hot Topics: Science, Sex and Schooling in British Columbia, 1910–1916.' MA thesis, Department of Sociology, University of British Columbia, 1999.
Szeto, Eric. 'Universities Not Wild about *Girls Gone Wild*.' *The Ubyssey* 87, 4 (16 September 2005): 3.

Tait, Kathy. 'Wreck Beach Skinny-Dippers Raided.' *The Province*, 13 August 1970: 1.

Tallentire, Jenéa. 'Everyday Athenas: Strategies of Survival and Identity for Ever-Single Women in British Columbia, 1880–1930.' PhD diss., Department of History, University of British Columbia, 2006.

Tate, Jane. 'Organizing Homeworkers in the Informal Sector: Canada.' In M. Hosmer Martens and Swasti Mitter, eds, *Women in Trade Unions: Organizing the Unorganized*, 75–82. Geneva: International Labour Office, 1994.

Temple, Annie. 'R.I.P. The Drake Showlounge.' 31 May 2007. Available at www.yonilicious.blogspot.com.

Thomas, Sandra. 'Strippers' Money Not Good Enough.' *Vancouver Courier*, 7 February 2007: 9.

Thompson, Peter. 'Nudism Soaring in Popularity as Club Membership Doubles.' *The Province*, 30 March 1957: 12.

Thompson, William, and Jackie Harred. 'Topless Dancers: Managing Stigma in a Deviant Occupation.' *Deviant Behaviour* 13 (1992): 291–311.

Thomson, Ann. *Winning Choice on Abortion: How British Columbian and Canadian Feminists Won the Battles of the 1970s and 1980s*. Victoria, BC: Trafford, 2004.

Todd, Ian. 'Liquor Laws Unrealistic, Says Booth.' *Vancouver Sun*, 11 December 1964: 37.

Tong, Benson. *The Chinese Americans*. Westport, CT: Greenwood Press, 2000.

'Topless Dancer and Boss Fined.' *Vancouver Sun*, 31 March 1967: 3.

'Topless Dancers Don Coats to Picket City Nightclub.' *Vancouver Sun*, 17 October 1967: 3.

Tracey, Lindalee. *Growing Up Naked: My Years in Bump and Grind*. Vancouver and Toronto: Douglas and McIntyre, 1997.

Trautner, Mary Nell. 'Doing Gender, Doing Class: The Performance of Sexuality in Exotic Dance Clubs.' *Gender and Society* 19, 6 (December 2005): 771–88.

Trower, Peter. *Dead Man's Ticket*. Madeira Park, BC: Harbour Publishing, 1996.

Tucker, Sherry. *Swing Shift: 'All Girl' Bands of the 1940s*. Durham and London: Duke University Press, 2000.

Turner, Michael. 'Fred and Ethel.' In Grant Arnold and Michael Turner, eds, *Fred Herzog: Vancouver Photographs*, 135–49. Vancouver: Vancouver Art Gallery and Douglas and McIntyre, 2007.

Tyler, Carol-Ann. *Female Impersonation*. London and New York: Routledge, 2003.

Urry, John. *Consuming Places*. London: Routledge, 1995.

- *The Tourist Gaze: Leisure and Travel in Contemporary Societies.* London: Sage, 1990.
Valverde, Mariana. *The Age of Light, Soap and Water: Moral Reform in English Canada, 1885–1925.* Toronto: McClelland and Stewart, 1991.
- *Diseases of the Will: Alcohol and the Dilemmas of Freedom.* Cambridge: Cambridge University Press, 1998.
- *Law's Dream of a Common Language.* Princeton and Oxford: Princeton University Press, 2002.
Valverde, Mariana, and Lorna Weir. 'The Struggles of the Immoral: Preliminary Remarks on Moral Regulation.' *Resources for Feminist Research* 17, 3 (1988): 31–4.
Van Gelder, Lawrence. 'Ann Corio, a Burlesque Queen on Broadway, Is Dead.' *New York Times,* 9 March 1999: C27.
Vertinsky, Patricia, and Gwendolyn Captain. 'More Myth Than History: American Culture and Representations of the Black Female's Athletic Ability.' *Journal of Sport History* 25, 3 (1998): 532–61.
Volkart, Carol. 'City's Strippers Hint Strike over Pay, Working Conditions.' *Vancouver Sun,* 15 November 1977: B7.
Walkowitz, Judith. *City of Dreadful Delight: Narratives of Sexual Danger in Late-Victorian London.* Chicago: University of Chicago Press, 1992.
- *Prostitution and Victorian Society: Women, Class and the State.* Cambridge and New York: Cambridge University Press, 1980.
Ward, David, and Gene Kassebaum. *Women's Prison: Sex and Social Structure.* Chicago: Aldine Publishing Co., 1965.
Ward, Peter. *White Canada Forever: Popular Attitudes and Public Policy toward Orientals in British Columbia.* Montreal and Kingston: McGill-Queen's University Press, 2002.
Warner, Tom. *Never Going Back: A History of Queer Activism.* Toronto: University of Toronto Press, 2002.
Wasserman, Jack. 'About Now: Gypsy Takes Off for Jack – On Various Topics, That Is.' *Vancouver Sun,* 30 April 1959: 25.
- 'Along the Triviera.' *Vancouver Sun,* 23 April 1963: 19.
- 'The Booze Who.' *Vancouver Sun,* 15 March 1967: 29.
- 'City Cabarets Facing "Ruin."' *Vancouver Sun,* 8 April 1954: 1.
- 'Flesh Tones.' *Vancouver Sun,* 1 October 1974: 19.
- 'Flesh Tones.' *Vancouver Sun,* 17 December 1974: 41.
- 'Night Spotter's Notebook.' *Vancouver Sun,* 13 January 1970: 25.
- 'The Passing Parade.' *Vancouver Sun,* 8 March 1976: 31.
- 'Saloon Crawler's Notebook.' *Vancouver Sun,* 19 October 1971: 29.
- 'Tale of a City.' *Vancouver Sun,* 5 August 1959: 25.

– 'Tale of a City.' *Vancouver Sun*, 13 August 1959: 25.

– *Vancouver Sun*, 6 December 1976: 23.

Waterhouse-Hayward, Alex. 'Closing Time: A Fan Bids a Fond Farewell to the Marble Arch Pub and Showroom.' *Vancouver Sun*, 2 March 2002: H2.

Watts, Jill. *Hattie McDaniel: Black Ambition, White Hollywood*. New York: Amistad, 2005.

Weeks, Jeffrey. 'The Sexual Citizen.' *Theory, Culture and Society* 15, 3-4 (1998): 35–52.

– *Sexuality*. 2nd ed. London and New York: Routledge, 2003.

Weingarten, Tara. 'I'm a Dancer, Not a Stripper.' *Newsweek* 141, 22 (6 February 2003): 71.

Weintraub, William. *Crazy about Lili*. Toronto: McClelland and Stewart, 2005.

– 'Show Business: Lili St. Cyr's Town – and Al's and Oscar's.' In *City Unique: Montreal Days and Nights in the 1940s and '50s*. Toronto: McClelland and Stewart, 1996.

Weissman, Aerlyn, and Lynne Fernie, dirs. *Forbidden Love: The Unashamed Stories of Canadian Lesbians*. Documentary film. Distributed by the National Film Board of Canada. 1992.

Wente, Margaret. 'Why Is Canada Pimping?' *Globe and Mail*, 30 November 2004: A21.

Whitaker, Reg, and Gary Marcuse. *Cold War Canada: The Making of a National Insecurity State, 1945–1957*. Toronto: University of Toronto Press, 1994.

White, Julie. *Mail and Female: Women and the Canadian Union of Postal Workers*. Toronto: Thompson, 1990.

– *Sisters and Solidarity: Women and Unions in Canada*. Toronto: Thompson, 1993.

– *Women and Unions*. Ottawa: Canadian Advisory Council on the Status of Women, 1980.

Whitehall, Brenda. 'Stilettos and Strap-Ons: Infusing Burlesque with Queer Femme Flair.' *Xtra! West*, 13 April 2006: 19–20.

Wiseman, Les. 'Not Your Average Joe.' *Vancouver* (April 1982): 60–4, 68, 84.

– 'Young, Sexy and Well-Heeled.' *Vancouver* (March 1982): 29–31, 33–5, 145.

Women's Bureau. *Women in the Labour Force*. Ottawa: Labour Canada, 1984.

Women's Council. *Women in the Labour Force, 1971, Facts and Figures*. Ottawa: Labour Canada, 1971.

Wood, Damien. 'Ping-Pong Prowess Is Making Mitzi Rich.' *The Province*, 5 September 1982: A14.

Wood, Daniel. 'Missing.' *Elm Street* 4, 2 (1999): 15–22.

– 'The Naked and the Dead: Truth Isn't the Only Victim in the 50-year Penthouse Saga.' *Vancouver* (December 1999): 102–15, 122, 145–6.

Woodward, Jonathan. 'The Battle to Keep B.C. Beach Bare.' *Globe and Mail*, 12 August 2005: A7.

Wynn, Graeme. 'The Rise of Vancouver.' In Graeme Wynn and Timothy Oke, eds, *Vancouver and Its Region*, 69–148. Vancouver: University of British Columbia Press, 1992.

Wynter, Sara. 'WHISPER: Women Hurt in Systems of Prostitution Engaged in Revolt.' In Frederica Delacoste and Priscilla Alexander, eds, *Sex Work: Writings by Women in the Sex Industry*, 66–70. Pittsburgh: Cleis Press, 1987.

Yip, Brandon. 'Rockin' Back the Clock.' *Vancouver Courier*, 7 July 2004: 1–5.

Young, Clara. 'Le Strip, C'est Chic.' *Globe and Mail*, 22 June 2002: T1, T4.

Yung, Judy. *Unbound Feet: A Social History of Chinese Women in San Francisco.* Berkeley: University of California Press, 1995.

Zarlengo, Kristina. 'Civilian Threat, the Suburban Citadel, and Atomic Age American Women.' *Signs: Journal of Women in Culture and Society* 24, 4 (1999): 925–58.

Zumsteg, Beatrix. 'Promoting Censorship in the Name of Youth: The Council of Women's Activism against Vaudeville in the 1920s and 1930s in Vancouver.' Unpublished paper, Sociology Department, University of British Columbia, 1998.

List of Interview Narrators

Retired Striptease Dancers

Virginia, interviewed in Vancouver, 28 August 1998.
Klute, interviewed in Vancouver, 19 September, 1998.
Roxanne, interviewed in Vancouver, 20 April 2000.
Bonnie Scott, interviewed in Vancouver, 19 June 2000.
Shalimar, interviewed in Vancouver, 2 July 2000.
Shelinda, interviewed in Vancouver, 6 July 2000.
Foxy Lady, interviewed in Vancouver, 12 July 2000.
Cascade, interviewed in Kelowna, B.C., 24 July 2000.
Jasmine Tea, interviewed in Kelowna, B.C., 24 July 2000.
April Paris, interviewed in Vancouver, 30 August 2000.
Coco Fontaine, interviewed in Vancouver, 20 September 2000.
Miss Lovie, interviewed in Vancouver, 22 September 2000.
Tarren Rae, interviewed in Vancouver, 5 December 2000.
Princess Lillian, interviewed in Burnaby, B.C., 26 January 2001.
Bambi, interviewed in Vancouver, 21 June, 2001.
Choo Choo Williams, interviewed in Vancouver, 4 February 2002.
Nena Marlene, interviewed in Vancouver, 27 February 2002.
Sarita Melita, interviewed in Vancouver, 15 December 2004.
Scarlett Lake, interviewed in Vancouver, 25 February 2005.

Retired Dancers (non-strippers)

Christine Chipperfield, interviewed in Vancouver, 8 November 1999.
Tricia Foxx, interviewed in Vancouver, 27 September 2006.

Dancers Who Performed Post-1980

Shawna Black, interviewed in Vancouver, 15 June 2000.
Carson Lee, interviewed in Vancouver, 25 February 2002.
Tiana, interviewed in Vancouver, 6 December 2004.
Honey Rider, interviewed in Vancouver, 8 December 2004.

Retired Club Owners

Ross Filippone, interviewed in Vancouver, 15 June 2000.
Richard Walters, interviewed in Vancouver, 8 July 2000.
Ernie King, interviewed in Vancouver, 4 February 2002.
Gary Taylor, interviewed in Vancouver, 22 June 2007.

Retired Choreographers

Jack Card, interviewed in Vancouver, 28 January 2000, and 14 March
    2000.
Patrick Kevin O'Hara, e-mail interview, from Paris, France, 18 June
    2007.

Retired Journalists

Patrick Nagle, interviewed in Victoria, B.C., 28 July 2000.
Denny Boyd, interviewed in West Vancouver, 2 August 2001.

Retired Club Staff

Megan Carvell Davis, interviewed in Vancouver, July 20, 2000.
Ron Small, interviewed in Vancouver, 22 September 2000.
Della Walters, interviewed in Vancouver, 20 September, 2001.
Buddy, interviewed in Victoria, B.C., 26 May 2006.

Musicians

Gord Walkinshaw, interviewed in Vancouver (by Kim Greenwell and
    Michelle Swann), 27 June 2000.
Dave Davies, interviewed in Vancouver (by Kim Greenwell and
    Michelle Swann), Vancouver, 27 June 2000.

Doug Cuthbert, interviewed in Vancouver (by Kim Greenwell and
  Michelle Swann), 5 July 2000.
Gerry Palken, interviewed in Delta, B.C., 18 February 2002.
Mike Kalanj, interviewed in Vancouver (by Kim Greenwell and
  Michelle Swann), 5 July, 2000.
Sean Gunn, interviewed in Vancouver, 18 March 2004.

Retired Booking Agents

Jack Card, interviewed in Vancouver, 28 January 2000, and 14 March
  2000.
George Paidy, telephone conversation, Vancouver, 19 June 2000.
Jeannie Runnalls, interviewed in Coquitlam, B.C., 21 June 2000.

Patrons/Aficionados

Norman Young, interviewed in Vancouver, 13 December 1999.
Lynne Ross and Bob Stork, interviewed in Abbotsford, B.C., 29
  January 2000.
Larry Wong, interviewed in Vancouver, 18 March 2004.

Photo Credits

Colour Plates

1 Photo by Glenn Baglo, courtesy of the *Vancouver Sun*.
2 Program cover, 1966, courtesy of Jack Card's private collection.
3 Photo by Ian Lindsay, courtesy of the *Vancouver Sun*.
4 Advertisement, courtesy of private collection of Danny Filippone.
5 Photo by Alex Waterhouse-Hayward, courtesy of Alex Waterhouse-Hayward's private collection.
6 Photo by Gerry Kahrmann, courtesy of *The Province*.
7 Photo by Rice and Bell, cover photo for the February 1948 issue of *Maclean's* magazine. Available at www.collectionscanada.gc.aa/obj/002026/flscott.jpg Library and Archives Canada.
8 Cartoon by Dan Murphy, courtesy of Dan Murphy's private collection.
9 Photo by Ryan Crocker, courtesy of Ryan Crocker's private collection.

Figures

Preface

P1 Cartoon by Adrian Raeside, courtesy of Adrian Raeside's private collection.

Chapter 1

1.1 Sally Rand, courtesy of the Library of Congress, LC-USZ62-112037.

Chapter 2

2.1   Map of Vancouver's West End, courtesy of Rachael Sullivan.
2.2   Photo by John Uter, courtesy of Nena Marlene's private collection.
2.3   Photo courtesy of the City of Vancouver Archives, 1184-3470.
2.4   Photo by D. Patterson, courtesy of Vancouver Public Library, VPL, 40652.
2.5   Photo by Ross Kenward, courtesy of the *Vancouver Sun*.
2.6   Photo by Ross Kenward, courtesy of *The Province*.
2.7   Photo by Ross Kenward, courtesy of Vancouver Public Library, VPL 69069.
2.8   Photo by Ian Lindsay, courtesy of the *Vancouver Sun*.
2.9   Photo by Dan Scott, courtesy of the *Vancouver Sun*.
2.10 Photo by NOGRADY Paris, courtesy of the private collection of Patrick Kevin O'Hara.
2.11 Photo by John Denniston, courtesy of *The Province*.
2.12 Photo by Steve Bosch, courtesy of the *Vancouver Sun*.
2.13 Photo by Daniel O'Neill, courtesy of the Vancouver Public Library, VPL 53715.
2.14 Photo by Alex Waterhouse-Hayward, courtesy of Alex Waterhouse-Hayward's private collection.
2.15 Photo by Peter Hulbert, courtesy of *The Province*.
2.16 Advertisement, courtesy of the *Vancouver Sun*.
2.17 Advertisement, courtesy of the *Vancouver Sun*.
2.18 Advertisements, courtesy of the *Vancouver Sun*.
2.19 Advertisement, courtesy of the *Vancouver Sun*.
2.20 Photographer unknown, courtesy of Ernie King and Choo Choo Williams's private collection.
2.21 Photo by Ralph Bower, courtesy of the *Vancouver Sun*.
2.22 Photo by Ian Lindsay, courtesy of the *Vancouver Sun*.
2.23 Photo by Alex Waterhouse-Hayward, courtesy of Alex Waterhouse-Hayward's private collection.
2.24 Photo by Ian Lindsay, courtesy of the *Vancouver Sun*.

Chapter 3

3.1   Advertisement, courtesy of the *Vancouver Sun*.
3.2   Photographer unknown, courtesy of Getty Images.
3.3   Photo by John Uter, courtesy of Nena Marlene's private collection.
3.4   Photographer unknown, courtesy of the private collection of Jack Card.
3.5   Photo by John Uter, courtesy of Nena Marlene's private collection.

3.6 Photo by Theodore Wan, courtesy of the Theodore Wan Collection, Vancouver Art Gallery.

3.7 Photo by James Loewen, courtesy of James Loewen's private collection.

3.8 Photo by Bob Thomas/Popperfoto, courtesy of Popperfoto/Getty Images.

3.9 Advertisement, courtesy of the *Vancouver Sun*.

3.10 Photographer unknown, courtesy of Ernie King and Choo Choo Williams's private collection.

3.11 Advertisement, courtesy of the *Vancouver Sun*.

3.12 Advertisement, courtesy of the *Vancouver Sun*.

3.13 Photo by Saralee James, courtesy of Mark, Susie, and Jonathan James's private collection.

Chapter 4

4.1 Photo by John Uter, courtesy of Nena Marlene's private collection.

4.2 Photographer unknown, courtesy of Ernie King and Choo Choo Williams's private collection.

4.3 Photo by Rachael Sullivan, courtesy of Rachael Sullivan.

4.4 Photo by Rachael Sullivan, courtesy of Rachael Sullivan.

4.5 Photo by James Loewen, courtesy of James Loewen's private collection.

4.6 Photo by Garth Pritchard, courtesy of the *Calgary Herald*.

4.7 Photo by Steve Bosch, courtesy of the *Vancouver Sun*.

Chapter 5

5.1 Photo by Les Bazso, courtesy of *The Province*.

5.2 Photo by Theodore Wan, courtesy of the Theodore Wan Collection, Vancouver Art Gallery.

Chapter 6

6.1 Barbara Ann Scott Doll Photo © Canadian Museum of Civilization, artifact 983.29.23, image S89-1870.

6.2 Photo by Ian Lindsay, courtesy of the *Vancouver Sun*.

Index

Performers' stage names are alphabetized by the first word of the name. Illustrations are indicated by italicized page numbers.